Desegregating Private Higher Education in the South

Desegregating Private Higher Education in the South

DUKE, EMORY, RICE, TULANE, AND VANDERBILT

Melissa Kean

LOUISIANA STATE UNIVERSITY PRESS ✳ BATON ROUGE

Published by Louisiana State University Press
Copyright © 2008 by Louisiana State University Press
All rights reserved
Manufactured in the United States of America
FIRST PRINTING

Designer: Amanda McDonald Scallan
Typeface: Palatino
Typesetter: J. Jarrett Engineering, Inc.
Printer and binder: Thomson-Shore, Inc.

Library of Congress Cataloging-in-Publication Data

Kean, Melissa, 1959–
  Desegregating private higher education in the South : Duke,
Emory, Rice, Tulane, and Vanderbilt / Melissa Kean.
      p. cm.
  Includes bibliographical references and index.
  ISBN 978-0-8071-3358-3 (cloth : alk. paper) 1. College
integration—Southern States—History. 2. Segregation in higher
education—Southern States—History. 3. Private universities and
colleges—Southern States—History. I. Title.
  LC214.22.S68K43 2008
  379.2′630975—dc22
                                                          2008007397

For Steve

Contents

Acknowledgments

I happily acknowledge that I could not have written this book on my own. I would never even have begun it if not for the warm welcome and encouragement I received years ago from the faculty in the History Department at Creighton University, especially Dennis Mihelich, Dick Super, and Ashton Welch. At Rice, first as a graduate student and then as University Historian, I have always been surrounded by able, interesting, and generous colleagues. Many of them have read and commented on pieces of this book. Carl Caldwell offered particularly useful criticism early on. Joel Wolfe and Tom Haskell read chapters, and Randall Hall helped edit the entire manuscript. John Boles, who first suggested the topic to me, has read and commented on every draft.

I am especially grateful to the people who helped me identify the research materials I needed and make productive use of them. Archivists at all these schools guided me through their collections and made me feel welcome. William King and Tom Harkins at Duke, Ann Case and Robert Sherer at Tulane, and Kathy Smith at Vanderbilt were generous with their time and knowledge. Ginger Cain at Emory was especially persistent in tracking down often odd bits of information. I owe a special debt to Nancy Boothe and Lee Pecht at the Woodson Research Center, who gave me the opportunity to explore the Rice University archives in great depth. Bill Barnett and Charles Szalkowski of Baker Botts in Houston helped me find important Rice trial records. Others spent hours talking with me about the intricacies of desegregation on these campuses. Gary Hauk helped provide perspective on Emory, Paul Conkin at Vanderbilt was generous with his time and insights into the history of that institution, and Clarence Mohr offered me aid and comfort from the very beginning of this project. I also talked with some of the participants in the desegregation story, most off the record, a few on it. I visited Harvie Branscomb near the end of his life, and he was very gracious and quite open. Walter Martin also spoke freely about his time at Emory, always with great affection and concern for that institution. The most important person I met in connection with this work, though, was Judson Ward at Emory. Dr. Ward was not merely helpful to me, although he was extraordinarily helpful, but he also showed an unflagging honesty in thinking about these difficult events coupled with a generosity of spirit that I hope is mirrored in this book.

My dear friends Deb MacDonald and Neal Gerstandt have been a constant in my life and have always sustained me in whatever I do. My colleagues on the staff and faculty at Rice have also helped in more ways than I can list. In particular I need to thank Jim Pomerantz, Mary McIntire, Mary Bixby, Lee Pecht, Philip Montgomery, and Amanda Focke. Above all, I will never forget or cease to be grateful for the friendship of the late Gil Whitaker. My husband, Steve Kean, and our daughters, Maggie and Nora, never stopped being curious and excited about this book, which made it possible for me to complete it.

Desegregating Private Higher Education in the South

Introduction

This is a story about how a group of very powerful people—the leaders of the South's elite private universities—came to do something that many of them did not want to do: admit black students. This story is quite different from the one that played out in the region's public institutions. Here, no federal court ordered these schools to admit black students; no troops or marshals arrived to enforce desegregation. However, to suggest that desegregation at Duke, Emory, Rice, Tulane, and Vanderbilt was voluntary would be deeply misleading. The desegregation of the private universities in the South was coerced—by northern foundations, professional academic associations, accrediting bodies, faculties that began to vote with their feet, divinity students and professors who felt called to oppose racial discrimination, alumni who withheld contributions, and by new federal contracting rules. Ultimately, behind all these pressures was the grassroots civil rights movement, led by southern blacks, which created a national crisis of conscience.

Before the schools bowed to the inevitable, though, each one endured nearly two decades of internal argument about how best to respond to these demands for change. The arguments ran hot and cold, touched on everything from global politics to personal antipathies and friendships, and revealed the same serious divide within the power structure of each university. This divide was partly the product of contemporary conditions. As changes of every sort swept through the postwar South, many, especially among the university trustees, fought to hold on to the world they had been born into. At the same time, the presidents of these schools struggled to seize the opportunities presented by so much change to force their slow-moving institutions into the national mainstream. Other aspects of this divide were more lasting and are perhaps even permanent features of American higher education. The American reliance on outside trustees as the final arbiters of university policy leaves these institutions in the well-meaning hands of alumni who often do not share the values, or even any meaningful understanding, of the world of scholarship and instruction. These boards are usually (often overly) cooperative with administrative leaders when it comes to managerial decisions about running a research university, matters on which administrators have acknowledged expertise. On broad issues of mission, goals, and policy, however, trustees commonly feel themselves on firmer ground and more forcefully assert their preferences. On the campuses of these five schools, the conflict over segregation that followed World War II gradually escalated into a direct clash between the needs of the academic enterprise and the values of the outside community.

This conflict emerged gradually over a period of several decades as these schools began, haltingly, to transform themselves from sleepy undergraduate colleges into research universities patterned after schools like Stanford, the University of Chicago, and the best of the Ivies.[1] Their leadership understood that American higher education was changing and saw that it might be possible to build nationally prominent universities in the South. Their efforts to establish reputations outside the region, focused mainly on the development of graduate programs and research, were in many ways astonishing and required vision, commitment, and resources almost beyond imagining.[2] At the same time, each school remained committed to its role as a leader of the South and protector of southern traditions, including segregation. The presidents and trustees took seriously and cherished their identity as southerners and believed that the private southern universities had an obligation to maintain their southern character and to lead the region in its drive to catch up economically to the rest of the country.

Conflict between these two goals—national prestige and regional leadership—remained muted until after World War II. Then, tensions appeared very quickly, with segregation at the heart of the problem. In the wake of a war fought in part against Nazi racial ideology, the oppression of American blacks became increasingly unacceptable to larger numbers of Americans. Even more pressing, in the early 1950s the threat of Soviet Communism made segregation particularly troublesome. As the defense of American institutions as more democratic, efficient, and virtuous than their Soviet counterparts took on the hallmarks of a crusade, a glaring flaw like segregation became a weakness in the fight against Soviet domination. Segregation flew in the face of the American creed of equal opportunity, relegating an entire group of people to second-class status by birth. Southern blacks, no matter what their abilities, were denied the chance to advance socially or economically, denied even the right to participate in American democracy. The rest of the nation and a few scattered individuals in the South saw the persistence of segregation as dangerous, in no small part because it allowed the Soviet Union to use the issue of the mistreatment of American blacks in the propaganda war for the loyalties of Africa and Asia.[3]

But the system of racial segregation that had been installed in the aftermath of Reconstruction was firmly entrenched in the South. To many, including the alumni and trustees of these schools, it seemed timeless, natural, and right. As wide and deep changes began to transform the South's economy and demographics, anxiety about the continuity of traditional institutions, including segregation, began to rise.[4] In the eyes of many white southerners any challenge to the enforced racial hierarchy constituted an attack on *their* America and the stability of their society. They could only see calls for change as attempts by the Soviet Union to destabilize and weaken the United States. In short, while the federal government and most of the nation saw segregation as a growing embarrassment and a hindrance in the war on Communism, in the white South anti-Communism meant a defense of segregation.

By the 1950s the campuses of Duke, Emory, Rice, Tulane, and Vanderbilt had changed significantly. The federal government poured money into research and several national foundations made the improvement of southern higher education a prominent goal. Successful fund-raising and sustained focus on improvement led to the dramatic growth of new and better graduate and professional schools, which some feared were beginning to dominate the campuses.[5] The student body too was changing, as the use of standardized testing began to improve its quality and recruitment efforts increased its geographical diversity. The small, tightly knit regional and local colleges, focused on classical undergraduate education, had evolved into legitimate, though still minor, research universities. They now competed with universities throughout the nation for resources, faculty, and students.[6]

At the same time, efforts to bring change to race relations began to have a real impact on these campuses. Some of the new pressures were distant and faint. The Truman administration, for example, proved unwilling to turn its back on American blacks and began a series of minor but real loosenings of racial restrictions in the federal government. The NAACP's lawyers produced a steady stream of successful challenges to segregation in public higher education. The Truman Commission on Higher Education began the era with a ringing condemnation of segregation and a call for broader democracy in American schooling. Other changes were far more immediate. National professional organizations and accrediting bodies, both critically important in the drive to build reputation, grew reluctant to tolerate racial discrimination in their memberships. The painstakingly recruited faculties, now often including many northerners, began to speak out against the color bar. Professors and students alike became increasingly vocal about the immorality of banning blacks from their schools for no reason other than their color.

Opponents of desegregation on campus fought these changes, basing their objections on the sanctity of southern tradition. The force of this stance would weaken over time, as the South was pulled inexorably into the American mainstream. The schools' own success in recruiting faculty and students from other regions, the growth of industry and urbanization in the South, demands for national unity in the cold war—all meant that discrete regional traditions could no longer exist in isolation. The power, and the desire, of individuals and institutions outside the South, as well as previously weak groups within it, to influence policies and events on campuses increased enormously.[7]

In the late 1940s and early 1950s the presidents of these private southern universities tried to negotiate a path through all these clashing needs and desires while pursuing the two overarching institutional goals of national prestige and regional leadership. During this era most of the race-related controversies that arose at these schools did not directly involve the problem of whether to admit black students. Rather, as thoroughly segregated institutions, these schools now constantly faced a whole range of new and troublesome situations that complicated their "Negro problem." The changing position of blacks in American society increasingly brought the private southern universities into contact with new and different blacks—not the cooks and janitors that they had always known, and sometimes loved, but chemistry professors, university librarians, and college football players. How to handle these "new" kinds of blacks was the most common focus of argument at the private universities in the early postwar period.

Although the precise circumstances surrounding this debate were new, the essence of the argument can be traced back as far as George Washington Cable. Cable, writing in the 1880s as segregation was being fashioned, argued repeatedly that the arbitrary imposition of a line based on color was immoral, both unfair to the refined black middle classes and a betrayal of the South's own heritage of class hierarchy.[8] Asserting the reasonableness and morality of a society based on class distinctions that recognized individual achievements, and condemning one based on the utterly arbitrary distinctions of color, Cable asked supporters of rigid racial segregation, "then tell us, gentlemen, which are you really for, the color line, or the line of character, intelligence, and property?"[9]

The answer that Cable received from the white South, most famously in a published rejoinder from Henry Grady, was somewhat confused but unmistakably hostile. While the white elite was prepared to tolerate some measure of black progress, as its embrace of Booker T. Washington indicated, there were also clear indications that it was determined to retain white supremacy no matter what black southerners could accomplish.[10] In fact, the rise of the black middle class was in large measure responsible for the intensifying white insistence on segregation. Without slave status to mark them as inferior, blacks, especially successful blacks, must be set apart in other ways. Thus, there was always the insistence that no matter what a black accomplished or owned, no matter how he dressed or how much she had learned, he or she was still inferior and deserved to be kept apart from whites of any class.[11]

This, in a nutshell, was the argument that played out at the private southern universities over the decade and a half that followed World War II. One side was dominated by those with the greatest concern for national reputation and academic achievement, most importantly the presidents of these schools. They argued that "exceptional" blacks ought to be treated as exceptions and could be accommodated on campus.[12] Critical to this position was a broad commitment to white control of the process of black uplift. The pace and scope of racial change, these men argued, must rest on the judgment of the educated white establishment. This group was differently comprised in each city but consisted generally of the loose aggregation of lawyers, businessmen, and some religious leaders who dominated local decision making—and who often sat on the boards of these universities. Unlike outsiders (northerners in general and the federal government in particular), these leaders believed they understood that disaster could result from pushing too hard or at the wrong time. Black progress was possible and even desirable, but only the educated white men of the South could decide how and when.

The other side, including many alumni, some older faculty members, and most trustees, was more concerned with local traditions than with joining the national mainstream. More fearful of their neighbors' anger than the disapproval of northern foundations or the condemnations of academic societies, they remained convinced that racial separation was both necessary and proper and demanded that black students, no matter how talented, stay in their own schools. Neither side was at all interested in the mass of poor, ill-educated black southerners or, for that matter, similarly situated white southerners. The debate was solely about the place of the black elite in southern society and in the most ambitious southern universities.

Before the Supreme Court's 1954 decision in *Brown v. Board of Education,* this debate took place in an atmosphere reasonably free of urgency. Although pressures for change in campus race relations were growing and the presidents of these schools were increasingly concerned, this pressure was still sporadic. The men who led these schools, both administrators and trustees, retained a sense of control, a sense that they had matters in hand. Even as the South was transforming around them, they believed that there was plenty of time to make decisions.

But even by 1950 the social, demographic, and economic changes in the region had begun to erode this sense of control. As the decade wore on, escalating tensions with the Soviet Union, the outbreak of the Korean War, and fears of domestic treason further ate away at the entire nation's confidence. Finally, in the aftermath of *Brown v. Board of Education,* the calm sense of mastery of the South's future that had allowed unhurried debate about the proper place for the "exceptional Negro" on campus was utterly destroyed. During the second half of the 1950s and the early 1960s, as the social and political atmosphere of the South became one of crisis, the notion that southern racial change could be quietly controlled by a small group of white men became completely untenable. The rise of both the grassroots civil rights movement and the massive white resistance that accompanied it cut to the very heart of this notion, as these groups forcefully seized control of events and denied in word and deed that any small group had the authority to make decisions for everyone else in the city or on campus. There was now unremitting pressure on these universities, accompanied by intense media interest that made every move an occasion for criticism from one side or the other. While tension had been growing between regional leadership and national prominence since the end of World War II, only now did these paths come to seem incompatible. Simply put, there was no longer any way for these schools to please both the white South and the rest of the country.

In response, the recalcitrance of the university boards only grew. Although at each school there were at least some trustees who supported change, many others expressed a willingness to sacrifice the gains their schools had made in order to keep the schools white. They blustered and talked tough, openly resentful of the pressure from "outsiders." But in the end, when the major foundations and the federal government made it clear in the early 1960s that segregated universities would no longer receive desperately needed funds, the boards simply capitulated.

What they would not do, however, was admit that they had capitulated.

Repeatedly, trustees and administrators claimed that they had not been compelled to change but had done so voluntarily. They insisted that their authority remained intact and that no Yankees, blacks, or federal bureaucrats had any power over them. Over the decade and a half of struggle their idea of compulsion, once exquisitely sensitive, had narrowed to include only court orders and military force. Thus, they could and did maintain with straight faces that their schools had volunteered to admit blacks, despite their years of gymnastic efforts to avoid exactly this outcome.

The organization of this book is chronological. The development of racial policy at these five institutions was slow and cumulative—apart from the 1954 decision in *Brown v. Board of Education* there were few dramatic events around which to organize a narrative. Matters are further complicated by the nearly constant interaction among the presidents of the schools, which makes it impossible to neatly separate one story from another. At the same time there were major differences, especially in the local social and political contexts, that shaped each institution in singular ways. The chapters are thus arranged by year, beginning with the immediate post–World War II era and ending with the final decision to desegregate, and they are divided into sections that analyze each school separately and, where appropriate, in relation to each other. Each chapter covers roughly a five-year span, with the exception of the discussion of the schools' reaction to *Brown*. This organization allows the gradual buildup of urgency to emerge naturally—the changes that took place in any given year (apart from 1954) are negligible, but over a five-year span significant differences in mood are readily discernible. Internally, each chapter is organized so as best to convey the major developments of the period, and there is thus no specific order in which the universities are treated.

Finally, a note about sources. This book is based almost entirely on written sources. Although there are quite a few people still living who participated in these events, I conducted no formal interviews, in large part because—unsurprisingly—most did not want to talk on the record. Many were, however, happy to talk off the record and I did have dozens of conversations with people involved in these events in one way or another, including two of the presidents. These conversations were extremely helpful in providing me with background and context, as well as in pointing me to fruitful archival sources. Notes from most of these conversations are in my possession.

1

Intelligent White Men of the South
The Late 1940s

T he presidents of Duke, Emory, Rice, Tulane, and Vanderbilt, charged with leading these universities into an uneasy post–World War II future, found themselves in the 1940s at the center of gradually growing controversy on campus. Each of these schools nurtured strong traditions and was deeply proud of its roots. Their alumni revered the founders and early leaders and the philosophical foundations of southern higher education that they had laid. The trustees, who had often known the giants of the past during their own days at school, saw these foundations—the nurturing of undergraduates, strong leadership in the South, a commitment in the denominational schools to Christian education—as guideposts for their own stewardship. Other ideals were unspoken but exerted no less influence. The older men who sat as trustees—locally powerful businessmen, bankers, attorneys, and clergymen—saw their schools as extensions of their private domains, places for their children and their friends' children to make important social and business contacts under the paternal gaze of trusted guardians of the status quo. They valued academic excellence and a strong national reputation, but usually rather less than they valued a good football team. Strict standards, but not exclusively academic ones, they believed, should guide admissions decisions. These should include the same kinds of standards that operated at the country club. Family background and ties, religion, good character, contributions to the community—all were easily as important as intelligence and ability in their definition of merit. These values endured among alumni and trustees long after World War II, even as American higher education as a whole was being completely transformed. As the years passed, these beliefs came under sometimes subtle but insistent attack as the southern universities were drawn into the national mainstream. More rapid and dislocating still were the changes to the larger southern economy and society. Trustees and older graduates felt buffeted and exhausted by this change, as the South and the schools they had known as boys disappeared.

The presidents of these five schools experienced the rapid changes after the war in a very different way from the trustees. While always carefully respectful of the past, they were more eager to embrace the future. Highly educated, they all had significant experience outside the region. Every one of them knew perfectly well that there was no university in the South that could even approach the attainments of any number of schools in the Northeast, the Midwest, and California. They also grasped that the new financial realities in the postwar world presented them with a rare chance to build real academic excellence, to join the top ranks of American higher education. They seized the opportunity presented by massive postwar federal research funding and continued philanthropic interest in southern education, engineering a leap forward in the quality of both teaching and research on these campuses. As they succeeded, these schools became far more cosmopolitan places, with more complex bureaucracies, professors and students from all around the country, and an increasingly sophisticated outlook on their place in the nation.

The presidents, with their broad view of the changing national academic landscape, conceived of these vast changes on their own campuses as the modern fulfillment of the founders' aspirations. They were uniquely situated, though, to grasp the depth of the opposition to new ways. All but one (Rice's William Houston) were themselves sons of the rural South who needed no instruction in the importance and subtleties of family relationships, social hierarchies, and local traditions. The social aspects of their roles as university presidents gave them a clear view of the world of the local leadership, with its private clubs, close-knit social scene, and loyalty to settled ways. From this vantage it was easy to see how a threatened and angry group of alumni could, in their reverence for the past, understand the postwar changes not as a fulfillment, but as a betrayal.

Thus, there was a growing gap between the presidents (and most of the faculty), who embraced the important changes in higher education as well as the changes in the social and economic climate of the nation and the South—and most of the trustees, who saw no reason to abandon a system that had given them happy and productive lives and that all their friends approved of on moral and social grounds. In order to be successful, university presidents must be adept at balancing the interests and desires of a variety of constituencies. No president has ever had the power to simply act as he or she thinks best. Not only trustees and alumni, but also faculty, students, administrators, financial backers, even local townspeople—all must be consulted, appeased, or squelched in accordance with changing needs. While their relative importance varies across time and circumstance, none of these groups can be safely ignored in making policy decisions. After World War II this problem became acute. The era began with intimations of change, and that change soon grew deeper than anyone imagined. The presidents of these institutions struggled to persuade the trustees, who held the final decision, to accept new curricula, a new emphasis on graduate studies, and an atmosphere of intellectual openness that many of them found suspect and even, at times, anti-American.

Among the changes brewing at these five schools was a new pattern of race relations. There had always been plenty of black people on campus. They were gardeners, porters, janitors, cooks, and laundry workers. A few held skilled positions as glass blowers for chemistry labs or machine shop technicians for engineers and physicists. Their roles on campus were carefully circumscribed, although with the usual local variation in segregation customs. In short, race relations on campus were an extension of race relations in Durham, Atlanta, Nashville, New Orleans, and Houston. This seemed ordinary and perfectly comfortable to the whites involved. In the postwar ferment, though, strange things began to happen. Blacks, becoming better educated and more prosperous by the year, started to come to campus for other reasons. Although there was not yet any real push to open admissions to black students, black townspeople sometimes came to hear concerts or lectures. The occasional black professor attended a scholarly meeting. At times, black ministers were invited to address campus groups, usually student religious organizations that earnestly debated issues of social welfare.

Even these minor changes enraged many alumni and trustees. While they accepted, grudgingly, the raft of substantive changes in the academic focus of the schools, race was a different matter. To many older alumni, faculty, and trustees the former seemed matters of judgment and debate, the latter examples of naked coercion. Hence, small breaches of established racial etiquette could trigger almost comically oversized fears. The presence of a single black speaker on campus could set off paroxysms of anger toward blacks who didn't "keep in their place," bullying northerners, and university administrators who cravenly submitted to their demands. There was, in this view, simply no predicting where it would all end. If no one would, or could, hold the line, these tiny breaches would end in a flood.

The presidents, however, remained focused on the job—building nationally respected academic institutions. Their daily lives were dominated by the tasks required to improve the schools' research and teaching enterprises. It was precisely because of this ambition that they remained ever mindful of the changing racial climate in the larger nation. In particular, each president kept close track of the growing anti-segregation sentiment among the federal agencies and private northern foundations that provided much of the money needed to improve the school. A struggle to reconcile the trustees to the new patterns of race relations was inevitable. To this end, the presidents adopted—each in his own way and each to his own particular purposes—a flexible rhetoric of moderation, one that turned on the critical proposition that in spite of growing outside pressures the white southern elite remained in firm control of race relations in the region and at these schools. This malleable, even ambiguous, rhetoric allowed those who feared change to articulate a seemingly moderate basis for caution, but it also helped the presidents who sought change to create the climate of calm they believed would allow them gently to nudge trustees forward.

I

Harvie Branscomb, chancellor of Vanderbilt, succeeded in clearing a path through the thicket of conflicts. Before the Vanderbilt Board of Trustees settled on Branscomb as the school's new chancellor, they had approached President Rufus Harris of Tulane about the job. Although tempted (and flattered) Harris turned them down, suggesting that his temperament was perhaps wrong for Vanderbilt. "Character, personality and temperment [sic] prescribe generally one's way of getting things done, and I do believe that mine would scarcely be effective or proper in concluding the issues and adjustments that appear to me to be necessary at Vanderbilt. . . . I am made aware that it will take a gentler hand than mine to do this." While it may be true that Harris's oversized personality would not have worked well in sedate Nashville, if Vanderbilt's trustees believed that they were getting a "gentler hand" in Harvie Branscomb they were greatly mistaken.[1]

In 1946 Branscomb was fifty-one years old and at the height of his considerable powers. He was a keenly intelligent man, strong willed, energetic, self-confident, and a subtle and astute politician. He had a powerful vision of what a great southern university could be and a powerful conviction that he was just the man to build one. From the moment he arrived on the Vanderbilt campus, Branscomb resolutely pursued what he believed to be the school's best interests with any means at his disposal, often to the discomfort of the trustees and alumni who sometimes fought change almost as ferociously as Branscomb sought it. From the start of his tenure, Branscomb was personally convinced that segregation's days were rightfully numbered; that it was both wrong and a terrible drain on southern society. He was also eager to gain Vanderbilt a national reputation and completely cognizant that these things were linked. Thus, among his efforts to improve Vanderbilt during the immediate postwar years Branscomb included steady work, often behind the scenes, to change the university's relationship to the black community. Almost from the moment Branscomb set foot on campus he began signaling that changes in relations with Nashville blacks were afoot. (Quietly reversing long-standing policy, for example, very early in his tenure he let Fisk University faculty know they were welcome to attend events at Vanderbilt's Neely Auditorium.)[2] Branscomb articulated a rationale for controlled, limited loosening of racial restrictions that convinced the trustees to allow a series of minor but meaningful adjustments. Carefully positioning himself not as an active proponent of change but rather as a sober, responsible southern leader, Branscomb pushed through moderate measures by arguing that southern whites had a duty to see to the best interests of the region's blacks and that failure to do so invited the intervention of people with more extreme views who could well do real damage. Branscomb's moderation was moderation with content. He staked out the middle ground in an effort to move all sides toward real, workable change.

Branscomb came from Alabama. He was born in Huntsville in 1894 and grew up in rural Alabama towns where his father, a Methodist minister, led congregations. Later in life he pointed to his father as an early model for his own beliefs about race in the South. His father, Branscomb reported, was "slightly more liberal on matters of race than most other citizens," an attitude he put into practice by inviting local black ministers to attend his weekly "Preachers Meeting." Probably wisely, few chose to attend, but the lesson was not lost.[3] As a young man Branscomb went off to study at Birmingham College, run by the Methodists of northern Alabama, and earned his B.A. in 1914. It was, he later noted, "a useful institution, struggling to become a superior one," but while he was there it remained the "kind of college where lunch was sometimes late because we had to wait for President Simpson to come out from town on a street car with the bread under his arm."[4] The contrast must have been staggering when Branscomb arrived at Oxford as only the second Rhodes scholarship winner from Alabama.[5] He spent three years there and earned a distinguished M.A. in biblical studies.

Branscomb left Oxford to serve with Herbert Hoover's Belgian Relief

Commission and then returned to the United States in July 1917, ready to enter the military. After trying and failing to join the air force, he instead went to work for the army YMCA at Camp Wheeler in Macon, Georgia. There, he spent a brief stint with Will Alexander, noted for his progressive ideas about racial justice in the South, who ran the YMCA's pastoral and social service efforts at southern army camps.[6] Branscomb did then enter the army briefly, returning home in 1918.

In 1919 Branscomb took a job as a philosophy instructor at the infant Southern Methodist University in Dallas. After a year, he became an associate professor and moved over to teach in the School of Theology. With characteristic confidence Branscomb believed that the post–World War I era held real opportunities for progress, and he was convinced that teaching theology put him in position to exert important influence on the course the South would take. With the region "facing in the next decade a choice of roads, reactionary resistance to change or acceptance of new ways of thinking and acting," Branscomb thought that the education of the South's next generation of ministers was critical. "No progress in the South could be made," he believed, "without the major Protestant churches . . . going along." Although this analysis had much to recommend it, Branscomb's estimation of the South's readiness for significant change was wildly optimistic.[7]

Branscomb's departure from SMU in 1925 provided ample evidence of the conservatism that continued to permeate the South, its churches, and its institutions of higher education. When a colleague in the School of Theology was fired for exposing students to what were deemed unacceptably liberal theological teachings, Branscomb fought the school's administration. His defense of the fired teacher was both too public and too stubborn, as well as completely ineffective. Branscomb himself was summarily fired. Although his opposition to the school's actions was absolutely consistent with his intellectual leanings, his intensity was probably explained by the fact that he already had a job offer from the Duke University Divinity School. It was simply time to leave.[8]

Branscomb arrived at Duke at the age of thirty and stayed for twenty-one years, leaving only to finish his doctoral dissertation in 1927 and for a year of study in Europe. Fortunately, his early performance as a campus politician at SMU did not turn out to be typical. As time passed he revealed a strong streak of political acumen, and in 1944 he became the dean of the Divinity School. Harkening back to his father, when he assumed that position he opened the school's chapel services to black ministers, who were sometimes invited to participate. Branscomb left in 1946 when he assumed the chancellorship at Vanderbilt.[9]

Vanderbilt University had been established, after several false starts, in 1873. It was organized by the Methodist Church, led by the powerful Bishop Holland McTyeire, but funded largely by Cornelius Vanderbilt. A bumpy beginning gave way to a period of vigorous growth and steady improvement. By the early 1900s, however, Vanderbilt's ties to the Methodist church had become a hindrance. The church leaders who controlled the board were increasingly unhappy with the school's movement toward becoming a broader, more secular institution that accompanied its strides in quality. At the same time, the church did not provide Vanderbilt with enough funds, which forced the administration to look outside for money. This too was a problem, as non-Methodist donors were wary of the school's strong denominational ties. The result, in the middle of the 1910s, was a bitter legal battle that ended with the church and the university severing their official relationship. By the 1930s, Vanderbilt was on fairly solid footing, due largely to huge grants from the Carnegie Foundation, the Vanderbilt family, and the General Education Board of the Rockefeller Foundation. Still, the school remained, in Paul Conkin's words, a "thoroughly conventional" regional institution. It struggled with academic quality and with the balance between its powerful, northern-funded Medical School and the rest of the university. The Depression and World War II kept Vanderbilt from more than incremental growth in size and quality.[10]

When Branscomb arrived as chancellor in 1946, what he had to work with did not look promising. Vanderbilt was too small, with woefully inadequate facilities. Outside its Medical School, it had no really prominent faculty. Its immediate neighborhood was steadily deteriorating. Lacking even minimally adequate housing, it had become nearly a streetcar college. Half of its students came from Nashville, two-thirds from Tennessee. Its enrollment in the fall of 1946 of about three thousand, swollen with returning veterans, was its largest ever by over 50 percent. Worse, in spite of the fact that Vanderbilt had no debt, its finances were in truly awful shape, with an acute shortage of income. Unrestricted gifts for the year following the war totaled only $8,358, despite four high-pressure fund-raising campaigns in the previous eight years with another one in progress when Branscomb arrived. Still, he took the job with a sense of anticipation, "convinced that the time had come to establish a great university in [this] part of the South."[11]

Branscomb wasted no time in getting on with the work. He set out on the road, speaking to Vanderbilt alumni groups in Washington, New York,

Chicago, St. Louis, and finally Memphis. In every city he highlighted the same themes. First, he stressed the critical role of higher education in preserving the "American democratic ideal." No democracy, he declared, can survive without a moral basis. "This is the critical issue which directly involves the university," he said, and "Vanderbilt stands firm, and will continue to stand as a great exponent of the liberal tradition which has been the creative force in the western world." Second, Branscomb noted that postwar changes would inevitably transform Vanderbilt's identity and goals. While Vanderbilt would certainly remain a school with a southern identity and retain a leadership role in southern education, Branscomb explained that the South was now closer to the rest of the United States economically, politically, and even culturally than it had been in a century. He expected it to grow even closer in the years to come. Thus, Vanderbilt had an obligation to expand its circle of influence and to make a national contribution.[12]

This argument was the bedrock of Branscomb's efforts to create a top-flight university over the next two decades. Progress, both for Vanderbilt and the South, meant movement toward the national mainstream. To pull inward in the face of sweeping changes would lead only to isolation and irrelevance. Branscomb truly believed, just as he had in the wake of World War I, that the region and its educational institutions should embrace new ways of thinking and acting. This time, however, he recognized that this would not simply happen by itself. Better understanding the resistance to change, he also better understood that he had to carefully prepare the Vanderbilt alumni (and board) to accept new ideas. Thus in his speeches and correspondence he presented change as something challenging but not overwhelming. He was a good speaker who could sound gently wistful for the South of his boyhood and then finish with a clear-eyed assessment of the need for different ways of doing things. Above all, he stood up for the region's dignity. There could be no progress, he maintained before all sorts of audiences, without other regions respecting the South's contributions to the nation. A real respect for southern tradition was almost a precondition for change, as the region's economic growth, political health, and social progress all depended on identifying and exploiting the region's strengths.

In the wake of World War II, though, Vanderbilt's most pressing problem was not the region's, or even the university's, place in the nation. It was money. If Vanderbilt were ever to become more than a good regional school, it would need a lot more of it. Branscomb's first move was to reorganize Vanderbilt's financial administration. He also quickly adopted more aggressive investment strategies and began a concerted effort to spur alumni giving. These changes did help the school increase its income, as did the tuition revenues that grew along with postwar enrollments. But the real boost came from the federal government and private foundations. Branscomb's pursuit of funds from these sources was immediate and energetic, and success came quickly. In 1949 the Rockefeller Foundation's General Education Board gave $1 million to endow the Graduate School, a key component in the drive for national prestige, with another $200,000 to follow over a five-year period.[13]

Already, however, it was becoming clear that this money would have strings attached. The philanthropic foundations and the federal government were growing uneasy about segregation on southern campuses and were considering changes in their funding policies in order to discourage it. No federal agency or major private philanthropy had yet made desegregation a requirement, but the handwriting was on the wall. Branscomb maintained quite a few personal relationships with administrators at the large foundations, which allowed him to understand that they were not going to abandon their concern about racial discrimination on southern campuses and that this would result one day in restrictions on grants.

Race relations at Vanderbilt upon Branscomb's arrival were simple. He noted in his memoirs that when he arrived in 1946 he was told "no black man had ever been on the Vanderbilt campus except in a menial capacity."[14] He judged this to be not strictly accurate but understood it as a statement of the school's broad official attitude. (The city of Nashville in the 1940s was thoroughly segregated, and the separation of the races was so ordinary as to require no comment.)[15] Branscomb's position on race relations, though, was more complex. Although he rarely advocated change on the basis of democratic or Christian principles, Branscomb was offended by the daily unfairness of segregation. His experiences in England and back in the United States with the YMCA after World War I, coupled with his strong Methodist faith and upbringing, had done much to shape his belief that southern blacks must be allowed to rise as far as they could. His devotion to southern progress led him to scorn segregation's waste of black talent as an unaffordable sin in a backward region.

Without question, however, Branscomb believed that changes in the practice of segregation could happen only slowly and only at the "level of the exceptional Negro." He showed real discomfort with lower-class blacks, even suggesting that there were limits to their ability to grasp basic concepts of health and hygiene. Branscomb's personal unease with racial mixing was never more evident than in a 1954 episode in which he discovered that Vanderbilt ROTC boys were sharing barracks space at Fort Campbell with blacks from Ohio. Although assured by the students that it was fine with them, Branscomb was clearly upset as he wrote of his "sense of surprise and almost shock" at the situation.[16] Similarly, in the late 1940s Branscomb opposed the mixing of black and white children in public schools. (Not surprisingly, his position on this would change over time.) He argued that most blacks had capabilities so much lower than even poor whites that it simply made no sense. "Opportunities," he believed, "must be given in some sort of relationship to capacities to use them and the mixing of populations must be on some general levels of approximately equal and similar social backgrounds and mores."[17]

The treatment of educated, middle-class blacks, however, seemed unreasonably harsh to Branscomb. This harshness he understood to be the product of historical change.[18] Branscomb saw two stages of race relations in the South. "The first was the slavery pattern, the second the one which grew up under the unrealistic idealism and sheer cynicism of the carpetbagger governments. This second pattern was worked out to deal with an uneducated inexperienced race which had just been released from slavery." Contemporary unfairness resulted from the fact that many southern blacks no longer resembled in any way the "uneducated inexperienced" freedmen of the Reconstruction era. For the good of the entire region, a third pattern in race relations should now evolve. "Negroes of education and ability" must be not merely accommodated but encouraged. "The South," Branscomb declared, "must have ways of enabling the educated Negro to take his place in and make his contribution to the work and advancement of the South."[19]

There was a critical qualification, though. Control of the gradual demise of segregation must remain in the hands of the white southern leadership. Only educated southern whites, who understood both the power of southern tradition and the need for change, had the mature judgment to steer a course that avoided the real danger of massive white violence. Only they had a practical sense of how much change the white South would peacefully accept. Practicality thus counseled slow, cautious movement toward a gradual reconciliation of progress and tradition. In Branscomb's view anyone who pushed an "idealistic agenda" was dangerous, because idealism clouded judgment and elevated principle above a "realistic" assessment of danger. Thus northerners, the NAACP, "militant" black students, and overeager white ones all (ironically) blocked progress by advocating it too strongly, thus setting off a defensive reaction among white traditionalists. These groups, in Branscomb's opinion, were the real enemies of racial conciliation. "The more I travel north and south," he wrote to Vanderbilt professor Donald Davidson, "the more I am convinced that the only hope for reaching a sensible solution to [the race] problem lies with the intelligent white men of the south."[20]

Branscomb treaded with caution in his first years at Vanderbilt. There was real tension between his natural optimism and boldness, which made him impatient for change, and his assessment of what was possible—that is, what he could convince the Vanderbilt board to accept. Branscomb almost always resolved this contest in favor of prudence, but he did not use prudence as an excuse to avoid action. He wanted action. His concern was how best to bring it about. Here, the fate of a proposal for a new graduate center that Branscomb drafted in 1949 is instructive. In planning for substantial growth in graduate education at Vanderbilt, Branscomb concluded that the black colleges, underfunded and inadequately staffed, were unable to provide first-rate graduate education to the most talented southern blacks and that state institutions, currently all white, would likewise fail them. This situation was grossly inefficient and harmful to the region. His solution was ambitious: a graduate school, operated by Vanderbilt but separate physically and organizationally from the rest of the campus, that would admit the best students in the region without regard to race.[21]

Branscomb was far from innocent about the likely reaction. "It must be anticipated that such a move would involve—unless compelled by legal action—resignations from the governing board, the reduction of enrollment at the undergraduate level, and quite possibly a lawsuit enjoining the action." While he thought "such unhappy and strife-laden consequences" were unavoidable, he also claimed to believe that they could be kept to a minimum. Acknowledging the difficulties posed by the actual physical presence of black students (who were regarded as "unclean" by many whites no matter how smart they were), he proposed following the pattern of German universities, which assumed no responsibility for the housing and social aspects of students' lives.[22] Branscomb, ever the optimist, hoped that if this project were launched "on a scale broad enough to capture the imagination," it could be done without serious damage to Vanderbilt and could—in a single stroke—change the future of southern race relations. Further, he thought the rest of the country might take it as a sign that the South was willing to begin dismantling segregation, and thereby lessen regional bitterness.[23]

Branscomb sent copies of this preliminary proposal, in confidence, to O. C. Carmichael, his predecessor at Vanderbilt who was now president of the Carnegie Foundation for the Advancement of Teaching, and to Robert Calkins at the General Education Board of the Rockefeller Foundation. Both returned lengthy favorable comments. Carmichael was especially enthusiastic, arguing that based on the easy desegregation of the Law and Medical Schools at the University of Arkansas, "there will be more praise than blame for the action throughout the south."[24]

Yet Branscomb abandoned the proposal and his reasons for doing so are clear. Even to submit it to a funding agency would require the blessing of the Vanderbilt Board of Trustees, a blessing that Branscomb knew would not be forthcoming. Branscomb both liked and respected the trustees who had chosen him as chancellor, but he understood from the beginning that his views on the South's racial practices put him at odds with the traditionalists on the Vanderbilt board. "The race issue," he wrote in his memoirs, "was one from which I anticipated trouble when I came [to Vanderbilt]. I regarded myself as liberally inclined, and I had traveled around enough to know that this issue would have to be met. . . . I remember thinking that the inclusion of Negroes in the educational services which Vanderbilt would bring to the South might well be an issue on which a break with the institution's constituency could occur."[25]

When Branscomb began his tenure at Vanderbilt in 1946, the board had thirty-two members, plus the chancellor. Of those thirty-two, seventeen were at least sixty-five years old and ten of those were at least seventy. The term of office was eight years, at the end of which all were regularly reelected. They were all alumni, all businessmen or professionals, and all devoted to Vanderbilt. They were also, he noted, "fine men who belonged to that second generation after the War Between the States, men who had worked hard and achieved positions of prominence and, in several instances, of affluence."[26] The trustees indeed loved Vanderbilt, but they "had reached the age when most of them preferred to relax and enjoy the pleasant things their years of labor had brought." It was plain, Branscomb wrote in 1970, that "the Board needed an infusion of new ideas, the addition of some younger men, and greater contacts with the national forces so important in the development of any university."[27]

Predictably, the board put up some resistance to greater contacts with national forces. In 1947 two new trustees were elected, one being Henry Alexander, a banker who would become the chairman of J. P. Morgan. Branscomb was very happy with this choice, as Alexander represented precisely the kind of new influence he had in mind. Still, opposition within the board to the addition of a New York banker, even though he was a Vanderbilt graduate, was troubling.[28] So Branscomb, in what may well have been the shrewdest political move of his career, took matters into his own hands. He convinced Harold Sterling Vanderbilt—a grandson of the university's founder, a New Yorker, and a billionaire—to join the Vanderbilt Board. Harold Vanderbilt was, of course, enormously wealthy, but it was not primarily for his wealth that Branscomb sought him out. (Branscomb in fact surprised Vanderbilt by not asking him for money at all in the course of his overtures.) Rather, it was his general view of the world, which was infinitely more cosmopolitan than that of the local Nashville trustees, and the vast influence that his name and stature would have on their actions. When he was able to get him on the board, in early 1950, Branscomb secured his own ability to gain trustee approval for the changes, racial and otherwise, that were necessary for the university to move forward.[29]

In 1949, however, the Vanderbilt board was still dominated by its Nashville faction— conservative, traditional, and led by the outspoken publisher of the *Nashville Banner,* James Stahlman, who had already vowed to oppose any effort to break down the color line on campus. Branscomb's abandonment of his proposal for integrated graduate education was thus a bow to reality. However much he might have wanted Vanderbilt to break the path for the rest of the South, he realized that this approach would never even get past his own board. Rather than start a fight he surely knew he wouldn't win—and which might well destroy his credibility with the board in the process—Branscomb backed away and decided to take another tack. If it wasn't possible to deal with segregation at Vanderbilt in a sweeping stroke, he would instead undermine it one small piece at a time.

Branscomb described this general approach in a 1949 letter to Joseph W. Holley,[30] the founder and longtime president of a black college in Georgia, Albany State. "We are living in a critical time in which I believe that the progress of the Negroes in the United States is being greatly accelerated. It is extremely important that this progress not change into the form of a conflict between the ideal and the practical. The most important thing, it seems to me, is to preserve that attitude of good will and cooperation which you have personified so fully, to preserve every forward step adding to them steadily as time goes on. It is a situation in which character and ability to take advantage of every situation are the primary requirements for leadership."[31]

"Taking advantage of situations as they arose" and adding steadily to each forward step, as Branscomb wrote to Holley, became his standard procedure when racial issues popped up on campus. Over and over, he came to the trustees with tiny "difficulties" that they could solve by simply relaxing some specific segregation policy without giving up their commitment to segregation. He always made it easier for the board to give in than to fight by making a careful case that flexibility would be prudent and rigidity damaging. Raising the practical over the ideal was Branscomb's stock-in-trade, although his notion of the ideal and the board's could hardly have been more different.

Branscomb was always careful to raise these racial issues on his own terms and in his own time. While his general strategy was to wait for minor issues to present themselves and then use them to induce minor changes, from time to time he dodged questions, judging, apparently, that sometimes even making an argument was politically unwise. Always, he was careful to preserve his political capital with the Vanderbilt board. For example, when approached in January 1949 by the Tennessee Philological Association (which was about to invite language and literature teachers at the state's black colleges to join) regarding the possibility of someday scheduling a meeting at Vanderbilt, Branscomb simply put off deciding. Since the association did not yet actually have black members, he wrote, the issue of how Vanderbilt would handle such a meeting had not yet arisen and so Vanderbilt did not have to establish a policy.[32] Similarly, explaining why he did not want Charles S. Johnson, the president of Fisk and his personal friend, to join the heads of the other local colleges on the podium at a University Center event, Branscomb wrote that granting Johnson any "special prominence" was sure to "create a misimpression." He went on to explain that Vanderbilt has "tried to be as helpful as we can to the Fisk and Meharry [the city's black Medical School] faculties, and have occasionally had one of them take part in a conference or program where there were specific reasons why they should be present. Where there are not such reasons, we have tried to avoid bringing them in unnecessarily."[33] Avoiding arguments like these, where there was little to be gained in any event, allowed Branscomb to maintain his credibility when he came before the trustees with claims that change was necessary.

By the same token, if Branscomb saw the possibility of some strategic gain, he might discreetly let it be known that he would support a move. For example, he sent a note to the faculty head of the Vanderbilt Medical Society, Dr. James Ward, mentioning that he had heard discussion about the society possibly inviting members of the Meharry faculty to the group's scientific meetings. Although he suggested that it would be better if such attendance were on "some informal and non-publicized basis," Branscomb directly told Ward that whatever the medical society chose to do, he "would be prepared to defend the Society's action in case there should be any difficulties concerning it."[34]

Branscomb made his first attempt to move Vanderbilt off center in racial matters in early 1948, addressing the issue at the board's February meeting. He began by pointing out that while race relations was hardly a new problem in the South, it had recently become a matter of new prominence in higher education. He ran through a list of events that seemed to portend change—the newly issued report of the Truman Commission on Higher Education, federal court decisions in Missouri and Oklahoma, and rumors of a possible call by the Association of American Colleges for the elimination of segregation. In keeping with his broad strategy, Branscomb first carefully soothed the board, reassuring them that he personally was not in favor of any dramatic changes in race relations. (While this wasn't precisely a lie, neither was it strictly true. As his aborted proposal for the integrated graduate school shows, Branscomb was in favor of changes that would have seemed more than dramatic to these men.) He flatly stated his agreement with those who dissented from the Truman Commission's call for an end to segregated higher education, and he again tried to reassure the trustees that "[segregation] has been the policy of the leading educational institutions of the South, and it remains the cardinal principle of the policy we are trying to carry out at Vanderbilt."[35]

However, Branscomb also told the trustees that for reasons of both principle and practicality Vanderbilt could no longer maintain "a purely negative position." He used an ingenious rhetorical maneuver designed to deflate their anger at perceived "outside" coercion on race. Appealing to their loyalty to embattled southern ways, Branscomb suggested that the only effective way to resist pressure from outside the region was to remain true to southern tradition. That tradition, he then argued, was never one of hostility to blacks but rather a paternal one of responsible care. Being "helpful to the Negro institutions in our City, and to the needs of the individual members of those institutions," Branscomb explained, "has always been the attitude of the best southern leadership. We would, it seems to me, be false to our position if we repudiated it under present conditions and pressures."[36]

Branscomb fleshed out his definition of *helpfulness* by describing some recent events on campus. Librarians at Fisk and Tennessee A&I had asked to use the Library of Congress catalogue held by the Joint University Library at Vanderbilt. Branscomb urged the black schools to buy the recently printed edition of the catalogue, but he let them use Vanderbilt's catalogue until their set arrived and anytime thereafter when the bound set didn't provide what they needed. This solution, he told the trustees, held to his two main principles, "to endeavor to be helpful, and yet not to establish regular recurring inter-racial patterns." The board agreed.

Branscomb avoided mentioning a fact that the trustees certainly understood. The Joint University Library, a cooperative venture involving Vanderbilt, Peabody, and Scarritt colleges, was funded by the GEB, an organization with a deep commitment to black education and from which Vanderbilt was about to seek a major gift for its Graduate School. Apparently wanting to avoid any suggestion of coercion, Branscomb never mentioned that permission for black librarians to consult a catalogue could hardly be refused without running the risk of angering one of the largest donors to southern higher education.

Branscomb closed his report with an argument that returned to the heart of his strategy for measured, practical racial change. "Wise southern leadership," he argued, "has felt that one of the essentials for the handling of this problem has been the encouragement and support of those temperate and realistic leaders of the Negro race who were willing to face the realities of this problem." By working with "the best type of Negro leadership," men who were "endeavoring to lead their race along the slow path of hard work, educational advancement and moral improvement," Vanderbilt could prevent worse problems. Give-and-take with reasonable black leaders would help ensure that unreasonable demands for deep change would not present a threat. Failure to encourage these leaders, failure to make the "realistic" small concessions that would help them lead their race forward, would only weaken them and, in the end, "play into the hands of the radical and revolutionary" black leaders.[37]

Branscomb convinced the trustees that such minor matters could be dealt with flexibly. On larger issues, however, they remained immovable. In late May 1949, both the admissions office and the chancellor's office received a request for admission to the School of Law from a black veteran named Robert Williams. This friendly and honest letter caught Branscomb's attention and he approached the university's attorney (and board member) Cecil Sims, for an opinion as to whether Mr. Williams could enroll. Sims replied almost immediately. "In answer to your recent inquiry, you are advised that Tennessee law especially forbids the attendance of white and colored persons in the same school, academy, college, or other place of learning." Branscomb, perhaps sensing an opportunity to begin softening the board's attitude, approached the executive committee with the application, arguing that while Williams must be notified that his application could not be considered, the words "at this time" ought to be appended. The committee overruled him.[38]

II

In May 1948, Harvie Branscomb sent a copy of his statement to the Vanderbilt board on race relations to Goodrich White, the president of Emory University. White strongly approved of it, telling Branscomb that he was "in thorough accord with the general principles you state."[39] To anyone familiar with Goodrich White's tenure at Emory, this seems almost shocking. Where Branscomb worked hard to lay the groundwork for loosening racial restrictions, White never urged the Emory board to take a single step in that direction. Quite the contrary, his position on segregation in general and at Emory in particular led him to downplay any need for change on campus. In part, this simply reflects White's personality. He was warm, strong, and stable, but much less aggressive than Branscomb. He was deferential to the Emory trustees and personally conservative. White also harbored a very real fear of southern white backlash, a fear fed by Georgia's volatile racial politics. Thus, where Branscomb believed that Vanderbilt should begin a process of gradual desegregation, White supported in Atlanta a "fairer" segregation, one that would provide more opportunities for able blacks within black institutions. It was White's judgment that at Emory the balance between change and tradition had to be found closer to the side of tradition.

These differences, however, did mask a degree of underlying agreement. White and Branscomb concurred that the appropriate people to decide where this balance lay were men like themselves, the "intelligent white men of the South." Implicit in this was a shared understanding that local conditions in different cities, on different campuses, and at different times would naturally lead to different judgments. It was up to each man to decide when to go and when to stop, and it was only to be expected that this would not be the same in Georgia as it was in Tennessee.

When forced to confront racial issues, then, White could use precisely the same argument that Branscomb made to the Vanderbilt trustees—outsiders cannot understand the subtleties of this problem, cooperation with the black elite is essential, and the ideal cannot be permitted to conflict with the practical. It is critical to note here, though, that Branscomb used this argument as a tool to coax change out of reluctant trustees, but White seemed to seize on it as a way to slow change down, to forestall the racial disaster that he feared. It is also important to note that the language itself will fairly bear the divergent uses.

Goodrich Cook White was born in 1889 and spent his boyhood in Griffin, a county seat town in middle Georgia. In 1959 he wrote a biographical sketch, possibly a draft for a speech, in which he reminisced about the world of his youth, a world he described as "closer in time to the Georgia of Longstreet's Georgia Scenes than to the Georgia—at least to the Atlanta—of today."[40] It was a world of cotton tenancy and sharecropping, with a mill village across the railroad tracks from town, and Saturdays spent around the courthouse square. White grew up in town, working at a general store and happily attending school, at which he excelled. His family lived in a tight circle that revolved around the Methodist Church, where his grandfather was pastor.

It was also a world of racial segregation. "Jim Crow," White wrote, "was in practice an established fact, whether by law or otherwise." Although blacks had not yet been completely disenfranchised, White considered that "during these years the Negro had been 'put in his place' and it was pretty well assumed that he would stay there. It was hardly necessary to feel contempt for him." That place was clear: "There were two 'nigger towns.' I knew where they were, but that was about all. There were Negro schools and Negro churches. That they were any of my concern was never suggested. We saw Negroes every day. They worked in the kitchens and in the yards and gardens; as nursemaids; as porters and waiters in the two small hotels; they drove the drays." Despite White's recollection of a Sunday afternoon lynching, which greatly disturbed his grandfather, for a young boy these arrangements were simply beyond questioning. "The Negroes' status was fixed," he explained, "and as far as I knew there was no 'race problem.'"[41]

White went off to Emory College, in Oxford, Georgia, and earned his A.B. in 1908, at the age of eighteen. A fraternity member and a fair athlete, he was more noted for his academic achievements and his skill as an editor and a debater.[42] (Remarkably, apart from the first six years after his graduation White spent his entire adult life affiliated with Emory.) He worked briefly for the Methodist Publishing House in Nashville, and then went to New York to study at Columbia University for his master's degree in psychology, which he received in 1911. After two years teaching English at Kentucky Wesleyan and one teaching psychology at Wesleyan College in Macon, Georgia, he returned to Emory in 1914 as an associate professor of "mental and moral science." During World War I White was a lieutenant in the psychological division of the U.S. Army Medical Corps. He administered intelligence tests to southerners, both black and white, in an effort to identify those who were unfit for military duty. This effort yielded results that deeply puzzled analysts who would spend years trying to explain them away: many black soldiers from the North scored higher than white southern farmers. These results apparently fascinated White, who kept his original copies of some of the early reports in his files.[43]

After the war White returned to Emory, now relocated in Atlanta and christened a university, where he proved a stalwart administrator. He assumed increasing responsibility, serving as dean of the College of Arts and Sciences beginning in 1923 and taking on the additional duties of the dean of the Graduate School in 1929 (after a leave of absence to earn his doctorate in psychology from the University of Chicago in 1927). He held these positions concurrently until 1938, when he resigned as arts and sciences dean upon his appointment as the university's vice president. He retained that post, as well as the deanship of the Graduate School, until he became Emory's president in 1942.[44]

Fiercely devoted to Emory, White nonetheless understood that the school he led was not as prestigious or academically advanced as Duke, Tulane, Rice, or Vanderbilt. To be fair, its horizons at this time were simply set somewhat lower. The Georgia Methodists had established Emory University in 1838 as Emory College. Slowly, it became a good regional college, with a classical curriculum and a strong commitment to Christian education. Its major turning point came in 1914, when in the aftermath of the split between the Methodist Church and Vanderbilt University the church turned its attention to establishing a new Methodist university in the southeast. Strongly influenced by Bishop Warren A. Candler and his brother, Coca-Cola founder Asa G. Candler, a church commission decided to locate the new school in Atlanta, with Emory College forming its undergraduate core. A gift of $1 million from Asa Candler helped the transition, and this time the churchmen carefully drafted the charter to ensure that Emory University would remain in their hands.[45] With this support, the university grew steadily, opening the School of Theology, Medical School, Law School, the School of Business Administration, and the Graduate School as well as expanding and improving the undergraduate faculty. Finances, while also improving, remained a chronic problem, and the Depression hit Emory particularly hard.[46]

At the end of World War II, Emory was still struggling. It was hampered by the fact that until 1946 it offered no work at all toward the doctorate and only limited work at the master's level, which had been suspended during the war. Although a postwar boom quickly propelled the school toward a major expansion of its graduate program, including the addition of Ph.D. programs, Emory began this era far behind its peers. Too, Emory was still officially and quite tightly tied to the Methodist Church. The influence of the Methodist hierarchy on the Board of Trustees was strong.[47]

Equally strong was the influence of the Atlanta business community, which provided nearly all of Emory's non–church affiliated board members and which maintained a firm grasp on the politics of the city and the state. A study of the state's political process, done in 1947 but unpublished until 1998, concluded that Georgia's large corporate interests, based in Atlanta, had mastered that process to such an extent that they were the de facto rulers of Georgia. This study focused on the city of Atlanta and found that a mere forty people, nearly all businessmen, effectively ran the city. Ivan Allen Jr., mayor of Atlanta for most of the sixties, later echoed these findings, claiming that the power structure in Atlanta included "the leaders of the top fifty or so businesses in the city." These were all rich men, and all were "white, Anglo-Saxon, Protestant, Atlantan, business-oriented, non-political, moderate, well-bred, well-educated, pragmatic, and dedicated to the betterment of Atlanta."[48]

Still, as president of Emory, Goodrich White faced a political reality very different from the one Harvie Branscomb encountered in Tennessee. Long before segregation became an incendiary issue in the politics of other southern states, Georgia's gubernatorial contests revolved around race. Controlled by the Democratic Party, the state saw intense competition between the party's two main wings even though there was little of substance to distinguish them. Both supported economic growth and modernization but coupled this with resistance to any social change that would upset the traditional order. This contradictory stance led to severe conflict later, but even in the 1940s it brought race to the forefront of politics.[49]

Georgia's "county unit" election system created a sort of state-level electoral college. Each county had two, four, or six votes, determined by population. Those votes were delivered as a unit to the candidate who garnered the most popular votes in the county. This system was designed to prevent urban areas from completely controlling the state, and it did so very effectively. Biased against the most populous counties from the beginning, that bias grew larger in lockstep with the growth of the cities and kept politicians from winning by simply courting the support of the powerful commercial interests in Atlanta.[50] Although this support was indeed critical, so were the votes of the rural, traditional, and increasingly frightened counties of southern Georgia. Politicians soon learned that full-out racial demagoguery and a fervid insistence on maintaining southern traditions in the face of perceived federal encroachments gained the votes of the "wool hat boys." And, while sophisticated businessmen in Atlanta may have felt distaste at the vigor and style of this invective, they were unoffended by the core of the message and willing to go along, as long as politicians continued to serve their economic interests.[51]

As early as 1942 Ellis Arnall made race a campaign issue in gubernatorial politics. He defeated incumbent Eugene Talmadge, helped in part by Talmadge's heavy-handed attempts to purge the faculty of the University of Georgia of "integrationists" the year before. The resulting loss of accreditation dealt a blow to the state's reputation and, more important, posed a threat to Atlanta's business interests.[52] Thereafter, the key issues in Georgia politics were race and segregation. The 1946 Democratic primary — the only election that counted — was a three-way contest that pitted two progressives against the traditionalist Talmadge. The campaign was a savage one fought largely over white supremacy. Talmadge seized on a recent Supreme Court decision, *Smith v. Allwright,* which invalidated the white primary, to conjure up images of federal tyranny and black rule. Robert Mizell, a longtime Emory administrator and a confidant of Coca-Cola president Robert Woodruff, summed up the situation in Atlanta in February 1946: "Not since the Atlanta riots some forty years ago has the race question been such an inflammable issue as now." Talmadge's victory, although followed almost immediately by his death, set the tone for Georgia politics well into the 1960s. His son Herman became governor in 1948, again campaigning on a promise to reinstate the white primary, raising the specter of miscegenation and intimidating black voters away from the polls. This series of divisive elections did much to keep racial fears at a boil throughout the 1940s and beyond.[53]

Goodrich White spoke and acted while he was president of Emory with full, nuanced understanding of these political realities. His personal beliefs about southern race relations also played an important part in his actions. He was not nostalgic and did not pine for the region's "glorious heritage," which as an adult he came to suspect had never existed. In his brief 1959 memoir he expressed regret at the persistence of the social and psychological characteristics of his early century, small town southern upbringing into the modern South, and at the failure of the region to confront its racial troubles. By the time he wrote this sketch, White, who as a child knew nothing of the race problem, believed that "the Negro has been *the* problem of the South throughout virtually its entire history. The problem cuts across every aspect of our life." In one particularly direct passage White revealed his own confusions about race and the South's relation to its traditions and to the rest of the country.

> There have been times when I thought—perhaps it was only wishful thinking—that the South was well on the way to mastery of its [race] problem and the attainment of maturity, properly cherishing whatever is admirable in its past but not trying to live *in* it and *on* it, facing the issues of the day as Americans, divided perhaps among ourselves but not always having our positions brought to the test of whether or no they are properly "Southern." But I can no longer delude myself or even cherish the hope. We have been set back—how many decades I do not dare to say. I would like to get off the defensive. I find it very hard to be patient with the haters of the South—or even with those who, personally tolerant and sympathetic, or at least polite, utterly fail to understand. Often defense is extremely difficult. And it is hardest of all to satisfy my conscience and to define the fine line between patience, wisdom and justifiable prudence on the one hand and cowardice on the other.[54]

This fine line White chose to walk as president of Emory. He approached any racial issue with extreme caution. White quite clearly believed that segregation as practiced led to gross injustices. Surrounded by the able and accomplished men and women in Atlanta's black colleges as well as in the city's growing black business class, he was not blind to the unfair treatment meted out to them in the name of tradition.[55] Believing himself, however, constrained by political circumstances, by the heavy weight of tradition, and by demagogues' manipulation of that tradition, White consistently chose a guarded path. Rather than make any attempt to break down the color line at Emory, he turned his attention to the improvement of Georgia's segregated institutions. No hypocrite, White served for years on the board of Clark College, a black undergraduate college in Atlanta, and worked throughout his adult life with other black institutions in the area on a more limited basis. Improving these schools, he believed, was the only racial progress that white Georgians would peacefully accept.[56] Much as he acted on his belief that enlightened whites should work to advance the black race within the bounds of segregation, behind the scenes he sometimes led the university to do what it could to bolster black institutions. In 1947 Emory donated a piece of land adjacent to its teaching hospital, Grady Memorial, for a new, desperately needed black hospital. Emory's Medical School also pledged to take responsibility for training black residents and interns at that facility, which would remain segregated. (Unsurprisingly, the school reneged on that commitment when the complications of maintaining segregation in a teaching hospital ward proved to be more than it could deal with.)[57]

White cogently articulated his views on segregation in higher education when he served on President Truman's Commission on Higher Education, organized in the summer of 1946. In an acknowledgment of the changes that swirled in the wake of the war, this group began a formal reexamination of the "objectives, methods and facilities" of the American system of higher education "in light of the social role it has to play." Charged with producing recommendations on a wide variety of subjects, the commission quickly split into subcommittees.[58] In October 1947 the subcommittee on "Equalizing and Expanding Individual Opportunity," chaired by Milton Eisenhower, presented its draft report to the full commission and called firmly for the complete elimination of segregated higher education in the South.

White did not speak up until it was time for the full commission to approve the subcommittee reports, and even then he tried to keep as low a profile as possible. He wrote George Zook, the chairman of the commission, "I have no wish to try to persuade the Commission to change its mind. That would be futile. . . . I have kept silent during the discussions of this issue, though at times smarting under an occasional utterance, because of a sense of the futility of any protest. I now simply wish to be recorded as dissenting."[59]

In his dissent from the commission's recommendation and in personal correspondence, White laid out his reasons for rejecting the group's judgment. Most important, the people making this recommendation, he believed, were not qualified to do so. The northerners who dominated the commission lacked experience with southern realities and their naivete, White argued, led them to sunder common sense from theory. Despite good intentions, they were unable to put aside their ideology long enough to understand that the lived experience of the South was different enough to require special handling. The commission's insistence on the immediate elimination of segregated higher education thus amounted to zealotry, the refusal to acknowledge the practical limitations of the laudable principles of democracy and equality. In both his letter to Zook and the dissent itself he made this plain, arguing that the recommendations, while inspired by "high purpose and theoretical idealism," were "wholly doctrinaire positions which ignore the facts of history and the realities of the present."[60]

White was not insensible to the problem. His dissent acknowledged that for southern blacks "gross inequality of opportunity, economic and educational, is a fact." He urged, "as rapidly as possible conditions should be improved, inequalities removed, and greater opportunity should be provided for all our people."[61] The heart of White's objection to the commission's conclusions was that they proposed to improve educational conditions for southern blacks by eliminating segregation at a stroke. Such a shock, he argued, would have the opposite effect than the one desired by the commission—it would incite furious white opposition to any black progress at all. Only an incremental, unthreatening course would lead to the improvements that they sought. "There are men of good will in the South," he told Zook, "who are concerned about inequalities and injustice and who are working quietly and persistently . . . to strengthen existing institutions of higher education for Negroes. . . . These men are sometimes (and this applies to some of our Negro leaders) subject to attack by extremists on both sides of the issue. It is my own conviction that their patient and persistent 'gradualism' is the only way to accomplishment without conflict and tragedy."[62]

White's insistence that the good works of well-intentioned southern whites would take care of the problem was not terribly persuasive to most other commission members. While the patience of most southern gradualists was beyond question, their persistence was another matter. Despite White's efforts to avoid open discussion of his dissent, other members of the commission raised the subject at the next uncomfortable meeting. The reasons for White's reluctance to debate the issue were clear. On one side was Goodrich White, on the other, everybody else. Although three other commission members out of twenty-seven ultimately joined White in his dissent, none of them was present. (White was not surprised that President Arthur Compton of Washington University in St. Louis, President Lewis Jones of the University of Arkansas, and Douglas Southall Freeman shared his beliefs about the impracticality of eliminating segregation in the South. These, after all, were the only "members of the Commission who are really in position to understand the problem through firsthand acquaintance with it.")[63]

The other members of the commission argued forcefully that the principles of democracy and equality under the law required them to challenge the practice of segregation in higher education. Failure to do so, they argued, would be "unfair and an insult to the whole of the South—Negro and white." The commission then took the opportunity provided by White's formal dissent to strengthen further the report's condemnation of segregation.[64]

This precise scenario, although in a slightly different context, was described by both Harvie Branscomb at Vanderbilt and Rufus Harris at Tulane in letters to White at about this time. In early 1948, in response to the Truman Commission's report, the Association of American Colleges was debating a resolution condemning segregation in southern higher education. Southern schools narrowly avoided a vote by calling for a committee to study the problem. Guy Snavely, executive director of the association and former president of Birmingham-Southern College, approached Harris and Branscomb to serve on that committee. Both refused. Branscomb, in a letter to White, explained why. "I refused to go on Snavely's minority rights committee. I wrote him that I saw no value to be gained in having the majority of that committee, with their minds already made up, ignoring the position of a minority of the schools of the country, this in the name of minority rights." Harris sent White a blind copy of his own letter to Snavely. He was, if anything, more emphatic. "I feel that it would be fruitless to accept assignment on this Commission since the basic principle of segregation is not accepted by the Commission. The vote on a matter touching segregation would always be ten to two or nine to three. I have no desire to be a whipping boy for a hostile press, nor do I wish to lose my usefulness here in my own section."[65]

The pressure that was building from outside the region on the race issue in higher education filled White with foreboding. He expressed it to virtually every correspondent he had at this time. For example, White lamented to James Dombrowski, head of the Southern Conference Education Fund (SCEF) and an Emory alumnus, the methods and positions on segregation taken by the SCEF. "I feel very definitely and positively that the agitation of this question is really a tragic mistake." Similarly, to Centenary College president Joe J. Mickle, White wrote that this "whole issue is a very live one and I am afraid that the situation is becoming ominous. My chief concern is that the progress we have made and the efforts which are being continued to improve conditions are put in jeopardy. Beyond this we may be facing truly tragic possibilities. I am deeply concerned and troubled over the whole development."[66]

White received only a few letters from alumni and other members of the community after the report was published. He fashioned rather long replies to those who disagreed with him, attempting to explain his stand. To one alumnus, White wrote a long letter explaining that attempts to impose the "ultimate solution" to racial problems would only make solutions more difficult to come by. To those who wrote in support, however, White's replies were short, nearly curt, and reveal more than a little discomfort with the company in which he found himself. "Thank you for your letter of December 18 which I have read with interest" was his entire reply to one correspondent who praised the Emory president for what he regarded as his strong defense of white supremacy.[67]

On the Emory campus itself, race relations were hardly a pressing problem in the years following World War II. When the issue did arise it was never because of White's deliberate choice, and he did not view it, as did Harvie Branscomb, as an opportunity to coax gradual change. White did not push the Emory trustees to change, ever. Rather, he responded, warily, when circumstances demanded it. Always, his responses underscored the belief that people who did not grow up in the South could never fully understand southern racial problems and did not grasp that they played with fire when they pushed the South to change. He himself wished that things could be different but feared (not entirely without reason) that too much pressure would ignite a violent backlash.

Throughout the late 1940s segregation at Emory was thorough. Blacks came on campus as menial workers or as entertainers at fraternity parties. The school, though, did not remain completely isolated from the currents of change. On rare occasions blacks spoke on campus, usually at the chapel or the Candler School of Theology.[68] In 1945, for example, Dr. Rufus Clement, president of Atlanta University, was invited to address a forum called "What Next in Race Relations" sponsored by the Emory Inter-faith Church Night program.[69] By the late 1940s a handful of blacks had applied for admission, but their applications were simply returned.[70] A few times during this era the student newspaper, the *Emory Wheel,* editorialized in favor of limited changes in race relations. In February 1948, for example, the *Wheel* editor wrote, "Emory could show it is one of the South's more liberal private universities by aiding the Southern Negro's adjustment by the restricted admission of Negroes to some of its schools."[71]

Also in February 1948, the Freshman Emory Christian Association invited Reverend Harrison McMains, a local white minister active in interracial church activities, to speak on "The Teachings of Jesus as Applied to Race Relations." This led in turn to an invitation to the dean of Morehouse College, a black man and an economist, to discuss Christianity and labor relations. In the course of that evening, several ECA members remarked that they had never met a black college student and the group agreed that they would like to invite Morehouse students to the next meeting. The sensitivity of a dinner meeting with blacks was apparent even to freshmen, however, and after a series of consultations with several levels of the Emory administration (including the assistant to the president), they decided not to issue the invitation.[72]

The mere prospect of such an event, however, was enough to enrage at least one alumnus. John A. Dunaway wrote a scathing letter of protest, expressing strong agreement with White's dissent to the Truman Commission Report and implying that the president was a hypocrite if he allowed mixed meetings on campus. "I do not think . . . that we ought to do anything at Emory which would tend to break down the barriers which tend to prevent the intermingling of the racial bloods," he wrote, "and I am firmly of the opinion that social dining together of the races will tend to break down these barriers quicker than anything in the world. . . . If Emory's present policy is to destroy this barrier or to weaken it in any wise, I am ready to give my diplomas back to Emory University and forget that I ever went to the institution."[73]

Dunaway complained loudly to trustee Henry Bowden, who sat on the board's executive committee. Bowden suggested that Dunaway, a lawyer, prepare a synopsis of Georgia segregation law "in order that Emory might conform fully." Interestingly, there was very little to report, and nothing whatsoever that would prevent the sort of meetings that Dunaway found so offensive. (It is impossible that Bowden, a sophisticated and canny attorney, did not know this already.) Nonetheless, Dunaway accurately insisted that although segregation in Georgia was "not a matter of written law" it was certainly "inherent in our background and training." In the end, after finally receiving a mild scolding from White's assistant Boisfeuillet Jones, Dunaway backed off, claiming that he had merely been concerned with Emory's reputation.[74]

In this case, where the students who began the episode did not mean to upset anyone, White was willing to defend their right to hear whatever speakers they chose. He was much less patient when students seemed deliberately provocative. On the campuses of all the private southern universities, student supporters of Henry Wallace's 1948 bid for the presidency were a thorn in the side of the president. The heads of these institutions saw vocal student support for Wallace as a magnet for unwanted outside attention at a time when failure to conform to political orthodoxies could be extremely dangerous. So when, in March 1948, the Emory University Wallace for President Club passed a "Resolution on Discrimination in Education" urging White and the trustees to give "careful consideration of the admission of Negroes to the University on all levels,"[75] White responded with a letter meant to cut off any further debate. He first calmly outlined his personal commitment to black progress, citing his service on the boards of three black institutions and his "many real friends among the Negro educators." But White then forcefully chastised the group for making a public fuss, arguing that "peaceful and practicable solutions are being incalculably delayed by the pressure tactics now being resorted to." Finally, White arrived at the bottom line. "It is obvious that, holding these convictions, I shall not recommend the admission of Negroes to Emory University."[76]

III

In 1949, Hollis Edens hit the Duke campus like a breath of fresh air. He was only forty-eight years old, handsome, charming, and warm, if a bit reserved. Edens came to Duke with a young man's energy, extensive contacts in the philanthropic community, and substantial administrative experience. Ready for change following several years in the doldrums, the Duke community met his arrival with enthusiasm. Soon after Edens took up his duties, though, almost before he had a chance to truly settle in, he faced a test of his attitude toward racial matters at Duke. This challenge arose from the students and faculty of Duke's Divinity School, who carefully articulated the academic rationale for desegregating the South's institutions of higher education. In handling this matter, Edens revealed almost nothing of his own thoughts about race. This personal reticence would prove typical, as would the caution with which he approached a potentially explosive issue and his sensitivity to board and state politics.

Hollis Edens was, like Harvie Branscomb, the son of a Methodist minister. He was born in 1901 in the parsonage at Willow Grove, Tennessee, and spent his childhood in the hills of central Tennessee. Edens scrambled hard for his higher education, alternating between work and school. He earned his bachelor's degree from Emory in 1930, at the age of twenty-nine. He completed an M.A. eight years later, teaching school off and on while he studied. He stayed at Emory as an associate professor of history and head of the University's Valdosta campus until 1942. At the same time, he began doctoral work in public administration at Harvard. Clearly talented, Edens continued to rise in the Emory administration, moving to the main campus and serving variously as acting dean of the Business School, associate dean of the undergraduate division, and dean of administration. In 1947 he was appointed vice chancellor of the University System of Georgia, leaving there only a year later to become the associate director of the influential General Education Board of the Rockefeller Foundation in New York. Here he came to the attention of the Duke University trustees and in 1949 they selected him for the top job at Duke.[77] Edens worked hard to forge strong ties with the alumni and the Durham community. He also cared deeply about Duke's historic, if now unofficial, ties to the Methodist Church and attempted to strengthen them.[78]

The roots of Duke University reach back to tiny Trinity College, founded in 1839 in the North Carolina piedmont as a one-room Methodist school for men. Trinity struggled to survive, nearly folding more than once before American Tobacco Company owner Washington Duke and his sons Ben and J. B. took an interest in it in the late 1880s. Contributions from the Dukes allowed Trinity to move to Durham in 1892. By World War I, under President John Kilgo and then William Preston Few, Trinity had become one of the South's foremost liberal arts colleges.[79] Then, in December 1924, James Buchanan Duke created the $40 million Duke Endowment, giving the school about one-third of the endowment's annual income in addition to an initial $6 million gift. For many years this annual contribution made up almost half of the university's budget.[80]

Few and J. B. Duke consciously undertook the creation of a national university. It was a massive job, complicated by the fact that even the endowment money was not enough to pay for the vast expansion in offerings. But the indefatigable Few steered the school steadily forward—building a medical school, a law school, a divinity school, and expanding and improving the arts and sciences curriculum—until his death in 1940. Still, at the heart of Few's vision remained a commitment to the careful education of undergraduates and a dedication to the South's religious tradition, which he regarded as a corrective to the problems of northern universities.[81] Robert Flowers, who had been at Trinity College since 1891, succeeded Few in 1940. Students, faculty, trustees, and alumni all loved Flowers, and he had worked closely with Few for his entire career. However, he was already elderly when he became president. Without energetic leadership, Duke began a period of drift that worsened during and immediately after World War II. When Edens arrived in 1949 after Flowers's retirement, the campus was more than ready for change.

Even after the years of dormancy Duke was academically strong compared to its peers in the region.[82] Duke offered work leading to the doctorate in twenty fields, and there were plans to add at least one more. It also supported three professional schools: law, forestry, and medicine. Robert Calkins of the Rockefeller Foundation's General Education Board, a close observer of the region's educational scene, believed that Duke's status as a graduate school was "considerably beyond that of any other institution in the south" and that the university was ready to "take the next step of becoming first rank, at least in a number of graduate fields, nationally."[83]

Still, despite this strong position, Duke faced formidable problems. The campus was overcrowded, with enrollment in 1946 reaching a new high of 5,121. Sixty percent of the incoming freshmen were veterans. Loss of faculty and a growing inability to recruit outstanding new professors was becoming a serious problem. In a survey completed that year, the Duke faculty lamented its heavy teaching load and low pay, the tiny stipends offered to graduate students (which made it difficult to compete with universities in the rest of the country), and the lack of funding for research and new facilities.[84]

Duke had long enjoyed a reputation as a wealthy institution, and most alumni assumed that the Duke Endowment could more than adequately provide for the school's financial needs. While there may have been some truth to this before the war, it quickly became clear in the postwar years that Duke had to find new sources of income if it were to continue to improve. In 1947 the trustees hired Kersting, Brown, a professional fund-raising firm. Their report to the board in November of that year touched on two points that were then novel and controversial, but that would prove to be of lasting importance. First, the university must become adept at controlling public relations. Second, Duke should pursue its relationships with the federal government and with industry, but not at the expense of "pure or fundamental research." It should rather be Duke's objective to "help close the wide gap that now exists between industry and education." On a more practical level, the report also included a long list of pressing and expensive needs: new dormitories; classrooms and laboratory space; recreational facilities; basic maintenance that had been neglected during the war; higher salaries, fellowships, and stipends; and finally, money for research. Paying for and directing these improvements would become the largest part of Hollis Edens's job.[85]

Race relations at Duke were no different than those at Emory and Vanderbilt. Although there was nearly no official interracial interaction, individual faculty members sometimes had informal contacts with their counterparts at black schools. When Harvie Branscomb headed the Divinity School, beginning in 1944 he opened its chapel services to black ministers, who were sometimes invited to participate, although they were seated separately.[86] Otherwise, segregation on campus was routine, but not total. Black researchers worked in the Duke library, but they had to use scarce segregated toilet facilities while on campus. Black staff members also had to use these inconveniently located restrooms and they were not allowed to eat at campus food services. Both the auditorium and football stadium had separate black sections.[87]

The first open challenge to segregation at Duke began in the spring of 1948, before Hollis Edens's arrival. The student body of the Divinity School circulated a petition requesting that the school consider allowing blacks as day students in that division. In this brief petition the students noted that blacks in the Durham area lacked opportunities to receive the kind of ministerial training offered at Duke. The real focus of their argument, however, was quite different. In an early iteration of a now standard "diversity" argument, they asserted that by not admitting blacks, Duke failed its own students. "We are now a part of a segregated Divinity School community," the students complained, "which does not afford us opportunity for understanding and appreciating Negro Christians preparing for the ministry." They desired "the fellowship, stimulation, and fuller Christian cooperation we feel would exist here if Negro students were to join us in our common Christian study as ministers of the Gospel."[88]

The students also attempted to anticipate the Duke administration's concerns. In particular, they grasped the need to keep a low profile. They stressed that limited admission of black religion students was not novel in the South, that any action would of course be tightly controlled, and that they meant to include only the Divinity School. Further, they asked only for the admission of black day students, an implicit acknowledgment of the difficulties caused by the physical proximity of black and white students.[89] One hundred and seven students in the Divinity School signed this petition and presented it to the dean, Harold Bosley, in May 1948. Thirteen students in the Graduate Department of Religion also signed the petition, and fifty members of the campus preministerial fraternity signed a separate petition to the same effect.[90]

In response, the Divinity School faculty formed a committee to study the issue. When polled, thirteen of seventeen full-time faculty members favored the change, one was undecided, and three opposed it. Still, even supporters had serious concerns about how such a change might be implemented, what sorts of problems it would create, and even whether it might be detrimental to the interests of the university as a whole.[91] The committee met with the university's legal counsel and with the vice president in charge of public relations. Although neither could point to anything in North Carolina law or Duke's charter that would prohibit the enrollment of black students, they were not encouraging. They asserted that despite the lack of specific language in the charter, segregation was assumed in that document and would be adhered to unless a different policy was explicitly adopted. They also noted that the authority to make such a change was not vested in the Divinity School, but in the university's Board of Trustees.[92]

Undaunted by this brush with reality, the committee continued its investigations. Two major issues arose. First, the faculty was troubled by the potential for the personal humiliation of black divinity students. Duke's extensive limits on the use of its facilities by blacks made that possibility quite significant. Second, they were uncertain about how the region's black theological schools would react to a white school drawing off their best students. Concerned, the faculty voted against the immediate delivery of the student petition to the trustees. Instead, they requested that the committee's head, Waldo Beach, study these issues in greater detail.[93] That these particular issues should have stopped the progress of the petition seems almost bizarre. The very real political problems that would be involved in convincing Duke's board to admit blacks were completely ignored, while the divinity faculty focused its attention on the possible embarrassment of nonexistent students and theoretical harm to black divinity schools.

Nonetheless, Beach set about his task. He queried the heads of some of the most important black theological schools in the area.[94] To a man, they expressed support. They had no fear that their own institutions would be undermined and little hesitation about sending black students to a school that still remained segregated to a large degree. Although this latter was somewhat troubling, the consensus was that "to ask all the doors to open (or all the barriers to fall) at once appears . . . somewhat utopian."[95] Beach also sought the advice of the heads of other southern theology schools that had already admitted black students. Here, Beach seemed much more conscious of what kind of information he might need to convince the Duke board to allow black day students to enroll in the first place. He specifically asked whether any unfavorable publicity had resulted from the enrollment of blacks. "It is on this question, of course," Beach noted, "that our university administration is rightly skittish."[96] The encouraging response was that there had been little publicity of any kind, and what there had been was generally favorable.

On June 1, 1949, the committee led by Beach submitted its final report and the faculty met to decide on the next step. The report was a cautious document. It did not entirely dismiss the early concerns but concluded that "the areas of possible difficulty and embarrassment are not so great as to outweigh the values that would be achieved in the admission of Negroes." The committee also agreed that "the number of Negroes who might qualify for admission would probably be very small, perhaps at the most two or three students in any one year. In the interests of gradualism . . . it would seem desirable that the number be thus limited."[97]

In the end, though, even this restrained recommendation was simply too much. Fearful of a direct challenge to the Duke board, most of the faculty preferred less provocative action. After considerable discussion they voted to form a new committee, led by future dean Robert Cushman, to draft a statement that would ask for the creation of yet another committee, this one composed of Divinity School faculty, administrators, and trustees, to study the question together.[98]

Overnight, Professor Cushman crafted a very subtle statement. In attempting to persuade Duke's new president to bring the matter before the board, Cushman managed to be both idealistic and politically astute.[99] He began with a clever appeal to the spirit of Duke's finest hour, the refusal of the Trinity trustees to fire historian John Spencer Bassett in 1903 for unpopular opinions on racial issues.

This faculty entertains the conviction that the purpose and intent contained in the student petition . . . is in accord with the high idealism and courageous actions of Trinity College, now Duke University, which have been manifest here for nearly a half century. This institution rightly takes satisfaction in holding a place in the forefront of those universities which have dared to stand firmly for the right in many areas of contemporary controversy. . . . It is nationally and even internationally known for the great stand which it has made for academic freedom. It would be natural and in accord with its tradition, its cosmopolitan constituency, its honorable past, and its reputation for devotion to right—irrespective of the consequences—that Duke University should be in the vanguard of those institutions which make a definite stand for a more equitable relationship between the races.[100]

Cushman then turned to the Methodist *Discipline* of 1948, which called for all church-related institutions to evaluate policies based on racial discrimination, and finally, the "Christian gospel, that, in the Church, as the Body of Christ, there are no distinctions of persons nor any barriers between brothers under God." The statement requested only the appointment of a joint committee.[101] Dean Bosley transmitted it, along with the original student petition, to President Edens on June 4, 1949. It had been more than a year since the students first presented their petition.[102]

Edens's reply was anticlimactic. In a brief letter, he acknowledged all the careful work that had gone into producing the "thoughtful and tactful" approach and assured Bosley that he understood the faculty's "attitude in wanting to work toward 'a more equitable relationship between the races.'" But, Edens concluded, "I do not think that the interests of either the negro race or of Duke University will be served at this time by raising for discussion the question of admitting negroes to the Divinity School." He never presented the petition to the board.[103]

Given Edens's habitual deference to the trustees, however, he almost certainly discussed the petition privately with board members. Like the Emory and Vanderbilt boards, the vast majority of the Duke trustees were older alumni who had always lived in the South. Many were leaders in the tobacco, textile, and lumber industries. In the summer of 1949, the board was led by prominent attorney Willis Smith, a graduate of Trinity College and the Duke University Law School, who had joined the Duke board in 1929. When he was elected chairman in 1946 he led a powerful new wave at Duke, taking control of fund-raising, hiring outside consultants, and beginning the nationwide search that would bring Hollis Edens in as president. Smith was eager and fully prepared to take advantage of any opportunities for Duke to advance in reputation and in quality.

Smith also had political ambitions. In 1950, while president of the American Bar Association he entered the race for one of North Carolina's Senate seats. His opponent was Frank Porter Graham, who had served as president of the University of North Carolina for nineteen years before he was appointed in 1949 by Democratic governor Kerr Scott to fill a Senate vacancy. Graham was beloved in the state, but as a genuine economic and racial liberal he was vulnerable to charges that he would not represent the wishes of most North Carolinians. The campaign—actually the Democratic Party primary—was one of the most intense in the history of twentieth-century North Carolina. Although Smith apparently did not relish it, his staff ran a campaign characterized by both red-baiting and race-baiting, suggesting that Graham would promote interracial sex and marriage and that his left-wing associations rendered him unfit to hold public office. Graham was no Communist, although he belonged to organizations that probably had Communist members. His racial stands, although outside the mainstream, were of the same moderate and gradualist stripe as most other southern liberals. In threatening times, though, this was enough. Smith was elected in a close race.[104]

With Willis Smith as head of Duke's board, Edens was undoubtedly correct that no good could come from raising the issue of desegregation. Even if Smith were personally willing to allow the admission of black divinity students, it would have been politically impossible. It was even conceivable that if confronted with the question, the board might decide to tighten Duke's heretofore unwritten rules about how and when blacks were allowed on campus. Such a move would rob the administration of all flexibility in making accommodations for the occasional black visitor and pave the way for potentially disastrous incidents.[105] The pragmatic Edens was probably right—at Duke in the late 1940s the issue was simply best left alone.

IV

During and after World War II, Rufus Carrolton Harris presided over Tulane University. Like Harvie Branscomb at Vanderbilt, Harris was a man with powerful convictions, a large personality, and boundless self-confidence. Born in 1897 in Monroe, Georgia, and raised a devout Baptist, Harris graduated from Mercer University in 1917 with a major in Latin and Greek. He served in Europe in World War I and was awarded the Purple Heart after surviving a gas attack. Upon his return from the war he attended Yale Law School, earning his LL.B. in 1923 and a J.D. in 1924. After graduation Harris immediately returned to Georgia to take up the reins as dean of Mercer's Law School, a post he held until 1927. He arrived at Tulane that same year and set about reinvigorating its struggling Law School. His success at this enterprise led the Tulane Board of Administrators to choose him as president in 1937.[106] Harris was an ambitious man and quite certain of his own abilities. A natural and phenomenally skilled politician, he had a biting wit, a decisive nature, and many loyal friends. He remained close to the Georgia political scene, in addition to Louisiana's, throughout his tenure at Tulane and continued to spend as much time as possible in his boyhood home of Monroe, returning for several weeks each summer and at Christmas.

During his years at Tulane, Harris staked out a position on race almost identical to that of Harvie Branscomb. Perhaps even more than Branscomb,

Harris was personally offended by the unjust treatment of able blacks under segregation. He clearly saw that change was coming whether the white South wanted it or not. But also like Branscomb, Harris argued—for strategic reasons—that racial change had to be "realistic." In a 1948 letter to J. W. Holley, the president of black Albany State College (with whom Branscomb also corresponded), Harris laid out this position, arguing that "the Negro has been unfairly treated in some respects" and that, for the good of the entire region, "we should all work together to improve the lot of the race." Harris embraced, as did Branscomb, the idea that the white South would in the end accept the contributions of talented and educated blacks. The problem, both believed, was that southern blacks had not been able to cultivate their talents to the degree necessary for most whites to realize their worth. The solution to the region's racial woes, then, was to provide able blacks with the resources they needed to thrive. "I feel," wrote Harris with breathtaking optimism, "that if the Negro is given educational and economic opportunity, social unfairness largely will take care of itself."[107]

Harris was active in racial matters throughout his career and kept a fairly high profile, although not always intentionally. In 1941, as chairman of the Commission on Institutions of Higher Education of the Southern Association of Colleges and Secondary Schools, he was closely involved with the revocation of the University of Georgia's accreditation after Governor Eugene Talmadge's purge of faculty and administrators he considered "soft" on integration.[108] In 1943 Harris found himself alone on the Louisiana State Board of Education in recommending higher salaries for black teachers in the state's segregated schools.[109] His willingness to spend time and energy in the service of black advancement was a constant. Even in declining an invitation to speak to the Louisiana Colored Teachers' Association in 1946, Harris volunteered to speak at the next meeting and asked the association's president to call on him if he could help in any other way.[110]

Harris believed that he had a realistic opportunity at Tulane to create an important national university, and he had the tenacity and drive to seize that opportunity. Although he would at times despair over the difficulties involved, and more than once considered leaving, throughout the 1940s and 1950s he held firm. Tulane was far stronger when he left than it had been when he arrived.[111]

From its beginning Tulane was an urban school, located in New Orleans, with a bent toward professional education. The university was created in 1884 when a $2 million gift from Paul Tulane was combined with the assets of the defunct University of Louisiana, which were deeded over to the school by the state legislature. Tulane opened with an undergraduate college for men, a Law School, and a Medical School. In 1887, Mrs. Josephine Newcomb funded the establishment of an undergraduate college for women. Tulane added professional schools in architecture, engineering, business administration, and social work, but through the 1930s it put little emphasis on graduate education or faculty research in the sciences and humanities. Its vision was limited, as it sought to serve the social and professional needs of New Orleans's upper classes rather than to strive for standing as a national university.[112]

On Harris's arrival Tulane was in dire financial straits. Faculty salaries were far too low, the physical plant was inadequate, the student body too local.[113] Extremely conservative management of the endowment left Tulane slipping behind the other southern private universities, with resources that did not even approach adequate for the kind of growth and improvement that Harris had in mind. Even after relatively successful fund-raising campaigns in the late 1940s, it was only large infusions of money from the federal government and the big northern foundations, the General Education Board and the Ford Foundation in particular, that allowed Tulane to improve.[114]

Harris, however, was not completely comfortable with the new relationship between the federal agencies and private higher education. In a 1949 letter he expressed his qualms. "I have been troubled by federal aid to education. There is much agitation in my mind because the needs of education are so great, and I do not like that way of responding to those needs. The choice seems a tragic one to me for there seems no other way for education to look, and yet I believe that such aid likely will compromise further our ideals both of government and of education. . . . There is a frightening association between subsidy and decadence in my notion of ideal values in education."[115] Harris's fears about the new relationship between the universities and the federal government would be born out with a vengeance at Tulane, and soon.

In the late 1940s the political environment that surrounded Tulane became explosive. The university found itself at the center of serious controversy time and time again.[116] Harris would spend much of the latter part of the decade scrambling to defend the school, and his vision of a commitment to free inquiry at the heart of American higher education emerged in tatters.[117]

It was faculty involvement with the interracial Southern Conference for

Human Welfare (SCHW) and with the 1948 presidential campaign of Henry A. Wallace that fueled high-profile right-wing attacks on the university. Several Tulane faculty members had ties to the SCHW, which had moved its headquarters to New Orleans in 1946. They participated in its conference there in November of that year and in various other educational activities under its general auspices. This in itself caused only a little stir, but it did attract the attention of a New Orleans group called the Young Men's Business Club, which was determined to expose and destroy Communists and Communist sympathizers in the area.[118] Tulane's troubles began to escalate in 1947 when the SCHW invited former Vice President and Secretary of Agriculture Henry Wallace to speak in New Orleans. He spoke three times, once to the SCHW, once at Dillard University (one of the city's black schools), and once on the Tulane campus. In response to the negative publicity that followed, Harris set out a defense of academic freedom in a published letter to alumni. This letter strongly asserted that free inquiry was the cornerstone of American democracy, but Harris still felt compelled to forswear any approval of Wallace or the SCHW.[119]

Harris was not really thrown back on the defensive, though, until a long-time Tulane law professor, Mitchell Franklin, agreed in 1948 (against Harris's advice) to run Wallace's presidential campaign in Louisiana. Much of the Tulane constituency identified Wallace with socialism and integration, and they abhorred both. Tulane alumni and board members were furious that the university continued to employ a man who would bring it into this kind of disrepute, again forcing both Harris and the law dean, Paul Brosman, to defend intellectual freedom on campus.[120] Still worse was to come. The Young Men's Business Club had alerted Louisiana congressman and member of the House Un-American Activities Committee, F. Edward Hebert, to Franklin's activities. Hebert attacked Franklin from the floor of the House and during questioning in the Alger Hiss case went so far as to declare of Tulane that "there are more Communists who infest that place than Americans."[121]

Hebert named several other Tulane professors he considered subversive. The link between support of racial equality and charges of disloyalty was clear in this list, which included one professor because he was active with the Americans for Democratic Action (ADA). Hubert Humphrey, Joseph L. Rauh, and others had organized the ADA in 1947 from within the Democratic Party specifically as an anti-Communist liberal organization.[122] Hebert declared this group subversive based on its forcing the inclusion of the civil rights plank in the 1948 Democratic Party platform, a plank that he claimed was "almost word for word similar to Josef Stalin's 'All Races' provision of the Russian Soviet Constitution."[123]

After Harris objected to the characterization of Tulane faculty as Communists, Hebert issued a sharp rejoinder, claiming that he had never actually said that they were members of the Communist Party, only that their "so-called 'liberal' activities have taken the Communist line." Rather than Communists, Hebert suggested, they were most likely "dupes." Although he agreed with Harris that the ADA was "vocally anti-communist," Hebert condemned the group and its supporters at Tulane because, despite their rhetoric, "in practice they adhere and advocate the very thing which Communism stands for." Again, Hebert explicitly equated support for civil rights with support for Stalin.[124]

Harris was in an incredibly difficult spot. He could not afford to allow Tulane to be identified as a haven for subversives. Not only federal money, but also the support of alumni and the retention of faculty and students were potentially at stake.[125] At the same time, however, other arms of the federal government and the major philanthropies were beginning to push for an end to racial discrimination in higher education, suggesting that funding might soon be denied to institutions that failed to desegregate. Hebert's public attack left the university exposed to the threat of funding losses from all sides. In another letter to alumni, Harris again expressed his strong belief that freedom on campus was necessary to preserve democracy, but by this time circumstances were so treacherous that his defense of academic freedom was seriously diluted with apologies and assertions that Tulane did not and would never in the future harbor Communists.[126]

This was the atmosphere when in February 1949 several Tulane students and faculty members, many of them associated with the Henry Wallace campaign, attended an interracial party at the French Quarter apartment of one of the students. Students from Xavier and Dillard, local black colleges, also attended. The party came to the attention of Tulane officials, and of everyone else in the city, after the police raided it, arresting sixty-five people for disturbing the peace. Harris dedicated his next *Letter from Tulane*—an occasional one-page publication sent to Tulane parents, high school principals, the university's faculty, and others—to a discussion of the school's official view of the matter.

This letter was a carefully worded document whose purpose and genesis are deeply revealing about the early postwar arguments on desegregation used by Harris, Branscomb, and White.[127] Here, in an environment of rather extreme political danger, Harris was trying to thread a needle. He needed to mollify an already hypersensitive community that included everyone from board members to faculty to alumni to the United States Congress, while still leaving room for progress on race relations, without which Tulane's future as a nationally important research university was in doubt.

To this end, Harris meticulously combed through the statements on race that Harvie Branscomb and Goodrich White had already made, which themselves had been meticulously crafted, to find precisely the right words.[128] This was all supremely ironic. Harris, who wanted racial change, was using arguments that Branscomb had written to induce Vanderbilt's trustees to allow change in order to calm the fears of opponents of change at Tulane. More surprising yet, Harris seamlessly blended Branscomb's 1948 report to the Vanderbilt board, which argued *for* change, with White's dissent to the Truman Commission Report and his letter to Henry Wallace supporters at Emory, which argued *against* change. This maneuver starkly displayed the underlying ambiguity of the argument.

In the letter Harris roundly condemned the students' behavior, even as he acknowledged that they had not engaged in the "rowdyism or misbehavior" with which they had been charged. His complaint was by now a familiar one—that by engaging in provocative behavior, no matter how well intentioned, the students made racial progress more difficult. Harris explained, in language that came directly from White's April 1948 letter to the head of the Emory Wallace Club, that such delicate matters ought to be left to "the men of good will of both races in the South . . . who are willing to work patiently and quietly at the racial problem in an effort to find practicable solutions without strife and conflict."[129] Harris also took sentences from White's dissent to the Truman Commission Report, altering them only slightly. "I disagree with the theoretical idealism of many persons who feel that democracy can be achieved only by imposing laws which would level the masses. To ignore the facts of history and the realities of the present will not contribute constructively to the solution of difficult problems of human relationships."[130] Again, practicality, rather than a commitment to such abstractions as equality and democracy, was presented as the only way to bring about change. Harris outlined what sort of progress he had in mind by using the words of Harvie Branscomb's 1948 report to the Vanderbilt board. "Since the close of the War Between the States most educated Southerners have felt one of the essentials for handling of the race problem has been the encouragement and support of those temperate and realistic leaders of both races who are willing to face the realities of this problem. We should not hesitate to recognize, encourage and assist those individuals who are endeavoring to lead all Americans along the slow path of hard work, educational advancement, and moral improvement which are the only roads of progress for any race."[131]

Harris thus reflected the growing consensus about racial progress among the leaders of southern private higher education. Calls for any bold steps, or even attendance at a gathering with black students, were certain to impede change; and the opponents of change could take heart from the assurance of Tulane's president that "temperate and realistic leaders" would remain in control of the progress down a "slow path" of improvement.

Despite the shared rhetoric, however, there were significant differences between Goodrich White on the one hand and Harris and Branscomb on the other. All of them used the same language, but they did not use it for the same reasons. White, conservative and apprehensive, used this argument because he believed it. He feared the consequences of too much rapid change and hoped against hope that disaster could be avoided through skilled leadership. Harris and Branscomb, on the other hand, both strongly favored change. They were also much more aggressive, much more impatient, and much more canny. Further, they likely believed this rhetoric, to some extent, but were always mindful of larger goals and the strategies adopted to reach them. In the end, both Harris and Branscomb used this argument because they thought it would work. They did not have to deny that change would come, or even that change was necessary, but by downplaying the influence of outsiders and insisting that control could be kept in their own hands they could soothe the fears and anger of those who opposed change—specifically, members of their boards. For Harris and Branscomb, the central problem with open racial agitation was that it upset and inflamed the trustees whose consent they needed in order to desegregate their campuses.

Apart from this one rather spectacular incident, smaller problems with race relations were arising on the Tulane campus itself. In these situations, which took place outside the glaring spotlight that made the interracial party episode so perilous, Harris behaved differently. Here, he pushed the board to make accommodations rather than attempting to calm their fears. Even so, however, he took great care not to push too hard. In February 1948, as New Orleans was preparing to host a foreign policy forum, faculty members suggested that Tulane use the opportunity to hold a student gathering. The problem of whether to invite delegates from black colleges inevitably arose, and the proposed solution is revealing. After much discussion the Tulane administration agreed that blacks should be included, but only blacks from the local colleges, Dillard and Xavier. These students would be ideal, as the sensitive problem of housing would be avoided and, as locals, they "could be expected to behave properly." To avoid embarrassment, no mention of segregation was to be made at any sessions.[132]

A year later, in the fall of 1949, the president of Dillard, along with a prominent rabbi, asked to use Tulane's McAlister auditorium on an integrated basis for a speech by black political scientist Ralph Bunche.[133] Harris approached the Tulane board, but they refused permission. Harris took the opportunity to warn the board that this was something they were going to have to deal with soon, probably within the next ten years, and it was time for Tulane to begin thinking about its own role in the process of racial change.[134] October 1949 also saw a speech scheduled at Tulane by Ralph McGill, the editor of the Atlanta *Constitution,* cancelled and moved next door to Loyola University because of Tulane's refusal to allow black Dillard and Xavier students to attend.[135]

Harris was increasingly troubled. At the December 1949 board meeting he discussed a recent incident and warned that it was likely to recur. Tulane had been given the opportunity to host a national meeting of social workers and was compelled to turn it down because faculty members from Fisk, Atlanta University, and other black schools were going to attend. Black membership in professional and scholarly organizations, Harris told the board, was increasing and Tulane would simply have to work out some way to cope with this. He disclaimed any desire to tell the board what it ought to do but pointed out that the national philanthropies, the federal government, and the national scholarly bodies were all intent on doing whatever they could to eliminate segregation. He also gave the board a laundry list of all the quiet desegregation that had already taken place in higher education in the South without problems.[136] Still, the Tulane board was not willing to change anything at all, however minor. This was the beginning of a pattern that would continue through the 1950s. Much as Branscomb did at Vanderbilt, Harris repeatedly came to the trustees with the latest small problem that an inflexible stance on segregation had caused the university. He offered them simple solutions that would require only small adjustments in Tulane's segregation policies. He made the serious consequences of failure to adapt clear. But unlike Branscomb, who had the support of a powerful board chairman, Harris's efforts would be stymied by a majority of his board, a group of powerful local men who prided themselves on not bending tradition for anyone.

V

The Rice Institute was different from these other four schools in almost every important way. For one thing, Rice was tiny. Unlike the others, it had no medical school, no law school, and no school of theology. Its only purely professional program at all was architecture. Intensely focused on science and engineering, for decades Rice had only skeletal offerings in the humanities and social sciences. It was also created later than the others, a school of the new century rather than the old. In 1891, Massachusetts-born businessman William Marsh Rice signed an indenture establishing an "Institute for the Advancement of Literature, Science and Art" in Houston, the city where he had made much of his fortune. But Mr. Rice did not want any action taken toward opening the school before his death, and after he was murdered in 1900 court proceedings kept the institute's Board of Trustees from acting for several more years. The Rice Institute did not begin holding classes until 1912, and its character was shaped less by southern tradition and the desires of local businessmen than by the bold and expansive vision of its first president, Edgar Odell Lovett. Lovett, formerly a professor of mathematics and astronomy at Princeton, planned from the very beginning that Rice would be a university to rival the best in the world. He pursued excellence with a passion and saw that the future of American higher education lay in graduate training and research. He also made certain that Rice hewed to far stricter academic standards than most of its peers. Lovett immediately began recruiting a faculty of real distinction, looking throughout North America and Europe for talented researchers. He insisted on strict admissions requirements and refused to coddle students, or their parents, who were often surprised and disconcerted at the difficulty of the Rice program.[137] Rice was also quite firmly, almost aggressively, secular. Here, there was no commitment to retain the influence of the South's religious heritage. Similarly, the social aspects of student life were played down by the school's leadership. The fraternity and sorority life that occupied such a large place on the other southern campuses, mimicking the social world of the students' parents, was entirely absent.[138]

And yet, whenever the presidents or trustees of Duke, Vanderbilt, Tulane, and Emory discussed their peer group, they always included Rice. Almost from its birth, its powerful leadership and commitment to real academic excellence marked it as one of a small group of southern colleges that had the breadth of vision and the resources to become an important national university. Under Lovett's guidance, Rice matured rapidly, awarding its first doctorate, in mathematics, in 1918. The board's conservative financial policies slowed the institute's growth by the late 1920s, however, and then the Depression and World War II crippled its rapid ascent. At the end of the war, Rice remained essentially a regional college, although a highly respected one.

The Rice Institute began the post–World War II era in a significantly different position than the other private southern universities. Although Rice had, of course, experienced many of the same wartime difficulties as these other schools, from loss of faculty to deferred maintenance to a campus overrun with military trainees, it was able to attack its problems from a far more comfortable position.[139] Rice was still much smaller than the other schools, with annual enrollments typically around 1,300, and still completely dominated by its strong science and engineering departments. It had no professional schools aside from architecture, and only a rudimentary graduate program.[140] Events during the war, however, had clearly demonstrated what Rice's 1945 long-range plan called "the vital contribution of broad scientific training to national security and the general welfare," and as a predominantly scientific and technical school, Rice stood to benefit a great deal from the government's continuing support of such research.[141]

Rice had also been the beneficiary of several financial windfalls during the war years. First, the nephew of the school's founder died and left a bequest to the university of more than $2 million. Second, properties owned by Rice in Louisiana were found to have significant oil and natural gas deposits. Third, and by far the most important, the institute acquired a 35 percent interest in the Rincon oil field in Starr County, Texas, which would nearly double the school's average annual income. These three developments also doubled the school's assets within the brief span of five years.

Rice trustee Harry C. Wiess, president of the Humble Oil and Refining Company, regarded the Rincon oil field purchase as "the most important financial event in the recent history of Rice." The board's handling of the acquisition, however, demonstrates the deep conservatism of that group, a conservatism that would endure throughout the 1950s and 1960s and would at times profoundly hamper the school.[142] The opportunity to make this investment came to the trustees by chance. A Rice alumnus, Harris County Judge Roy Hofheinz, had before his court a complicated estate case that involved the Rincon field in the Rio Grande valley. Hofheinz realized that a deal involving Rice, which was not subject to the steep corporate taxes that were burdening the field, could work to the benefit of all parties and could prove to be a financial boon to the institute. Rice need only provide an initial payment of one million dollars in cash, half of which was quickly raised by friends of the school. In order to complete the deal they would have to borrow the other half of the purchase money.

Rice's charter, however, included a provision forbidding the trustees to incur debt. The cautious trustees, fearful of potential legal consequences, filed suit in district court seeking authorization for the venture. The court quickly agreed, and the Rincon oil field proved to be almost phenomenally profitable for Rice. The income generated by this investment was crucial to Rice's postwar expansion, allowing for increased faculty salaries, the hiring of more faculty, and growth in course offerings. It would also reduce the level of worries on campus generally, allowing Rice to develop both a false sense of financial well-being and a certain detachment from the currents that shifted around it in the late 1940s and 1950s. This detachment and the continuing caution of its trustees would inhibit change throughout those decades.[143]

By the late 1940s Rice's President E. O. Lovett was an old man. He had informed the trustees of his intention to retire several years earlier, but the outbreak of war had made finding a replacement impossible.[144] Thus, while Lovett certainly remained a shaping influence, the future of Rice now lay in the hands of its board as they searched for a new president. Wiess and the rest of the Rice trustees had a good grasp of the institute's practical position, since they themselves had formulated a broad strategic plan for its immediate future. In 1945, anticipating the end of the war, they adopted a long-range development program that revolved around substantial new building, including a library and a president's house, an increase in the number of faculty, and better faculty compensation.[145] The plan also envisioned the development of broader course offerings, while retaining a commitment to scientific and technical education, and it indicated support for expanding the graduate program, especially in science. It explicitly stated the intention of the trustees that Rice remain small, providing "especially good training for a limited number of students."[146] The trustees anticipated a transition period of about two and a half years but expected by 1948 to be able to begin implementing this plan.

The board, however, was under no illusion that it knew how to direct the general plan itself. When Harry Wiess addressed Rice's alumni association in November 1945, he detailed the board's vision for the institute's future in the broadest possible terms. Like Tulane's Harris, Wiess argued that universities had a duty to "take stock of their role in the community and set forth on a course that will add to the progress and welfare of humanity."[147]

Unlike Harris, Wiess had no firm notion of what that course might be. As a trustee his job was to help select someone who could lead Rice down the path to its postwar future. A new president would have to be installed to carry the program forward.

The man the trustees finally chose to succeed Lovett was William V. Houston, a physicist at the California Institute of Technology.[148] Unlike Branscomb, Harris, White, and Edens, Houston was a northerner. He was born in Mount Giliad, Ohio, in 1900 and remained in Ohio throughout his boyhood. A strong commitment to and love of science, a love he attributed to the gift of a crystal radio set when he was a boy in Ohio, characterized Houston above all. He pursued scientific learning all his life, graduating from Ohio State University in 1920, then leaving for the University of Chicago, where he received the master's degree in 1922. He married Mildred Harriet White in 1924 and finished his Ph.D. in physics at Ohio State in 1925. Houston became, upon graduation, a national research fellow at Cal Tech where he remained as a professor and then as department chair until he assumed Rice's presidency in 1946.[149]

Houston continued through the years to be a dedicated and distinguished scholar. He studied in Germany on a Guggenheim Fellowship in 1927, working with Werner Heisenberg and others on the development of quantum theory. During World War II he took leave from Cal Tech to work at Columbia University's Division of War Research. While there he conducted studies that proved critical in improving the effectiveness of America's undersea warfare capabilities, including the development of the first homing torpedo. For this work Houston was awarded the U.S. Navy's Medal of Merit. Other work included pioneering efforts in atomic spectroscopy and solid state theory. Houston's interest in his research never waned. He accepted the Rice presidency on the understanding that he would also be named a professor of physics and would be allowed to continue running his lab.[150]

In an early address to the Rice community, Houston laid out his plans for the institute's future. These plans closely followed those set forth in the long-range development plan adopted by Rice's trustees in 1945. Houston outlined his support for the building program, for keeping enrollment low until the faculty could be expanded, and for working assiduously to recruit more and better faculty. Above all, Houston was concerned with the state of the Graduate School. He himself set about the tasks required to build a first-rate research program, designing the first graduate bulletin and recruiting poster and announcing the availability of generous stipends and the remission of fees for new graduate students.

During the late 1940s President Houston simply did not deal with matters of race relations. It seems impossible that it never came up, but neither the exceptionally discreet board minutes nor any other records contain any reference to trustees or administrators discussing racial matters before the late 1950s. A good part of the explanation for this is that Rice simply lacked many of the things that pulled Duke, Emory, Tulane, and Vanderbilt into contact with racial problems. It was by far the smallest of these schools, it tended to be inward looking, and throughout this period its intellectual life revolved around the engineering and science disciplines. Its leadership was ambitious, but because it lacked the size, diversity, and broad scholarly firepower that made a place like Duke believe that it was only inches away from becoming the Harvard of the South, there was less concern for the good opinion of outsiders. It had no law school, no divinity school, and no medical school, divisions that often brought faculty and students at the other schools into at least semiregular contact with parts of the black community. After its Rincon oil field deal Rice was also in better financial condition than the other schools, and thus less dependent on the goodwill of northern philanthropies. In addition, William Houston's lack of familiarity with southern racial customs may have led him to defer more completely to his board on these matters. He also had none of the long-standing personal ties that the other presidents had with each other and was never a real part of the general circulation of information and concerns that they shared. Above all, Rice's charter contained clear language to the effect that the school was to be for whites only.[151] The school's board had previously shown itself to be extremely cautious about violating the charter in any way, taking rather extreme steps to ensure their compliance even when a financial windfall was at stake. In the late 1940s it would have been difficult to imagine how anything would force this conservative southern board to challenge the clear language of its own charter on the issue of race.

But even at Rice the issue of racial change could not remain dormant forever. In late 1948 the editors of the student newspaper, the *Thresher*, decided to stir the pot. Editorializing on the need to end segregation and to base admissions to Rice solely on merit, *Thresher* editor Brady Tyson began a dispute that ran for several months, drawing in first the local Houston papers and then others around the region.[152] Letters to the editor arrived from Governor Strom Thurmond of South Carolina, the executive secretary of the Houston branch of the NAACP, James Dombrowski of the Southern Conference Educational Fund, the editor of the University of Texas's *Daily Texan*, and a host of concerned Texans on both sides of the issue.[153] President Houston let this go on for quite a while. Finally, however, in mid-February 1949, with the controversy still brewing he sent his own letter to the editor. In this very brief note Houston merely stated some facts and let them speak for themselves. "I have concluded," he wrote, "that some of THE THRESHER staff, as well as most of your correspondents, must be unaware of the provisions of the Rice Institute charter. The Rice Institute was founded and chartered specifically for white students. The question of the admission of negroes is therefore not one for administrative consideration, and the discussion in this connection is entirely academic." Astonishingly, the contents of this letter were reported a few days later in the *New York Times*.[154]

President Houston's appeal to the authority of the founding charter brought a quick, though by no means permanent, end to this small tempest. Although the discussion soon trailed off, the challenge would not be withdrawn. The *Thresher* continued reprinting, without comment, editorials from other student newspapers on the topic of campus race relations.[155] Other indications that the matter, in the end, would not be so simply disposed of came from outside the Rice hedges. The student paper of Texas Southern University, Houston's black school, quite astutely put its finger on the flaw in President Houston's reasoning. The "students at Rice," the *TSU Herald* noted, "have not attempted to attack the legality of the situation, rather the morality."[156]

In some ways, this skirmish at Rice illustrates what would soon be a constant and severe problem for the presidents of the South's flagship private universities. Again and again in the years to come some racial controversy would arise on campus and would come to the attention of the larger community, quickly snowballing into a major matter of public attention. The press, first local and then national, seemed actively to seek out stories with racial angles, playing them up as much as possible. For the men who were trying to run these universities, any coverage at all would only make their jobs with the trustees more difficult. As opinion became more and more polarized and communities quicker to anger, any publicity resulted in controversy, for no matter what had happened someone would be upset. Conservative board members and alumni were frequently angry over stories that indicated any support, by students, faculty, or the administration, for any relaxation of traditional segregation. At the same time, publicity that suggested racial recalcitrance was also embarrassing, as the major foundations were looking for progress in race relations on the campuses to which they sent money. The heads of all these universities realized that they desperately needed to avoid drawing any attention to either change or the lack of change in any school policies that had anything to do with segregation.

Unavoidably, controversy came. The 1948–1949 *Thresher* debate was exceptional only in the ease with which it was ended and in its head-on confrontation of the issue of black admissions itself. Under most circumstances, embattled presidents did not hold the kind of trump card that President Houston did, but they quickly developed a variety of tactics to minimize the damage from press coverage of their racial debates and incidents. A nimble sort of double-talk, in which the president would appear to agree with whomever he was writing to, while never actually stating his position, was one such common tactic. Another was the careful cultivation of newspapermen, both publishers and reporters, who could be counted on to help out in a public relations emergency.

In the late 1940s, however, these problems were still minor. Nothing had yet occurred to draw real wrath from large segments of the community. Pressures to give way on racial matters were still sporadic, still minor enough to be ignored or downplayed or simply dismissed. What changes were taking places on these campuses seemed tiny adjustments, flexible adaptations that were often so small as to be all but invisible to the general public. But the forces that brought on these changes were still in motion, and they would not stop as the new decade opened.

2

"The Sense of Security No Longer Exists"
The Early 1950s

As the 1950s opened, change pressed on the South with growing intensity. The victory of the Communists in China and the beginning of the Korean War brought global challenges to American power into sharp focus. At home, an aggressive anti-Communism arose to counter the perceived threat of subversion from within. In the South itself, deep changes spread through the economy, demographics, and culture.[1] New manufacturing industries entered the region, drawing agricultural workers to rapidly growing cities. By 1950 there were thirty cities in the South with 100,000 or more people; ten of those had at least 250,000. The region's population as a whole had increased by nearly 4 million since 1940.[2]

In 1950, on the occasion of Vanderbilt's seventy-fifth anniversary, Harvie Branscomb spoke of this transformation with pride and hope.

> The South is no longer the [n]ation's acute economic problem, though we are far yet from attaining the average individual income of the nation as a whole. The progress in this part of the United States within the last two decades has been impressive. The farms are being mechanized; the one crop system is gone. More and more power dams are being built on our rivers. Industries are springing up. Barge lines now move up the Tennessee and the Cumberland. Vast installations of government are now coming into the region. One only has to drive across the country to see that the physical form of the old South has ceased to be, and that the new South which we have talked about so long is in process of realization.[3]

Branscomb believed that these ongoing changes presented southern universities with even greater opportunities to lead. The region's new vitality, he said, meant that southerners

will be able to build educational institutions of the first rank. The resources for a great university in this region are now to be found at
home. . . . There is almost daily evidence that the thoughtful lea[d]ers
of the country believe that sound foundations have been laid here for
a great university and that this is the proper location for one. This is
the meaning of the recent election of Vanderbilt to the Association of
American Universities. It did not mean that our advanced teaching
and research had reached its full or proper limit. It did mean a ver-
dict by our peers that the graduate school . . . is sound and worthy,
and that we should be called upon to represent and strengthen scholarship and science in this part of the country.[4]

Change continued also in southern race relations, often quietly and beneath the surface of daily life. While much seemed the same—schools,
parks, and transportation all remained segregated; most southern blacks
still worked in menial occupations—within the region's black communities
a new resolve to fight their demeaning treatment emerged. By the summer
of 1951 the five cases that would later be consolidated as *Brown v. Board of
Education of Topeka* had all been filed. A little more than a year later lawyers
argued these cases in front of the United States Supreme Court.[5] The desegregation of the region's public graduate and professional schools, also insti-
gated by NAACP legal challenges, continued at a steady pace.[6]

Not every white southerner, of course, embraced these changes with the
same sense of optimism as Harvie Branscomb. The scope and pace of the
transformations left many angry and disoriented, but even more jarring was
the erratic nature of the change. As southern cities were being rapidly trans-
figured, smaller towns and rural areas were often left with many of their
traditional ways intact. This clash added to the anger and sense of lost control, as people struggled to understand what was happening and why.[7]

Something of this state of mind can be seen in a speech that Hollis Edens
gave in early 1950 to the Men's Fellowship Club of the Main Street Methodist Church in Gastonia, North Carolina. The *Gastonia Gazette* reported his
uneasy remarks. "Time ceased to march 60 years ago, Dr. Edens said figu-
ratively, and 'now it catapults.'" His remedy for the unsettled state of affairs was to turn around, to "double back" and "fill the pockets that were
left open in that march of civilization." Edens insisted that "we need to go
back to teaching our young people more history—the history of this country
and the history of other nations. We must teach them of the rise and fall of
other civilizations, so that they won't easily surrender the tenets that our

forefathers held to."[8] This impulse to turn back in the face of change, to hold fast to tradition, provided a counterpoint to the forces that pulled the South and its universities away from the past and toward the rest of the nation. Even Branscomb and Tulane's Rufus Harris, the two of these presidents most willing to see change as opportunity, repeatedly invoked the importance of tradition. In the same seventy-fifth anniversary address that celebrated change, Branscomb noted, "I said that I cannot foretell the future, but some things about our future are determined by our past." As these two currents—devotion to tradition and rapid but uneven change—increasingly clashed at these institutions, their leaders struggled to find a clear path forward.

I

At Duke in the early 1950s, there was no reason to believe that any relaxation of racial restrictions might be impending. Hollis Edens was by nature a cautious man, more than a bit unnerved by the changes roiling the South. His daily life was dominated by efforts to improve and expand Duke's academic capabilities, efforts that ultimately depended on the support of the conservative Duke board. Unsurprisingly, his leadership on racial issues was hesitant. Although he certainly understood that large forces were eroding traditional southern racial arrangements, he made little effort to reconcile the highly traditional Duke board to the inevitability of change. Unlike Harvie Branscomb, who used nearly every racially pregnant incident as an occasion for nudging the Vanderbilt trustees toward desegregation, Edens downplayed the need to change, bringing the matter before the board in a serious way only once during the early part of the decade. On the whole, avoiding trouble, rather than positioning Duke for change, drove his actions. When he finally did delicately suggest a minor adjustment and the Duke trustees refused, he quickly retreated to his former inaction, and the possibility of Duke playing a meaningful leadership role in southern race relations faded.[9]

Edens began the decade just as he had begun his tenure at Duke—by neatly disposing of a call for the relaxation of the color bar in the Divinity School. In the fall of 1951 a new group of Duke Divinity School students presented Edens with a report on segregation in southern theological education. In their "Summary of Social Action Study" they issued a clear and strong moral statement. "Although we have participated in a segregated society throughout most of our lives, we have come to view segregation as sinful. . . . We believe that segregation in theological education vitiates our unity in Christ and obscures our dedication to a common task. We believe the exclusion of students from the Duke Divinity School on the basis of race alone to be contrary to the teachings of Jesus and the dictates of the Christian conscience."[10] The students were alarmed that Duke was now being left behind even in the South. More than twenty private schools in the region and all but three of the private seminaries had by now desegregated. This change, along with growing court-ordered desegregation of public institutions (including the University of North Carolina's Graduate School) meant that Duke looked increasingly like a laggard.[11] Just as in 1948, the student committee asked Edens to appoint a group of trustees, faculty, and administrators from the Divinity School, along with members of the Divinity School student body, to study the issue further. Edens handled this request as he had the previous one. Although he met with the students, and acknowledged the growing acuteness of the problem, he refused to take the matter up with the board and ended with a concise demurral: "Honesty compels me to tell you in advance that I do not anticipate any change in this policy at this time."[12]

Around the same time the Association of American Law Schools (AALS) presented a much more aggressive challenge when it raised the possibility of withholding accreditation from segregated law schools. As early as 1948 the AALS expressed the conviction that racial restrictions in legal education had to end. At its annual meeting in 1950 the membership resolved that the association opposed "the continued maintenance of segregation or discrimination in legal education on racial grounds, and asserts its belief that it is the professional duty of all member schools to abolish any such practices at the earliest practicable time."[13] At the same meeting the Yale Law School proposed an amendment to the association's articles that would make nondiscrimination in admissions a requirement for membership.[14]

This so-called Yale Amendment was received with surprise and varying degrees of anger at Duke, Emory, Vanderbilt, and Tulane. (Edens, Branscomb and Harris consulted with each other frequently throughout the several years of this controversy, both about the specific issue of law school desegregation and about the general issue of the power of accrediting bodies.)[15] Edens sent a short statement to the Association's Special Committee on Racial Discrimination, which had been constituted to investigate the issue.[16] He argued vehemently that segregation had no impact on the soundness of a law school and that "accrediting agencies should be concerned with the kind of work carried on in a school. They are treading on dangerous ground when they concern themselves with administrative policies that have nothing to do with the quality of work done within the institution. . . . It is absurd to assume that this perplexing question [segregation] has anything to do with the kind of instruction a school offers."[17] While this argument is not nonsensical, it is impossible not to notice here the narrow scope of Edens's conception of the university's role in southern society. Activism in promoting the progress of the region is gone, replaced by a defensive insistence that Duke's proper role entailed nothing more than the competent instruction of individual students.

The Duke Law School dean, J. A. McClain, followed this up with a blistering response of his own, highlighted by an extended and accurate condemnation of anti-Semitism at northern law schools.[18] Hollis Edens actively endorsed McClain's comments and forwarded them to Duke's trustees.[19] Always a pragmatist, though, Edens pointed out to the board that the AALS threat was not yet concrete. "It is hardly probable," he wrote, "that developments will reach a critical stage this year, but this is a sample of the increasing pressure which we may expect in the years ahead."[20]

Edens was right on both counts. The special committee's report to the AALS annual meeting in December 1951 concluded that segregated law schools should not be forced out of the association. Still, the AALS would debate what to do about segregation for several more years. Through it all the loss of accreditation never really did become imminent, but the problem of the pressure and the accompanying embarrassment remained a live one for southern law schools throughout the early 1950s.

Other racial issues surfaced on a regular basis during these years, and Edens addressed all of them with deep caution and an unwillingness to rock the boat. A particularly revealing incident took place in early 1950, when two interns at the Duke hospital wanted to purchase lots owned by the university. They were veterans and thus eligible to buy the land on very favorable terms under the GI Bill. The deeds, however, contained a racially restrictive covenant, which meant that the lots could not be bought with federal funds. The interns asked Duke to remove the restrictions, and their request passed through several layers of administration before finally landing on Edens's desk in April.[21]

The United States Supreme Court's 1948 decision in *Shelley v. Kramer* addressed this precise issue. There, the court definitively declared that racial covenants in deeds were unenforceable. The restrictions on the Duke deeds were therefore legally meaningless—they could never be enforced and so it made absolutely no difference whether they were there or not.[22] But Edens did not conclude that he could remove them. Instead, following the advice of Duke's business office, he seized on a Missouri case that challenged the Supreme Court's reasoning in *Shelley*.[23] Although he surely knew that the Supreme Court was not going to abruptly reverse itself, Edens used this as a justification for retaining the racial ban.[24] Almost incoherently, he asserted that "it seems we are bound by the covenant which appears in other deeds in the same area and I doubt that we would have a legal or moral right to change the deeds on subsequent sales."[25]

Edens's handling of the problem of the restrictive covenants was unusual in that he actually took a clear, almost brazen, stand. His typical response to people who expressed unhappiness with segregation was quite the opposite. For example, as the 1950s opened, alumni began to complain more frequently about Duke's restricted admissions policy. His replies to their letters are almost comical smokescreens of platitude and misdirection. One alumna wrote Edens about the ongoing fund drive. While she was grateful for all that the school had done for her and intended to donate funds, her contribution awaited his answer to one question: "What steps has Duke taken—or is it planning to take—to assume leadership in the South in admitting negro students to its student body?" Unable or unwilling to simply answer her, he reeled off a string of non sequiturs. "The question you raise involves a problem of tangled human relations which apparently cannot be solved quickly and easily. It will require patience and mature judgment. It is easier to crystallize one's personal attitude in the matter than to obtain a workable solution in society. . . . I wish I could point to a clear solution of the problem which confronts us."[26] To the director of the Methodist Student Movement of North Carolina, who had written urging the end of segregation in Methodist schools as "a great witness to Christianity," Edens replied, "It is difficult to judge the proper timing in the hesitant steps of social progress."[27] Some of the most interesting examples of Edens's sometimes heroic obfuscation are in his responses to blacks who applied for admission, wherein he somehow managed to tell them that they could not be admitted without ever giving any particular reason, or directly mentioning something so awkward as segregation. "You perhaps are familiar with the past history of Duke University and its policy concerning requests similar to yours. There has been no change in policy."[28]

A relative handful of pushy alumni and students, noisy accreditors, Duke employees with their own agendas—these were not constituencies that had any real power and their challenges were easily disposed of. The faculty, on the other hand, possessed significant, if usually latent, authority. They were the heart and soul of the university, and their cooperation and goodwill were vital to its health and future. The faculty's understanding of the region's racial problems and of the university's duties to address them was evolving rapidly during these years and would ultimately prove to be a far more formidable threat to the president's—and the board's—control of the stream of events. The faculty could not be simply brushed off. They would have to be dealt with.

If Edens was unable to control the faculty by the same means he used on others, it was not for lack of trying. By the early 1950s the Duke faculty was talking about black admissions openly and often, in a wide range of situations. In a December 1952 meeting of the University Council, an advisory group chaired by Edens, the issue was raised during a discussion about broad planning for the university.[29] Edens remarked briefly on goals for the size and scope of Duke in the near future, including stabilizing total enrollment at about five thousand, finishing the school's building program, and recruiting students from a wider geographic area. He was quite specific, quoting facts and figures, until asked about the possible admission of blacks. Then, Edens turned to the sort of shapelessly murky statements that were his stock-in-trade. Noting the obvious—that the trustees and executive committee of the university "are aware of and are informed on the problem to date"—he assured the council that they were thinking about the issue, which was complicated and thus "should be most seriously examined."[30] Two months later, pressed again by faculty members in the same forum, Edens simply cut off debate with a crisp "discussion of the admission of Negroes to the University [is] not indicated for the immediate future."[31]

Edens understood, however, that dealing with the incipient problem of faculty unhappiness with segregation would require more than this. He began openly to use his wide network of personal and professional contacts to screen job candidates for racial attitudes as well as for accomplishment and potential. For years this network had been the primary means of recruiting talented new professors to all these schools, and the matter of whether a man would "fit in" in the South had always been relevant information. As they began to compete for the best faculty in the country, though, rather than merely the best in the South, willingness to go along with southern racial arrangements became a more pressing consideration. At the level of deans, this criterion was even more important. Concerned with finding a new head for the Duke Divinity School before the fall of 1950, Edens called on his friends for suggestions and advice about particular candidates. Writing to his close friend from his days at Emory, Ernest Colwell, who was then president of the University of Chicago, Edens asked for comments on one appealing prospect. Although "a man of great talent in many fields," Colwell responded, this man would not be suitable for Duke. The problem was "an inflexible position on the matter of race relations. I remember he said to me some years ago, 'I could never again live south of the Mason and Dixon Line because of the way the Negro is treated.'" Thus ended the candidacy.[32]

But such screening could never be wholly effective, nor could it touch the evolving opinions of faculty who were already on campus. By now many professors were from outside the South and many were involved in their discipline's professional societies, which were national in scope. Others were lifelong southerners who had simply come to believe that segregation was wrong. By the early 1950s a number of the Duke faculty were anxious and embarrassed about the increasing isolation of segregated institutions. Many also remained deeply committed to the idea of Duke as an important regional leader. At least some of the faculty contested at the deepest levels Edens's understanding of Duke's role in fostering social progress. In 1952 William B. Hamilton, a longtime member of the History Department, spoke to the local chapter of the American Association of University Professors (AAUP).[33] He expressed a powerful vision of the university as an institution with an abiding responsibility to lead. Hamilton explicitly linked this duty to the notion of academic freedom that was defended by the Trinity board in the Bassett affair. "In respect to freedom of expression," Hamilton told the AAUP, "we at Duke draw our strength from the past of our own institution. . . . We must remember, as we exercise our function of leadership here, that Trinity College and Duke University have based their self-respect, their reputation, and their hope of greatness not on subservience to surface currents of public opinion but on principles that frequently seemed in conflict with some strata of the society around them. This institution grew rich and powerful not by trying to follow, but by boldly leading."[34]

But bold leadership was in short supply in the Durham of the early 1950s. In Edens's February 1952 report to the trustees he made his uncertainty explicit. "I scarcely need to remind you that the impact of national and international developments continues to bear heavily on universities. The sense of security which once was present no longer exists. Doctrines that frighten us are abroad in the land. Minority groups everywhere are pressing for recognition. The conflicting viewpoints represented in these issues present problems which we must meet almost daily."[35] His determination to slow things down was even more evident at the May 1952 board meeting. Emphasizing that true understanding of a problem comes slowly, that it "cannot be hurried any more than friendship or love or prayer can be hurried," Edens argued that the movement of an educational institution must also be deliberate. "Such a philosophy must be maintained at Duke somehow in spite of kaleidoscopic change and hurried national and international movements which seem to catapult us along at a most uncomfortable speed."[36]

Edens was deeply ambivalent, but his real concern for his first priority — Duke's growth and national reputation — led him finally in February 1953 to speak formally to the board about the consequences of its racial policies. He told the trustees that the daily problems caused by segregation were multiplying. Sometimes they were caused by those with "vicious motives," but more often they simply arose from "normal and unpremeditated incidents." In either case, the university now had to deal with these problems "in a glass house of publicity." Edens neither asked for nor got any action from the board, but he had put them on notice.[37]

Then, in the late summer of 1953, Board Chairman Willis Smith died. Smith was far from alone on the Duke board in his commitment to southern racial traditions, but his death opened up at least a possibility of relaxing Duke's segregation policy. Hollis Edens grasped this chance and for the first time argued for specific, carefully calibrated change. This sudden willingness to push (if gently) suggests that Edens did grasp the strategic importance of desegregation for Duke's advancement but felt constrained by opposition on the board. Oddly enough, one of the few relatively clear expressions of his own views about segregation at Duke is found in a letter he wrote to an alumna between the time of Smith's death and the next board meeting. Helen Morrison had written him a passionate letter, vigorously opposing segregation at Duke with a combination of moral arguments, concerns about international politics, and a heartfelt appeal to the idea of Duke as a leader of the South. Perhaps he knew her, or perhaps something she said simply struck a chord. For whatever reason, he actually gave her an answer. (Although, almost reflexively, Edens also left her with a fair measure of his usual blather.) He wouldn't predict how soon Duke might change, and he complained that the state schools had the easy way out of the problem because they were forced by the courts to open admissions. More tellingly, he tacitly admitted that he knew change would come but also revealed a complete unwillingness to get out in front of that change, which would seem to be a prerequisite for leadership. "I am a 'gradualist,' which is a hated word in many quarters. It is my firm conviction that Duke University can and should admit negroes only when the community and constituency are prepared for it. We have an obligation to foster social progress, but we have a larger responsibility for maintaining an intellectual atmosphere where all controversial subjects can be debated."[38]

At the first board meeting without Smith, in February 1954, Edens made a gradualist case for beginning desegregation at Duke. His trepidation in making this approach could not be any clearer. Every aspect of his argument seems crafted to avoid angering or offending the board, but this thorough caution with the trustees feels very different than the kind of ordinary dodging that Edens did with others and different as well from his ordinary deference to the board. There is a real sense of danger that, even with Willis Smith gone, the Duke board might be capable of doing something very bad. (Whether Edens feared damage to Duke's future, or the possibility of losing his own job, or something else altogether is not clear.)

He began by insisting that he didn't want to be talking about segregation. "I raise [this issue] again," he said, "not because I desire to agitate the question but because it is ever present whether I will it or not." He described recent events on campus that had brought the problems of segregation to his doorstep, foremost among them the annual meeting of the National Physics Society. During the planning stages of the conference, someone realized that there were black physicists in the group. Duke, Edens went on, then "had to decide whether to suffer the embarrassment of refusing to entertain on our campus this national meeting of scholars or work out an acceptable plan which would not embarrass the negroes." These kinds of issues, Edens insisted, would continue, and they were "genuine problems of academic life" rather than false issues that had been whipped up by "troublemakers and cause-serving religious fanatics." Forthrightly, he informed the board that "we are less embarrassed now by professional agitators and planted problems than by the stream of events." Edens also shared with the trustees some of the many changes that were now sweeping through southern higher education, demonstrating that Duke was part of a rapidly shrinking rear guard.[39]

Finally, Edens ventured a tentative suggestion. "I cannot foresee the necessity at any time in the foreseeable future of admitting negroes at the undergraduate level. Neither do I think it would be wise to admit negroes into all of the graduate and professional schools now." However, "if I were called upon to name the spot where one or two negroes could be placed in Duke University with the least amount of friction I would suggest the Graduate Department of Religion."[40] Edens walked a fine line here, trying to explain why action was necessary in a way that minimized the importance of outside pressure and stressing that control over events resided no-where except with the Duke board. He acknowledged that outside pres-sure was at work but affirmed that the Duke trustees had the authority to respond in whatever way they chose. It was precisely concern for their in-dependence, Edens suggested, that led him to advocate movement toward desegregation at this time. His greatest worry, he claimed, was "how best to prevent Duke University from being maneuvered into an embarrassing position either by delaying too long or moving too swiftly."

One more time, Edens emphasized his reluctance. "Now, I wish to has-ten to say again, lest you think I am pressing the question, that I have no desire to precipitate the problem unnecessarily. We would be more com-fortable if we could maintain our position of leadership and respectability and still preserve the status quo. Nevertheless, I do feel it my duty to tell you that I think we should review our situation soon to determine whether or not we should make some small gesture toward de-segregation."[41] The board chose to take no action, and Edens did not dare press further.

Word of Edens's approach to the Duke trustees about the possibility of some change in the school's racial policies soon spread on campus. In April 1954, he heard from Divinity School professor Waldo Beach, a strong pro-ponent of desegregation and a key figure in the preparation of the religion faculty's 1948 petition on that subject. Beach told Edens that the Divinity School dean, James Cannon, had read part of Edens's report to the board in a faculty meeting. "I simply want to indicate to you personally my own hearty approval of both the intention and tone of your treatment of a diffi-cult issue. As you know, it has long seemed for many of us on the Divinity faculty a matter of acute embarrassment that Duke University has main-tained its policy of segregation where it might have voluntarily assumed a position of Christian leadership on what seems a fairly clear moral issue." Avoidance, Beach suggested, might no longer be possible, and in any event might no longer serve the school's interests. "Measured by the criterion of national prestige," he wrote, "the real danger now is not that Duke Univer-sity will move too fast but that it will move too slowly. I am very glad that you are pointing the Board of Trustees to the necessity of action since at this juncture of events neutrality is in a sense impossible, and 'not to choose be-comes a form of choice.'"[42]

But throughout the early 1950s Duke refused to choose. As long as pro-ponents of change did not force the issue, the strategy of avoidance slowly degraded Duke's leadership role but kept the school away from open con-flict. By the time of Edens's next report to the trustees, however, in June

1954, *Brown v. Board of Education* had been decided. Quietly avoiding a choice would no longer be possible.

II

In contrast, at Vanderbilt Harvie Branscomb had long since chosen. Where Hollis Edens was passive, Branscomb was active. Where Edens was cautious and uncertain, Branscomb was bold, convinced that there was nothing here he couldn't handle. Branscomb actively raised broad issues of racial policy with the trustees, regularly talking with them about the continuing and largely uneventful desegregation of the public graduate schools in the South, including the University of Tennessee.[43] He carefully planned his messages, steering the trustees in the general direction he wanted well before he came to them with any specific request.

Through 1951 Branscomb asked for no changes in Vanderbilt's admission policy. In early 1952, though, he developed a greater sense of urgency. In the spring and summer of that year the issue of admitting black students to the School of Theology of the University of the South (Sewanee) had almost torn that institution apart. Front-page headlines chronicled its near disintegration, as almost the entire theology faculty resigned in protest over the board's refusal to allow even small steps toward open admissions.[44] Although he knew well that the possibility of a similar incident at Vanderbilt was remote, Branscomb acted to use Sewanee's troubles as a wedge to open up Vanderbilt's theology program. In confidence, Branscomb asked Jack Benton, dean of Vanderbilt's School of Religion, to prepare a detailed study of which southern divinity schools had begun admitting blacks.[45] Benton sent inquiries to fourteen southern seminaries and received responses from twelve. All of the twelve reported that they allowed interracial meetings in seminary buildings, sometimes with the requirement that the meeting be sponsored by the school. Overwhelmingly, these schools also allowed blacks to be admitted as regular students who attended classes with white students and received the regular seminary degrees. Only Emory University's Candler School of Theology and the Duke University Divinity School still did not enroll black students.[46] Dean Benton also inquired about the sensitive matters of social discrimination against black students. Here, the results were more mixed. In eight of the ten seminaries that admitted blacks, they were allowed to eat with other students in seminary dining rooms. In six, they lived in regular university housing. In five schools blacks were simply "accorded the same educational and social privileges as white students without discrimination."

Branscomb also planned to bring the ongoing tussle over the American Association of Law Schools' Yale Amendment in front of the board at the same time. Like Hollis Edens, Branscomb was unhappy with the AALS pressure. Unlike Edens, he delivered a very measured response. Recognizing that there was no immediate threat, Branscomb kept his communications with the AALS to minimal statements of the school's admissions policy and firm but polite protestations that the university could handle this problem itself.[47] In part, Branscomb wanted to outline these developments for the board in anticipation of the day when a decision would have to be made. Another consideration, though, was surely that the discussion, especially if it remained safely hypothetical, could only serve to reinforce the lessons of the Sewanee disaster—that the pressure would continue to rise, and that passivity was an ineffective response.

By September, another piece of good luck fell into Branscomb's lap. Scarritt College president Hugh Stuntz told Branscomb that two black graduate students would begin attending Scarritt that semester and asked if this would require the termination of the exchange arrangements of the Nashville University Center.[48] Under the terms of this agreement, which had been in place since 1936, the blacks enrolled at Scarritt would be eligible to take classes at Vanderbilt and at Peabody Teacher's College. Suddenly, Branscomb had a real problem rather than a potential one—and it was conveniently small—to raise with the Vanderbilt trustees.

When the board met in October, Branscomb brought his whole package of issues—the possibility of admitting black graduate students to the School of Religion, the incipient threat to the accreditation of the School of Law, and the proper response to the desegregation of Scarritt College—to the table. (A fourth issue related to racial policies was also discussed but was brought before the board at the request of Tulane's President Rufus Harris. Branscomb told the board that "I have received a telephone call from the President of Tulane University stating that he had discussed this matter [black admissions] with the trustees of his institution and that he was instructed to inquire whether Vanderbilt University would be disposed to act either with Tulane in admitting a few negro students to their Graduate School or in acting jointly with a larger group which might include Duke University and Rice Institute." The Vanderbilt trustees declined.)[49] In his 1978 autobiography, *Purely Academic*, Branscomb claimed that he presented the Scarritt matter to the board as a simple issue of upholding contractual obligations and then asked them to live up to the agreement. They unanimously consented, he reported, "without passion or obduracy."[50] While this is probably at least close to the truth, it is also likely that the chancellor had to marshal some pretty convincing arguments.

The clearest expression of his reasoning around these issues is found in a letter to an angry alumnus, who telegraphed Branscomb objecting to the decision and demanding that ties with Scarritt be severed. In a long reply, Branscomb argued that the costs of failing to allow the two black students to attend classes were simply too high to pay. It was not possible to expel Scarritt from the University Center and it would be foolish for Vanderbilt to withdraw. "We would have to relinquish our part of the ownership of the Joint University Libraries and all books purchased since the signing of the indenture. My guess is that the property involved in this is worth now from three to five million dollars. Do you think the two negro girls in Scarritt College are worth that? Frankly I do not."[51]

Branscomb continued on in the same vein, taking up what at first seems to be a moral argument and then turning it into an accounting of the high cost of opening Vanderbilt up to charges of religious hypocrisy. Referring to the fact that the students involved were graduate students in religion, Branscomb noted that:

> The School of Religion is dedicated to the teaching of Christianity and the training of preachers, missionaries, and other workers in the Christian faith. It sends its missionaries to Asia and Africa to preach the fatherhood of God and the brotherhood of man. I agree with you that one can believe in this principle, and at the same time recognize the acute social difficulties in the situation. On the other hand when these students who are involved in this action are residing at Scarritt College, return to Scarritt for their meals, get no credit toward a degree at Vanderbilt University, cannot belong to our alumni association, have no claim on our physical facilities, can we say that we will spend millions of dollars to send missionaries abroad but refuse to let these two students sit in a class room in America and hear a professor expound the principles of the Christian gospel?[52]

Branscomb also pointed out that the furor over Sewanee's refusal to admit black students to their School of Theology had painful consequences for that institution, including a national outcry against the school. He implied that a similar fate would befall Vanderbilt were it to remain recalcitrant. Again, Branscomb specifically avoided taking a moral position. "The point of this," he wrote, "is not that Sewanee is right or wrong. It is not my business to try to answer that. I am suggesting, however, that on practical grounds as well as those of fundamental doctrine of Christianity, our Trustees have felt that this action is the only one we can take in the basic interest of Vanderbilt University." In an apparent afterthought, Branscomb finished off with a quick swipe at geopolitics. "I can whole-heartedly defend [this action] first of all in the interest of Vanderbilt University, and secondly, from the standpoint of the principles involved which have world-wide implication in the present struggle against communism."[53]

Branscomb made these same arguments at the October 1952 board meeting, although with a lot less color. He convinced the trustees to allow the University Center agreement to stand, thus opening the possibility of black students taking courses at Vanderbilt. They took no action on the AALS matter and reserved judgment on admitting black students to the graduate program in religion.[54] Again, all of Branscomb's arguments, even those made in favor of desegregating the School of Religion, were based on the costs of failing to change, not on emotionally charged social questions. Branscomb argued very explicitly that the price for refusing to make small adaptations would be prohibitively high and appealed to the most pressing "practical" need of all.

> Among the honest and sincere proponents [of desegregation] are a number of important national philanthropic foundations. Some of these, for example our good friends in the General Education Board and the Carnegie Corporation, have not made this an issue in their grants. The Ford Foundation appears to be doing so, although they have not been explicit in this matter. Nevertheless, one of our good friends in the Carnegie Corporation, an alumnus of this University, has told me quite frankly that he believes that within five years no national foundation will be in a position to make grants for general support to institutions practicing segregation.[55]

These considerations would be Branscomb's standard weapons when arguing for racial policy change in the future. He was always quite willing to give tactical ground on the morality of segregation in order to have his "realistic" positions carry the day. When it came to hardheaded professional judgment about what was best for Vanderbilt's progress, Branscomb would admit no conclusion other than his own. Here, he had angry alumni, community members, and even trustees at a profound disadvantage. Anyone could have an informed opinion on matters of faith and religious practice (or could at least believe that their opinion was as valid as any other); but when it came to managing a research university, all opinions were not equal.

At some level Branscomb understood that his calm, reasonable calculations of the costs and benefits of token desegregation at Vanderbilt were far from neutral. To him, two black students in a Vanderbilt classroom were obviously not worth the loss of millions of dollars and credibility with northern patrons. To others in the community and on campus, though, even the smallest crack in institutional segregation was a frightening threat, an exception to the rules that would ultimately bring the rules crashing down. To these people—quite reasonably—Vanderbilt's action seemed a calculated betrayal of southern tradition, conducted in exchange for money.

Fearing backlash from this constituency—alumni, southern donors, and the Nashville community—Branscomb and the board agreed they would not announce publicly that black Scarritt students were eligible to attend class at Vanderbilt. However, much of the benefit of the decision would be lost if the foundations were unaware of it. So, according to Branscomb, "we did let it be known in certain quarters that this had been decided."[56]

Predictably, it did not take long for news of the board's action to become public, and it was in a manner guaranteed to heighten tensions. On February 12, 1953, the Very Reverend James A. Pike, dean of the Cathedral Church of St. John the Divine in New York, issued a statement refusing an honorary degree from the University of the South (Sewanee). Pike's public rebuke of Sewanee for its continuing resistance to the admission of blacks to its School of Theology included, by way of contrast, praise of Vanderbilt for its handling of the matter with Scarritt.[57] The *Nashville Tennessean* accused Branscomb of a cover-up, and the incident nearly exploded.

Branscomb stemmed the trouble with a statement to the *Nashville Banner*. He began by complaining that the issue had ever been made public, a complaint perfectly in keeping with his wariness about any newspaper coverage of racial issues or incidents. The board's decision not to release any statement on their October vote was "admirable," he insisted, "since such statements usually lead to misunderstandings." Only the publication of "certain unauthorized statements" (that is, Pike's comments) led to the reversal of that decision. Branscomb emphasized the narrowness of the issue and the fruitfulness of the University Center arrangement. He also made a brief, and rare, appeal to Christian morality. "The particular point determined was permission for these students to take courses in the Vanderbilt School of Religion. The Board voted without dissent that this should be done. We felt that this was right both because of the values of the Scarritt-School of Religion relationship, and on its merits. The School of Religion studies and teaches the Christian Gospel. Christianity is not the sole or private possession of any one race or nation, as every missionary movement since the dispersal of the first apostles to the far corners of the earth has witnesses. We were not willing in this simple issue to vote against this principle."[58]

Apart from a bit of angry correspondence, this ended the matter. The Vanderbilt trustees admired Branscomb's steadiness in handling the negative public attention. Board member James Stahlman wrote Branscomb approvingly that "your ability as a figure skater, on very thin ice, puts you in a class with Dick Button and entitles you to consideration for a spot on the Olympic winter sports team."[59]

As accomplished as Branscomb's public relations maneuvers were, however, his correspondence with the Reverend Pike was much more interesting. In the aftermath of this minor tumult, the two exchanged several letters in which Branscomb openly expressed his willingness to ignore state segregation laws.[60] In explaining the details of the Scarritt decision, Branscomb acknowledged that Vanderbilt recognized that "we might be legally enjoined on this matter, since we are teaching them [black students] in the same classrooms with the other students." If this were to happen, and "I now express my own judgment and not an official action, we would accept any suit and appeal it to the United States Supreme Court for decision." Branscomb elaborated on this position in a second letter. "Those who cite Tennessee law are, I think, appealing to a very dubious authority. In the light of the Supreme Court rulings, it is very doubtful whether this Tennessee Act is still law. On that point, the courts simply have not made a formal ruling, and our own attorney, also Sewanee's attorney, has advised me that if we do have a suit and we appeal it, he feels confident that the Supreme Court would declare the Tennessee law no longer binding." He concluded with a statement that must have haunted him later. "I see no moral strength in the argument that we are bound to abide by the established local but probably invalid ruling."[61]

Branscomb's reasoning here, it should be noted, was precisely the opposite of Hollis Edens's at Duke. Branscomb used the rapidly changing legal status of segregation in order to argue that standing Tennessee law was probably unconstitutional and thus there was no real compulsion to obey it. Edens, on the other hand, insisted that even in the face of a Supreme Court decision, the barest possibility that racially restrictive covenants might be legal forced Duke, as a matter of morality, to retain one. The difference is less one of legal philosophy than of goals and strategies, and even of personality. Hollis Edens was ambivalent about change, hesitant as a leader, and almost certainly could not have convinced the Duke board to change in the early 1950s even if he had pushed it very hard. Thus, he gratefully seized any excuse to avoid action. Branscomb, on the other hand, was both extremely sure of himself and eager to remove the stumbling block of segregation from Vanderbilt's path to national prominence.

This position would be tested again at the very next meeting of Vanderbilt's board on May 1, 1953. That April, Dean Jack Benton of the School of Religion had come to the chancellor with an exceptionally well-qualified black applicant. The Reverend Joseph A. Johnson was president of the Phillips School of Theology, run by the Colored Methodist Episcopal Church in Jackson, Tennessee.[62] With degrees from Texas College in Tyler and the Iliff School of Theology in Denver, Colorado, Rev. Johnson had already been admitted to graduate study at Yale, the University of Chicago, and Union Theological Seminary, but he preferred to attend Vanderbilt in order to be near his wife and three children. Benton's letter to Branscomb took pains to convey that Johnson was not one to cause problems for the school. "He is," wrote Benton, "a mature man of 39, a fine person, and a man of poise and good sense. He is a Southern man with complete understanding of the social patterns that prevail in the South, and I believe he would adjust himself with complete sincerity to our situation." Addressing possible concerns about any racial activism, Benton told Branscomb that "in conversation with him he said 'I have no interest in publicity and I do not seek entrance at Vanderbilt for any reason except that I want to know more about the New Testament, so that I can teach it better.'" Benton concluded with an irreducible statement of the issue: "Our only reason for not accepting him at once is that he is a Negro."[63]

Branscomb approached the trustees with Benton's letter and after considerable debate the board unanimously approved Johnson's admission.[64] This action provided the occasion for a critical statement of Vanderbilt's official racial policy. At the October 1952 meeting, when the board dealt with the Scarritt matter, the trustees asked Branscomb to articulate exactly how far he proposed to go down this path. The general policy that he now offered was simple and shrewd. Vanderbilt, he argued, should admit extremely well-qualified black students to those programs that were unavailable to them at black institutions in the area. Given the presence in Nashville of Fisk, Tennessee State, and Meharry College of Medicine, the number of such programs was very small, consisting only of graduate departments of religion, law, and a few academic subjects. With their decision to admit Reverend Johnson, the trustees endorsed this strategy.[65]

This plan met all of Branscomb's needs—it helped the local black elite, it would keep the number of blacks on campus quite low, and it could be fairly said to the funding agencies that the school did not deny opportunity to qualified blacks in the Nashville area. Most important, Branscomb also believed that the more traditional members of the Vanderbilt community, as well as the larger southern community, could live with this formulation. Positioning himself between the forces that demanded change and the forces that defended tradition, Branscomb insightfully identified instruction for the Christian ministry as an area of possible compromise. He worked to persuade the trustees that this adjustment was one they could make in good conscience.[66] His role was essentially that of a mediator—he found a place where even the most tradition-bound board members could conceive of making an exception and showed them how doing so would work in the best interests of Vanderbilt, the South, and southern blacks all at once.

The limits of Vanderbilt's new policy, however, were stark. The carefully crafted prescription for admitting blacks to Vanderbilt, while it benefited the Reverend Johnson, excluded far greater numbers of qualified students than it included. Nonetheless, by treating an "exceptional" black man as an exception rather than as black, Vanderbilt took the first real step toward the destruction of segregation on campus. The simple idea that any black man could be "qualified" to attend Vanderbilt contained within it the seed of an entirely new conception of merit.

The trustees were understandably nervous. Taking a lesson from the earlier uproar over the Scarritt matter, they made a public announcement of the new policy. There was little reaction, although some alumni grumbled.[67] On campus, active disapproval seemed limited to only one or two faculty members, most notably Donald Davidson of the English Department, who sent Branscomb his "emphatic protest" at the admission of Johnson. Although Branscomb dismissed Davidson as a "prima donna" who "seems to have soured on the world," charges that contained some truth, Davidson's letter went directly to the heart of the issue and demonstrated how differently the price of desegregation could be calculated by someone who held a different set of principles.[68]

Davidson insisted that the justifications for the admission of the black student were "spurious and indeed absurd" and was adamant that traditional southern race relations should be retained precisely because they were traditional. In Davidson's mind, the physical presence of blacks along-side white students was objectionable, a violation of whites' right to choose their associations and even a threat to their safety and health. No "practical" considerations about the usefulness of the University Center, about funding from foundations or the federal government, or about Vanderbilt's reputation outside the South were, in his view, even relevant to the issue. Davidson understood that the heart and soul of segregation was the refusal to make exceptions. Johnson, "no matter how plausible his 'qualifications,'" should not be admitted to Vanderbilt because Vanderbilt was for whites. The legalities of the situation were also beside the point. Davidson deplored the action of the board and the administration even as he acknowledged that the admission of blacks might be declared legal by the courts. The problem, he accurately observed, was that the admission of Johnson seemed "clearly and obviously contemptuous" of the "customs, and deeply ingrained sentiments of the State of Tennessee and other Southern states, relating to the separation of the white and negro races."

As to the moral issue, Davidson was equally clear in his rejection of Branscomb's reasoning. "I know of no tenet of Christian belief," he wrote, "that requires the education of whites and negroes to be conducted in the same institution. As a professing Christian, I am obliged to regard the invocation of Christian principles in this case as an unworthy exploitation of our sacred religion for purposes that are certainly not religious." In the end, though, Davidson could only object. As an isolated faculty member he had no power to influence in the slightest way a board decision that he believed "to a lamentable degree is scornful of the public interest in the University as well as of the more intimate interests of students, alumni, and friends."[69]

Although Davidson was not alone in his sentiments, there was also positive reaction to the Johnson decision.[70] Branscomb felt confident that the path the board chose in 1952 and 1953 was not only the best course for Vanderbilt but also the one most likely to be accepted. "We must decide what we think is right," he wrote, "and rely upon the Vanderbilt family to support us in that."[71] In the atmosphere that still prevailed in the South in the early 1950s this was a reasonable stance. While there was increasing unease over racial issues in the region, and a growing anger at rapid change, it still seemed that white southern leadership, if vigilant and active, could exercise some degree of control and that with some minor accommodations the pace and direction of change might be wisely guided. Certainly, no one doubted in 1953 that Harvie Branscomb directed Vanderbilt's course.

III

At Tulane, Rufus Harris maintained an aggressive stance on loosening campus racial policies that was quite similar to Branscomb's—in theory. In practice, however, Harris had little success in moving the stubborn Tulane board. Still, Harris made good progress in other areas. Tulane grew steadily in size and quality during these years. Harris's notable success in raising money from the federal government and foundations helped with the growing problem of maintaining adequate faculty salaries and teaching loads and allowed the expansion and improvement of the Graduate School.[72] This outside support was also, according to Harris, "a clear recognition of the leadership Tulane had attained in the region."[73] In a statement to the Atlanta bureau chief of *Time* magazine, Harris expressed his deep concern for southern advancement and singled out the improvement of colleges and universities as the most important development of the previous decade. Keeping talented and ambitious students in the region and reducing expensive inefficiencies and duplicative offerings, he believed, were crucial to improving the quality of life in the South. He also regarded as crucial the "admission of Negroes to many state and some private institutions of higher education." He noted that although this change had taken place "under pressure and with dire predictions of revolt, no insoluble problems have arisen, and, on the whole, there have been satisfactory relationships between white and Negro students." This "more realistic pattern of race relations," Harris believed, suggested not only that the South was maturing but that it might also assume the mantle of leadership in race relations nationwide.[74]

On campus, however, there was little reason for such optimism. Tulane's Board of Administrators demanded strict control over the presence of blacks on campus. At the same time, contacts between Tulane professors and students and those of the city's black colleges were increasing, as were the number of blacks coming on to campus for a variety of events. This created an enormous number of headaches for Harris, who was forced to ask the board time and again for policy adjustments. Although the board rarely granted these requests, by 1953 the problems were both frequent and severe enough that they began to consider alternatives.

This consideration was complicated by the president's rocky relationship with the new chairman of the board. In 1950 the board's longtime head, Esmond Phelps, died. Phelps, the son of a former Tulane board member, earned both his undergraduate and law degrees at Tulane and had served on the board for more than thirty-five years. He had led the board since 1926. When he died, Rufus Harris lost a warm personal friend. He also lost Phelps's balanced judgment and calming influence. Worse, the choice of Joseph Merrick Jones, a prominent and powerful New Orleans attorney, as the new head of Tulane's board was a disaster for Harris.[75] Less judicious and generally less well disposed to Harris, when Jones was elevated to the board's chairmanship there was an almost immediate surge in tension. Moreover, the Tulane board was far more involved in routine matters on campus than most other boards. It was heavily dominated by New Orleanians and met monthly, rather than the more typical quarterly. This close involvement with the university's day-to-day affairs created even more opportunities for annoyance and irritation.[76] Another area of serious conflict was opened up by Jones's avid support of Tulane athletics. This enthusiasm often brought him and other "boosters" on the board into conflict with Harris, who tried throughout his presidency to downplay big-time sports.[77] In short, Harris, whose thinking on desegregation closely resembled Branscomb's, began to lose effective control of his board just as Branscomb gained control of his with the arrival of Harold Sterling Vanderbilt. Although Harris would always have allies on the board, he spent the rest of his tenure at Tulane treading very carefully around Jones, who often treated him as an employee rather than as a partner in managing the university's affairs.

During the early 1950s pressure to change Tulane's racial policies came from several directions. Most persistent here was the growing insistence of academic and professional societies that they would no longer condone segregation. The Association of American Law School's proposal to exclude segregated schools from membership threatened Tulane's Law School, like its counterparts at Duke, Emory, and Vanderbilt. Tulane's response, like Vanderbilt's, was measured. Tulane's law faculty did vote against the Yale Amendment as well as the original AALS resolution that declared nonsegregation an objective for member schools, but the group exhibited a wide range of views, "all the way from approval of segregation generally to disapproval of segregation both generally and at Tulane." And all but one were able to agree that Tulane's admissions policies should not be the concern of the AALS. Harris scrupulously kept this matter in front of the board as it slowly unfolded.[78]

Insight into Harris's thinking and his own political situation can be gleaned from correspondence between Monte Lemann, a prominent local attorney who also taught at Tulane's Law School, and Edmund Cahn of

New York University Law School, a member of the AALS's investigating committee. While Lemann also took the position that the AALS did not have the authority to force schools to adopt any particular admissions policy, he made clear his own, and Harris's, sympathy for the association's underlying goal.

> I agree with you entirely that racial segregation is on its way out, at least on the graduate school level. In another two generations it may be out all the way down the line. If the decision were left to me and to President Harris, the Tulane Law School would not I think oppose the resolution of the A.A.L.S. but President Harris is governed by the rigid instructions from his Board, many of the members of which are not yet in accord with the ideas that you and I and indeed most of the graduate students themselves today entertain. Many of the older men in the South have not yet forgotten the evils of the reconstruction days, especially in sections where Negroes (then largely illiterate) were in the majority."[79]

Whatever Harris's personal inclinations he was indeed governed by the board.[80] The letter that he wrote to the AALS outlining Tulane's position on the Yale Amendment reflected this reality. In contrast to Dean McClain of Duke, Harris was brief and temperate. "Tulane University does not admit Negroes. This policy has been in effect throughout the University's lifetime. There may be legal as well as other obstacles to such admissions. This conclusion has been considered constantly and there is no immediate likelihood of it being changed."[81]

The attendance of blacks at Tulane events became a constant sore point. Harris repeatedly had to outline to the board the convoluted procedure for handling this. "When calls are received over the telephone, the office tries to discourage in a polite way those Negroes making inquiry about admission to campus events. It is explained that we do not have the necessary facilities for mixed meetings. If a Negro does come to an auditorium, we have a competent doorman who escorts him to a place where he is immediately understood to be segregated. If such a person should insist on sitting where he pleases (no such incident has yet occurred), the doorman is instructed to allow him to do so."[82] By late 1953 this policy was the source of increasing difficulties. Some of these were fairly minor problems of community relations. Tulane's McAlister Auditorium was frequently the site of general cultural and religious events that drew black New Orleanians.

Concerts, lectures, and special programs such as the jubilee celebration for New Orleans's Archbishop Rummel in 1952 attracted many black patrons. Every year local blacks attended the Easter sunrise service at Tulane's New-comb College, which caused no dilemmas in fair weather, "when they are seated together in the open and are at once considered to be segregated," but which did become a problem when rain forced the service indoors.[83]

Other problems caused by the official policy of excluding blacks from public events on campus had the potential to damage the university's academic reputation or its ability to provide its students with a fully rounded college experience. Harris outlined some of these problems at a meeting of the board in December 1953 in an attempt to convince the administrators of the need for a change in the policy. The New Orleans Association of Commerce asked Tulane to sponsor and conduct a Ford Motor Co. museum of scientific exhibits on the campus in early 1954. "This is an important exhibit," Harris told the board, "but the museum was unwilling that we conduct it without admitting Negro children as well." Worse, "owing to the present rules of the University, the student International Relations Club had to decline the sponsorship of the annual convention of the southern student International Relations Club . . . the students were denied the credit for leadership in the [organization] which would have come to our Tulane group had the meetings been held on the Tulane campus." This experience, the president continued, had become common in trying to arrange other student meetings as well, especially the regional conventions of student religious groups. "It is increasingly difficult to explain to the modern student," Harris said, "that mixed meetings are not possible when the purpose of such meetings is as serious as religion."[84]

Harris may have also touched on the increasing frustration of Tulane's faculty with the policy of excluding blacks from campus gatherings. AALS pressure on Tulane's Law School was only one manifestation of the growing desegregation of the professional associations that were at the center of the academic disciplines and the administration of higher education. In 1952, for example, there was a joint meeting of black and white representatives from the region's institutions of higher learning at the Southern Association of Colleges and Universities (the regional accrediting agency) gathering in Memphis. This was interpreted by the association's membership, including the Tulane delegates, as a definite step toward merging the two sections. The faculty increasingly recognized that the learned societies were no longer going to expose their black members to meetings in segregated facilities and was aware of the increasing rarity of totally segregated universities. In February of that year the dean of the Graduate School, Roger McCutcheon, proposed that "it would be appropriate for the University to take some positive action on a policy of permitting professional meetings to be held on campus without regard to the presence of Negroes in the group and with no attempt at segregation." McCutcheon's suggestion was strongly supported by the other deans, who "agreed . . . that the University is being avoided by some organizations because of this problem."[85]

Finally, Harris asked the board to adopt a clear policy of allowing blacks to attend public meetings on campus. He stressed that this would solve these several problems without giving rise to new ones. "I believe this should be done quietly and without publicity. I do not believe any incident will occur, but if it should I feel that it could be met if the Administrators would be willing to support the university administration in a statement to anyone who may complain that the University had decided to permit members of other races to attend cultural and religious meetings on campus." Harris also addressed the issue of dining and bathroom facilities, a perennial concern of white southerners. Here, Harris was surprisingly relaxed. "If those in attendance at such [mixed] meetings are using the cafeteria," he proposed, "either at a banquet or as a group, the colored members of the group could be permitted to join them. In the use of toilet facilities, one booth in the rest rooms could be marked for colored." Unsurprisingly, the board refused, leaving the problem of integrated meetings to fester for a while longer.[86]

At this same meeting, Harris referred to another, more ominous source of pressure to drop segregation. "Mr. Winthrop Rockefeller recently told one of our solicitors that he would not contribute to Tulane's Endowment Fund since the university would not admit Negroes."[87] Although this was a matter of Rockefeller's personal contribution, Harris surely knew, and the administrators could not fail to understand, that the threat of lost foundation support was real. Given Tulane's dependence on the major foundations in its drive to become a national university, that loss would be catastrophic.

Equally catastrophic would be any loss of federal funding. By 1950 the Tulane Medical School was receiving a considerable number of research grants from the federal government. These contracts could only be signed by the president, and when Harris left New Orleans for the summer he asked the board to authorize Dr. Clarence Scheps, the comptroller of the university, to sign for him. After some debate, they agreed that he could, but the administrators had words of caution. "The most pertinent considerations to be kept in mind by the President of the University, the Comptroller and the Secretary of the Board are to avoid financial liability against the University for performance or non-performance of the contract and commitments which might contravene the University's policy on matters of race."[88]

Harris's position on the need for federal funds at Tulane was clear. "From time to time," he wrote, "I receive some violent expressions on the part of our alumni and friends against the University 'seeking' or 'accepting' Federal funds or support. It is not my opinion that most of these persons mean exactly what they say when they state that they desire none of them. Some of them have requested a declaration from the University regarding such funds and imply that if we seem to favor them they will have nothing more to do with us. The reason I state that I am not sure that they feel the way their words imply, is that we would be in a bad way already without such funds." The inclusion of nondiscrimination clauses in a growing number of federal contracts sent unmistakable signals that this source of money was also endangered.[89]

Tulane began another important involvement with the federal government in January 1952 when it established the Tulane Center at the Pensacola Naval Air Training Center. This was a cooperative venture, begun at the request of the U.S. Navy. Tulane offered regular college courses, provided full-time teachers, and awarded credit toward Tulane degrees. The navy provided all other facilities. Inevitably the matter of enrollment of black naval personnel surfaced. In a letter written in 1961 to Rufus Harris's successor as Tulane's president, Herbert Longenecker, John Dyer (director of Tulane's University College, which was responsible for the administration of the Pensacola campus) outlined his clever response to this problem. "After a series of discussions between Tulane authorities, the Naval Air Station and the Bureau of Naval Personnel, a plan was evolved which permitted negroes to take courses with the understanding that they could not receive credit for these courses at Tulane. As I recall it, they did fill out an enrollment form, but this enrollment form did not become a part of Tulane's official records. That is to say, their records were kept in a separate file in the Naval Air Station's files. It was provided, I believe, that in case a negro wished to transfer any credits earned by him, that this transfer of credits would be from the Naval Air Station program and not from Tulane's Center there." Somewhere around a dozen black students attended classes at the center and "sat in classes with the white naval personnel."[90]

According to Dyer, this arrangement was never committed to writing. Further, while Dyer was clear that Harris approved the plan, he was unsure whether it had ever been reported to the Tulane board. While there was much discussion of other aspects of the program, there is, in fact, no evidence in Harris's written reports or in board meeting minutes that it was discussed. Still, given the stakes it is inconceivable that Harris would have taken such a step without consulting anyone. Most likely he did talk the issue over privately with some members of the board and they agreed to keep the arrangement quiet. The Tulane Center at Pensacola was a major success for the university, cited by the Southern Association of Colleges and Universities as a model for off-campus instruction, until financial constraints at the Naval Air Station led to its closing in 1955.[91]

Although the board may have been unaware of this particular situation, the continuing racial ferment on campus combined with Harris's aggressive advocacy of change led the trustees to start thinking about loosening racial restrictions. The immediate occasion was an application for admission from a well-qualified black man.[92] In April 1952, Mack J. Spears, a school principal who already held a B.A. from Dillard and an M.A. from Xavier, applied to enter Tulane's Graduate School. While the board informed Spears that it could not admit him "at this time," new board member and former Harris law student Marie Louise Snellings agreed to produce a report on the board's legal options in light of Tulane's racially restrictive charter.[93] From this point on, legal considerations were the focal point of board discussions about segregation and the board's legal committee was the center of debate.

Marie Louise Snellings distributed her seventeen-page report nearly a year later on April 8, 1953. Most of this document simply detailed the gradual breakdown of segregation that had already taken place in the South. Snellings outlined the NAACP legal victories in public education, voting rights, housing law, and transportation. She analyzed cultural issues as well, devoting several pages to a summary of Gunnar Myrdahl's *An American Dilemma*. Finally, in a brief conclusion Snellings stated flatly that there was no legal barrier to the desegregation of Tulane, and neither was there any legal compulsion. Two considerations led her to this conclusion. First, there were linguistic ambiguities in the racial restrictions in Tulane's founding documents. Second, the status of the university as private was also ambiguous. Some of Tulane's assets were originally those of a public school, the University of Louisiana, which the state had turned over to the Tulane Board of Administrators in 1844. Tulane still had some arrangements of governance and financing that, as Snellings pointed out, gave the university "certain public aspects." These considerations, she concluded, left Tulane free to determine its own position on admitting black students.[94]

The Tulane board may well have been free, but in spite of clearly approaching trouble it was not willing to decide. Segregation on campus was becoming more difficult to maintain. Further efforts to maintain it would possibly threaten Tulane's ability to raise funds and to improve its research and teaching. Even in the face of these problems, though, it seemed to most of the trustees that things were progressing well and that there was plenty of time to survey matters before they would have to make a decision. The Board of Administrators was ready to talk about change but it was not yet ready to allow any.

IV

At Emory, the early 1950s were years of relative calm in race relations. Most of the administration's energy was directed toward fund-raising, particularly for the Graduate School. In 1951 they received a $7 million grant from the General Education Board, primarily for the improvement of graduate studies, which was conditioned on the university raising an additional $25 million. Progress was difficult, but they slowly pressed forward. By 1955, nine departments offered the doctorate, and forty-five Ph.D.s had been granted since the approval of the first program in 1946. The university was exercising great care in approving new programs, attempting to ensure that an Emory degree would be worthy of respect.

In keeping with Goodrich White's stated beliefs about the proper — slow — pace of racial change in the South, Emory took no steps toward loosening racial restrictions in admissions or in any other aspect of campus life. The 1950–1951 academic year did see some interest from the student newspaper, the *Emory Wheel*. On January 27, 1950, the paper ran an editorial entitled "Negroes Should Be Admitted to Grad School on Limited Basis." In this piece, editor Reese Cleghorn argued that the "separate but equal" standard in southern education was seriously flawed. Laying out the total failure of Georgia to fund black and white education equally, Cleghorn provided a litany of the malign economic and social results of the South's failure to adequately educate its black citizens. Ending with a call for Emory to lead the way to a more equitable and sensible future, Cleghorn concluded that "Emory students by and large would not object to having a few Negroes sit in their classrooms. Nor would faculty members or financial benefactors. This is one chance for Emory to prove her reputation as a progressive institution. It is a chance for Emory to show her practicality."[95]

Student papers get a new editorial staff every year, however, and the following fall the *Wheel* sounded quite a different note. Questioning the wisdom of court-ordered desegregation of the South's public graduate schools, and calling into question the reasoning of the January 27 editorial, the paper expressed concern for the black students admitted under these circumstances. "We wonder," the editors said, "if the intolerance and prejudice which exists, and unfortunately it does exist in the South, will not make a living hell of the life of those Negroes who are admitted to Southern graduate schools."[96]

Although Emory's official records show little of the turmoil that was arising in the religion departments of Vanderbilt and Duke, there are hints that the Candler School of Theology felt similar currents. In 1951, their student council wrote the board about the "problem of racial discrimination in our School," arguing that "the problems of our age demand forthright, determined, and courageous action in accordance with the principles of Christ. We cannot fail the expectations of our God nor miss any opportunity for the highest in human achievement."[97]

Throughout these years President Goodrich White's formal reports to the Emory Board of Trustees contain no mention of race, not even of the AALS pressure to desegregate the Law School. This is not to say that the trustees never discussed racial matters, for some aspects were simply unavoidable. However, no available records indicate who framed the response to the AALS, for example, or what it was.[98]

A few other sources, though, suggest what the school's official stance might have been. The attitude of the board's chairman, Charles Howard Candler, was critically important. Candler was the son of Asa G. Candler, founder of Coca-Cola and chairman of Emory University's trustees from the day the board was organized in 1915 until his death in 1929. He was also the nephew of Methodist Bishop Warren Akin Candler, who was instrumental in the creation of Emory and served as the university's first president. The younger Candler assumed the leadership of the board upon his father's death and held it until his own in 1957.[99] He was an extremely generous donor to Emory and a very active chairman. Candler, though, ruled the board with an iron hand.[100] His successor as chairman, Henry Bowden, later described (politely) how the board had worked under Candler. "At meetings of the Board when he would announce something that had been done he would ask if there were any questions about it or differences of opinion. In most cases there was a solemn nodding of the head in acquiescence. Committees reported but there was seldom any heated discussion. They knew that his long experience and judgment would protect Emory's interests."[101]

Candler's thinking on race can only be characterized as deeply traditional. Even the smallest breach of Atlanta's segregation etiquette offended him, and he saw no reason to keep his unhappiness to himself. A conference on "The Churches and World Order" scheduled to be held at Emory's Glenn Memorial Methodist Church in April 1953 presented one occasion for Candler's wrath. By 1953 the presence of a few nonmenial blacks on campus was generally accepted, and student and faculty contact with their counterparts at the city's black colleges was fairly routine. The pastor of the Wheat Street Baptist Church, Dr. William Holmes Borders, for example, spoke at vesper services in the Alumni Memorial building during Brotherhood Week in February. In October, the Emory Wesley Fellowship sponsored a weekend retreat with delegates from six colleges, including Morehouse.[102]

It isn't clear why Candler would object to the April church conference and not to these other events. Most likely, he simply never became aware of them. But someone took the trouble to send him a brochure announcing the conference and when he discovered that the organizers planned to welcome "all persons, regardless of race," Candler fired off an angry and vaguely threatening letter to Goodrich White. "This sort of thing naturally disturbs me and some of your other associates who are concerned about the effect such things may have on our relationship with the church [Glenn Memorial] and with Emory," he complained. Candler concluded the note with instructions to cancel the conference and to prevent "any such function" in the future.[103]

Despite Candler's warning, White did not cancel the meeting. He promised to look into the matter but wrote the board chairman with barely cloaked irritation and insisted in the clearest possible terms that he would not rescind permission for the conference just because Candler wanted him to. Attempting to keep a minor event from becoming a major source of trouble, White snapped back: "At present I must say that I cannot, on my own initiative, take any steps looking to the cancellation of this engagement. To precipitate an issue over this meeting would, in my judgment, be unwise, unjustified, and hurtful." Nonetheless, White acknowledged where the ultimate authority lay. "I am, of course," he wrote, "subject to orders; and if I am instructed by the Executive Committee of the Board of Trustees to cancel the arrangement for the use of Glenn Memorial for this meeting I will do so. My future course in such matters, as long as I am in office, will conform to any instructions the Executive Committee gives me."[104]

Later the same afternoon White drafted a longer letter to Candler, which he apparently decided not to send. He opted instead to raise the matter when the executive committee next met on April 16th. The letter, though, shows his thinking on racial matters as they affected Emory at this time. Typically, White's reasoning was cautious but far from reactionary. He began with a defense of the conference that was the immediate issue. White first pointed out that it had been scheduled at the request of Dean H. B. Tribble of Emory's School of Theology, but that despite a close relationship with the university, the pastor of Glenn Memorial Church had always been free to schedule what he saw fit without Emory's approval. He also noted that it would be "discourteous and embarrassing" for Emory to force the cancellation of the event, which was sponsored by some of the most prominent and respectable Protestant organizations in the city. He stressed that there was to be no "social intermingling" between blacks and whites at the event—that is, no "housing or meal service" was to be provided.[105]

White also described his own stance on interracial activities at Emory in general. This statement was a characteristically amorphous attempt to avoid alarming, upsetting, or embarrassing anyone rather than a firmly held position derived from principle. He was obliged, of course, to first avow his distaste at having to deal with the matter at all. "I have wanted," White declared, "to avoid agitation of the 'race question' as it affects Emory." Circumstances, though, forced White to deal with the matter more and more frequently. His method was to scrutinize each situation on a case by case basis, rejecting some meetings and allowing others. "I have quite recently vetoed two proposals for large meetings under the University's auspices because some of the conditions would have violated established and necessary conventions. Some time ago I had to turn away the Judicial Council of the Methodist Church, which wished to meet at Emory, because a Negro is a member of the group. This, you know, is in effect the Church's 'supreme court.'" On the other hand, White admitted that he had authorized "occasional, relatively small" interracial meetings, "religious or professional in character," on the Emory campus.[106]

The basis for White's decisions in these cases is obscure. What is clear is his sense of being caught in the middle. "I have tried to act wisely and firmly in the interest of the University, despite criticism and the implicit charge of 'cowardice' in some instances and 'going too far' in others." In a real gesture of futility, White tried to explain that opinion on campus was almost totally opposed to that of the board chairman. "It is a fact," White insisted, "that there are many of our own people, faculty and students, who wish to go further in 'race relations' than I think wise. These people are not 'radical' and agitators. Their position is based on sincere conviction as to the proper Christian attitude."[107] Thus, White sat between the board, unwilling to alter traditional racial patterns, and the faculty and students who wanted change. In spite of his contention that his position on the matter was "reasonably clear," White was unable or unwilling to articulate any clear prescription for deciding when some flexibility was appropriate and when it was not. Examination today seems to yield only the principle that if proposed contact between blacks and whites could be accomplished without attracting attention or controversy to Emory, then it was acceptable. What White seemed to want above all was the ability to deal with these issues as they arose with no pressure or interference from either the board or the faculty. Whatever the mysterious reasoning for his decisions, the president believed that he knew how to make these decisions and that interference would lead only to that which he most wanted to avoid: public controversy. He was probably right.

V

At the Rice Institute the early 1950s were a time of growth and improvement but little discussion of racial issues. By 1950 the school had largely met the goals of its 1945 long-range plan. Its endowment had grown to over $30 million. New buildings dotted the campus, including, for the first time, an adequate library. Enrollment was still around 1,500, with just over 150 graduate students. The faculty numbered 114, many of them nationally prominent. And, as the faculty grew, Rice's graduate program also expanded, although in 1950 the doctorate still was offered only in science and engineering disciplines. This expansion continued throughout the decade, fueled by successful fund-raising and an active board and administration. Rice remained a small school and it continued to have problems keeping faculty salaries competitive. Still, while Rice was not rich, it was in a solid financial position.[108]

There were also changes in the composition of Rice's board. In 1949 the seven-member Board of Trustees voted to expand, creating an additional eight-member Board of Governors to advise and help with the work of overseeing the institute's affairs. (The governors would not, however, have voting rights, which meant that control of the institute remained in the hands of the seven trustees alone.) In 1950 chairman Harry Hanzsen died, and Houston businessman George R. Brown was named his successor.[109](The Rice trustees would remain remarkably stable over the next decade or so, with only two changes in membership between 1950 and 1963.) The selection of Brown, a sophisticated businessman with a national outlook and close ties to rising Texas politician Lyndon Johnson, was critical for the future of

Rice. Brown's leadership of the Rice board would be central to the school's growth in quality and prestige throughout the next two decades.[110]

The city of Houston had changed dramatically over the course of the previous decade. Explosive economic growth took place during the 1940s as the petrochemical industry became firmly established in the area. Industrial employment soared, wages surged upward, and rapid urbanization changed the face of the city almost overnight. By 1950 Houston was the sixteenth largest city in the United States, with a population of almost 600,000, and the largest city in the South. About 125,000 Houstonians, over 20 percent, were black.

The 1950s in Houston were also a time of nearly hysterical fears of Communist activity.[111] Several right-wing organizations closely monitored the city's schools and other organizations searching for evidence of subversion. School board candidates ran on "anti-UNESCO" platforms, vowing to "save the schools from Socialism."[112] Again, this fear and hatred of Communism was frequently linked to fears about changes in traditional racial patterns. In February 1952, for example, Dr. Rufus Clement, a prominent black educator who had been president of Atlanta University for fifteen years, was invited to Houston's First Methodist Church to speak on Race Relations Sunday. This news was received in Houston's organized anti-Communist circles with horror. For days before Dr. Clement was to speak, these groups organized protests, distributed materials claiming that Clement was an active member of Communist front organizations, and threatened to disrupt his talk. Clement's history contained nothing that could reasonably give rise to the belief that he was a Communist or Communist sympathizer. On the contrary, he was an extremely conservative man, the epitome of Harvie Branscomb's "responsible Negro leadership." The only reason to suspect Dr. Clement of subversive tendencies was that he was a black man speaking to a white audience. The controversy reached as far as Duke, where Hollis Edens was queried about Clement's reputation. Edens vouched for Clements's loyalty and character, calling him "a gentleman of the highest order" and stating that "I have never heard his character or reputation questioned."[113] This kind of active, radical anti-Communism that characterized the city of Houston during the early 1950s was one factor in the near total lack of open debate over racial issues on the Rice campus.

Of greater importance, however, was the nature of the Rice Institute itself. Rice was still by far the smallest of these schools and it remained heavily dominated by scientific and engineering departments that focused on educating undergraduates. While the graduate program was steadily growing, it too was dominated by hard sciences and engineering. These programs attracted few blacks and were also unlikely to produce research that challenged the community's social or racial beliefs. Even more important, Rice was an almost aggressively secular institution and had no school of religion or theology. Thus, one of the major strains of anti-segregation thought, Christian morality, had no institutional presence at the school. Whatever the private beliefs of faculty members, there was no dean of theology to approach the president about admitting black students and no divinity school student body eager to petition for change.[114]

Finally, Rice did not have a law school. As much as the theology schools, by the early 1950s the law schools of the private southern universities were lightning rods for challenges to the racial status quo. In part, this was due to the NAACP's strategy of using the courts to break down traditional patterns of segregation.[115] This strategy placed lawyers at the heart of the battle over race relations and made American constitutional law another major strand of anti-segregation thought. The argument over the meaning of equal protection was naturally a subject that would be discussed in the curriculum of the region's private law schools. More immediately, the threat from the American Association of Law Schools to withdraw accreditation from segregated schools forced the other private southern universities to debate the issue of discriminatory admissions policies internally. Rice, lacking a law school, was protected from this current, one which pulled the other schools into the thick of conflict.

Rice was not totally sheltered from the problems of changing race relations, however. President William V. Houston's awareness of the issue of easing racial restrictions is seen in his work with the Council of Southern Universities. This council was established in October 1952 as a forum for the heads of the region's most prestigious institutions to come together to consider their common problems in an intimate setting.[116] It was a small group, comprising at its first meeting Duke, Emory, Tulane, Rice, Vanderbilt, the University of Texas, the University of North Carolina, and the University of Virginia.[117]

As a member of the council's executive committee, William Houston helped prepare the agenda for the first meeting. High on the list of topics was segregation. The tentative agenda proposed a discussion of "the possibility of a working understanding among our constituent institutions, especially the private ones, with reference to the problem of possible future enrollment of negroes at the graduate and professional school level."[118] The meeting did include "extensive discussion" of the admission of black students to the private schools. In particular, the presidents were interested in the possibility of some sort of joint resolution, a notion that must have been attractive to many, providing as it would some political cover. After much discussion, however, the members decided that because of "the diversity of problems, it appeared impractical to make any general statement at the present time." They also "agreed that the five private institution members of the Council should undertake to keep each other informed with respect to developments along this line."[119]

With Rice hosting the 1953 gathering of the council, President Houston again outlined an agenda. Once more, "trends with relation to the problem of segregation" occupied a place on that agenda.[120] And again, the private universities could reach no consensus on how to handle the issue. Although the same problems were arising on each campus (with the exception of Rice)—the AALS situation, the matter of black applicants to the divinity schools—the details were often quite different. In particular, the members focused on "the general attitudes of the boards of trustees" as the key area of difference. (Interestingly, when Houston reported to the Rice board about the activities of the Council of Southern Universities, he focused on the group's efforts to obtain and administer grants and did not mention the discussions of racial matters.)[121]

Other racial matters that arose at Rice were so minor as to be incidental. The construction of a new football stadium, completed in 1950, was the occasion for one board discussion. "The matter of allocating space in Rice's new stadium for a limited number of colored people was also discussed and it was the sense of the meeting that space be allocated if provisions can be made without disrupting present plans."[122] Occasionally a speaker would discuss race in a lecture or forum, but no black speakers came to campus. In 1952, for example, Rice assistant professor of history Edward Phillips gave the fall faculty lecture on "The Problem of Race in the World Today." Phillips was concerned primarily with international affairs and claimed that America had to solve its racial problems "as an example" to Asia and Africa, the two "breeding spots for Communism."[123]

Rice students were not deeply interested in racial issues during the early 1950s, although there were some exceptions. In 1950 the assistant editor of the *Thresher*, William P. Hobby Jr., editorialized about a cross burning at the University of Texas Law School after the enrollment of black student Hemann Sweatt.[124] Speculating that the burning and the "KKK" graffiti painted on the law building were in fact the work of the Klan, Hobby hoped that this action represented "the last gasp of the bigoted, hate-blinded cowards who form the organization." Hobby tied this horrible event to Rice and directly challenged the racial status quo and the reasoning of President Houston in the 1948–49 *Thresher* controversy. Houston quickly ended that controversy, in which *Thresher* editors argued for the admission of black graduate students, with an assertion of the Rice charter's unambiguous ban on blacks. Hobby was unconvinced by this technical prohibition. "The question of admitting Negroes to Rice," he wrote, "was fought out in these columns several years ago. The result of that fight was a temporary victory for those who would maintain segregation. That the victory was temporary is a certain fact—made temporary by the trend of judicial and public opinion which has in the past few years so diminished racial hatred and prejudice." If Rice would not lead, Hobby implied, it would have to follow. "It will not be many years, we feel sure, before the Rice Institute will admit qualified Negroes, whether under orders from the courts or voluntarily."[125] There was no public response to this editorial either from Rice students or the administration. In 1951 the Rice student council voted with only one dissent to instruct the school's delegates to the Texas Intercollegiate Student Association to vote in favor of a resolution allowing black schools to join the organization.[126] In 1953 a poll, with almost half the student body responding, found that almost 52 percent supported the admission of "properly qualified Negroes."[127] These episodes, however, had no impact on the thinking of Rice's leadership. Like the 1948–49 *Thresher* controversy, they faded away on their own.

At Rice, then, the campus remained quiet. In spite of the rapid physical transformation of the city and the campus, the pressures to drop segregation from academic life that came from funding agencies and learned societies, and the political turmoil that percolated within Houston, the university remained an island, seemingly untouched by real debate over race. With both the board and the president inclined to leave the matter alone for as long as possible, it was difficult to see what might make them act.

During the early 1950s, the presidents of these schools experienced growing difficulty in navigating among their various constituencies. Partly this was because more constituencies began to raise their voices on race relations. Much of the growing impetus for change came from outsiders, such as professional and accrediting groups, and from internal constituencies, such as students and segments of the faculty, that were at the margins of official power. Public attention to the refusal to admit black students was also growing, as the NAACP's legal victories and heavily publicized episodes of conflict at other schools kept the issue on front pages. As ever the press stood by, eagerly waiting for stories of either any action or any failure to act on racial issues. While the courts had not taken any direct action against private universities with racially exclusionary admissions policies, it was clear that the time was rapidly approaching when some sort of public justification of these policies would be demanded. In response, many trustees began to dig in their heels. In this growing welter of competing demands and pressures, the presidents were called upon to find a way through. Although they always framed their institutions as regional leaders, the ongoing desegregation of the public universities made that status seem more and more doubtful. And still these presidents misunderstood how far change had already progressed and how quickly it would advance. Their sense of control and their confidence that the South's educated white men could effectively lead change began to evaporate and they grew increasingly careful and defensive. Their timid behavior, for all these schools save Vanderbilt, led inexorably to the loss of the regional leadership role that had been such a cherished part of the schools' identity. The South was changing without them.

3

The Backlash against Brown
1954

On January 15, 1955, Rufus Harris wrote to an old friend in his hometown of Monroe, Georgia. Wearily, Harris told him, "I watched the old year go out without regret. It went out burdened with fears, hates, scandals, and some bumbling stupidity. It had seen a premium placed on hate as a way of life with organized hate-mongers setting neighbor against neighbor for political gain and scaring the wits out of millions of Americans. . . . The new year scarcely will see such a low descent into darkness, I hope. So to 1954 I wanted to say goodbye and good riddance!"[1]

Harris was far from alone in his eagerness to leave 1954 behind. It had been a difficult year, particularly in the South. On May 17th, in the culmination of the NAACP's legal assault on Jim Crow, the United States Supreme Court unanimously declared state-enforced segregation in public education unconstitutional.[2] Although the decision was not unexpected, its announcement still shocked many whites. In some southern states, particularly in border areas, political leaders initially reacted to *Brown v. Board of Education* with restraint and urged upset whites to "wait and see" what the Supreme Court's enforcement edict would require. This initial moderation, however, was not shared by all. Many Deep South politicians such as Georgia's governor Herman Talmadge answered *Brown* with immediate defiance. Still, an early period of relative calm during the court's deliberations on how to enforce the decision suggested that the grudging cooperation of southern whites might be forthcoming.

These early hopes for peaceful progress on desegregation proved almost wholly misplaced. President Dwight D. Eisenhower's failure to support publicly the Supreme Court's decision and the open determination of an increasing number of southern politicians to evade its clear intent made defiance seem reasonable even to respectable middle-class whites.[3] The rise of massive resistance transformed the political and social atmosphere of the region to one of crisis. Segregation became the central, almost the only, issue in southern politics and public life. Opposition to racial change was entangled with resentment of outside pressure, mistrust of the federal government, fears of creeping socialism, and a general disquiet spawned by the enormous changes that had come to the South since World War II. As Adam Fairclough has pointed out, "between 1944 and 1954 whites had, in fact, accepted a degree of change that would have been unthinkable fifty or even twenty years earlier."[4] The *Brown* decision provided a focal point for all the frustration, fear, and anxiety that simmered as a traditional way of life was replaced by something new and uncertain.[5]

For the elite private universities in the South this atmosphere severely complicated their struggle to provide regional leadership and attain national prominence. While there had always been tension between these goals, only after *Brown* did they come to seem incompatible. In the rest of the country, including prominently the academic community and its patrons, interest in southern race relations became newly intense and tended strongly toward condemnation of segregation and insistence on its elimination. Within the South, resistance to *Brown* soon meant resistance not only to public school desegregation but also to any move to relax racial restrictions of any kind whatsoever. This presented a deepening dilemma for these universities, which needed support from both sides in order to move forward.

The dilemma was made even worse by increased public attention. Before *Brown* the private southern universities made decisions in relative seclusion. The local press was certainly interested in developments on campus but ordinarily covered what the schools asked it to with a minimum of investigation. The schools' status as elite institutions set them apart somehow from their communities, just as their campuses—green, shady enclaves— were set off from the cities that surrounded them. Their status as private institutions further shielded them from the direct processes of politics that often intruded on public universities. This insularity had allowed the trustees the luxury of unhurried debate on many issues, not just their racial policies. Even at Vanderbilt, where Chancellor Harvie Branscomb had enough clout with his board to make some small adjustments, the pace of change was hardly urgent. At the other schools discussion of desegregation focused on the vague future, when it was acknowledged at all. There was time, the boards believed, probably decades, to decide on the proper course.

After *Brown* this aloof stance was almost impossible to maintain. Angry and organized, southern whites exercised new vigilance in defense of racial orthodoxy. They searched out, identified, and denounced even minor deviations from accepted practices wherever they found them, including on the campuses of the region's most prestigious universities. Both inside and outside the South the press grew more keenly attentive, eager to find and publish evidence of the latest outrage (however defined). The constant scrutiny rendered every discussion of race on campus—whether by trustees, faculty, or within student religious organizations—potentially explosive. In short, the vise that had been slowly squeezing around the South's private universities since the end of World War II now tightened dramatically. The old atmosphere of fretful wariness was replaced by something near panic as the true impact of the region's economic and social transformation began to dawn.

The presidents of these schools, trying to deflect pressure from all directions, repeatedly pointed out that the *Brown* decision pertained only to public education and had nothing to do with them at all. But no one was fooled. No matter the specific legal issues involved in the decision, *Brown* had to do with everything. It raised issues that had been quiet before, it shone a light on places that had remained hidden, it forced decisions that had been coaxed along slowly. Just as with the myriad changes that otherwise transformed the South, there was simply no evading it.

Even before the *Brown* decision became public Harvie Branscomb was involved in a project that aimed at chronicling its consequences. On May 11, 1954, he attended the first meeting of the board of directors of the newly founded Southern Education Reporting Service (SERS) at Peabody College in Nashville.[6] The SERS was financed with nearly $100,000 from the Fund for the Advancement of Education, an agency of the Ford Foundation. The grant, made to Peabody for a one-year period beginning in July 1954, paid for "the gathering and distributing of objective facts about developments in education in the South as a result of Supreme Court action." These developments would be reported in a regular publication, *Southern School News,* which was set to release its first issue in September.[7] The SERS board was filled with prominent, mainly white, southern educators and journalists. The few black members came entirely from the class that the white establishment considered "responsible black leadership." In addition to Branscomb, board members included Henry Hill of Peabody College, Charles Johnson of Fisk, and other prominent academics and editors like Virginius Dabney of the *Richmond Times-Dispatch* and Coleman Harwell of the *Nashville Tennessean.*

The press release that announced the gift included a statement by Dabney that explained the group's purpose. Above all, this statement displayed continued faith in the South's civic and commercial leadership and the firm belief that they would be the ones to see this problem through to its eventual solution. Dabney also articulated the unshakeable conviction—indeed, the reason for the publication—that providing "objective facts" to decision makers was the key to navigating through the crisis. Accurate reports on how others were handling the change would, in this theory, provide the basis for intelligent choices everywhere in the South.

> We are convinced that a major contribution can be made at this time to the advancement of education and to the general public interest by an impartial reporting service which provides accurate and unbiased information concerning the adjustments which various communities in the southern region make as a result of the Supreme Court's recent opinion and forthcoming decrees in the five cases involving segregation in the public schools.
>
> We believe that the primary burden for making these adjustments rests with the school administrators and other leaders, both public and private, of each individual community. . . .
>
> The Southern Education Reporting Service has therefore been established with the aim of assisting responsible local and state leaders, and particularly school administrators, in developing practical and constructive solutions to their own particular school problems by supplying them with objective facts about the developments in other communities.[8]

The collection of "objective facts" would soon become almost an obsessive habit among board and faculty committees, as well as the SERS. While the actual "objectivity" of these facts should well be questioned, another problem would prove to be even more troublesome.[9] Without a clear set of principles with which to assess the importance of any particular "fact," policymaking floundered. A barrage of reports and studies that identified issues and described the actions of others did nothing to help decide the right, fair, or even practical course to follow.

At the South's private universities, the trustees ultimately lacked the will to choose any alternative at all without first knowing how the political winds would blow. It was not at all clear that the federal government would try seriously to enforce desegregation in the South, and even if it did it was not clear that southerners would allow it to happen. So, in spite of a busy cottage industry devoted to the collection of "objective facts," the real decision makers on the private campuses—the boards—sat stock still. The end result of *Brown* and its aftermath was to halt all movement in the direction of racial liberalization on these campuses. Differences between the most aggressive and the most passive leadership evaporated for a time as everyone waited. At this moment of crisis those who claimed to lead the region retreated to the safety of neutrality. At Vanderbilt, Harvie Branscomb stopped pushing the trustees for change. At Tulane, in the days immediately before *Brown* the board's law committee agreed, after long and careful deliberation, that Tulane had the authority to open graduate school admissions to blacks, but this was as far as they got. The announcement of *Brown* sent them into headlong retreat, and as the environment in Louisiana and New Orleans gradually moved closer to chaos in the years ahead, Tulane remained paralyzed. At Emory, there were still no signs at all of change. Its cautious leadership stood by and watched Georgia respond to *Brown* with furious defiance. Similarly, the Rice board did not even contemplate any change on campus. Surprisingly, at Duke the usually circumspect Hollis Edens was somewhat emboldened by the crisis. While his statements about racial change to the press and correspondents remained as opaque as ever, Edens spoke more candidly to the Duke trustees. The rapid transformation of race relations throughout the South, he argued, made the issue of segregation at Duke seem minor. This might be exactly the time to make small changes. His forthrightness, however, carried no weight. Duke's conservative board listened but refused to act.

Even in the face of their complete inability to fashion effective responses to the turmoil that surrounded them, these men remained unshaken in their faith that only they and others like them could solve the region's racial problems. If anything, they believed that their responsibility to guide the region became more pressing after *Brown,* as the threat of disorder grew. This belief was complicated, though, by the fact that much of the South's white leadership was behaving irresponsibly. With racial issues now occupying center stage to an extent not seen since the turn of the century, many white politicians turned to outright demagoguery. At the same time, the middle-class membership of the White Citizens Councils made massive resistance respectable. *Responsible* white leaders, then, ought to provide an alternative to the kind of stubborn refusal to change that was sure to provoke head-on, and unwinnable, clashes. As educators these men seemed perfectly positioned to lead in a productive way. Clearly, men like Branscomb, Rufus Harris, Hollis Edens, Goodrich White, and William Houston understood the inevitability of desegregation. They stood able to educate the children of the white establishment in responsible behavior on this issue. Yet as the momentum of change gathered and old ways of life were swept aside, those who claimed to be the natural leaders of the region failed to act as the examples they thought others needed to guide the way.

I

Tennessee received word of the *Brown* decision with relative equanimity. Governor Frank Clement almost immediately issued a temperate statement, accepting the authority of the court and urging the people of Tennessee to wait and see what the implementation decree would bring. Clement's calm response was rewarded later that summer, when he easily defeated two rivals for the Democratic gubernatorial nomination (tantamount to election even in Tennessee) who made opposition to the decision the cornerstone of their campaigns. Similarly, in the senatorial primary Estes Kefauver sought reelection without taking any real stand on segregation, arguing that it was a local issue that had no place in a race for federal office.[10] His opponent, Congressman Pat Sutton, was an outspoken supporter of state's rights and the separation of the races. In this contest too, appeals to whites' racial fears were ineffective and Kefauver won by a comfortable margin.[11]

At Vanderbilt, when the *Brown* decision was handed down the undergraduates had already left campus for the summer. When they returned in the fall of 1954, it was apparent that, in general, they accepted that segregation was finished and were willing to begin exploring practical solutions. Somewhat surprisingly, a significant portion of Vanderbilt's largely southern-born and conservative student body supported desegregation, at least on their own campus. An October poll of ninety-three Vanderbilt students revealed that 45 percent (forty-two respondents) were in favor of desegregating the school's undergraduate college, although only 29 percent opposed segregation in general. The students too had faith in the ability of Vanderbilt's leaders to control racial change. According to the *Hustler* the students were willing to defer to the wisdom of their elders, expressing "full confidence in Vanderbilt's administrative officials" and the certainty that "the type and caliber of Negro which the administration would let enter the undergraduate school would be suitable fellow students." Another eleven students refused to characterize their opinions as either definitely for or against segregation, offering a variety of reasons for their stances. Christian brotherhood figured strongly in their thinking, as did notions of merit—"people should be educated according to ability and not color."[12]

It was this idea that was uppermost in the minds of the *Hustler* editors when they called for the inclusion of Fisk University in Nashville's Joint University Center. The editors acknowledged that most Vanderbilt students came from families that harbored strong objections to desegregation but rejected this as a reason to maintain segregation at Vanderbilt, concluding simply that "eligible persons of all races and creeds deserve the chance to receive top-rate educations." The editors did take more seriously the possibility that suddenly dropping the racial barrier to entry into Vanderbilt's undergraduate college could harm both Vanderbilt, which stood to lose money and students, and Fisk, which might well see a decline in enrollment as its most able students left for Vanderbilt. The solution that they advocated in an October 22 editorial was to admit Fisk into the Vanderbilt-Scarritt-Peabody arrangement that allowed students enrolled at one to take classes at the others. While at least one Vanderbilt board member supported this idea, it seems never to have been seriously considered.[13]

Student interest in issues of race continued through the fall. Commenting on a series of campus talks and meetings to discuss segregation, the *Hustler* editors said that "the increasing awareness on this campus that segregation is no longer to be ignored, and that educational institutions must look for some gradual conformition [sic] to the Supreme Court's doctrine, is indeed refreshing. The plans for a solution to the integration problem are innumerable and will eventually cause some sharp breaks and hot tempers. But at Vanderbilt no voice has growled—as did the irascible Mr. Talmadge—for the policy of immovable opposition."[14]

Still, while Tennessee whites were willing to wait for the Supreme Court's enforcement order and Vanderbilt students expressed a cautious acceptance of change, *Brown* left powerful unease in its wake. Although Branscomb was far from upset personally about *Brown*, he understood the southern situation as unsettled and he was uncertain about what course things might take. A friend from Alabama startled him with a note that anxiously raised the possibility of fraternities being forced to accept black members. Branscomb was at first skeptical but admitted that the problem of fraternal organizations "may hit me at any time." Mulling over the possibilities, he rejected the notion that college administrators could dictate, as had already happened at a few northern schools, that segregated fraternities would not be allowed on campus. But logical as ever, he also acknowledged that if a fra-

ternity elected "a colored brother, the university would have no right to interfere." The slightest lack of certainty crept into his tone as he assessed the
situation at Vanderbilt. "At present, unless our fraternities elect someone
from Fisk, the problem could scarcely arise, but it would be a brave man today to say where and how this issue may not arise."[15] Branscomb did realize
that the hardening of positions in the wake of *Brown* and the open division
of people into angry camps made it harder to pursue his usual strategy of
using small tacking maneuvers to get where he wanted to go. Yet, interestingly, he also believed this problem would be temporary and so never completely stopped his behind-the-scenes planning.[16]

Branscomb did, though, back away from the one direct opportunity to
press the issue that arose in 1954. The absence of any legal training for blacks
in Nashville meant that the Law School was clearly within the bounds he
had outlined earlier for deciding where Vanderbilt should open admissions
to blacks. Further, continuing pressure from the AALS had kept the matter
in front of the university's leadership for the last few years, and the threat
of loss of membership was real. With the successful enrollment of Reverend
Joseph Johnson and another black student in the School of Religion, Branscomb was eager to admit black law students.

In November, after consultation with Branscomb, the dean of the Law
School, John Wade, sent Branscomb two versions of a memo, leaving it to
him to decide which one to present to the board.[17] Branscomb chose the
longer version, which laid out the reasoning behind the law faculty's request for an end to racially restrictive admissions.[18] In a tour de force, Wade
touched on morality and practicality, compulsion, outside interference, idealism, and the need to retain control of both the institution and the region in
the hands of a properly educated elite. It was now time, he argued, for the
loose group of civic and business leaders who effectively ran the community to include blacks.

Dean Wade invoked the Supreme Court's decision in *Brown* and pled for
respect for the law, claiming a special responsibility for legal educators. "It
seems to us," he argued, "that the Supreme Court decision should have peculiar significance for a law school. While the narrow holding applies only
to state supported schools and not to a private institution like Vanderbilt,
we who teach law and seek to instill a feeling of respect and reverence for
the law, must be concerned not only with the strict letter of the law but with
its true spirit."[19]

Wade next appealed to one of Vanderbilt's most cherished roles—the
education of leaders. He wrote that the Law School "has consistently re-

garded its goal as the training not of mere craftsmen in the law, but of real leaders in their community. We think it is well to teach our students by example to meet and to take a position on impelling moral issues once the bases for reaching a proper judgment have been determined." The dean did not hesitate to address the more practical aspects of this concern as well. Citing the school's exemplary record in supplying white leadership to the South, he suggested that "Negroes in the South need leaders too, and will obtain them from their own race" and that these leaders are likely to come from the ranks of the legal profession. Wade followed this reasonable observation with a warning. "If these [black] lawyers attend law school outside the Southern region where they live and practice, their ideas and leadership may prove more extreme and less realistic than those which would be produced by the more moderate and better balanced position which we should hope to inculcate."[20]

Finally, Wade addressed the issue of the American Association of Law Schools' stance toward segregation. In 1951 the AALS adopted a requirement that its member institutions must provide "equality of opportunity in legal education without discrimination or segregation on the ground of race or color."[21] He pointed out that although the AALS allowed a period of adjustment for noncomplying schools, that "grace period" was likely to end soon and he was clear about what must be done. "It will thus be necessary," he stated as though no other conclusion were possible, "for action to be taken sometime soon if we are to retain our accredited status." Perhaps to make this more palatable to the board, Wade focused on the fact that there was still time to accomplish the change before the compulsion would be obvious. Vanderbilt might actually get something in return, he argued, if they would just go ahead and act now. "Voluntary action may inure to the credit of the School in many circles of importance and may add to the prestige of the School in the Nation as a whole." Stressing finally the matter of internal control of the process, he ended with this: voluntary desegregation "affords the opportunity of controlling more completely the details involved in the selection and admission of students."[22]

Wade stressed that the law faculty was unanimous in these opinions. This group was certainly motivated by several things. First, the acceptance and approval of the national legal community was important to them. Loss of AALS accreditation would harm the reputation of the school mainly in academic circles; the state bar associations had more to say about whose graduates could practice law. It was the professors, then, rather than the students who would be most hurt by AALS sanctions, embarrassed in front of their peers.

The law students, though, also supported the change. An informal poll conducted by the law school newspaper, *Dicta,* found that 53 percent favored opening admissions to qualified blacks and 63 percent would not object to such enrollment.[23] Wade saw in this acceptance evidence that the transition to a desegregated student body would be a smooth one, a conclusion bolstered by the experience of other southern law schools that had recently integrated. He admitted that some prospective students would not come to Vanderbilt if admissions were opened to blacks but predicted that the number would be small. He also predicted that the number of black students who enrolled would likewise be small, as Vanderbilt's "high standards, both for prelegal work and for work in the Law School, would be likely to keep the number of eligible applicants low."[24]

Branscomb, however, did not use this powerful memo to push the trustees hard. He submitted Wade's memo at the fall meeting but did not ask for any action on the Law School's request. Rather, he offered only a brief statement that focused not on race at all but on the freedom of the faculty to communicate with the board.

> The Chancellor stated that several days before the meeting of the Board of Trust he was asked whether the School of Law could present a memorandum to the Board concerning the admission of qualified negro students to that School, and he had replied that any faculty of the University could at any time present any communication to the Board which it wished. He stated that the School of Law was not endeavoring to determine this issue but only to advise the Board of Trust, the responsible body, of their views on this matter. He asked what disposition the Board wished to make of this document, and it was moved, seconded and carried that it be received and filed.[25]

Branscomb seems to have gone into the meeting intending to urge the desegregation of the Law School but sensed the board's mood of resistance and backed away. In a 1955 letter to David Cavers, a Harvard law professor and head of the AALS Committee on Racial Discrimination in Legal Education, Branscomb explained that "I think I would have succeeded in opening the Law School to Negro students . . . last fall except for the complications of the Supreme Court ruling. . . . I presented to the Board a memorandum which Dean Wade and I had worked up on the subject, but they would hardly listen to it."[26] Despite this tactical retreat, Branscomb remained committed to moving Vanderbilt slowly away from racial restrictions. If nothing else, the Wade memorandum let the board know that they would soon have to face the racial problem in the Law School, even if it could still be put off for a while.

The slow course of desegregation that Branscomb had set, in fact, bore fruit in 1954, when the first black student admitted to the School of Religion, Rev. Joseph Johnson Jr., received his B.D. degree at the end of the summer session.[27] (The Religion School continued to admit black students although the partial nature of the changes at Vanderbilt required some creativity.)[28] Convinced that Vanderbilt was moving in the direction that would allow for its continued growth and improvement, Branscomb paused after the announcement of *Brown*, but it wouldn't be for long.

II

In Georgia the *Brown* decision hit like a bombshell. *Southern School News* summed up the situation:

> Anticipation of an eventual U.S. Supreme Court decision on segregation in the public schools and the knowledge that the ruling would have great impact on the state had laid close to the hearts and minds of all Georgians, white and colored, for several years.
>
> But when the high court de[c]ree was announced on May 17, it found all of Georgia's important state government officials and a great number of Georgia's white citizens totally unprepared to accept or to follow the Supreme Court decision outlawing segregation in the public schools.[29]

Georgia's Governor Herman Talmadge had been working to preserve segregation for years. He based his strategy on "equalization," believing that racial separation could be preserved by actually providing "separate but equal" schools. In 1951 Georgia implemented a retail sales tax whose proceeds were used to increase teacher salaries, reduce the pay gap between white and black teachers, and provide other benefits to black schools. In 1952 a State School Building Authority helped raise money for school construction.[30] By 1953 the Georgia legislature began taking action to support the state's constitutional ban on financing integrated education, setting up a Commission on Education to plan for public schooling "consistent with the state constitution" and passing a proposed constitutional amendment that would allow the state to discharge its educational responsibilities through grants to individual students. This "private school plan" was controversial. Many Georgians, concerned about the quality of their children's education, strongly opposed it. Many others, more concerned about race mixing, supported it.[31]

The November 1954 election would determine the fate of the proposed amendment. Also at stake that fall was the governor's seat. The September Democratic primary, the real election, was hotly contested, and segregation was the most important issue; the announcement of the *Brown* decision "built a fire under an already hot Georgia gubernatorial campaign." Of the nine candidates only one advocated compliance with the Supreme Court decision.[32] The other eight offered different plans to evade the law. The eventual winner was Lieutenant Governor Marvin Griffin, a member of the Talmadge faction who ran on a platform of preserving both segregation and the county unit system, and whose mandate to do so was strengthened by the easy passage of Talmadge's "private school plan."[33]

As ever, control of Georgia depended on control of the rural base along with the cooperation of Atlanta's business community. But as race relations came to supersede all else, the interests of those two groups diverged. In the traditional, rural, agricultural counties, any tampering with segregation remained anathema and it took no great effort to whip the white people of these counties into a near frenzy over the possibility of integrated public schools. Atlanta, though, was a different story. The city was more and more dominated by large corporations and had become the largest transportation hub in the South. Atlanta was also home to prominent black colleges, powerful black churches, and influential black leaders. The city's large black population had a small but real voice in the city's politics.[34] Relatively smooth race relations prevailed, the product of cooperation between black and white leaders. This cooperation was prompted in part by a shared concern about maintaining a stable environment for business. Thriving Atlanta was led by aggressive entrepreneurs like Coca-Cola's Robert Woodruff, who cared deeply about economic growth and building a national reputation for the city. These things depended on the existence of a good racial climate, which made investment in the area attractive and made Atlanta seem like a good place for executives and employees to live. Whatever their private opinions about blacks, Atlanta's leaders valued calm more than strict segregation and national influence more than the esteem of south Georgia crackers.[35]

This pattern was nowhere more visible than at Atlanta's most prestigious university. Emory shared the desire for the approval, the embrace really, of the rest of the nation. By 1954 it had made impressive strides in improving the quality of instruction, especially in the critically important Graduate School. Emory was still hampered by chronic financial problems, but in April the university received a check for $2 million from the General Education Board of the Rockefeller Foundation, the first payment on a conditional grant of $7 million to improve the graduate program.[36] The year before Emory had begun participating, along with Duke, Vanderbilt, Tulane, and UNC, in a program sponsored by the Carnegie Foundation for the Advancement of Teaching that provided funds to increase salaries of outstanding professors working in the Graduate School and to increase stipends for promising graduate students. Together, these two grants did much to raise morale and develop the reputation of the Graduate School at Emory.[37]

The enhanced ability to attract and retain prominent professors in an increasingly national job market was not without social side effects. Faculty came to Emory in ever greater numbers from outside the South. Although these faculty members were of primary importance in Emory's struggle to meet the standards of the broader academic community, they brought northern habits of mind along with their research and teaching skills. By 1954 some Emory professors interacted regularly on an informal basis with the faculties of Atlanta's black colleges.[38] Emory faculty also analyzed the issues that surrounded desegregation more rigorously than did the administrators, at least in public forums. One example of this was a symposium on segregation published in the Law School's *Journal of Public Policy*, the first really scholarly discussion of the legal, social, economic, and educational questions that were raised by the *Brown* decision. Here, professors from several disciplines, many of them from Emory, prodded on a deeper level. "What is the South? What is equality in a democracy? What will it cost to end segregation in schools? What are the problems on the level of the local school boards? What are the social issues involved? The economic issues? The personal issues?"[39] This kind of searching attention to the problems of segregation on the part of faculty would only increase in the future as overt racial discrimination came to be both rare in higher education and ever more important in Georgia's politics.

Emory students were also outspoken in their reactions. Classes were still in session when the *Brown* decision was announced, and the student newspaper quickly moved to open debate. The May 20 edition of the *Wheel* devoted nearly the entire editorial page to discussion of the Supreme Court action. "The Court Has Ruled," said the headline, and the editors had strong feelings about the ruling. They accepted that change was inevitable and recognized that segregation was, in effect, finished. They hoped that graceful, if gradual, integration would be possible. But while segregation was clearly "on the rocks," the manner of its demise was still undecided. Here, the students stressed the danger inherent in the decision, echoing the objections that had long been standard fare for white southerners who resented northern interference in southern race relations. "While progressives are congratulating themselves," they warned, "Southern demagogues will exploit the situation to the fullest, particularly in the rural areas. Truthfully, little exploitation will be needed. In many parts of the South opinion of the Negro has remained the same since the Civil War."[40] Another article contained man-on-the-street polling of students and faculty. The faculty members and administrators who were interviewed seemed to be of a single mind on the issue. All stressed the rightness of the decision, its "inevitability." However, most also focused on the need for more time. Political science professor Ronald Howell pointed out that because there was no active case before the courts involving Georgia, "there is thus time enough for wise planning directed necessarily towards obedience to the high court's decision. All will not change overnight." Floyd Watkins of the English Department was in general agreement: "A large number of years will be needed to put the system into effect. There may be violence in some rural communities."

Not surprisingly, student opinion was divided, with most expressing some degree of skepticism. There is little evidence to suggest that the new visibility of segregation as an issue among students was anything of real consequence, however. The general apathy of Emory students toward political matters, even segregation, was apparent in their failure to turn out for a debate about the best way to preserve segregation. Held in Emory's Glenn Memorial Auditorium and featuring four gubernatorial candidates, the debate was the only time that fall's political campaign came directly onto campus. "On the whole," reported the *Wheel*, "the Emory student body was conspicuous by its absence. The most liberal estimate of the 'crowd' was 150, with most of it being made up of outsiders and faculty members."[41] The feelings of most Emory students about the furor over *Brown* were probably best expressed by Sam Clark, "college senior and man-about-the-Library-steps," who asked, "What effect will the decision have on the Kappa Alpha fraternity?"[42]

The public reaction of Emory's administration to *Brown* was muted. In a speech to the Phi Beta Kappa chapter on May 21, Goodrich White shared his thoughts on the last twenty-five years in higher education. He identified the "beginnings of a break-down of racial segregation" as one of the major trends of those years. White did not engage in any detailed discussion of racial change yet made it clear that he believed the issue would not go away and that it had become in the last several years part of the broad mix of social, political, and economic changes that would demand adaptation from higher education in the future.[43]

Apart from President White's brief remarks, there is little evidence of any discussion of the matter, let alone any serious consideration of what Emory ought to do about it. In his October report to the Board of Trustees, White made no mention of segregation or of the *Brown* decision.[44] It was discussed only briefly at the inaugural meeting of the "Committee of One Hundred," a group of Methodist laymen headed by Emory trustee (later chairman of the board) Henry Bowden and organized by the university for fund-raising purposes. This group included Goodrich White, Emory trustees James V. Carmichael and Bishop Arthur J. Moore, and many prominent Emory alumni. In a wide-ranging exchange of views about the university's goals and prospects, someone raised the matter of black enrollment. The notes on the meeting are terse but revealing: "Discussion of Emory's position on admission of Negroes developed the normal objections, as well as the further fact that under the laws of Georgia admission of Negroes would cause the University to lose its tax-free status, which would have a ruinous effect financially."[45]

The best evidence of the thinking of the university's leaders at this time is probably the editorial penned by *Emory Alumnus* editor Randy Fort that led the October issue of that magazine. While Fort had an independent streak and was given a fairly free hand in producing the *Alumnus,* there is every reason to believe that such an important—and cautious—piece of writing was discussed with the administration and approved before publication. The editorial suggests something of the quandary that the school was in. It weaves back and forth between facts that seem to mean that Emory will have to change and facts that seem to indicate that it won't, while providing no basis for deciding which sets of facts ought to prevail. While Fort's stated goal was neutrality, the overriding impression that the piece gives is of hazy uncertainty and paralysis of will.

"What's Emory going to do? This question had been asked over and over again by Emory alumni—and, for that matter, by faculty members, students, and other friends of the University—since the U.S. Supreme Court's

May 17 decisions on segregation in the public schools." Fort cast himself as a neutral party, dispensing "points of information" to readers who were lacking critical facts. Ever since the *Brown* decision, he claimed, "practically every leader in the State of Georgia has been admonishing everyone else to approach the H-bomb of segregation calmly and coolly. We shall here take this excellent advice and do our utmost to tackle the question in a calm, cool, and reportorial manner."[46]

Fort's tone was indeed calm, even reassuring, as he outlined five "points of information." First, he noted comfortingly, the *Brown* decision did not require Emory, a private school, to do anything at all. Fort immediately offset this, though, with another hard fact. "At the same time, as much as many among us might wishfully think it, the problem isn't going to just go away and leave us alone. It must be faced sooner or later, and since May 17 it has looked like sooner." Fort then went through the roster of formerly segregated schools that had already come to terms with the issue. Eighty-two in all, including substantially more private than public institutions of higher learning, had opened their doors to black applicants in the last several years.[47] When Emory finally faced matters squarely, Fort seemed to imply, the resolution was foreordained.

Fort's second point seemed, again, designed to soothe fears. "The president and other administrative officers of the university, the faculties of the University, the students, the alumni—any of these can recommend courses of action or express their opinions, individually or collectively," he stated. "But the trustees make the decisions." Those Emory trustees, Fort pointed out, were all "Southerners by birth or rearing, and in almost every case by both." Of the thirty one current trustees, twenty five were alumni of the University.[48]

In his third point Fort returned to facts that muddied the waters. He described the provisions of Emory's charter and by-laws that relate to the purposes and beneficiaries of the institutions. These documents make no reference at all to race, stating simply that the sole purpose of the university is "to give, promote, and extend under Christian influence and under the auspices of said Methodist Episcopal Church, South, instruction and education in theology, and in the arts, sciences, and professions, and to encourage and promote research and study in all the branches of learning."

Fort also discussed Georgia's segregation laws. The critical legal matter for Emory was its status as a tax-exempt institution, which was granted by a state law that allowed such exemption only as long as schools that had been "established for white people" remained for the exclusive use of white people (and conversely, that schools founded to educate blacks, or "colored people," as the Georgia code had it, continued to educate only blacks). The law was unequivocal: the issue now was whether the May 17 Supreme Court decision meant that the law was unconstitutional. If not, disobedience would have catastrophic results. The best estimates put Emory's potential tax bill at between $2 million and $2.5 million, about half of the university's annual budget. According to Fort, the consensus of Emory's attorneys was that the law was unconstitutional but that a test case would have to be mounted before blacks could be admitted. Fort offered another troubling piece of information. The Georgia code did not refer to "Negroes" but rather to "colored people," and by the code's own definition "colored people" included not only blacks, "mulattoes," and "mestizos," but also all Asians and natives of India. He noted accurately that "probably every white institution of higher learning in the state, public and private, for decades has been admitting Japanese or Chinese or Asiatic Indians or all three."[49]

Finally, the *Alumnus* editor concluded with a statement about the relationship between Emory and the Methodist Church, and a discussion of that church's evolving position on segregation. Emory's bylaws were clear—Emory "belongs to the Methodist Church." The church had the right to approve the appointment of all trustees and the right to "direct" the administration of the university. The most recent *Discipline of the Methodist Church,* published in 1952, spoke directly to racial segregation in Methodist institutions. "Ours is a world church. As such its responsibility is to unite in one fellowship men and women of all races and nations. As Christians we confess ourselves to be children of God, brothers and sisters of Jesus Christ. This being true, there is no place in the Methodist Church for racial discrimination or racial segregation. . . . We propose that the church seek to free itself utterly from racial discrimination and segregation."

After this wandering disquisition Fort ended with a repetition of his earlier warning. "This is not a problem which will just fade away and leave us, for too many publics—too many institutions, organizations, and individuals—are interestedly watching and asking questions."[50] Emory had no way to even begin answering these questions.

III

At Tulane in early 1954, it looked like something might happen. On Monday, April 12, about 100 of the 155-member graduate school faculty attended a regular meeting to discuss the microfilming of doctoral dissertations, the summer school, language requirements, and the machinery of the new

Graduate Council. The final order of business was introduced by Professor James Feibleman, chairman of the Philosophy Department, who requested that "full discussion be given to the problem of admission of Negroes to the Graduate School."[51] There was apparently not much in the way of disagreement: all or nearly all of the comments were "favorable to the admission of colored students." Dean Fred Cole made a brief motion. "In view of the great need of all Southerners for opportunities to receive specialized training, the Faculty of the Graduate School recommends that steps be taken to clarify the policy of admission to the Graduate School in order that admission of Negroes might be facilitated." This motion passed easily.[52] In interviews with New Orleans newspapers a spokesman for the faculty explained the reasoning behind the resolution, citing concern over the lack of adequate graduate and professional education for blacks in the area and carefully noting that there was no such difficulty with undergraduate training because of the presence of Dillard and Xavier.[53]

The graduate faculty sent copies of the resolution to Harris and to the editors of the student newspaper. The students responded with a long editorial urging support. "Negro students should be admitted to Tulane. They should be admitted freely and graciously, as early as possible, before the air is tensed by a Supreme Court order demanding that the color line be dropped." Noting the already significant numbers of black students attending previously all-white graduate and professional schools in the South, the Tulane students asserted that "the walls are definitely tumbling down. Some places they are being pounded down. Other places the builders are carefully taking them down. We should do that at Tulane and set the pace for the Deep South."[54] This editorial and the graduate faculty's recommendation were picked up by the press.[55] As publicity mushroomed, board chairman Joseph Jones released a statement. Jones stressed that Tulane's racially restrictive admissions policy was already under consideration, in fact had been for some time, and that the faculty resolution changed nothing.[56]

Rufus Harris was not pleased. He had been unaware of any movement within the faculty to request desegregation and he was caught by surprise. At the May 20 meeting of the Dean's Council he made his displeasure clear. President Harris "felt it would have been helpful if this matter had been discussed with him prior to the faculty action. In the future he requests that such a course be constantly observed."[57] Harris's remarks to the deans echoed Jones's statement to the press. "The Administrators had been giving careful consideration to the matter of the enrollment of Negro students to graduate study long before the recent resolution pertaining to this was presented by the graduate faculty," and "a committee of the Board had already been appointed and a meeting date set to consider the legal aspects of the matter before getting to other considerations."[58]

While it is certainly true that the subject had come up before, it had been a year since Marie Louise Snellings submitted her report on the legal issues surrounding desegregation at Tulane. The board had taken no action regarding that report and there is no record of any further deliberations on the matter. It seems quite unlikely, then, that a meeting to discuss desegregation of the Graduate School a month after the faculty resolution and a week after the *Hullabaloo* editorial was unrelated to these events.[59] In any case, on May 13 the board's legal committee did meet in the offices of its chairman, J. Blanc Monroe, to discuss the admission of black graduate students. This discussion turned entirely on the legal ambiguities in the university's founding documents. The 1882 charter included a letter from Paul Tulane reserving the income from his donations for "the promotion and encouragement of intellectual, moral, and industrial education among the white young persons in the city of New Orleans, State of Louisiana." The committee noted, though, that the actual instrument of donation (which did not technically include the letter) did not use racially restrictive language at all, and furthermore it made clear that the Board of Administrators had the authority to acquire income from other sources and to use it on whatever terms its donors requested. (This was, in fact, exactly what happened in 1884 when the Louisiana legislature gave the Tulane board the property that had previously belonged to the University of Louisiana.) The law committee then unanimously agreed that the school's charter did not prevent them from admitting blacks to Tulane.[60] In the wake of this meeting Joseph Jones began to prepare a statement and readied himself to announce action that would allow the admission of qualified blacks to graduate study at the university.[61]

Four days later the *Brown* decision was handed down. Reaction in Louisiana was swift and belligerent. The tone of segregationist rhetoric was immediately harsh and it escalated over the next several years to a fever pitch of hysteria and hatred. To contradict in the smallest degree the bitter-end posturing of Louisiana politicians was to risk financial, social, and career suicide. Although the governor, Robert Kennon, seemed inclined to accept the decision, the state legislature was another matter.[62] Within three days of the *Brown* announcement both the Louisiana House and Senate passed resolutions by overwhelming margins that censured the Supreme Court for "usurpation of power." Within a month, three bills intended to thwart the decision had passed and a new Joint Legislative Committee to Maintain Segregation had been formed to plan strategy for the fight.[63] No holds would be barred in their efforts to beat back the twin menaces of federal intervention and racial amalgamation.

Like the legislature, it did not take long for the Tulane Board of Administrators to react to *Brown*. Marie Louise Snellings, Harris's closest ally on the board, wrote him on the very day of the decision to express her doubts about the wisdom of changing any racial policy under these new circumstances.[64] The response of Louisianans to the publicity about the graduate faculty's resolution and the *Hullabaloo* editorial could not have helped. By the time of the June 9 board meeting Harris had received seven letters, of widely varying degrees of literacy, expressing disapproval. The president was distressed that none "made the distinction that consideration was being given to admission of Negroes to graduate work only, but the idea seemed to be that Negroes would be admitted to any department, including Newcomb College [the women's college]."[65] In the reply Harris drafted to handle these complaints, he carefully explained this point. That it mattered to his correspondents hardly seems likely. In the weeks and years that followed the *Brown* decision, most whites in Louisiana were in no mood to split hairs. The point of segregation was to keep blacks out. The notion that it was somehow acceptable to destroy segregation if it were destroyed slowly, beginning with blacks who already had more education than most whites in the state, would have been less than compelling.

Little evidence remains of Rufus Harris's thoughts during this critical time. Clearly, he desperately wanted the admissions policy changed and no doubt worked carefully behind the scenes to help bring this about. Responding to Snellings's growing hesitation about changing Tulane's racial policies, Harris took pains to downplay any suggestion of urgency. "The Negro admissions resolution of the Graduate Faculty does not constitute any crisis nor seem so monumental to me even yet," he assured her. Stressing the positive aspects of the situation, Harris pointed out "the ancient Chinese meaning of the word crisis: a dangerous opportunity." But in closing he again returned to the message that there was no reason at all to act hastily or from a sense of emergency. "I think Tulane's decision should be unhurried—as usual."[66] He was nervous, plainly, about upsetting what must have been a very delicate balance on the board, and one that began eroding quickly after the announcement of *Brown*. His remarks to the Dean's Council on May 20, for example, reveal his anxiety about the faculty abruptly intruding into the discussion without first talking to him. In concluding those remarks Harris hinted at the delicacy of the deliberations when he "expressed the opinion that caution should be observed to avoid any similar resolutions by any other faculty as they would only serve to give a further agitative appearance of pressure upon the Board."[67]

This statement stands in stark contrast to Harvie Branscomb's remarks to the Vanderbilt board and the faculty of the Vanderbilt School of Law about their resolution requesting that the Law School be desegregated. In that case Branscomb was able to tell both the professors and the trustees that the voices of the faculty were welcome at all times in board meetings.[68] This difference reflects the underlying contrast between the relationship of Harris and the Tulane board and that of Branscomb and the Vanderbilt board. Branscomb was operating from strength, even during the difficult year of 1954. He was an effective leader who had a close working relationship with his board. Harris was also a strong leader, but he was saddled with a board chairman who disliked and disrespected him, who filled vacancies on the board with his cronies, and who was not inclined to follow the president's lead even when (as was almost always the case) it would be the wise thing to do. Disagreements over other policy issues such as the proper place for athletics within the university also contributed to the disintegration of Harris's personal relationship with Jones and the erosion of his influence with the board. At its next meeting on June 9, the Tulane board tabled the issue of desegregation.

In the aftermath of this near miss, Tulane was left with the same set of growing problems. If anything, southern resistance to *Brown* triggered a parallel increase in pressure from other quarters, such as the professional organizations and the foundations. By October, for example, Harris was back in front of the board with correspondence from the chairman of the Association of American Law Schools' Special Committee on Racial Discrimination. Tulane was now one of only seventeen law schools in the country that retained bars on black admissions. Harris warned the board that "with only a few schools continuing to refuse to admit Negroes, the possibility of being dropped from the accredited list is a very real one."[69] In spite of Eisenhower's tepid response to *Brown*, the federal government also demanded compliance with hiring regulations designed to provide equal economic opportunity for blacks. On September 3, Eisenhower signed an executive order mandating the inclusion of a new nondiscrimination clause in all federal contracts. By December, government agencies were sending notice of the new clause to its research contractors, including Tulane (and Duke, Emory, Rice, and Vanderbilt as well). Tulane's story, which they stuck to here, was that they did not discriminate in employment, as anyone could clearly see the large number of blacks who worked on campus. Nearly every one of them was a janitor, gardener, cook, or other service worker. In 1954 this was enough to satisfy federal requirements, but Tulane's leadership could not have failed to recognize that they would not be allowed to get away with this forever.[70]

Pressure continued to mount inside the university as well. Despite Harris's deteriorating relationship with the board he managed throughout the 1950s to maintain an extremely open environment on campus. His defense of academic freedom during the 1949 attacks by Congressman F. Edward Hebert was heartfelt and earned him the trust of the faculty. Their sense of safety and freedom, even when dealing with the controversial issue of race, is evident in matters that surfaced in the wake of the administrators' decision to continue excluding black students. At the October board meeting, Harris passed on to the administrators a letter from the director of libraries that discussed the problem of providing research facilities for black patrons. Garland Taylor, the library head, wrote Harris seeking explicit sanction for the apparently long-standing policy of quietly supporting the research efforts of the few blacks who needed access to Tulane's collection. Taylor seemed quite proud of the fact that "in spite of the limitations which we put upon the complete freedom of our Negro patrons," at least four of them were able to complete master's theses based on research done in Tulane's Howard-Tilton Library. Two recent developments, however, prompted Taylor to seek "assurance of backing from the University in this area of service." First, through its Urban Life Research Institute, Tulane now employed two "professionally trained colored persons . . . in intellectual work." As associated staff, Taylor assumed, they were "entitled to have the same library privileges which other members of that staff have. And in absence of specific orders to the contrary the Library expects to give them these privileges."[71]

The second item of concern was closely tied to the debate over admitting black graduate students and strongly suggests the determination of the faculty that racially discriminatory admissions policies be changed. Taylor summarized the problem for Harris.

> The second situation relates to an exceptionally well qualified recent Negro applicant for admission to the Graduate School. Admission has been denied him . . . but the candidate's training and qualifications are such as to make service to him a matter of serious concern

to the Department to which he applied and to the Dean of the College. We have accordingly agreed that we will try to assist in the carrying out of a reading program to be arranged under informal graduate faculty direction. It should hardly be necessary to add that the student in question cannot carry out such a program at any other library in New Orleans. It is my proposal to do everything that we can to help in what I think is a real responsibility here."[72]

In spite of some concerns about the possible "reluctance of some staff members to serve Negro customers" or the chance that patrons might be "offended by the presence of Negro readers in our midst," Taylor felt that the university "must not flee" from its responsibility. What he wanted was for Tulane to "formally back us in this view." To fail to do so, he argued, "is to throw staff members to the wolves." Taylor was quite aware of the racial turmoil that was already gripping New Orleans in response to the *Brown* decision but had made his own decision on where it would ultimately lead. "Perhaps it is not timely now to formulate long range policy," he closed, "but I hope it may be possible to give thought to this also, since the handwriting is upon the wall."[73]

The board, however, was unwilling to make any formal statement on racial policy of any kind. They took no official action on Taylor's request, although they allowed Harris to give him private assurances.[74] The handwriting may have been upon the wall, but Tulane's board was going to need its law committee to conduct another study of it.

IV

At Rice, the *Brown* decision drew no official reaction. There were no reports of President Houston's response in any area newspapers. The trustees and administrators were not spurred to reconsider their stance on admitting blacks. There was not a single mention of blacks in any board minutes or president's reports throughout 1954. The combination of the 1891 charter language that clearly forbade the admission of blacks, the lack of serious internal pressure for change, and the hostile political climate in Houston and Texas were major factors in this passivity.

In Houston, the election of two moderates to the school board in 1954 momentarily confounded the far right-wing groups that had come to loudly dominate the city's politics, but it did not end their powerful influence. Even as the most overwrought fears of Communism seemed to fade among the city's general population, the anti-Communist extremists, abetted by Houston's upper classes, continued to hold sway.[75] The Supreme Court's decision in *Brown* was unpopular with whites in Texas, and the preservation of seg-regation was an issue (although not the major one) in the state's 1954 gu-bernatorial contest. Incumbent Governor Allen Shivers, running for a third term (against Texas tradition), campaigned for the Democratic nomination on a platform of racial prejudice and anti-Communism. Despite early indi-cations that Shivers might take a moderate stance toward the court's decree, a closely fought primary battle led him to race-bait and red-bait his main opponent, Ralph Yarborough. Yarborough never took a strong position on *Brown,* stating that he opposed "forced commingling of races in our public schools" but refusing to defy the Supreme Court.[76] Shivers won reelection, and his use of red scare tactics as governor kept the political climate of the state fearful and uncertain.

At Rice, this fevered political atmosphere would have made any thoughts of removing racial restrictions quite unappetizing. But, in fact, no one there seemed to be having thoughts of that nature. Partly this was the result of the near total absence of concern with the issue from any department or school in the institution. This absence persisted even as the organizational pres-sures on the other campuses began to spread. Again, the fact that Rice did not have a law school or a theology school greatly contributed to its isola-tion from critical currents of change that were present on other campuses. By 1954, though, the other schools were feeling pressure from other internal sources as well. Medical schools and nursing colleges at Emory, Tulane, and Duke were pressed to consider how to respond in areas where training for black physicians was painfully inadequate and hospital care for black pa-tients was almost recklessly bad.[77] But Rice had neither a medical nor nurs-ing school. At Tulane, the School of Social Work became an active center of engagement with racial change as the faculty began to take seriously its re-sponsibility to serve the whole community. Rice, though, had no school of social work. In a similar fashion sociology, anthropology, and economics departments in all these other universities became lightning rods for race matters as faculty began to give more consideration to the practical aspects and consequences of segregation and to the possible effects of integration. At Rice, the humanities and especially the social sciences had long been ne-glected; there were no graduate programs in either. There simply was no department of anthropology. Sociology (with one part-time professor) and economics were afterthoughts, appended to the Department of Business Administration, with no prospect of immediate expansion or improvement. Rice was still primarily a technical institute, its curriculum focused almost entirely on science and engineering, areas that neither dealt with racial issues nor attracted large numbers of black students at the time. Thus, there was still no real source of organized agitation inside the institution.[78]

Financially too Rice remained much less subject to pressure from outside funders to change its racial policy. Although not as rich as people assumed, Rice was in reasonably good financial shape and, importantly, during the 1950s it began to actively solicit major support from industry. Contributions from northern foundations were limited until the end of the decade, and although Rice received substantial research money from the federal government, without a medical school to support even that money was not so desperately needed. Reliance on industry made more sense: given the institute's focus on engineering and science, Rice faculty and graduate students were admirably qualified to help businesses solve their practical problems. And this reliance on industry, often local energy companies and almost always businesses with major operations in the South, freed Rice from the fear that failure to desegregate would result in the tap being shut off.[79]

Rice students, however, expressed growing interest in racial changes even before the *Brown* decision was announced. In April the *Thresher* conducted a poll that asked, "Do you think Negroes should be admitted to this school on the same basis as other students? Why or why not?" Thirty students indicated approval of opening admissions to blacks and sixteen opposed it. Those in favor of desegregation stressed the need to "do away with childish, archaic prejudices" as well as the community's need for all people to develop to their full potential. "The Negro who is prepared for college and has a sufficient desire to get as good an education as possible," said one student, "should be given every chance possible to be a more valuable citizen." Another reply also focused on desegregation as a benefit to the larger community. "An educational institution should devote itself to personal, national, and cultural improvement. Since increased educational advantages for Negroes is highly compatible with these aims, Rice should definitely admit them." Unfavorable replies stressed personal unhappiness at the prospect of blacks on campus. "I don't believe in mixing white and Negroes," one student stated simply. "It would prejudice many people against Rice," according to another, and "there would be much student objection," said a third.[80]

Student interest in race relations found other outlets. Predictably, religious organizations with a presence on campus were among the most active in creating interracial ties among students. The Council on Race and Education, for example, invited Rice students to three interfaith, interracial services in 1954.[81] In one mysterious episode, the *Thresher* announced that the Rice Forum Committee would sponsor a debate between the Rice and Texas Southern debate teams on the Rice campus, but, without any comment, the black debaters were excluded and the Rice team debated itself. Rice students also continued their involvement with the Texas Intercollegiate Student Association (TISA), which had begun admitting black members in 1951 and which also continued to issue statements favoring desegregation. Rice student Louis Israel was the president of TISA in 1954, and he defended the passage of a resolution calling for the end of segregation in colleges. "I personally think," said Israel, "that this resolution does represent the majority of the Rice student body's viewpoint." Israel may well have been correct, but the impact of student thinking on the matter remained the same as it had always been. Neither the Rice administration nor its board showed the slightest inclination even to officially notice that there was a problem, let alone take any steps to deal with it. But the growing frustration of the students, best seen in a short editorial that ran right after Rice's football game with Cornell, unmistakably heralded the coming of the day when the school's leadership would have to face the matter.

> A few weeks ago the Thresher received a letter from the Cornell Daily Sun in which the editor asked if we could help to secure the same sleeping and eating accommodations for the "Big Red's" negro player, Dick Jackson, which were provided for the rest of the squad.
>
> Unfortunately, we had to reply that regardless of our personal feelings and regardless of the United States Constitution and the Bible, the State of Texas maintains that this athlete is inferior (incidentally, the inanity of this contention was adequately demonstrated on the playing field Saturday night) and not entitled to equality with his white teammates.
>
> Thus again we must hang our heads in shame and say only that perhaps the day will not be far off when Rice and the State of Texas will welcome all men equally. Only then will we be able to be proud that we are part of the Rice Institute, and part of Texas.[82]

V

Two days after the announcement of the *Brown* opinion, several North Carolina newspapers carried brief stories describing the reaction of Duke President Hollis Edens. Characteristically, Edens was measured and calm. "I believe that the people of North Carolina are reasonable," he said, "and that they will take the Supreme Court decision in stride." As to the effect of the decision on Duke, Edens had less to say. The South's private institutions, he explained, "appear gradually to be taking care of the problem in their own way and in keeping with their own time schedules." The president "did not discuss what approach Duke may be using to the problem, nor did he say what time schedule may be in operation at Duke."[83]

Eden's placid response to *Brown* was in keeping with North Carolina's heritage. The state's politicians, while no less committed to segregation than their counterparts in the Deep South, were part of a political tradition that shied away from open confrontation about race.[84] North Carolinians continued to pride themselves on the smoothness of their race relations and on the polite "North Carolina Way" of doing business. This was reflected in the response of the state's political leaders to the Supreme Court decision. Although Governor William B. Umstead expressed disappointment over *Brown,* he also made clear that "this is no time for rash statement of the proposal of impossible schemes."[85] Umstead and Lieutenant Governor Luther Hodges, who became governor upon Umstead's death in November, acted instead by appointing committees to study the problem. On August 4, Umstead appointed a nineteen-member special advisory committee to "think through the various proposals and make a study of policy and program." Hodges, as head of the State Board of Education, set up a committee of that board to look at possible responses.[86] In the Democratic senatorial primary contested that spring, Kerr Scott, the former governor who had appointed Frank Graham to the Senate in 1949, defeated an opponent who tried to brand him as "soft" on race. Scott represented the more progressive wing of the party, which supported gradual movement toward both racial and economic justice. North Carolina believed in segregation, but hysterical reaction was simply not its way.

On the Duke campus, both students and faculty accepted the decision and the inevitability of desegregation, but neither group put real pressure on Edens or the board in 1954. Typical of the reaction of the students was an early October editorial in the *Chronicle* entitled "Time and Tide" about the resistance to desegregated public schools in Maryland and Delaware. Disturbed by the ugly scenes of protest in these border states, the *Chronicle* lamented that this was probably a signal that "the time when the Deep South will be able to forget the tattered dogma of white supremacy is farther away than even the least optimistic would guess." Still, the editorial concluded, the day would come when formal distinctions based on race would be abolished. "Those who refuse to face this reality are sadly like King Canute when he commanded the tide to stop."[87]

Duke administrators continued to have some flexibility in allowing interracial meetings on campus, and for the most part these gatherings were religious ones. The fall semester of 1954 saw the organization of a new student group, the Inter-Collegiate Fellowship for Religion in Life, an interfaith and mixed race organization open to the Duke, University of North Carolina, and North Carolina College communities. The group was founded to discuss the religious grounds for social action, including not only segregation but also academic freedom and personal responsibility for world issues. The group met in the basement of the Duke chapel, at least some of the time.[88]

Members of the Duke faculty remained concerned about race. Sociologist Edgar Thompson, for example, attended an international conference on race relations sponsored by the Ford Foundation in October. Reporting on the conference, Thompson argued that the problem needed to be viewed in a global context. He told the *Chronicle*, "The Supreme Court ruling on segregation is of worldwide importance in view of America's need for allies among dark-skinned peoples in other nations," and that "gigantic racial readjustments are taking place also in many other parts of the world today." Thompson warned that "the Soviet Union is seeking to exploit these changes, with considerable success so far." However, he added, "Our efforts toward democratizing race relations and doing away with second class citizenship in the United States are posing a great challenge to Russia."[89]

In December, another faculty member, professor of Biblical literature Mason Crum, discussed the Supreme Court decision in an article in the Methodist weekly, *The Christian Advocate*. Crum first established his bona fides as a true southerner, describing his descent from a confederate soldier and a slaveholding minister and his childhood in South Carolina. While acknowledging "the horrors of the Reconstruction period," Crum held up Booker T. Washington as an example of what blacks could accomplish and expressed his belief that white southerners were now "willing to tackle the problem" of desegregation for their own good as well as for the good of southern blacks. Thoughtful white southerners, argued Crum, had understood for years that segregation was insupportable on moral grounds and harmful on practical ones. "But now," he continued, "that which they knew in their heart was right and just, has been declared so by the highest court in the land. Churches that have been spiritually embarrassed for years have welcomed it." Echoing Washington's racial rhetoric, Crum stressed the limits of the *Brown* decision. "The greatest fear in the South is social equality, or social intermingling. But the Supreme Court decision has nothing to do with personal social relations. It is aimed at equality of opportunity in tax-supported educational institutions." And this, he wrote, was the only thing that the vast majority of blacks were interested in, despite what was suggested by the attention paid to "the aggressive wing of the Negro group." In the end, Crum was optimistic. Whites would cooperate, and the removal of racial barriers might be "the first great step in the direction of a new order in the South."[90]

One hopeful sign was Hollis Edens's growing willingness to discuss internally the manner and timing of Duke's approach to desegregation. The trustees convened for their year-end meeting a scant two weeks after the announcement of the *Brown* decision, and Edens used the occasion to make his clearest statement ever about desegregation at Duke. While conceding that *Brown* posed "no immediate problem for Duke University except that of increased pressure," Edens argued that whatever the details of the enforcement decree, segregation at all levels of public education was doomed. He directly addressed the divided nature of public opinion, which he acknowledged was more important to Duke after the Supreme Court's action.

> There are those who think it would be foolish or unwise for a university of Duke's national stature to attempt to evade the principle of the Court's ruling. They think the time will come soon when segregation in privately supported universities will be declared unconstitutional on grounds of tax-exempt privileges. Others hold to the belief that not only will privately supported universities not be affected but that means will be found locally to circumvent the Court's order in the public schools.[91]

Adding that there was likely to be local variation in the final outcome, Edens took a clear stand. "To assume that Duke University can remain permanently an island of refuge from the effects of desegregation," he stated, "would be unrealistic." He also expressed skepticism about the racial practices of northern schools and argued that their experience with black students suggested that white supremacy would serve as a natural check on black enrollment even if institutional segregation were banned.

I suppose I should apologize to those of you who are more idealistically inclined for approaching the problem in such a realistic way, but my observation of certain Eastern institutions, Princeton for example, leads me to the conclusion that they have admitted only the principle of non-segregation and that they have become very little involved in the practice. There are reasons for this beyond the desire to admit only a minimum of negroes. The fact is that relatively few negro applicants meet the admission requirements.

Finally, Edens tried to put the question of black admissions to Duke's graduate schools into perspective. Given the torrent of changes that had already come to the South, he argued, the refusal to make this small one was pointless and, by implication, likely to be counterproductive.

> To those of you who may be alarmed at the trend of my thinking, I would reply that the effect of non-segregation in universities is no longer significant in comparison to the developments elsewhere. The real change is taking place closer to you. More and more negroes are going to grade school and high school, they are serving on school boards, they are getting better jobs and earning more money as they disappear from the homes and kitchens of white employers. They are driving good cars and paying for the best accommodations on non-segregated public transportation. I could continue to spell out the change that is taking place. This is to say that university people generally do not look upon the admission of an insignificant few negroes with the same jaundiced eye as does the average man outside who is being faced with more revolutionary changes closer to home. This is to say that we may be straining at a gnat and swallowing a camel if we refuse to admit a few negroes at the graduate level of the University while being overwhelmed by the swift movement elsewhere.[92]

The president proposed again what he had suggested at the February 1954 meeting: "some small gesture toward de-segregation in the near future."[93] Duke's trustees were unmoved, but they did not close to door to future action.

By December, Edens decided that it would be worthwhile to have the University Council conduct a detailed study of the university's segregation policies and the policy changes that had taken place at other southern schools. "The preliminary discussion which followed [Eden's announcement of this plan] was largely confined to the question of the admission of negroes to the Graduate School and professional schools. . . . Vice President Gross directed attention to the possible effects of a continued policy of complete exclusion on the tax-exempt status of Duke University. With regard to faculty attitudes toward the admission of qualified negroes in the professional schools, Dr. Cleland felt that the faculty of the School of Religion would possibly be unanimous in favoring such admission in that School at this time. Professor Latty believed that the Law School faculty would on the whole be disposed to take the same position. The question will be again placed on the agenda of the January Council meeting for further exploration."[94] By February 1955 at Edens's behest the council would set up a committee to study the extent and experience of desegregation at other southern universities.

As 1954 closed, however, little had really changed. The decision to consider possible policy changes was a hopeful one, but here, as at all the other schools, no one had articulated a principle that would allow collected facts to be weighed appropriately and a judgment made. Too, Edens was still unable to speak forthrightly to off-campus constituencies. In December 1954 Edens received another letter from Duke alumna Helen Morrison, who had earlier expressed her unhappiness about segregation at the university. "So much has happened since I last wrote you about my concern for the integration problem," she told Edens, "that I thought you might have some news about what Duke's position is. . . . The day for shilly-shallying has passed. A brave, bold statement of our intention for integration is needed."[95] Edens, though, had nothing new to tell Mrs. Morrison. He fell back on the same sort of bland rhetoric that had always been his standby. "Undoubtedly, we shall attack the problem at the graduate level when we do move toward a change. I have had considerable conversation with members of my Board of Trustees and members of the University Council concerning this question, but no decisive action had been taken."[96] Thus, while Edens was the only one of these presidents to seize the *Brown* decision as an opportunity to push—however tentatively—for change, he found himself in exactly the same position as the others, and exactly the same position he had been in before.

The South's response to the *Brown* decision made negotiating a safe path far more treacherous for Duke, Emory, Tulane, Rice, and Vanderbilt. As race relations became the most important issue in southern politics, there was little room left to maneuver. Governors and state legislators blustered and schemed to thwart the Supreme Court ruling. Race was on the front pages of newspapers, with every suggestion of compliance or resistance a story. Positions hardened, anger boiled, and rhetoric was often explosive. Political agitation and an avid press utterly destroyed the private universities' sense of calm independence. They were more aware of the scrutiny of outsiders and of the weight of their actions in public opinion.

The *Brown* decision had a similar effect on students and faculty. Students, although certainly split on the issue and in general more concerned with dances than with politics, accepted the idea that segregation was going to end sooner rather than later. They were a very conservative group, mostly southern and solidly middle class, and they generally remained content to allow this process to work itself out without much participation. An outspoken minority, though, was invigorated by the decision. This minority would keep the issue of desegregation alive on campus, mainly on the editorial pages of the student newspaper and in the student religious organizations. The faculties were by and large convinced even before 1954 of the need to end racial restrictions in admissions policies. The *Brown* decision cemented this position and the turmoil that followed created situations that tested faculty members' willingness to remain at their schools.

The boards, though, maintained their bedrock caution and resisted change with determination. In general, the trustees had always feared the reaction of their friends, neighbors, and business associates to any loosening of racial restrictions on campus. They found in the hysterical atmosphere that followed *Brown* a confirmation of their good judgment in avoiding change in the past and a reason to avoid change in the future. This position was shared by many older alumni and probably most white people in the larger community, or at least in the social circles familiar to the trustees.

The presidents, no matter what their own convictions, spent a tremendous amount of energy trying to soothe the fears of opponents of desegregation and calm their own boards. Not surprisingly, most of the presidents, even those who favored desegregation, decided that prudence dictated at least temporary inaction. The fact that *Brown* dealt only with public schools gave them a tool to keep panic at bay and they used it, telling correspondents and trustees over and over that they were compelled to do nothing, that their fate remained in their own hands. To some extent this was whistling past the graveyard and these presidents knew it. But it was also true that they did still have time. For a brief moment there was something like equipoise—every force that pushed for change was offset by a counterforce that opposed it. What the boards chose to do with that time was to wait, to see how and where the balance would tip. While they studied alternatives and had committees gather information, they had no principles to guide them in making a move to one direction or the other. So they followed rather than led, hiding from small changes while southern society was transformed around them.

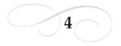

4

Unable to Lead
The Late 1950s

B y the late 1950s the worst fears of the private university presidents seemed to be coming true. Angry whites reacted violently to the pressing demands of southern blacks for some measure of justice. A now steady stream of highly publicized incidents—the Montgomery bus boycott, the acceptance and then expulsion of Autherine Lucy at the University of Alabama, the ugly mob scenes in Little Rock, the bombing of a high school in Clinton, Tennessee—had the entire region quivering with tension. At the same time, the nation as a whole was growing ever more determined that segregation should end. These presidents had long since grasped the essential political truth about segregation—the South did not have the power to prevent its demise. Under these circumstances, they understood, hanging on until the end could have grave consequences. Desperately needed money would be lost, painstakingly assembled faculties would disintegrate, opportunities would slip away. Decades of effort to overtake the finest universities in the nation would be wasted as growing national reputations began instead to erode.

Ironically, by the late 1950s most of the South's public graduate schools and many of its public undergraduate colleges had already peacefully enrolled blacks, even if they hadn't truly integrated them. Some smaller private schools had also lifted the color bar with little or no adverse reaction, either on or off campus. Although there were noteworthy exceptions and sometimes vast social distance remained, black students were generally accepted by their white fellows, joined campus government and other organizations, and settled in to the business of education with a minimum of disruption.[1]

There was no longer any question of the elite private universities being leaders in desegregation, although many on campus continued to talk as if this were still possible. The presidents now struggled to prevent disaster, and the struggle was with their recalcitrant trustees and older, often

prominent, alumni. Wedded to tradition and angrily determined that neither northerners nor blacks would tell them what to do, these men refused
to accept the reality of the changes around them. The exception remained
Vanderbilt, where another small measure of desegregation was accomplished in the Law School. Even here, though, in the fevered atmosphere
of the post-*Brown* South, the explosive reaction of alumni and community
members began to drain Harvie Branscomb of his will to move forward. In
the late 1950s, as the need for change grew acute, the ability to change con-
stricted.

I

By the late 1950s, decades of effort had resulted in the significant strengthening of Tulane University. A visiting committee from the Southern Association of Colleges and Universities reported that the school was "in a state
of dynamic ferment," with enthusiastic faculty members, impressive top
leadership, and a commitment to recruiting the strongest possible student
body. "There is evidence of a genuine faith," wrote one member of the committee, "that a university of national importance is being planned and that
the development of such an institution will succeed."[2]

Somewhat earlier, in late 1955 or early 1956, Rufus Harris had drafted a
short "proposed blueprint" for that development. What he used this for, or
whether he ever used it at all, is not clear. Harris's vision of Tulane's present and future was characteristically clear-eyed. He described the school's
postwar accomplishments without overstatement. "Despite great financial
handicaps and limitations in all kinds of facilities, we have managed to
gather a productive faculty of considerable distinction, to establish more
than adequate programs in our various fields of graduate and undergraduate training, and to win a measure of national prestige for the work
we are doing." Looking forward, Harris saw the possibility of true excellence. This depended, in his view, on four things. Raising faculty salaries,
adopting national entrance examinations, and scaling back the intercollegiate athletic program were all issues that he had raised before (and all issues that had led to conflict with the board.) The fourth matter too was
familiar—the admission of blacks. On this Harris was succinct. "Whatever
the quibbles and dodges now being used in some states to avoid compliance
with the Supreme Court ruling against segregation, Tulane should immediately admit qualified Negro applicants to its graduate divisions. . . . Private
institutions regularly boast that they are by their very nature the leaders in
educational matters and the pioneers in new departures. The whole country

knows that Tulane has as yet done no leading in this particular matter. Thus Tulane cannot hope for a place among the best universities in this country until we take this necessary step."[3]

Harris's argument was sound, but the social and political circumstances in New Orleans in the late 1950s made this "necessary step" all but impossible. The unfolding crisis of public school desegregation in that city kept racial animosities at a boil throughout the late 1950s.[4] Given this turmoil, it is not surprising that Tulane was unable to lead. On one hand, the school faced credible threats of sanctions from accrediting bodies and professional organizations, growing dissent among faculty and students, and the possibility of losing crucial funding from the federal government and foundations. On the other, white New Orleans was fervid in its opposition to racial integration and anyone who favored it. The aggressive meddling of organizations like the South Louisiana Citizen's Council worried board members, and the general state of affairs in the city kept them on edge.

Harris now regarded this turmoil as the major obstacle to desegregation at Tulane. The more worried the board was, the more threatened they felt, the less likely they were to do what was necessary. Harris spent most of the latter part of the decade trying to minimize urgency so the board could feel secure enough to act. But events unfolded so rapidly—in the courtroom, in the legislature, in the streets—that there was no way to preserve a sense of calm in the boardroom. The result was a peculiar mix of boldness and caution from the president, who desperately wanted Tulane to change but who saw stability as the best way to accomplish it. In private correspondence and with allies, Harris was clear that segregation had to go, and the quicker the better. With the board, though, he downplayed pressure for action and he tried to get others on campus to cooperate in this. Meanwhile the board vacillated, paralyzed with yet more fruitless legal analysis. Even after they decided in 1956 to retain their ban on admitting blacks, the issue would not go away. Outside pressures kept it alive, and worry continued to substitute for action.

In early 1955 the board's law committee was still considering the graduate faculty's request to begin desegregation that had been tabled in 1954. Marie Louise Snellings, whose 1953 analysis of desegregation seemed to portend just such changes, had done a complete about-face in the wake of *Brown.* In a January letter to law committee chairman Joseph McCloskey, Snellings outlined her current thinking. Arguing that legal issues did not control the decision, she instead cited the potentially "endless" problems that she believed would arise from the admission of blacks to the graduate schools. "The changes in policy," she predicted, "would create a furor in the South, where we have a numerical negro problem. Questions would arise concerning school functions, football tickets, banquets, concerts, and on down a list of situations that loom endlessly." Snellings believed that the Tulane board possessed the power and the wisdom to choose precisely the right moment to act, and she counseled that that moment had not yet arrived. "The trend of events," she admitted, "is in one direction and we will reach it, in time. I am not temporizing. I do not believe that it is a question of jumping right after Vanderbilt and right ahead of Washington and Lee. I am not in favor of trying to slip by in a crowd, of being clever enough to avoid leadership in the admission of negroes to private institutions in the South, and also to avoid delaying until statutory action or court decision compels us to a change of position."[5] Fellow law committee member George Wilson concurred in a letter of his own after reading Snellings's opinion. "Doubtless, within a period of not many years, we may reach different conclusions on the policy question, but I do not think that this is the time for Tulane to be instrumental in hastening the end of segregation."[6]

The following week the law committee reported to the full board. Dealing specifically with the resolution passed by the graduate faculty in May 1954, the committee again stated its belief "(a) that Tulane would have the legal right to admit Negroes to its Graduate School and (b) that Tulane would have the legal right to exclude Negroes from its Graduate School."[7] Full discussion yielded nothing that would break this stalemate. The board unanimously decided that Harris should tell the graduate faculty that "the admission of Negroes in the Graduate School has been under serious consideration for a long time and will continue to receive serious consideration."[8] Informed of this decision not to decide, the faculty considered asking for "a more explicit explanation" or taking further "steps towards expressing its views" but, most likely in an effort to avoid angering the board, decided to do nothing more.[9]

Other aspects of Tulane's racial policy gave rise to different problems. Yale University, for example, wanted to schedule a basketball game with Tulane the following season but had a black player on its team. Despite the athletic department's eagerness, the board refused. Citing their ongoing debate on "the whole broad problem of segregation," the administrators announced that they "did not feel disposed to act on the matter on a piecemeal basis." However, at the very same time Harris again raised the matter of the attendance of black members of professional societies at meetings on campus. In this case, the board voted to allow it.[10]

In the summer of 1955, a year after the *Brown* decision and just months after the law committee report, Board Chairman Joseph Jones suddenly became eager to take "definite action to dispose of the matter." The reason for this apparent willingness to make a decision seems to have been the discovery of new documents relating to Paul Tulane's original donation for the school.[11] Still, Jones was not about to take hasty action. The law committee, of course, would need to consider these documents and report back to the board in the fall. At that time, Jones directed, a decision would be made.

Unsurprisingly, the deliberations took considerably longer than that. Throughout the summer and into the following fall and winter, the members of the law committee wrestled—again—with the legality of desegregating the university. In July, Marie Louise Snellings prepared another lengthy report; now taking the view, directly contrary to her earlier opinion, that Tulane's founding documents prevented it from admitting blacks. Snellings ran down a list of deeply damaging consequences that would likely attend a failure to desegregate and suggested that, if the board decided as a matter of policy that it wanted to avoid those consequences by admitting black students, it should seek a court judgment that would allow it to do so.[12] Harris praised Snellings's legal abilities but dissented from her views. "I go along with you on the advisability of seeking a declaratory judgment on our legal rights in this matter, for the University wishes only to do the right thing and we need the matter clarified. Such a suit would serve to settle many pressures upon Tulane. After this judgment is declared, if it permits negro enrollment, it is my opinion that the Administrators then should refer the judgment to the President of the University to advise the faculties of the Graduate and Professional Schools that the matter of University admission qualifications is a faculty job and should be handled administratively by them with the Board's approval."[13] The problem, though, was that the board had not yet decided that it wanted to do this. Until the board stepped up and made its policy decision, a lawsuit made no sense.[14]

Meanwhile, debate intensified within the AALS over how to treat segregated law schools. The Special Committee on Racial Discrimination announced plans to submit a proposal that would make the admission of black students a condition of membership. This troubled Harris, who felt sure it would pass. In spite of indications that the AALS would "soften the blow" by taking no action to exclude a school until it had actually denied admission to a qualified black applicant, Harris understood that the passage of the resolution would itself prompt such an application.[15]

By November, Harris was deeply worried. He forwarded copies of the special committee's report to the board's educational affairs committee and urged them to discuss it at their next meeting.[16] He also asked for permission to invite the law dean, Ray Forrester, to speak with the committee.[17] When the committee met in December, they could reach no conclusion except that the problem "will necessarily require action by [the Law] Committee also and probably action by the whole Board at the Special Meeting to be called to consider the whole policy on Admissions question."[18]

The law faculty, after heated debate, decided to abstain when the AALS voted on the resolution at its annual meeting in December. Unexpectedly, it failed by a narrow margin. Harris, although clearly relieved, emphasized to the board that the issue was far from over. "Dean Forrester reports that the failure of this proposal means no lessening of the Association's purpose and determination as a principle to eliminate segregation in the law schools." The only meaning that the vote did have, according to President Harris, was "that we have another year for the consideration of the issue."

Other serious pressures were brought to bear during the fall of 1955. Elizabeth Wisner, dean of the School of Social Work and long a proponent of desegregating that school, explained to Harris that severe consequences for her program were on the horizon. After a trip to Washington where she met with a number of federal agencies, she feared that a decision to make desegregation a condition for receiving grants was near. Such a decision, she argued to the president, would "make it impossible for the Tulane school to operate as an accredited curriculum of any significance."[19]

As time passed and the board still did not act, Harris became more sensitive to anything that might upset the members. This concern is evident in some frank correspondence with a member of the newly constituted Tulane Board of Visitors. This group, comprising prominent Tulane alumni and friends, began to meet annually with the Board of Administrators to discuss policy issues affecting the university. At their meeting in March 1955 there was some talk about opening graduate admissions to qualified blacks. Dr. Robert Lambert of Greensboro, Alabama, took a special interest and in November wrote to Harris and Max Lapham, the dean of Tulane's Medical School, about the possibilities for educating black physicians and generally improving health services for blacks in New Orleans.[20] Harris was appreciative, but he also counseled caution about giving any impression of pressure to the board. "I hope," wrote Harris, "that some positive action may be taken. It is difficult to discuss these matters openly when any rumor emanating from executive sessions of the Administrators may well delay further progress. Even the recent interpretation of the law regarding the use of public recreational facilities may be a deterrent to a more favorable action of the Administrators, and I say this because I know each of them so well."[21] Harris assured Lambert that while the board thought things over, he was able to take small steps on his own, such as quietly opening the medical library to black doctors. Still, Harris concluded, "I know of your great interest in this serious problem and I do hope you know that it is of equally great interest to me. However, I would not like to take any step now that may delay action of the Administrators which may be broader in its scope than anything I may do by edict."[22]

At the December meeting of the board, Chairman Jones again indicated that he would like to "dispose of the racial question" very early in the next year.[23] The messiness of this question and the problematic nature of any answer were brought home to Jones when in February 1956 he received a letter from Dr. Emmet Irwin, president of the Greater New Orleans Citizens' Council. Irwin took Tulane to task for the actions of some of its faculty, who were "appearing in public or otherwise espousing the cause of integration of the races."[24] Jones was troubled by Irwin's letter, which purported to be a gesture of goodwill, intended only to let the board know that "considerable comment is being made in the community concerning this activity of Tulane people." Irwin scolded the university for allowing faculty members to appear on integrated discussion panels and blacks to lecture on campus, and for generally "leading the public to believe" that Tulane supported integration. Special attention was directed at Forest LaViolette, the head of the Department of Sociology and Anthropology, and the faculty of the School of Welfare. Anticipating claims of academic freedom, Irwin explained that "the open advocacy of integration in the classroom is certainly not considered academic freedom, but rather as prejudiced teaching advocating integration." Finally, Irwin stated flatly, "the time has come for each of us to take a stand and if we are not for separation of the races there is but one other category in which we might be placed."[25]

The Tulane board met on March 21, 1956, to try once again to decide how to proceed. They dispensed with the regular order of business and devoted their meeting "primarily to the consideration of the admission of Negroes to the graduate schools of the University." The law committee and the educational affairs committee, which had each considered the matter, stated their conclusions.[26] The law committee reported first, and after a year and five detailed legal analyses the committee had finally made up its mind.[27] By unanimous vote it agreed that "the admission of negroes at this time would not be free of complications and it, therefore, recommends that there be no change in the policy on that subject at this time."[28] The educational affairs committee, on the other hand, focused on the desire of the graduate divisions to desegregate. These divisions, the committee wrote, "are unanimous in their belief that there is a great need by qualified negro students seeking higher education for the educational opportunity available in the Graduate and Professional Schools at Tulane; that a great service could be rendered in undertaking the advanced education of these qualified students; that their faculties desire to undertake the education of these students, and that they believe that the students of the Schools involved would accept them if they were admitted." Dean Max Lapham of the Medical School also warned the committee that the loss of federal research funds that would inevitably follow a continued refusal to desegregate would also mean the loss of important faculty.[29]

The level of tension surrounding these questions was by now incredibly high. Just how tense things had gotten is suggested by the extraordinary statement made at this meeting by board member Edgar Stern. Stern, who had been instrumental in the creation of Dillard University and active for decades in improving relations between the black and white citizens of New Orleans, felt compelled "to openly deny the charges" that he supported the integration of the races in the public schools. Requesting the floor on a point of personal privilege, Stern acknowledged that he had received reports of "the undercover feeling" that he was promoting desegregation. "Even though he was confident that the Board members [did] not subscribe to this feeling," Stern felt compelled to reassure them. This was not an auspicious sign for desegregation at Tulane. Indeed, "after full and deliberate consideration" the administrators resolved, simply, "that there be no change in the existing policies relative to the admission of Negroes to Tulane University at this time."[30]

This decision would stand throughout the rest of the decade, although race-related problems continued to bedevil Tulane. Racial incidents on campus, uncontrollable contacts between black and white students, faculty and student agitation, and clearer warnings from funding agencies that they would not continue to give money to segregated institutions multiplied during the last years of the decade. Tulane's faculty in particular grew impatient. In May 1956 the graduate faculty tried a new approach, proposing consideration of "an administrative facility in New Orleans that would provide for non-segregated enrollment in graduate studies." Under the banner of some other entity besides Tulane, they may have hoped, desegregated graduate education might be possible. The Graduate Council, however, quietly killed this idea, deciding that "such a move is not feasible at this time."[31]

In the fall of 1957, faculty members seized on a recent resolution of the American Association of University Professors. Arguing that free access to educational opportunity was a crucial aspect of academic freedom, the AAUP resolved at its annual meeting that racial segregation "imperils the right of the teacher to teach, as well as the right of the student to learn." Further, the resolution affirmed the right of every teacher to act individually or within organizations to advance desegregation.[32] On December 2, 1957, a memo went out from Dean Lumiansky to the members of the graduate faculty informing them of a meeting on December 10 to consider, among other things, the AAUP resolution on segregation. President Harris was also notified, and he was frankly alarmed. "In the present situation it is not only not helpful in the local situation but may actually be detrimental to our own hope for an intelligent, dispassionate solution to this problem. It seems apparent that this solution may be reached only after a period during which there is no agitation. Perhaps we have started on such a period and I would regret if any action by the Graduate Faculty would cause its interruption."[33] Despite this warning, the graduate faculty went ahead. Following lengthy discussion, Professors Abram Amsel and William L. Kolb moved that the AAUP resolution be endorsed.[34] This motion carried, but the closeness of the vote (42 to 30) indicated enough division that it was withdrawn. Harris was still unhappy and was compelled to report these events to the board at its meeting the following week.

The threat of expulsion from the Association of American Law Schools was ongoing. At its 1957 meeting the AALS overwhelmingly voted to censure schools that still refused to admit qualified blacks, and by this time censure had the power to harm Tulane's Law School almost as much as expulsion.[35] Law dean Ray Forrester sent Harris a cogent summary of the problem.

> A censure has the effect of smearing an educational institution in the eyes of many people and may lead to permanent injury to reputation and standing. Leaving aside the merits of the basic issue of segregation, I do not want the Tulane Law School to receive a bad name nationally, and I feel that even many of our southern friends, although sympathizing with a segregation policy, would still choose to send their young people to a northern or eastern institution where no such national censure would exist. Furthermore, the Tulane Law School

is active in a national and international sense and, if it is to continue to occupy this position and to seek to strengthen it in the future, it must face squarely and realistically the implications of the segregation problem.[36]

In a remarkable turn of events John Wade, dean of Vanderbilt's Law School (which had by now desegregated), was now chairman of the AALS Committee on Racial Discrimination. In this capacity he wrote Forrester, asking if there was any way he or the committee could help Tulane. Forrester echoed Harris's wariness about applying any kind of pressure. "Under the present circumstances, I do not believe that there is much that any of us can do in the situation. In fact, it is my own conviction that too much activity at this time may actually aggravate the situation rather than help it."[37]

At the same time, the students began to show signs of abandoning caution. In the spring of 1958 Tulane students, along with some faculty members, were meeting with their counterparts from Loyola, Xavier, and Dillard at the Dillard University Social Science Club. Harris, reporting this to the board, anticipated objections and cut them off with a short statement. "I know of no effective way of forbidding either students or faculty personnel from attending any professional, cultural, or even social function which they may choose to attend."[38] To the board, though, even these kinds of minor contacts between Tulane students and black college students were objectionable. In 1958 John Stibbs, who was in charge of student activities, ran down a list of interracial student contacts that he knew about, noting that they "are on the increase most everywhere in the college world."[39] Harris in turn notified the board of these incidental contacts, which took place at ROTC rifle matches, National Student Association meetings, debate tournaments, and other similar venues. At times, Tulane students insisted that they would only participate in statewide or regional events if representatives from black colleges were also allowed to attend. Harris urged, and the board apparently agreed, that "it would be unwise to attempt to prohibit contacts with mixed groups as long as they do not involve meetings on our own campus."[40]

Other aspects of the problem popped up from what must have seemed every direction. Tulane students, for example, appeared in a theater production that held performances at black high schools in New Orleans.[41] The problem of athletic contests with teams that had black players was growing more difficult as more southern schools admitted blacks.[42] The *Hullabaloo* continued to editorialize in favor of desegregation, sometimes drawing hostile responses from the community. On January 11, 1957, for example, editor E. S. Evans wrote a bold piece that called for the complete disman- tling of segregation. "Yes, integration is coming," he stated. "It cannot be stopped, like it or not. Times change and as they do they crush those who try to cling to and live in the past." This forthright statement suggests that the neat "you're either with us or against us'" bifurcation perceived by op- ponents of desegregation was shared by many of those who supported it.[43] The administration of various national tests, such as the National Teacher Examination, which Tulane undertook with pride, meant that blacks sat next to whites to take the test in Tulane classrooms. This too brought objec- tions from off campus.[44]

Applications from blacks, some with excellent credentials, arrived with regularity during the late 1950s. In most cases Tulane officials simply re- plied with a standard letter expressing "sympathetic understanding" but refusing to consider the application. (Harris continued to tinker with this letter, making his last revision in April 1959.)[45] Occasionally, a slipup oc- curred. In late 1956 Ernest Morial, the first black graduate of LSU's Law School and later the first black mayor of New Orleans, had to withdraw his registration for two classes offered to practicing attorneys in Tulane's School of Law when he was mistakenly accepted by staff members who did not re- alize that he was black.[46] As always, Harris kept the board, and Jones in par- ticular, informed of each application.

In late 1958, years of conflict between Rufus Harris and the Tulane board finally took their toll. The president, not entirely of his own volition, in- formed the board of his impending retirement.[47] By the next fall, having been given to understand that there would be no role for him at Tulane, Harris accepted the presidency of his alma mater, Mercer University in Ma- con, Georgia.[48] From this moment on Harris, freed finally from the con- straints of trying to please unappeasable board members, reactionary alumni, restless faculty, and impatient students—although still bound by his love of Tulane—expressed his own opinions openly.[49]

Speaking to the Tulane chapter of the AAUP in December 1959, shortly before his departure from the university, Harris discussed his basic phi- losophy of higher education. Insisting that the entire purpose of a univer- sity is the discovery and teaching of truth, Harris asserted that

> The notion that the university can be whatever the students, faculty,
> administration, trustees, alumni or public want it to be is a serious
> error. If it is devoted to discovering and teaching truth, its mission

fails unless these groups . . . meet the conditions required of the mission. To the extent the conditions are not met, whatever the cause—whether by irrelevant and distracting student activities, by indifferent faculty members or officers of administration, or by restrictions of public support or trustee interference—to that precise extent the institution is something less than a university may or ought to be. Admittedly, no President can transform the conditions of American college life and the dispositions limiting education. But he can discourage them. The price of such discouragement may be the forfeiture of acclaim and popularity, though I suspect he will advance his claim to fundamental respect. Which he prefers is the test of his own character.[50]

To his everlasting credit Rufus Harris preferred respect to popularity. He made his decisions based on what he believed would enable Tulane University to come as close as it possibly could to fulfilling the true purpose of a university. As soon as Harris understood that the refusal to admit capable students because they were black was hurting Tulane—because it was costly, because it was immoral, because it was simply *beside the point*—he began to advocate ending the restriction. And in the end this advocacy, along with other positions he held for the same reasons, made him profoundly unpopular with the constituency he most needed to do his job, the Board of Administrators. The administrators, Harris understood, had a different agenda. The pursuit of truth carried somewhat less weight with them. The pleasures of a winning football team, the exercise of personal power, and increased status in the eyes of their peers usually counted for more than the often unpopular and uncomfortable striving for understanding that Harris saw as the very reason for Tulane's existence. Their neighbors' anger, the threat to their social position, and a resentful refusal to capitulate to "outside" pressures motivated the board far more than any concern for Tulane's proper role. On his copy of the address to the AAUP, Harris scribbled fragmentary notes on the role of the trustees. These notes capture in brief phrases the essence of his inability to persuade these people to do what needed to be done. "Feel a little sorry for them," he wrote. "They know so little. Their interference—unwittingly at times. Their EGO." Finally, and ironically, "most critical single factor in American Education's advancement." Simply, without the agreement of this group, nothing could be changed.[51] So, nothing was.

II

In the mid-1950s many, probably most, trustees of Duke University clung to a traditional vision of their university. One alumnus, objecting to the choice of Hodding Carter as commencement speaker in 1955, summed up this attitude succinctly: "I confidently expect Duke to continue to gain in stature among the leading universities of the country, and it is my fervent hope that in so doing it will retain those conservative qualities and traditions which have endeared it to generations of its sons and daughters."[52] By the late 1950s, however, the contradiction between maintaining southern traditions and growing in national stature was unmanageable. Conservative traditions were under siege. Just a few miles down the road, the University of North Carolina had admitted three black undergraduates without disruption.[53] Duke itself became home to persistent, organized agitation for the elimination of segregation. In October 1955, for example, more than 350 Duke students signed a petition protesting the school's refusal to allow black students from nearby North Carolina College to attend plays in Duke's Page Auditorium.[54] The student newspaper, the *Chronicle,* while still mostly interested in dances, student elections, and football games, grew more cognizant of the social changes that were transforming North Carolina. Articles on the progress of integration and editorials favoring it at Duke became common.[55] Black speakers, men like Ralph Bunche or President Alfonso Elder of North Carolina College, visited campus.

Hollis Edens seems by the late 1950s to have absorbed the changes in the South and in the South's relationship to the rest of the nation. His thinking on segregation, which began to shift after *Brown v. Board of Education,* was now firmly established. His commitment to do what was best for the university led him to conclude that segregation at Duke should be gradually abolished.[56] As with all things, Edens approached this challenge slowly, by degrees. At their February 1955 meeting Edens merely warned the trustees that the problem of desegregation was "actively before the University, and this Board should be prepared to hear more about it in the future."[57] He also began gathering information that might be of help to him in persuading the Duke trustees to make some adjustments.

In the late fall of 1955, the University Council, which Edens had authorized to conduct a study of desegregation in higher education, reported its findings.[58] After significant research, including confidential conversations with the heads of newly desegregated schools, the committee concluded that the transition had been almost uniformly smooth. All reports were that a small number of black students applied, few were qualified to enroll, and those who did were easily absorbed into the student body. Social difficulties had been few; there was almost no trouble over dining or other facilities.[59] The council passed a resolution at its next meeting, asking that "action be taken looking toward the admission of duly qualified Negroes in such areas of advanced study in the University as might be desirable."[60]

Also about this time Edens approached Harvie Branscomb with questions about how Vanderbilt was managing its slow process of desegregation. Branscomb explained the policy that provided for admitting blacks to the divisions of the university that had no counterparts in the city's black schools. Although Edens believed that there might be something useful in this strategy, he ended the correspondence on a pessimistic note. "We have made no move whatsoever here toward desegregation. I doubt if we can move for quite a while yet."[61]

The source of Edens's doubt, of course, was his Board of Trustees. Branscomb had Harold Vanderbilt, a close ally, as chairman of his board, and Vanderbilt was critically important in mitigating the influence of the conservative local trustees. Timing was also crucial. Vanderbilt's board had agreed to a principled basis for gradual desegregation in 1953, before the *Brown* decision was announced. Edens had the daunting task of trying to persuade the Duke board to begin desegregation in a post-*Brown* environment saturated with racial hostility. This, nonetheless, he now attempted to do. His messages to the board became increasingly pointed but always acknowledged the final authority of the trustees.

The February 1956 board meeting marked a turning point: for the first time, Edens openly argued for admitting blacks. Although he was careful not to force a decision, he left no doubt that he believed the change would have to be made sooner rather than later. Still, his concern for avoiding any kind of internal split or loss of support among the trustees guided his careful presentation. He began with remarks he had earlier made to the faculty, describing the many "fringe areas of this problem which confront us daily," the kind of "contact between the races in academic, religious and cultural activities" that had been steadily increasing both on and off campus since the end of World War II. The problem, according to the president, was that while these contacts continued to expand, "there is no clear guide" for how to deal with them.[62]

Edens carefully laid out for the trustees exactly what he meant. While assuring them that the faculty and students remained "calm and stable," he also made it clear that they were not "neutral or unconcerned." He briefly mentioned the student newspaper's agitation and included the entire text of the Divinity School's plea for desegregation. He reported the University Council's call for the admission of "qualified Negroes in such areas of advanced study in the University as might prove desirable and feasible." Edens saved the most critical issue for last: "our dealings with agencies of the Federal Government in accepting contracts for research and other academic programs." Here, he assumed the day would soon arrive when segregated schools would no longer be eligible to receive federal money, and he insisted that it was "unreasonable to expect a university of Duke's standing to cut its faculties off from such opportunities and it is becoming increasingly difficult to avoid the segregation question in such negotiations."[63]

Finally, Edens addressed the prospects for solving these problems. Here he became conciliatory, backing away from the powerful arguments that he had just made.

> Now, it is reasonable to assume that many of you would have preferred that I omit mention of this subject but the responsibilities of my office require that I keep you informed about all major issues which concern the University. I have at present no recommendation to make and I cannot predict when I shall have one. . . . In the meantime, I shall continue to express my views to the Committee as I have done in the past. As a matter of fact, all of you are well aware of the trend of my thinking. I do know, however, that problems of this kind require patience and time. Furthermore, decisions in a Board of Trustees for an educational institution should be by consent and agreement rather than by pressure and majority vote. And private discussions with members of the Board convince me that you are not ready for a major decision on this matter.[64]

Edens was only too aware of the deep hostility to desegregation among the members of Duke's board and the probability that even mentioning it would rouse ire in some. The fact that such a profoundly cautious man chose to raise it at all, chose to risk some part of his hard-earned goodwill, testifies to his realization that desegregation was now an absolute prerequisite for Duke's continued growth in national stature.

The response of the board was not encouraging, although it was unusually honest. Following his report, the board engaged in a long discussion of segregation. A motion was made and seconded that a special board committee be set up to further study the matter. Before the end of the discussion, however, the motion was withdrawn, as the trustees acknowledged that no new information would make them change their minds.[65] This was a rare admission, and it must have thrown cold water on any hopes Edens harbored for a smooth end to segregation at Duke.

At the same time, of course, others at Duke only grew more insistent that segregation be abandoned. By 1956 the Divinity School was increasingly preoccupied with this issue. Individual faculty members spoke and wrote in opposition to segregation in any number of public venues. Waldo Beach, for example, a professor of Christian ethics who had been involved in the school's efforts to desegregate since the first petition to Edens in 1949, wrote an essay in 1956 for *Christianity and Crisis* in which he discussed the severe polarization of opinion on segregation and the danger that "moderate opinion will remain latent, frustrated, and ineffectual unless soon it can find unified courageous leadership and a public voice."[66] In an attempt to provide some measure of that leadership, seventeen members of the Divinity School faculty issued a statement to the press affirming their "eagerness to admit suitably qualified applicants to regular courses of theological study without restrictions of race." The theologians cited the most recent General Conference of the Methodist Church, with which the Duke Divinity School was affiliated, and its call for the elimination of segregation in its institutions. While acknowledging "deep trouble of spirit," the faculty members looked "hopefully and prayerfully to the proper authorities of the University" for change.[67]

The "proper authorities of the University" were unimpressed. The only trustee response came from George R. Wallace, head of a fishery in Morehead City, who expressed sheer annoyance. "Speaking frankly and entirely of my own opinion," he wrote Edens, "I feel that this action is, to say the least, in bad taste." While he admitted that the Divinity School professors had the right to express their ideas, Wallace just could not contain his irritation. "I feel that if the gentlemen signing the statement which was made public do not agree with the policy of the institution at which they are teaching and if they are 'with deep trouble of spirit' then they should in good conscience disassociate themselves from such institution and align themselves with one more in keeping with their principles." For his part, Edens firmly defended the faculty members, stressing their good faith and loyalty to Duke.[68]

The convictions of professors outside the Divinity School were also becoming ever clearer. In April the Duke chapter of the AAUP passed resolutions supporting both the national policy statement condemning seg-regation in higher education and the University Council's call for an end to racially restrictive admissions at Duke. In June the entire faculty voted, without discussion, to approve the council's resolution. They insisted that the resolution be passed on to the Board of Trustees.[69]

Despite their focus on classes and social activities, the issue would not die among students, either. Many seemed now to be constantly debating, circulating petitions, or even writing letters to trustees. The Divinity School student body produced another petition to the board, signed by 150 (of 220) students.[70] The Women's Student Government overwhelmingly passed a resolution calling for the end to racial restrictions in admissions.[71] In late 1956 and early 1957 a group of undergraduates organized a campaign to write to each trustee individually to ask for desegregation in the Divinity School. Over a dozen students participated, but they received answers from only a handful of trustees. Most of these answers were not especially revealing—they politely explained that the matter was always being re-viewed by the board—but a few exchanges demonstrate the nearly com-plete lack of common ground between supporters and opponents of deseg-regation.[72]

The letters from the students made the now standard arguments for desegregation. That is, they argued that Christian morality, democracy, and academic freedom demanded that the white South change. Occasion-ally, but not often, someone would take notice that there were actual black people involved in the matter, asserting for example that "colored people should be given their chance to attain a way of life equal to that of ours." Even here, though, lurked the belief that few blacks would be affected by any such change. "I also feel that many of the members of the colored race are not ready for a sudden change in their way of living."[73] Ironically, even for proponents of desegregation living, breathing black people were rarely at the heart of the matter. The issue was always something else: their own willingness to accept a few black students, their own Christian morality, their own freedom to choose their students, their own reputation among their peers.

The trustees who opposed desegregation saw the question in starkly dif-ferent terms. There were few abstractions in their thinking. For them the is-sue was the physical presence of black people where they did not belong. Like Donald Davidson at Vanderbilt objecting to the admission of a black minister to the School of Religion, supporters of segregation at Duke rea-soned from a different set of principles than those who objected to it. Most of them grew up during an era when blacks received little education, were confined to menial occupations, and were perceived as physically dirty and dangerous. For these trustees, it remained unthinkable that any good could come from the breakdown of the strict bars that kept these threatening people away from whites, especially white youth. One opponent of desegregation thus responded to students urging black admissions with very concrete and pointed questions, including the following:

1. Should the Trustees of Duke University permit conditions at Duke that are not permitted in the homes of the students who comprise the student body of Duke?
2. Do your father and mother practice social and racial equality with the Negroes in your home?[74]

The answers to these questions were obvious. No decent white family would allow blacks to socialize in their homes. Duke, likewise, should not allow the presence of blacks within the circle of the "Duke family."[75]

The importance of these kinds of arguments can be seen in the debate at the February 1957 meeting of the Duke board, which came soon after most trustees had received these letters. There, another letter, from James Cannon, dean of the Duke Divinity School, provided the catalyst for the board's first formal vote on desegregation. Edens received this letter on February 13, 1957, exactly two weeks before the winter meeting of the trustees. The timing alone raises suspicion that Cannon and Edens colluded in its rather sudden appearance. Cannon, while not a die-hard segregationist, had opposed earlier Divinity School efforts to begin desegregation. His explicit acknowledgment of his reluctance on the issue and his admission that he and Edens had discussed the matter "a number of times" only deepens this suspicion of their collusion.

The dean's letter could not possibly have been better crafted to persuade a group of traditionalists. Cannon spent a good deal of time establishing that he himself was reluctant and that he had not been a supporter of earlier Divinity School petitions to the board. "Even now," Cannon explained, "I should much prefer to leave this thorny subject to my successor." He backed away from moral arguments, or any arguments based on abstractions, and argued only concrete, "practical" issues. The dean thereby positioned himself as a moderate, a man of reason as opposed to emotion, and one who understood the folly of extreme positions.[76]

Only urgent circumstances, he claimed, compelled him to speak out now. "It is my considered judgment that we should not and cannot longer postpone action on this question. Indeed, I feel that we are almost too late even if action is taken now." Cannon made clear that his foremost consideration was the "standing of Duke University," not any larger questions about the nature of the Christian gospel or American democracy. Indeed, he was careful to craft his statement so that it was really "about" the standing of Duke University (rather than "about" blacks and their rights). "As a national institution it is an embarrassment to be out of step with other institutions of our rank. I think I am correct in the observation that Duke is the only member of the Association of American Universities that does not admit negroes. I am impressed by the fact that all other major theological schools in the South except one (Emory) admit negroes or plan to do so at once."[77] Cannon also attempted to minimize the impact of the change he was asking for. "I am convinced that the problem of assimilating the few negroes who would be eligible for admission to the Duke Divinity School is a minor one compared to the problem of further delay."[78]

Edens strongly supported Cannon's recommendation and asked for "discretionary authority . . . to admit negroes to the Divinity School if and when properly qualified candidates should apply." He was careful to distance this request from the increasingly vocal student demands for change, stressing that this was all completely unrelated to a student petition that was also before the board. Edens reminded the board that, like Cannon, he was no zealot on desegregation. He only asked for this decision now because he believed the time had come to squarely face the issue.[79]

When the Duke trustees did squarely face the issue, they explicitly affirmed their commitment to segregation. Although the 10 to 13 vote was far closer than supporters of desegregation had dared to imagine, the end result was still a firm repudiation of racial change at Duke.[80] The trustees understood well enough that segregation was damaging the university. They certainly understood the possibility of far more serious harm in the future. They were only too aware that sentiment on campus strongly favored the desegregation of the Divinity School. But they were not going to give in. Edens's careful presentation, his efforts to downplay the broad implications of desegregation and to focus instead on a narrow solution to the specific problem, were wasted.

On the other hand, the trustees who supported Edens were certain that desegregation would come soon. Sidney Alderman, who introduced the motion to open admissions in the Divinity School, wrote Edens that "the present members of the board will live to be convinced, and very soon I fear, that they took the wrong action and an action which will hurt, rather than help, the national standing and reputation of our university." This was undoubtedly correct, but from the president's point of view there was something else that mattered almost as much. "I am convinced I was right," he answered Alderman, but "although the majority of the Board does not agree with me I think it highly important that the membership assumed as it did the responsibility of saying so."[81]

Edens took his orders from the board, even when those orders were misguided or counterproductive. The board had now spoken. In his 1975 memoir, former Duke chaplain Barney Jones recounted Edens's struggles. Edens, according to Jones, found himself in conflict with the "generally conservative and provincial" board only when he was able to "transcend his own provincialism" on the issue.[82] R. Taylor Cole, a long-serving administrator, later provost, agreed with this assessment. Cole described the "determined opposition of a large majority of the Trustees" and Eden's conclusion that "moral suasion . . . would not move them toward gradual desegregation, which as a Christian and a realist he had come to favor."[83] In spite of this disagreement, according to Jones, Edens was above all "determined that a wedge not be driven between himself and his Board."[84] There was nothing to be gained from a fight, and the 10 to 13 vote indicated the potential for serious division among the trustees in addition to possible erosion of the relationship between the board as a whole and the president. In Edens's mind, to undertake a campaign to force the trustees to accept racial change would have been to endanger everything else that Duke was trying to accomplish. Ongoing plans for growth and improvement, an ambitious development campaign, the recruitment of highly qualified faculty and students—everything—could be lost if a battle were to break out. Even if the fight were private, his ability to pursue these goals would be severely compromised.

As it was, the 1957 vote, even though it revealed an almost perfect split in opinion, did nothing to damage Edens's relationship with the board. Letters arrived afterward from both supporters and opponents of desegregation, all praising the president for his judicious handling of a delicate matter.[85] For the rest of the decade Edens scrupulously informed the trustees about the problems segregation caused at Duke but avoided inviting any conflict over the issue. "I should like to state here what is to me a maxim of administration," he told the board in his discussion of segregation-related difficulties during the February 1958 meeting, "— that the President of an institution must administer with integrity its policies as determined by the Board of Trustees. I shall expect to do no less."[86]

While the 1957 vote of the trustees effectively put an end to serious consideration of desegregation for the rest of the decade, it did nothing to end the demands for change.[87] Applications from black students arrived, to be politely rejected.[88] Students grew unhappier and more vocal. The law students took up the issue, voting in favor of integration in April 1957.[89] The *Chronicle* repeatedly returned to the issue, and other, less formal student publications also took up the cause of desegregation.[90]

Public attention seemed constantly to be on the university, almost always with embarrassing results. Perhaps the most unseemly spectacle came in the fall of 1957, when the Duke delegation to a mock assembly, the North Carolina Student Legislature, introduced a resolution to legalize interracial marriage.[91] It would be difficult to overstate the intensity of the reaction to this incident. Newspapers throughout the state carried the story, including the reaction of Governor Luther Hodges, who wanted all of North Carolina to know that he had nothing to do with it, and Congressman Harold Cooley, who claimed to be deeply shocked.[92] Back on campus, Edens was deluged with angry letters. He told one friend that "some of the letters which I have received are almost incoherent with hysteria and irresponsible accusations." (This is possibly generous.) Many were venomous in their contempt for the Duke students, with racial and sexual slurs coming from even the most educated correspondents. Edens's response was quite mild, a defense of students' freedom to be young and foolish that avoided issues of race almost entirely.[93] This ugly incident no doubt confirmed in the minds of the trustees the wisdom of their decision to keep black students off the Duke campus.

Divinity students and student religious organizations continued to clamor for change. Edens met with the Episcopal Student Fellowship in April 1957. They had formulated a statement on segregation declaring their willingness to accept and support black students "in their use of every facility of whatever kind the University offers to its students."[94] Annually at Christmas time the student body of the Divinity School sent a message to the Duke trustees, asking them to reconsider their racially restrictive admissions policy, citing the positions of the Methodist General Conference and the North Carolina Methodist Conference opposing segregation in church institutions and the need for Duke to exercise "wise leadership" on race.[95]

As the decade drew to a close, the situation worsened. In 1959 two more student petitions went to the board. One was from the graduate students and many of the faculty in the School of Arts and Sciences. Far blunter than previous pleas, this petition stated plainly that continuing to exclude students because of race "would be morally wrong, practically unnecessary, and incompatible with Duke University's responsibilities as a community of scholars and a leader among universities."[96] Approximately 73 percent of the graduate students signed this petition, along with nearly half of the faculty. Petition organizers claimed that another 10 percent feared reprisals if they signed.[97] At the same time the Divinity School student body drafted and circulated a similar petition, which was signed by 185 of the school's 225 students. Edens presented both petitions to board chairman Norman Cocke in advance of the February meeting.[98] When the board's executive committee met the day before, however, they instructed Cocke not to bring them before the entire board. It was the "judgment of the Committee that since the matter has been discussed thoroughly in the Board prior to this time the best interests of the University are not served by having the matter brought up again at this time."[99]

After the board ignored this latest petition, morale in the Divinity School began to erode deeply.[100] The pleas of both faculty and students for moderate and gradual racial change had now fallen on deaf ears for over a decade. Editorials appeared in two leading Protestant journals, *Christianity and Crisis* and *The Christian Century*, which were highly critical of the Duke trustees' stubborn refusal to listen. A need to respect the opponents of desegregation, *Christianity and Crisis* warned, "should not prevent a small group of powerful men, who have had a wide enough experience of the world to know better, from feeling the full weight of the criticism, from all parts of the nation, of the religious, moral, and intellectual incongruity of their policy."[101]

Anger seeped into discussions as the faculty thoroughly grasped both the board's intransigence and their own lack of institutional power. When Duke professor of Christian ethics Waldo Beach was asked by the Duke *Chronicle* for a response to the published condemnations, his brief reply prickled with resentment.

> If Duke does lay claim to be a national university it must be willing to be judged by national standards of enlightened Christian opinion. No one of us then can write this kind of criticism off as that of "outside meddlers." The trustees should be sharply conscious of the fact that many of us on the faculty are obliged to live under a policy which goes squarely against our Christian conscience. We regret also to see our national reputation skidding rapidly downhill. Though obviously we respect the conscientious divergence of opinion on this touchy matter, the least we can ask for, locally, is an exchange of views between the "absentee owners" who set the policy and those who must live with it.[102]

National press coverage exacerbated the situation. After the editorials were published, dozens of letters came in, some to Divinity School dean Cushman, others to Edens. They came from all over the country, from ministers, professors, businessmen, and alumni. Almost uniformly they denounced Duke for failing "to exercise any forceful moral leadership in this area"[103] and predicted that "the prestige of the school will suffer nationally as a result of the unfortunate action of the board."[104]

Dean Cushman was driven nearly to despair. For him, the timing of these events could not have been worse. In the spring of 1959 the Divinity School was actively seeking to hire new faculty members and the continuing turmoil over segregation was scaring them off. In fact, the last two hires had been convinced to come to Duke only after extensive correspondence about segregation and the prospect of its elimination.[105] Further, there would be an ongoing need to recruit, as current faculty members continued to resign at least in part due to their loss of hope for desegregation.[106]

Duke's Law School also confronted profound difficulties in hiring. By the spring of 1958 the Law School had been without a permanent dean for almost two years and no prospect was in sight.[107] Although candidates had a variety of often very personal reasons for declining the job, some, including the most prominent, cited segregation as a primary reason for not coming to Duke. Interim law dean E. R. Latty described a conversation with Robert Keeton of the Harvard Law School. "He frankly admitted that one factor in the situation at Duke seriously bothered him, that is, the attitude with respect to Negro applicants. He said that he certainly would not consider taking the Deanship without assurance that the Trustees were prepared to accept a qualified Negro student." Even more ominous was Keeton's warning about the effect of segregation on hiring generally. "He added, incidentally, that the outside understanding on the Duke attitude on the admission of Negroes is going to hurt Duke Law School not only in getting a Dean but also, as time goes on, in getting top-flight law professors and top-flight students from outside the South."[108]

What made this problem especially difficult was that it cut both ways. While Duke administrators clearly knew that segregation made it much harder to recruit good faculty, they also understood that desegregation was going to come sometime soon. When that day arrived, they could not afford to have a faculty full of staunch segregationists. A Stanford law professor urged Latty not to hire one particular candidate for exactly this reason: "I don't suggest that you should get a zealot for integration who would barge ahead though the heavens fall, but this is no time for Duke to have a dean who has an unreconstructed rebel's views on the race question."[109] Who, then, was left to hire? The *interim* was removed from Latty's title in June 1958.[110]

As the decade ended, impatient alumni also pressed the case for desegregation. In August 1959 Franklin H. Cook, a Duke alumnus who was a professor at Penn State, was startled when he tried to send one of his black students to Duke for a Ph.D. "Revelation of this restraint," he wrote, "shocked me profoundly as the secretaries in the office observed." Once over his shock, he sat down to pen a powerful letter to Edens, one that laid out exactly what his alma mater was courting.

> If Duke aspires to national recognition, it can attain stature in the academic arena by opening her doors to all students, thus assuming a position of leadership in the south. Duke by submitting to local pressures will tend to become a repository of inert ideas, which will undermine its position in securing excellent students, in attracting outstanding faculty, and in promoting the acceptance of programs such as the Law School's World Law project. . . . As a professor I value those institutions which unreservedly through teaching and research seek the truth. As a citizen and an alumnus of three universities I expect a university to produce graduates to live in a dynamic America.[111]

Even now, Hollis Edens was unable to answer such a letter candidly. "I have full appreciation of your point of view concerning the admissions policy of Duke University," he told Cook, and it was undoubtedly so. But all he could add was a feeble defense of inaction. "I would not have you believe that there are no complications in the problems which the swift moving changes present in the Southern states."[112] The swift moving changes did indeed present problems in the southern states, and the prospect that Duke could continue to grow in national stature while retaining its conservative traditions was well-nigh dead. The university was trapped by its own trustees, unable to lead, unable even to follow along behind the public colleges.

III

The late 1950s were a difficult time at Emory University. In March 1955 Goodrich White announced his decision to step down on September 1, 1957. Uncertainty and division followed and did not fade when the new president, Dr. S. Walter Martin of the University of Georgia, proved to be an unpopular choice. The death of the long-serving chairman of Emory's board, Charles Howard Candler, only two months after Martin's selection, further unsettled the university. Emory's chronic financial problems also worsened significantly. In White's remarks to the board at its November 1955 meeting he stressed that budgetary economies, while necessary to avoid continuing deficits, were coming dangerously close to destroying morale on campus. "Holding the line," he told the trustees, "has not been easy for a staff and faculty who are eager and ambitious for the University to continue its forward march."[113] At nearly the same time, Georgia's political leaders threatened to close Atlanta's public schools rather than allow even token desegregation. For the Emory faculty, many of whom had children, this was deeply disturbing. For the Emory trustees, on the other hand, the disruption in public education was nearly irrelevant. As a private school Emory was not bound by federal court decisions and thus could simply stand apart from the conflict. The battle, they believed, had nothing to do with them.[114]

Any public discussion of desegregation in any forum at Emory inevitably drew fire from angry alumni and board members who believed that the university could and should stay completely insulated. One revealing example is the reaction to a 1956 editorial in the *Emory Alumnus* about Georgia's plan to close any public schools that were ordered to desegregate by the federal courts. This piece, written by editor Randy Fort, likened closing schools in order to prevent integration to "cutting the throat to cure the cancer." The effect of such closings on Emory, Fort argued, would be disastrous on at least two counts. First, it meant "Emory's student body would deteriorate in quality, rapidly and steadily." Second, and perhaps more important, the university's faculty would also begin to erode. "Think this is idle talk? You wouldn't, if you could discuss the problem with several persons on the campus. A number of young professors already are laying plans to look for other jobs, should the public school system fall. And Emory officials already are finding it increasingly difficult to persuade new teachers to move into the state. A fine faculty is nothing to be put together or bought overnight. It takes years to build one, and newcomers to it are attracted not only by the reputation and offerings of the institution but by the opportunities its community holds out to their families."[115]

Predictably, the response was furious and not entirely coherent. One irate alumnus totally missed the import of Fort's argument. "My point is that it is no concern of Emory to become involved in the segregation controversy. . . . As time goes by, I believe it will become more and more apparent that one of [Emory's] greatest advantages lies in the fact that, as a private educational institution, it is not beset by the problems of integration and segregation which necessarily concern public institutions financed by public funds. In short, I think we are confronted with an excellent opportunity to mind our own business and stay out of this controversy."[116]

A copy of this letter found its way to the chairman of Emory's board, Charles Howard Candler. In a reply to its author, Candler, as usual, made himself amply clear. "I wish to commend your feeling about the unjustifiable use of the Emory Alumnus as a medium for propaganda," Candler wrote. The letter to Fort, he believed, was "timely, appropriate and eminently in line with the conviction of those most interested in Emory and one which I believe will restrain Mr. Fort if he is ever again tempted to publish in our fine magazine his personal opinion of matters which do not properly belong in it."[117]

But Emory *was* "beset by the problems of segregation and integration," despite its private status. That was Fort's point. And events on campus continued to bear him out. Throughout the 1955–56 school year *Emory Wheel* editor Larry Custer argued in favor of desegregation in Georgia and at Emory. He also printed a column written by former governor Herman Talmadge and a long letter by Georgia's attorney general, Eugene Cook, which, while denouncing integration in the strongest possible terms, kept the issue prominently visible. A Presbyterian student group, the Westminster Fellowship, submitted a statement to the *Wheel* that decried the possibility of closing the public schools in order to prevent desegregation.[118]

Officially, Emory continued its resolute refusal to consider change. In a meeting with a student development committee in early 1957, Goodrich White answered questions about desegregation with a succinct declaration of its impossibility. "There is no prospect for the admission of negroes to any division of the University." White's explanation was likewise simple — admitting blacks would end Emory's tax exemption and make continued operation impossible. That, it seemed, was that.

In the waning days of White's tenure as president of Emory, the faculty of the Candler School of Theology presented him with its first organized statement on race. While individual members of the theology and religion faculties had long been active in promoting better race relations, as a group they had seemed reluctant to press the case.[119] This changed in early 1957 when the dean of the school, William Ragsdale Cannon, appointed a special committee to prepare a statement of the faculty's views on how to respond to the South's changing racial situation.[120] This report resulted in the adoption of a faculty resolution that was submitted by the president to the Board of Trustees.[121]

This resolution was brief and very careful. The heart of their request was that the university—the administration and the board, that is—conduct a study of the "policies and practices" of the School of Theology "as they relate to race, making sure that these policies and practices are Christian." The basis of this request was the 1956 *Methodist Discipline,* which urged such a study in all church-related institutions. Looking forward to the admission of black theology students, the faculty also expressed a "willingness and readiness to have them as members of our classes and of the student body." Finally, they assured the trustees that the faculty understood the "complex and delicate nature of the problems involved in this request" and would thus treat the matter as confidential. Prayers would also be said.[122] In perfect keeping with his long-standing reluctance to press this issue, Goodrich White sent this resolution on to the trustees with a brief note: "I have no recommendation to make with reference to action by the Board."[123] The board took no action.

Perhaps understandably, it was the selection of Emory's new president, not the statement of the theology faculty, that dominated this board meeting. Immediately after adjournment, Chairman Candler announced the election of Dr. S. Walter Martin as the university's fifteenth president. Martin was a Georgia native, born in 1911 in the small town of Tifton in the southern part of the state. He attended a Baptist school, Furman, as an undergraduate, receiving his bachelor of arts in 1932. Martin was trained as a historian, first at the University of Georgia, where he received a masters in 1935 and joined the faculty, and then at the University of North Carolina, where he completed work for the doctorate in 1942. Martin remained on the faculty at the University of Georgia, moving steadily up the ranks. He headed the History Department from 1943 to 1945 and served as assistant dean of the faculties from 1945 to 1947. In 1949 he was named the dean of the College of Arts and Sciences, a position he held until he accepted the presidency at Emory.[124]

Martin was also a dedicated and active Methodist layman. He was Sunday School superintendent at the First Methodist Church in Athens for fifteen years, chairman of the church board of education, the church-campus relations committee, and the pastoral relations committee. He was vice chairman of the board of stewards and a member of that committee for eighteen years. Martin also served as district lay leader of the Athens-Elberton District and as a member of the Georgia Methodist Commission on Higher Education.[125]

This religious commitment, coupled with his record as an administrator at the University of Georgia, had led several smaller Methodist colleges to try to recruit Martin as president. Happy in Athens, he always refused. When the search committee from Emory approached him, Martin was swayed for the first time. Charles Howard Candler chaired the committee, which included two Methodist bishops, and he was determined that Emory's next president be someone who would strengthen the university's ties with the church.[126] Martin, nonetheless, was far from certain that moving to Emory was the right thing. He had spent his entire career at the University of Georgia and was highly regarded there. His family was well established in Athens, and he was comfortable in his church. To pull up stakes so abruptly and take on the presidency of a financially troubled private school, even the Methodist flagship, was not an easy decision.

Assured by Candler that he was needed, Martin could not say no. He was elected unanimously by the board and agreed to a starting date of September 1, 1957.[127] The unanimous vote, however, concealed deep fractures within Emory. It had been over a year since Goodrich White informed the board of his desire to retire, and in that time several internal candidates for the presidency appeared. They attracted varying degrees of support among the faculty, board members, and influential backers of the university. Although no one man had compelling support, these candidates were among the most powerful and able men on campus and several could reasonably entertain the notion of becoming president.

By contrast, when Walter Martin's name leaked out as a possible successor to White, howls of protest went up. Faculty members who could agree on precious little else agreed that a dean from the University of Georgia—a school they considered a "cow college"—was an inappropriate choice. A group of senior faculty members, most of them department chairmen, took the audacious step of writing to Candler with their objections. Claiming "the support of a substantial majority of [their] colleagues," they asserted that Martin did not "incorporate personally or professionally that combination of qualities so essential for vigorous and effective guidance of Emory's future destiny." Candler and the board simply ignored this letter.[128]

Oddly, while these faculty members were mistaken in many of their judgments about Martin, in some sense they were correct. Martin and Emory were not a good match, although not because of any lack of ability on his part. Martin was a reasonably good scholar, an able administrator, a dedicated worker, and a thoroughly honorable man. He was, however, a man who remained true to his roots, both social and religious. Martin was uninterested in Atlanta society and unimpressed by his new memberships, provided by Emory, in tony private dining and country clubs. He was, and would remain, a man more at home at a Methodist church supper than at the Piedmont Driving Club. Fairly or unfairly, this lack of interest in being "one of the boys" in Atlanta's upper crust would hinder Martin throughout his time at Emory.

Hearing of Martin's selection, President G. B. Connell of Mercer University welcomed him to "the aspirin fraternity."[129] Indeed, even apart from the copious fence mending he would need to do, Martin was in for plenty of headaches at Emory.[130] Well before he arrived on campus, he began to get an idea of the kind of serious problems that the school was facing.[131] In May, even as congratulations were still arriving, he received an ominous letter from Dean Rusk, then the head of the General Education Board of the Rockefeller Foundation. "I am anxious," said Rusk, "to have a long talk with you about the background and future of the General Education Board's grant for the development of graduate studies at Emory."[132] This grant, made in 1951, gave a desperately needed $7 million but required Emory to raise $25 million in matching funds. Emory had not been able to do it. This deeply embarrassing situation was a harbinger of what was to come for Walter Martin. Although he managed to return from his New York meeting with Rusk with a check for a million dollars and an agreement to quietly let Emory off the hook, Martin would be beset by fund-raising problems throughout his tenure. In his first brief report to the trustees, made less than three months after his arrival, he identified money as the most critical problem facing the university.[133] Much, probably too much, of Martin's time and imagination would be devoted to fund-raising during his term as Emory's president.

Martin's troubles expanded exponentially when Charles Howard Candler died within two months of Martin's selection as president. It was Candler who most wanted Martin at Emory and who was most sympathetic to Martin's strong religious views. It was also Candler who controlled the board. Without his dominating presence, Martin was hamstrung. Several trustees and prominent outside supporters were less than enthusiastic about the new president, hampering further his ability to get things done.

The change in Emory's president yielded no change in the university's stance on race. Like White before him, Martin was no advocate of integration and would never aggressively push the Emory board to open admissions to blacks. Even had he wanted to, his lack of institutional support would probably have made it unwise. Still, and again like White, Martin was not one to give in to calls to muffle the faculty or students. Contacts with black professors and student groups continued unabated during the late 1950s, and Martin never considered trying to stop them despite sometimes furious threats against the university from segregationists.[134] Rather, as the faculty and students continued inviting blacks to university events while many trustees actively objected, Martin tried to act as a peacemaker.[135] Like Hollis Edens at Duke during the early part of the decade, Martin saw himself as a "moderate" who could best avoid disaster for his school by keeping open division at bay. This was an incredibly difficult balancing act, even more so in the late 1950s when any day could bring an incident that would upset one side or another. Martin also resembled Edens in his uneasiness about the course of change in the South. The massive economic and social transformation since World War II unsettled him and made him fear that the postwar prosperity would result in moral decay. In one 1958 speech he expressed this fear and included race relations in a litany of American troubles.

> Last year you and I progressive Americans consumed 20 million aspirin tablets daily. Each night we swallowed 20 million sleeping pills; the next morning chasing them away with as many wake-up pills. American doctors will this year write nearly 40 million prescriptions for the anti-worry pills called tranquilizers, hoping to stave off the anxiety, the depression, and the fear that hamstrings our modern living. Juvenile delinquency is a common topic over our tea-cups; we have all kinds of social problems which we are unable to solve ranging from chronic drinking to integration. Such is the price of our wisdom and our sagacity. Slowly but surely in our land of bounty we are driving ourselves to a sort of prosperous desperation. . . . Many of us find ourselves American aliens mentally and spiritually displaced in our own native land.[136]

Martin said little publicly about race during the late 1950s. He managed, in speech after speech to alumni clubs, parents, students, and religious groups, to discuss in great detail the changes that swept the South after the Second World War and the changes that were coming to Emory, without mentioning blacks.[137] Also left unmentioned was the fact that the Atlanta community was in increasing turmoil over race. The city had remained calm for most of the decade, largely due to the desire of the business community for racial stability and economic expansion. Together with Mayor William B. Hartsfield, Atlanta's power brokers had been able to negotiate slow but steady progress in race relations during the 1940s and 1950s.[138] This progress was threatened by the rise of massive resistance after *Brown,* as the state's pro-segregation leaders gained the support of many white Atlantans. Segregationists like Roy Harris of Augusta had people in an uproar, and the state legislature continued to tinker with its "private school plan" to nullify the intent of *Brown.* Until matters came to a head, however, things continued as they always had in Atlanta.[139]

Finally, though, the crisis came. In January 1958 the NAACP Legal Defense and Education Fund filed a class action suit in the northern district of Georgia asking for the desegregation of Atlanta's public schools.[140] The outcome of the case was never in doubt, given the trajectory of federal court decisions following *Brown,* and most of Atlanta was probably ready to begin at least token desegregation. Georgia law, however, with its provisions for closing public schools rather than integrating them, stood in the way. The scene was set for several years of intense conflict between Atlanta and the rest of the state.

The now very real possibility that the schools would close had a galvanizing effect on Emory's faculty. As Randy Fort had argued in his controversial 1956 editorial, this was an issue that had the potential to uproot a carefully built faculty. The campus buzzed with talk about how to respond. In late November 1958 a statement bearing the signatures of the overwhelming majority of Emory professors was delivered to the *Atlanta Journal and Constitution.* Signatories included Goodrich White's son, Chappell, a professor in the Music Department; Judson Ward, dean of the faculties; William Archie, dean of the College of Arts and Sciences; Carl Pfeiffer, head of the Division of Basic Health Sciences; William Cannon, dean of the School of Theology; and Evangeline Papageorge, assistant dean of the Medical School. The statement objected vehemently to closing the schools. It suggested that closed schools would cause "irreparable damage" to the local community, the state, and the nation. Damage to individual children was certain. Echoing the reasoning of the business community, the faculty also argued that the loss of industry that would certainly follow closure of the schools would harm the economic welfare of the entire state. Any interruption in the educational system would eventually lead to a shortage of trained service providers, from doctors to county agricultural agents. Worse, closing the schools would allow "Russia's systematic attempt to overtake us educationally" to succeed.[141] The topic of race, though, was hardly mentioned.

The faculty's arguments were by now pretty standard fare—pragmatic appeals that focused on the increasingly high cost to whites of maintaining segregation. Perhaps more interesting than the statement itself was the reaction to it. It is impossible to imagine Charles Howard Candler responding to this with anything other than cold fury. Indeed, the faculty half expected that there would be consequences.[142] However, Candler's successor as chairman of Emory's board, Henry Bowden, was a thoroughly different sort of person. Affable and charming, Bowden had a trial lawyer's way with words and relied on persuasion in his dealings with the Emory trustees. No longer was there "quiet, nodding acquiescence on the part of other members of the Board." Rather, Bowden reported approvingly that "no sooner are reports made, decisions announced or aims projected than the air is filled with questions, discussions, counter-views and suggestions."[143] Bowden also had wide and deep ties to Atlanta's business community and shared its concerns and perspectives, including, no doubt, a resistance to seeing the city's schools closed by the state.[144]

Bowden's response to the publication of the faculty statement was sanguine. While he did not express approval of its contents, he defended the faculty's right to make it. In a talk to a group of professors he took pains to express his, and the board's, support for the right of the faculty to speak out, whether individually or as a group, on the issue of race or on any issue at all. He contrasted this respect for the faculty's rights with the situation at "tax supported institutions in our State," where professors who wanted to take similar stands were "thwarted by administrations which shuddered at the thought of reduced appropriations, open criticisms from politicians and embarrassing days ahead."[145] This calm response indicates how changed Emory's leadership was. Perhaps another subtle gesture of changes to come was an honorary LL.D. awarded at the 1958 commencement to Judge Elbert P. Tuttle of the Fifth Circuit Court of Appeals. Tuttle, who joined the court as an Eisenhower appointee, had already begun to raise hackles in the South for his part in expanding and enforcing the *Brown* decision.[146]

Despite the clear change in the tenor of the board's leadership and Bowden's tacit approval of the faculty statement, no changes were made in Emory's own policy. Fear of losing the city's public schools continued to fester as state politicians loudly proclaimed that all Georgia schools would close before one would integrate. Georgia's new governor, elected in the fall of 1958, was Ernest Vandiver, who showed no sign of backing down on desegregation. On campus the waters continued to roil. A forum held during the annual "Brotherhood Week" in February brought several speakers to campus to discuss "What Are the Basic Issues of the Racial Crisis?" including Dr. Harry Richardson, president of Gammon Theological Seminary, and James M. Dabbs of the Southern Regional Council of the Presbyterian Church. Both men were advocates of open schools and desegregation.[147] A special issue of the *Emory Alumnus,* "Crisis in the Schools," examined racial problems in Atlanta. Focused on an Emory evening course for adults organized by Dr. John A. Griffin, the *Alumnus* article lauded the university for being one of the very few places in Georgia where all points of view on segregation could safely be expressed.[148]

Both the speakers and the article quickly drew objections, although only from a small number of Emory graduates. One alumnus complained that the university was allowing a one-sided presentation of segregation, from the side that wanted to do away with it. And, although editor Randy Fort was careful to avoid taking sides, a small number of alumni insisted that the kind of open discussion he praised meant that the school had gone over to the side of the integrationists.[149]

In 1956, when faced with complaints about the *Alumnus* pieces on race, Chairman Candler had vociferously agreed with them. Now, Emory officials sprang to Fort's defense.[150] Alumni Director Walter R. Davis wrote a long letter to one furious graduate in which he attested to the critical importance of the issue to Emory. The loss of faculty, already begun and with the potential to snowball, Davis explained, "was of paramount importance here at Emory." Therefore, the *Alumnus* had every reason to report on the problem. Furthermore, the charge that Emory had become a hotbed of racial radicalism simply was not credible, according to Davis. Neither Bowden nor Walter Martin, Davis insisted quite reasonably, could ever be called a "wild-eyed liberal," and "the Emory Board of Trustees could . . . safely be characterized as 'conservative.'"[151] Thus, at the close of the 1950s Emory admitted that there was a problem, and that it must be discussed. No longer would the school simply claim that as a private institution it was immune from the racial turmoil that surrounded it.

Articles in the alumni magazine and seminars on campus, however, were not going to satisfy the proponents of racial change at Emory. In March the *Wheel* carried a short but portentous story. Twelve members of the Atlanta chapter of the Congress of Racial Equality (CORE), including several Emory students, picketed outside Rich's Department Store in downtown Atlanta. Emory faculty members were also reported to be involved with the group, which had proceeded with the demonstrations against the wishes of Atlanta's established black leadership.[152] This burgeoning threat to the city's economic climate only added to the pressures for racial accommodation. At Emory, Henry Bowden's leadership of the board was about to make accommodation possible.

IV

By the end of the 1950s Harvie Branscomb began to feel somewhat beleaguered. The optimism and sense of control that had characterized his actions on race relations seemed to slowly leak away in the new atmosphere of heightened tension. Branscomb did not give up—far from it—but his efforts took on an increasingly defensive tone. Where he had once envisioned integrated graduate education in Nashville "on a scale broad enough to capture the imagination," the chancellor now counted heads in the School of Religion, aiming to keep the number of black students to an acceptable minimum.[153] Much of this defensiveness sprang from the 1955 decision of the board to open law school admissions to qualified blacks, or rather, from the immediate, furious response to that decision.

Although in the spring of 1955 Branscomb was pessimistic about the chances of persuading the trustees to accept black students in the Law School, there were some good signs. The racial climate in Tennessee a year after the *Brown* decision was nowhere near as desperate as it was in Georgia or Louisiana. To be sure, there was resistance to public school desegregation. It was sometimes, in some places, even disturbingly violent. In Nashville, a cautious grade-per-year plan was adopted, but even this was not accomplished without disturbance. Still, there was no "massive resistance" encouraged by politicians. There seemed to be, rather, a quiet determination on the part of the state's leadership that the law would be followed, although with the smallest amount of desegregation possible. This attitude would prevail throughout the rest of the decade, even during crises such as the bombing of Clinton High School in 1958 and unrest during the desegregation of Nashville's public schools in 1957.[154]

In early May 1955 Branscomb decided to make another attempt to desegregate Vanderbilt's Law School. Once more, as in 1954, he sought and received a letter from Dean John Wade to present to the trustees.[155] This letter was short, to the point, and requested specific guidance. In light of almost certain AALS action requiring compliance with its antidiscrimination policy, Wade asked "what specific steps we should take in the event we receive an application for admission from a qualified Negro student."[156] In addressing the board, Branscomb focused on the threat from the AALS and emphasized that he believed that, rather than waiting, Vanderbilt ought to exercise the "dignity of voluntary choice."[157] After what was apparently a very lengthy discussion, the board agreed and unanimously asked Branscomb to inform Dean Wade that "no student otherwise qualified should be refused admission for reasons of race, creed, or color."[158]

Branscomb and the board regarded this as a specific application of the policy they adopted in 1953—that Vanderbilt would allow the admission of qualified blacks only to those programs otherwise unavailable to them in the Nashville area. In practice, this meant the Law School, the Divinity School, and graduate programs at the Ph.D. level.[159] Fearing a large influx of applications, the board instructed Branscomb to make no announcement of the decision. He confidentially informed the AALS and a handful of close colleagues at other schools, but otherwise succeeded in his efforts to "keep it quiet until [the first black student] turns up in the class on the first day of instruction."[160]

The public was unaware of the decision until stories appeared in the Nashville dailies about the admission of two blacks to the Law School in September 1956 (over a year after the trustees authorized the change).[161] Within two days a group of Vanderbilt law alumni, led by local attorney and counsel for the pro-segregation Tennessee Federation for Constitutional Government, Sims Crownover, announced an open meeting at a Nashville hotel to discuss possible responses.[162] This meeting resulted in the formation of a new group, the Independent Association of Alumni and Friends of Vanderbilt University, which stated its purpose to be the preservation of "the traditions of Vanderbilt University within the concept of a privately endowed school with the power to run its own affairs privately, free from interference of any type from Federal, State and local governments or private philanthropic foundations or associations whose aims may be contrary to the traditions of Vanderbilt University."[163] Although this group was terribly angry, it was not terribly effective. The Vanderbilt Alumni Association, though, and the Law School Alumni Association both planned to meet on campus during homecoming in October and both groups had the desegregation of the Law School at the top of their agenda.

Ironically, Branscomb had spent the late summer and early fall in South Africa, where he sometimes found himself entangled in difficult discussions of racial change.[164] He returned to Nashville at the end of September, just as the opposition was picking up steam.[165] In response, Branscomb began quite consciously to talk out of both sides of his mouth. To those who supported desegregation, like the AALS and the philanthropies, he stressed the deep implications of the Law School decision. To those who opposed it, he insisted that there were no long-term implications at all. Urging Law School dean John Wade to remove the words "solely because of race, creed or color" from a form letter he proposed to send to disgruntled graduates, Branscomb argued that this wording should be removed as it "would seem to the readers to be an affirmation of a wholesale program of admissions, that it would undercut the impression of carefully selected admissions we are trying to make." Unfortunately, this language was in the board resolution itself, but Branscomb wanted Wade to "quote the resolution if you wish only with the more responsible and important people."[166]

As Paul Conkin points out in his history of Vanderbilt, the opponents of this change were remarkably consistent in their objections. They did not stand on morality, religion, or the law, or on the principle of upholding academic standards.[167] Rather, their argument was the same one that Vanderbilt professor Donald Davidson raised in 1952 when the university agreed to maintain its relationship with Scarritt College after Scarritt began admitting blacks—it was wrong to admit blacks to Vanderbilt because, by tradition, Vanderbilt was open only to whites. When a Fisk University professor defended desegregation while speaking on the Vanderbilt campus, Sims Crownover registered his "solemn protest." He lectured Branscomb about both the "Communist sponsored and inspired" NAACP and about Vanderbilt's past: "Vanderbilt has had a proud heritage, one of the outstanding universities of this nation. I am sure that neither Chancellor Garland nor Chancellor Kirkland would have permitted such a meeting as this to take place on the hallowed ground of Vanderbilt University."[168]

Segregation, for these alumni, was not a matter for cost-benefit analysis. Neither was it susceptible to compromise—the presence of a single black student was as repugnant as the presence of dozens. "I don't like the argument that negroes have been admitted to *only* two departments," complained alumnus Wick Stubblefield. "Remember, Jackie Robinson a short time ago was the only black in the big leagues. I feel certain that the law and divinity students already admitted will make it easy to let down the bars in other places. The *only* place where a line can be drawn *and held* is where it was drawn in my day—in Dr. Kirkland's day."[169]

To these alumni, any crack in the wall of institutional segregation represented an intentional betrayal of the South's tradition, the result of cowardly subservience to some outside authority. This meant, of course, northerners, in any of their various and corrupt guises. The federal government, the big foundations, the NAACP (often described as a puppet of subversive whites), Eleanor Roosevelt—all were identified as the sources of pressure that caused the Vanderbilt board to "cave in." The Independent Association of Alumni and Friends of Vanderbilt University, for example, placed the blame for law school desegregation squarely on the shoulders of outside funding and accrediting agencies. "While we have no facts on which to base our opinion," they admitted with remarkable casualness, "we have had conflicting reports that negroes were admitted to the University due to pressure from certain philanthropic organizations and the National Association for Accreditation of Law Schools. We would violently oppose the University prostituting itself to any such groups even though it may mean considerable financial loss for some few years." The Independent Association, furthermore, was convinced that refusing to capitulate to northern demand for desegregation would be to Vanderbilt's great benefit. With the South's public universities forced by the federal government to desegregate, "there will be thousands of the highest type and well-to-do families of means throughout the South searching for a segregated school for their children. . . . We feel certain that the quest for a segregated school of standing will be so great that people of means from all over the South will donate more than sufficiently to compensate any loss of the socialistic, leftist money from the North." This statement reveals an almost comic misapprehension of the amount of money it took to run an elite university and of the desperate financial straits the various divisions of the university sometimes found themselves in even with a good deal of philanthropic and federal funding.[170]

Although many individuals and several chapters of the Vanderbilt Alumni Association voiced similar opposition to the admission of blacks, in the end most seemed to realize that the issue was not really as simple as the pro-segregation rhetoric would have it.[171] No one could fail to understand that there were real costs to maintaining social arrangements that were opposed by the rest of the country. Reflexive resistance to any change that northerners wanted would be self-destructive, and most people were not truly opposed to weighing consequences and reaching the best possible decision for the school. One alumnus, speaking at a meeting of the Memphis club, his voice "charged with emotion," tried to untangle what some of the costs might be. "I would hate, just hate, to give the NAACP any more to sink their teeth into than they already have. Whatever you do here, do it with a lot of sober thought because if we let this thing go to the point that where Branscomb is run out of Vanderbilt because he let in Negroes, it will be 50 years before Vanderbilt will live it down in academic circles."[172] Also troubled by doubts was the Board of Directors of the West Kentucky Vanderbilt Club.

They were clear that "as a matter of personal preference" they did not want any blacks at Vanderbilt. Beyond that, however, certainty evaporated. The group recognized that "some provision must be made somewhere, by somebody, to provide higher education for the demonstrably able negro," but they did not see why that had to be Vanderbilt. Finally, at a dead end, they decided that Vanderbilt's Board of Trustees was "perfectly capable of considering and handling any situation" and must have had good reasons for doing what they did.[173]

There was no danger of Branscomb being run out, though. In spite of all the noise, there was as much approval of the opening of the Law School as there was disapproval. More letters congratulated the school for its decision than complained of it, and many of the happy correspondents frankly carried more far weight than the alumni clubs. Dean Rusk, for example, president of the General Education Board of the Rockefeller Foundation, wrote Branscomb a brief but significant note about the furor raised by the law school alumni. The admission of the two black students, Rusk said, "was an act of courageous leadership of the sort which one would expect from Vanderbilt. Conversely, it would be disastrous were Vanderbilt to lead a retreat by changing its position in the face of real and distressing (but perhaps temporary) pressure. A university reaps much of its harvest in terms of decades. I haven't the slightest doubt but that Vanderbilt, twenty-five years from now, will look back with satisfaction to the action which your Board of Trust took in opening the doors of the Law School to qualified Negro students."[174] When the Vanderbilt board met in October, in spite of the concurrent meetings of the Alumni Association and the Law School Alumni Association that at times seemed mutinous, there was simply no question of not upholding the May decision.[175]

The trustees' belief in the limited nature of the change, however, was increasingly apparent. One wrote Branscomb with his hopes for the future of desegregation. "I thought the Board meeting went off very well and that the Law School matter was handled as well as possible under the circumstances. As stated, what I think the alumni are worried most about now is not the two students who are already in but about any future admissions which I hope we can postpone at any rate now that we have taken these two."[176] James Stahlman assured several correspondents that there was no possibility of opening undergraduate admission to blacks. He was, he said "quite certain that the Board of Trust as it is constituted at the present date would under no circumstances consider 'integrating' Vanderbilt University. Personally, I would not be a party to any such program."[177]

Although any immediate threat had passed after the October meeting, the atmosphere remained tense for years. Under pressure from alumni and with the South in turmoil, Branscomb too began to underscore that Vanderbilt's program of desegregation was "sharply limited." In a letter to J. D. Williams, president of the University of Mississippi, Branscomb described the course of desegregation at Vanderbilt, making clear how narrowly circumscribed it really was. "In May 1953 our Board of Trust, on my recommendation, approved the admission of a mature Negro minister to our School of Religion. Last year there were two and this year there are four such students. We are watching it carefully, and are not going to let the numbers grow very much, but in this matter one can cause almost as much alarm as a hundred."[178] His personal views seemed consistent with his vision of Vanderbilt's proper course. Discussing the talks he gave at universities in South Africa, he noted that "my lectures pleased nobody, since my view is that one must move steadily in the direction of full opportunity for individuals who qualify for said opportunity, but I don't go along with wholesale paper reforms by which we embrace all our brothers and sisters, whether or not they are embraceable. That kind of moral satisfaction is only possible for those who don't live with the problem in its acute form."[179]

Still, Branscomb was truly committed to the admittedly limited program of change that he had begun at Vanderbilt. He was one of the few whites whose calls for "moderation" did not ring completely hollow, precisely because his moderation actually meant something. That is, Branscomb was willing to chart a course of action, even though narrow and tightly controlled, that was meant to lead to real changes in southern race relations. Admitting a small number of carefully chosen elite blacks to a small number of carefully chosen academic programs, Branscomb believed, was a reasonable, moderate, step toward the gradual assumption by southern blacks of their rightful place in society.

It was a course, moreover, that he could fairly defend to anyone. When the dust began to settle after the law school admissions uproar, *Vanderbilt Alumnus* editor Robert McGaw convinced Branscomb that it would be wise to explain the decision in an upcoming edition. The result, entitled from a Branscomb quote, "A Policy the University Can Defend . . . in the South and in the North, in the Present and in the Future," highlighted the limited nature of the changes and a defense of the notions of fair play that underlie them.[180] Branscomb often appealed directly to southern pride and the need for responsible white action when he argued in favor of limited black admissions. Responding to an alumnus who was still angry in 1958,

Branscomb argued that the major reason for allowing blacks into the Law School was his "belief that the race problem in the South should be handled by Southern men, and that the best Southern tradition has always been to give to individual, worthy Negroes, under properly controlled conditions, such opportunities for which they could qualify. The northern politicians have alleged that we will do nothing about the Negro's needs unless they compel us to do so by law and by the policeman. As a Southerner, I do not admit this."[181]

Aside from the brief and dramatic law school episode, there was little agitation over racial topics at Vanderbilt during the late 1950s. The same pressures that Duke, Emory, and Tulane felt were, of course, also felt there, but their effect was minimized by the steps that had already been taken. In this sense, Branscomb's strategy of admitting small numbers of carefully selected black students actually worked. The token changes rendered the issue less acute both on and off campus. For example, the student newspaper showed interest in the unfolding events of the civil rights movement throughout the rest of the South but almost no concern about race relations on their own campus. The editors in the late 1950s tended to support some desegregation, but, like their elders, only on the South's own terms. Editorializing on Autherine Lucy's attempt to study at the University of Alabama, the paper expressed support for her effort but concluded "as southern students we ask for time to work out our problems without outside interference."[182] From year to year this remained the paper's basic stance, even as its editors changed. The *Hustler* came out squarely in favor of "patience and cool heads" and condemned "extremists," "radicals, or fanatics" who pushed too hard. This moderation, it should be noted, was completely unlike Branscomb's. The student editors had simply no idea of what concrete steps might be considered "moderate." Responding to the events in Little Rock, the *Hustler* announced that "we are in favor of moderation, not bayonets."[183] Displaying consistency, it also condemned the segregationists in Clinton for their resort to violence in trying to keep blacks out of the white high school.[184] Closer to home, the paper had little to say. The presence of black students in the Law and Divinity Schools left little room for agitation of the question. The only controversy to actually hit campus was whether to retain membership in the National Student Association, which many students wanted to abandon because of the NSA's condemnation of segregation.[185]

Otherwise, race-related problems were few. Occasionally there was difficulty when integrated groups wanted to meet on campus, although this was now only an issue when they needed dormitory facilities.[186] Applications from prospective black students arrived, apparently not in very large numbers, and were scrutinized with great care, not only for qualifications but also with an eye to campus politics. Thus, in 1957 Branscomb turned down a good candidate for the Graduate School because he was from Georgia. If Vanderbilt did not limit enrollment to blacks from the immediate area, he explained, "we would have students sent to us from all parts of the country, some of whom might not be coming for purely educational purposes."[187] While the problem of retaining faculty was less severe in a school that was partially desegregated, it did still exist and was troubling to Branscomb. The university lost an important sociologist not because of his own qualms about segregation, but because of the difficulty he was having as department chairman in recruiting young faculty to the South.[188]

One event that would have major consequences later was the death of Divinity School dean Jack Benton in the late summer of 1956. Benton had never been as aggressive as Branscomb on racial change, but he had been instrumental in building a powerful and respected Divinity School and was a reliable and steadying influence and a staunch friend and ally to Branscomb.[189] His loss left a large hole in Vanderbilt's administration, and replacing him would be difficult. Branscomb, with an eye to the long-term growth of the school's influence, settled on a young and energetic man as the next dean, a man who seemed just on the verge of "arrival" as an important administrator and an advocate for ecumenism. Robert Nelson was only thirty-six and came to Vanderbilt not from an academic job but from the staff of the World Council of Churches in Geneva, Switzerland. Branscomb could not contain his excitement at Nelson's prospects and the prospects for Vanderbilt's Divinity School under his leadership.[190] In a letter to James Cleland, dean of the chapel at Duke, Branscomb almost glowed as he listed Nelson's qualifications, but he did admit to one small twinge: "I know I am gambling again, as you put it. . . . The gamble, of course, is whether he can adjust to the southern scene happily."[191]

Nelson jumped into the dean's job energetically and from the first he showed a concern for race relations. The school continued work on a project begun by Jack Benton, a conference for ministers on racial segregation in the churches, and Nelson gracefully deferred to Branscomb's judgments about details of the proposal, particularly details that had the potential to accidentally inflame public opinion.[192]

At the same time, dissent over how much change was desirable and who would decide began to emerge from within the Divinity School. In 1958 a new applicant for graduate study presented problems that earlier black students had not—because she was a woman. Although her credentials were impeccable, Branscomb was reluctant to admit her. He wrote Dean Nelson a long, troubled letter, apparently trying to work the matter out himself as well as explain it to the dean.

> It must be recognized that the emotional center of the race problem so far as this part of the country is concerned deals with relations between the sexes. Vanderbilt University has undertaken to provide leadership in the South in voluntary action to eliminate segregation. To bring together young men and women of both races into the student body would be to carry out this experiment in the most explosive of all situations.
>
> My fear is that the Divinity School would find itself on the horns of a dilemma, that it would find itself forced into partial paralysis of efforts to weld the student body into a closely knit social unit, or alternatively, it would run the risk or probability of social episodes which would become the subject of wide discussion and violent reaction. It is my judgment that if this latter occurred, it would under present conditions sabotage the entire effort of the University in this area, and no efforts of mine or the Divinity School faculty could prevent this.[193]

In spite of this pessimistic analysis, Branscomb did not turn her away. A major consideration seems to have been that "certain members of the faculty had stated that they might resign if their view of this matter was not accepted." This prospect was a grim one, and it led the chancellor to give perhaps more ground than he would have liked. "I would be very unhappy over [the loss of faculty members over this matter], so much so that my best judgment might be over-ridden by my desires, both personal and official, in this respect. I would do anything which I could to hold together this fine faculty, in which I have the fullest confidence. I would only suggest, however, that a similar confidence is due in return, that the record would not indicate any grounds for the lack of confidence, and that the faculty together with the administrative officers should rather join together in an earnest endeavor to seek what is the wise and good course in this difficult area." Branscomb authorized the student's acceptance as a "special case."[194] At the same time he may have inadvertently created the impression that threats of resignation were an effective way to change his mind.

In the late 1950s, keeping a careful watch over every admission, Branscomb succeeded in maintaining a precarious balance at Vanderbilt. By allowing a limited number of blacks into two postgraduate programs, he greatly reduced the pressures for change. Through delicate explanations, he kept the opponents of desegregation at bay. This was an exhausting labor, though, and the stress of it was beginning to wear on him. A few years of peace would have allowed him time to regroup, but the growing determination of blacks throughout the South to take matters into their own hands, the growing anger of many whites over the change they had already been forced to accept, and the impatience of the divinity faculty with the slow pace of change would soon combine to destroy any semblance of peace at Vanderbilt.

V

Astoundingly, even during the late 1950s tiny Rice Institute remained an oasis of calm in the troubled South. Still largely insulated from the currents that swirled on the campuses of the other elite schools in the region, Rice went about its day-to-day business as though no revolution was taking place on the other side of its hedges. On campus, things were going well. Several important new buildings rose. Rice instituted a wholly new basis for undergraduate life with the opening of the residential colleges, including for the first time housing for women on campus, in 1957. If the new colleges did not immediately transform the intellectual climate, they did lead to improvement in the quality of life for students. The colleges created a warmer, more close-knit environment on campus and even helped begin the process of bridging the traditionally wide distance between the students and an often remote, research-oriented faculty. Student life in the late 1950s remained difficult, however, as a challenging curriculum combined with perhaps overly rigorous grading and professorial indifference to keep students preoccupied with their studies.[195]

At the very end of the decade new graduate programs in several departments of the humanities and social sciences broadened the scope of academic offerings. Even so, Rice's graduate curriculum still centered on its excellent programs in the sciences and engineering. Through 1959, Rice had awarded 261 doctorates, of which 246 were in science or engineering. Ninety-one of those, over one-third of the total, came from the nationally prominent Physics Department. By contrast, only fifteen Ph.D.s had been granted in the humanities, and only three humanities departments—History, English, and French—offered work toward the doctorate.[196]

While this intense focus on technical subjects left Rice free from the internal pressures to end segregation that were generated on other campuses by faculties in fields like religion, law, social work, sociology, and economics, there were changes afoot that would soon make even technical institutes vulnerable to social change. In 1954 Rice had been notified by the Atomic Energy Commission (AEC), a major source of funds for the Physics Department, of President Dwight D. Eisenhower's Executive Order 10557, which provided for a new nondiscrimination clause for use in all federal contracts. This clause was directed at discriminatory employment policies, and no one interpreted it at the time to require open admissions. Thus, Rice's administration continued to sign contracts with federal agencies.[197]

In 1957, federal efforts to enforce nondiscrimination took a more threatening turn. That May, the AEC notified Rice that a grant for the purchase of laboratory equipment contained a new clause. Rice was now required to agree that "no person shall be barred from participation in the educational and training program involved or be the subject of other unfavorable discrimination on the basis of race, creed, color, or religion." President Houston immediately called board chairman George Brown and sent him a copy of the new language. Concerned, Brown instructed Houston to send a copy to each board member. Houston also called trustee Malcolm Lovett, the son of Rice's visionary first president Edgar Odell Lovett and the school's legal counsel. Houston was alarmed, but not panicky. He suggested to Lovett that Rice could still sign off on this contract, as the only people eligible for the courses that used the equipment were fourth and fifth-year Rice students. If no blacks met this condition, Houston reasoned, no blacks could be discriminated against. The fact that the reason no blacks met the condition was because Rice discriminated against them in its admission process seems not to have occurred to him.[198] Malcolm Lovett agreed with this strained interpretation, and Rice's law firm sent Houston an opinion to that effect.[199]

Although this particular contract was executed without problems, Houston reasonably worried about the future. President Eisenhower had created an oversight committee, chaired by Vice President Nixon, which soon signaled that it would take a far more aggressive approach to contractor compliance than earlier committees.[200] The handwriting on the wall was visible even at Rice. Writing apprehensively to Malcolm Lovett, Houston fretted about where this was all heading: "Certainly, if we are not able to undertake activities of this kind [government sponsored training and research], we will soon find ourselves lagging far behind the general development of universities."[201]

Indeed, the need for federal funding had slowly become Rice's Achilles' heel. The acquisition of the Rincon oil field in the mid-1940s had given the Rice board a false sense of financial security. The income from that field was certainly substantial—enough to allow the trustees to indulge their ingrained suspicion of the federal government. Resting on this cushion of oil money, Rice did not pursue grants and contracts with anything like the zeal exhibited by Duke, Emory, Tulane, and Vanderbilt. By the mid-1950s, however, it had become obvious that the specialized technical research that was the institute's strength required equipment so expensive that it could only come from the federal government. An important example was the Bonner Nuclear Laboratory, which opened in 1953 and housed a six-million-volt Van de Graaf accelerator. Financial support from local and regional industry, while critical to Rice's expansion of its graduate and research programs, would never be able to provide nuclear laboratories. This belated understanding of the dynamics of the postwar funding boom meant that Rice now needed to play catch-up, and any threat to federal funding endangered the heart of the institution.

Even as Houston and the board were confronted with growing federal insistence on nondiscrimination, Rice was seeking another large infusion of federal money. In 1956 Congressman Albert Thomas, a Rice graduate and the representative from Rice's district, began pushing the Atomic Energy Commission to build one of its projects, a high-flux nuclear reactor, on land controlled by Rice just outside Houston.[202] The AEC turned the proposal down in August 1956, and throughout 1956 and into 1957 Thomas and trustee George Brown continued to pressure the commission to change its mind.[203]

In the summer of 1957 the congressman learned from a newspaper article that Rice was considering different plans for the land, plans that he thought lacked ambition. His inquiry to President Houston elicited an interesting response. Rice now contemplated, said Houston, establishing a center for marine geophysical work on the property, "with enough local and assured support" that the center would not become "entirely dependent" on federal funding.[204] While Thomas had no objections to a geophysical lab, he believed that much more could and should be extracted from the federal government in return for the valuable land. "May I respectfully offer the suggestion," he wrote Houston, "that we can get one of the big processing centers as easily as we can get this small specialized center."[205] This was advice that Rice's chairman, George Brown, hardly needed. Brown was an astute deal maker, experienced in national politics, closely connected to Lyndon Johnson, and not one to underplay a winning hand. He and his brother, Herman, had made canny use of government contracts to build their own company, Brown and Root, into a major international construction business.[206] Houston's concerns over the strings attached to federal funding, while accurate, were simply not enough to trump the huge leap in Rice's fortunes that would come with a major nuclear installation. The idea for the geophysics center soon died, and Thomas and Brown again pursued the proposal to the Atomic Energy Commission.[207]

Although Thomas was apparently close to a deal at one point, the AEC refused to fund the reactor after the head of the commission, Lewis Strauss, resigned in 1958.[208] Thomas, now more than a little angry, turned his sights to the newly established National Aeronautics and Space Administration (NASA) and its first administrator, T. Keith Glennan. Glennan had only officially been the head of the new agency for a few weeks when Thomas called him about the possibility of building a NASA facility on the Rice land. As head of the House Appropriations subcommittee that controlled NASA's budget, Congressman Thomas was in a stronger position this time. He was not shy about making this clear to Glennan. By 1959 both Thomas and Brown had met with the NASA administrator several times, and although no deal was agreed on, Rice had every reason to believe that a major federal research installation would be built on its land.[209] A bounty of government research and training contracts now seemed to be headed in the direction of the institute. The only potential obstacle was the government's stiffening stance on nondiscrimination.

Thus, by 1958 segregation finally became a critical issue at Rice. In July, Houston received a memo from C. A. Dwyer, assistant secretary to the board and business manager, "with reference to a recent decision of the Supreme Court relating to the rights of private Trustees to exclude negroes." At the request of trustee and university counsel Malcolm Lovett, Dwyer had written to the board of Girard College in Philadelphia. "We have been following with a great deal of interest the suit that was filed against your college with reference to accepting negroes," Dwyer wrote, and "[Rice's] Charter provides for white inhabitants and we will appreciate a letter from you advising us on what basis you were successful in maintaining your school 'For White Male Orphans.'"[210]

If Rice's trustees were determined to maintain their school for whites only, the Girard College decision would have given them confidence. In 1831 Stephen Girard left funds in a trust for the operation of a college, which was to admit as many "poor white male orphans" as the income would support. The will named as trustee the City of Philadelphia. In February 1954 two black students applied for admission and were rejected because of their race. Their lawsuit was ultimately unsuccessful, even though the Supreme Court ruled that the refusal of admission violated the Fourteenth Amendment. The critical point around which the decision turned was the status of the City of Philadelphia as trustee. Once the city, a governmental entity, was removed as trustee of the college and replaced with private citizens, Girard College was free to discriminate.[211] This decision was important for all the private southern universities, who now had legal confirmation that they were still protected from the direct impact of *Brown.* The indirect impact, however, was another matter. While Rice may have been able to continue protecting its segregated status, the loss of the benefits of a NASA installation that would likely follow made this seem less and less like a good idea.

On campus there seemed to be little strong desire for change, although neither was there especially strong opposition to it. The student newspaper, the *Thresher,* provided one of the few outlets for public debate on this topic. It varied slightly in its editorial stance toward race relations, depending on who was editor in chief, but was never especially vehement about segregation. Rather, the paper tended to deplore the violence and stupidity that often accompanied defenses of segregation. It thus condemned Arkansas Governor Orval Faubus for his creation of the crisis in Little Rock and declared that "what is needed on both sides is less demagoguery and more good faith."[212]

The student editors were realists when it came to the possibility of desegregation at Rice. When the University of Texas began admitting blacks in real numbers in the fall of 1957, the *Thresher* noted in an extremely astute editorial that "although the Rice Institute should logically be among the first to integrate it will probably be among the last. There are several reasons why integration has a better than average chance of success on the Rice campus. The selectivity of the student body is designed to insure that both Negroes and whites would be of high academic standing if admitted. . . . Past polls of the student body have each time shown them in favor of integration. Furthermore, Rice is not hampered by the caste consciousness of fraternity campuses." The editors, however, grasped the unwillingness of the trustees to make any controversial changes. "Rice has made no efforts toward desegregation and probably will not for some time. As a private institution, it will not be forced to open its doors to Negroes, and a voluntary effort in that direction for some reason does not seem likely. Yet, we can not help but hope that the force of student opinion will soon influence the Rice Institute, and that steps will be taken to admit Negroes."[213]

The *Thresher* took steps to demonstrate student opinion to Rice's administration. The paper organized a poll the very next month, and although it admitted that "desegregation of the campus does not seem imminent," it stressed (inaccurately) that the feelings of the student body were important in the decision-making process.[214] Over 61 percent of the 522 respondents favored desegregation at Rice, most gradually, and about 38 percent wanted to keep the school white.[215] Predictably, nothing came of this.

On the surface, little had changed regarding the possibility of desegregation at Rice since 1948. In the late fall of 1959 the chairman of the Commission on Human Relations of the Student Association of the University of Texas contacted the Rice Student Association with some questions about desegregation at Rice. The Texas students were concerned with their own efforts to integrate the dormitories and athletic teams at their own school and solicited information about the attitudes of Rice's student body and administration toward playing teams with black athletes. They also wanted "to more or less swap notes with [the Rice Student Association] concerning *any* work, problems, progress, etc., that is being carried on at our two schools relative to racial integration."[216]

The response of Rice's Student Association President Wayne Hanson gives a short but clear view of the university's public position on desegregation. Hanson began by answering the most immediate question.

> I have talked with the administration and found that integration would not cause a change in administrative policy toward the University of Texas. The integration of the University was discussed in our Student Senate meeting to determine the students' reaction. Most of the Senate members were either for or didn't express any strong opinions for either side. Those against integration were mainly opposed to dormitory integration, especially women's dormitories. Rice does not have any restrictions against playing teams with Negro athletes, and they are treated with the same consideration as any other member of the team.[217]

Hanson's answer to the more general request for sharing information on efforts to bring about integration was even more revealing. "We do not have a Board of Human Relations working toward the integration problems of Rice University," he wrote. Dismissing the matter, Hanson returned to the *Thresher* controversy of the decade before. "This integration problem was a big issue on the Rice campus in 1949, and Dr. W. V. Houston, President of the Rice Institute, wrote a letter to the school paper concerning this problem.

I believe Rice's stand on integration can be clearly explained by the following portion of that letter." Hanson closed with the succinct quote that had so quickly ended discussion of desegregation ten years earlier. "The Rice Institute was founded and chartered specifically for white students. The question of the admission of Negroes is therefore not one for administrative consideration, and the discussion in this connection is entirely academic."[218]

Just as in the past, Rice simply removed itself from the debate with an appeal to its charter language. Ten years after Houston first made his statement on desegregation at Rice, the school's *public* posture on race had not changed at all. "Desegregate? We can't." Behind this placid facade, though, the pressure of federal insistence on nondiscrimination in contracting, coupled with the ambition of George Brown and Albert Thomas to bring a major federal research facility to the Houston area, was forcing new consideration of racial restrictions at Rice. Houston and the Rice trustees were finally beginning to grasp the emerging new reality, and although the *Thresher* editors had no way of knowing it, Rice was about to position itself to make significant changes.

As the 1950s drew to a close, the situation at Rice was still fundamentally different from that at the other schools, although now in a new way. At Duke, Emory, Tulane, and Vanderbilt the escalation of conflict following the *Brown* decision, the increasingly loud and urgent debate about desegregation both on campus and in the wider community, made change more difficult. Their leadership remained or became paralyzingly cautious as political troubles swirled. At Rice, though, calm still prevailed. With little organized pressure coming from the campus, the board and administration had breathing space to consider in private the consequences of the new federal regulations for their expansion plans.

All of these institutions were by now in real danger of giving back at least some of the tremendous gains they had made since the end of World War II. Without the support of both their local communities and the larger national academic world, they could not possibly muster the resources needed to be among the country's academic elite. As the crisis over civil rights in the South continued to intensify, the middle ground where their leaders had sought shelter was disappearing. The trustees kept clinging to it, however, choosing inaction until the moment came when they finally discovered who really did have the power to force them to change.

5

Push Comes to Shove

The Early 1960s

B y the early 1960s the quickening pace of the civil rights movement
brought each of these schools to the same critical point. The moral
strength of opposition to institutionalized racial discrimination was
swaying opinion throughout the country. The Kennedy administration, while
not notably aggressive on civil rights, did use federal power to advance
equality of opportunity in areas where they could avoid getting bogged
down in dangerous public debates. President Kennedy issued a new executive order on nondiscrimination in federal labor practices that included a
much stronger commitment to equal opportunity regulations. The philanthropies that provided critical support to southern institution-building finally drew a firm line against supporting segregated universities.

Change, usually slow and cumulative on campuses, came abruptly. Three
of the presidents who led these schools during the 1940s and 1950s left office
in 1960. Hollis Edens of Duke, Rufus Harris of Tulane, and William Houston
of Rice left behind campuses that had been transformed during their service. Each of these schools was bigger, more sophisticated, and more highly
regarded than it had been on their arrival. Their successors, though, were
men of a different generation, who harbored the concerns and ambitions of
a new era. The notion that if it were to happen at all, desegregation had to be
carefully guided by the white establishment did not seem to carry any emotional resonance with the new presidents. To them, racially restrictive admissions policies were not delicate issues that required a fine hand to navi-
gate. They were anachronisms that hobbled the school's ability to get about
its proper business, and they should be abandoned as quickly as possible.

At Emory, Walter Martin was caught in the wake of the much bigger fight
over Atlanta's public schools. Martin's ineffectiveness at Emory and the extremely high political stakes in Georgia took the decisions about Emory's
future almost entirely out of his hands and left them with the board, par-

ticularly its powerful chairman, Henry Bowden. At Vanderbilt, Harvie Branscomb, now well into his sixties, remained. The turmoil that accompanied the civil rights movement seemed to him to confirm his belief that if responsible, educated white southerners did not exercise leadership in racial change, trouble would follow. But a dramatic and very public confrontation loomed between those—like Branscomb—who insisted on the duty of the white establishment to guide race relations and a generation of black youth who claimed leadership as their own. At Vanderbilt, this conflict played out when most of the Divinity School faculty, in sympathy with young Nashville sit-in participants, flouted the wishes of the Vanderbilt trustees. The press, enthralled with the drama, brought the events in Nashville to the entire nation.

The moment of crisis had arrived—finally—at the South's private universities. Their trustees had dodged demands for racial justice since the end of World War II, but by the early 1960s only a single choice remained: they could go along with the federal government, the national foundations, and the professors and thrive, or they could defy them and wither. Their power to control events had evaporated. The willingness of others to accept their authority—their right to make decisions for everyone else—was gone. In the end they capitulated, but not with particular grace.

I

In 1960 the threat of public school closures still hung over Georgia, as a clash brewed between Atlanta and the rest of the state. Following the federal court's 1959 decision ordering Atlanta's public schools to desegregate, the city's school board submitted a grade-per-year plan, beginning with twelfth grade. Judge Frank A. Hooper approved the plan but waited for the Georgia General Assembly to meet in January 1960 before he ordered implementation.[1] Atlanta's Mayor Hartsfield asked the legislature to repeal its mandatory school closure law and allow Atlanta to determine its own course on desegregation. Hooper's delay gave the state the chance to back off, but it was far from clear what would happen. Governor Vandiver, although publicly committed to resistance, had no taste for the consequences of closed schools. But in 1960 most white Georgians would rather close the schools than integrate, and most Georgia politicians vocally supported them.[2]

On Emory's campus, the uncertainty took a toll. At the end of 1959 President Walter Martin told the trustees that the public school situation "was without question an important factor in nearly all [faculty] resignations."[3] Replacing those who left was an almost impossible task. The *Emory Alumnus* reported that "Emory has had turndown after turndown from able young teachers it has wanted to employ from colleges in other states. They simply would not bring their children into a climate where the future of public education is uncertain. Nor will many professors now at Emory stay any longer if the situation grows much worse."[4]

In February, tensions began to ease somewhat when the General Assembly, with Vandiver behind the scenes, appointed a commission of prominent Georgians to hold statewide hearings on desegregation and the public schools. The head of the commission was John A. Sibley, president of Atlanta's Trust Company Bank, a partner in the law firm of King and Spalding, and former general counsel for the Coca-Cola Company. While Sibley loathed desegregation, he was a man of the Atlanta business community and understood that massive resistance would devastate the city. In complex and subtle ways, his conduct of the hearings during the late winter and spring of 1960 helped avert outright crisis.[5]

Meanwhile, other events contributed to the tense atmosphere in Atlanta. Martin Luther King Jr., had recently returned, bringing with him a reputation that worried and angered many whites. In early March students at the city's black colleges, inspired by the sit-ins in Greensboro and elsewhere, published a full-page "Appeal for Human Rights" in the *Atlanta Constitution*. The "Appeal" was shocking to many white Atlantans, with its declaration that "we do not intend to wait placidly for those rights which are legally and morally ours to be meted out to us one at a time." Demonstrations and protests continued throughout the spring, and students planned a boycott of Rich's Department Store.[6]

On the Emory campus, the issue of public school closures merged with broader faculty concerns about segregation. One incident galvanized faculty opposition to the school's racial policies and brought into sharp focus their distance from the trustees. In early March the board forced Emory's Glee Club to cancel an appearance at Tuskegee, citing the possibility of a violent reaction to a white choir singing—and staying overnight—at a black college. This was obviously a small matter, but it angered many in the Emory faculty. President Martin supported the cancellation but sent a somewhat conciliatory letter, which William Archie, dean of the College of Arts and Sciences, read to a faculty meeting in mid-March.[7] The letter provoked a wide-ranging discussion of Emory's racial policies. Archie warned the faculty that the deans believed the time was not "propitious to have the Board confront these issues officially," and given their recent Tuskegee decision, this may have been sound advice. But the arts and sciences faculty was in no mood to drop the matter. (Indeed, there was strong support at this meeting for publicly endorsing the black students' recent "Appeal for Human Rights.") On the unanimous vote of the faculty, Archie appointed a committee to meet with Martin and discuss "the Tuskegee episode and related questions of policy with respect to Faculty and student relations with the Negro community." Predictably, the group left that meeting unsatisfied.[8]

Martin found himself caught between the faculty and the trustees. Emory professors, including a large contingent from arts and sciences (which seemed at times to view itself as the "real" Emory), continued aggressively pushing for quick action, inviting students and faculty members from the black colleges to the Emory campus, participating alongside students in demonstrations, and drafting resolutions. The board, though led by the consummately practical Henry Bowden, still had a preponderance of traditionalists who were unhappy about public identification of Emory professors and students with integration. And Martin, a reluctant gradualist himself, was hobbled as a leader by campus and boardroom politics.

On March 31 Martin tried to calm tensions with a more formal talk to selected faculty members. He first warned them that, although they undeniably had the right to participate in important community affairs, that right must be exercised appropriately. He also disavowed any duty of Emory to help lead the state through this trouble and defended Emory's commitment to segregation.

> Emory University is subject to the customs and laws of Georgia. Some of you may wish that Emory were elsewhere, but it is the South. We simply cannot get too far out in front of the community in which we live, or else we ruin ourselves. History teaches that; nature teaches that. The climate must be right. I can easily see this University on the road to destruction if we get too far out in front. We are nurtured by our business and church friends, alumni, and yes, even the state government of Georgia. Suppose these friends and agencies turn their backs on us. . . . It is because of these facts that our Board of Trustees has said that we cannot schedule "open meetings" with Negroes, and that we must not have integrated meals or provide housing or sleeping for Negroes on the campus.[9]

Martin urged the faculty to drop their request that the trustees formally spell out their policy on race relations, as "the Board would have no choice but to rigidly interpret a policy of segregation." He returned again to the idea that the traditional racial beliefs of the "Emory family" could not be disregarded.

> I believe that the people who help provide the resources which pay our salaries and buy our facilities are part of the Emory family, too, and are entitled to some consideration. There is justification for being as considerate of the personal opinion of a trustee as of a professor. We should be willing to avoid embarrassing our friends, unless there is an overriding contrary interest at stake. I don't know how to spell out this policy in great detail, but I can cite an example or two: A formal concert by the Emory University Glee Club at Tuskegee, with an overnight stay in their dormitories, would destroy most of the good will and support our Alabama friends have worked to build up. Picketing of Rich's store by Emory students was a most unhappy choice, for the Rich Foundation is a member of the Emory family. . . . So, I call for an end to any such demonstrations on the part of Emory people, and ask the faculty to help in telling the students the damaging effects of these doings.[10]

It is a measure of how bad things had become that Martin thought this kind of lecture would quiet the faculty. The position he staked out was no different than Goodrich White's in 1948: idealistic insistence on racial change is unrealistic and self-defeating.

While some shared Martin's views, his efforts to control internal pressure for desegregation had no discernible effect.[11] Throughout the late spring of 1960, the College of Arts and Sciences pushed a resolution, passed on May 6, which called for an expansion of the policy of allowing mixed groups on campus "until it becomes feasible for Emory to make all of its facilities available without reference to race." In a direct challenge to Martin, the resolution stated that "in assessing the possibility of adopting such a policy it should be borne in mind that Emory has a national as well as a local constituency."[12] When the board met the following week, this resolution prompted "lively discussion," but the only result was a brisk letter from Henry Bowden saying that "the request . . . that Emory take the initiative in bringing together the races on our campus for joint work toward bringing about more inter-racial cooperation cannot be granted."[13]

Still, the faculty persisted. The University Senate had also been considering Emory's racial policies but had not yet reached any conclusions. On May 25 the arts and sciences representative offered an identical resolution along with a copy of Bowden's dismissive letter. This time, there was resistance. Representatives from other divisions had not seen the resolution before and were unhappy that they could not get an unambiguous explanation of its meaning. Still, with Martin voting against it, the Senate adopted the resolution by a 6 to 5 vote.[14]

The arts and sciences faculty set up a committee to study ways to implement the resolution and to communicate with the administration and board. Summing up the group's thinking, Dean Archie wrote Martin that "social, political, and allied changes are upon us. The committee feels that there is no way we can stop this tide . . . [and] the University ought to try to do something to accommodate itself to the change or to channel the changes that are coming in the best possible ways in order that we might not be engulfed by them." Archie reassured the president that the faculty committee was "not wild-eyed in any sense" and had "its feet firmly on the ground." The members understood that they needed the cooperation of the trustees and hoped to meet with some of them informally. From Martin's point of view, the best news in the letter was probably that the group did not plan to meet over the summer.[15]

By the time classes began again in the fall, Georgia's public school crisis was reintensifying. The Sibley Commission had issued its report in April, recommending that that state establish "a system of education within the limitations of the Supreme Court decision, yet one which will secure the maximum segregation within the law, which will vest the control of its schools in the people of the community." Judge Hooper again postponed implementation of his order desegregating Atlanta's schools in order to give the state a chance to repeal its massive resistance laws. The schools, he ordered, would desegregate the following fall. Although many, especially in rural areas and in southern Georgia, still vehemently insisted that segregation was more important than schools, the Atlanta business community strongly supported the Sibley Commission recommendations.[16]

That autumn also saw the resumption of demonstrations and sit-ins at downtown Atlanta lunch counters. On October 19 Martin Luther King Jr. was arrested along with fifty-one students for violating trespass laws after being refused service at the restaurant in Rich's Department Store. Mayor Hartsfield quickly negotiated the students' release from city jails and extracted from them a pledge that they would not hold demonstrations for thirty days in return for his efforts to get Dr. King released by DeKalb County (where Emory was located). Although it took an appeal from Robert Kennedy to secure King's freedom, the students honored their bargain. Demonstrations did not resume until late November.[17]

At Emory, Walter Martin had an interesting situation on his hands. A vocal contingent of students and faculty members were clamoring for change. Many on the board and among the alumni seemed unalterably opposed to change and they were just as vocal. And Emory was desperately in need of money—a lot of it—that he was expected to raise. Never really happy at Emory, Martin was by now miserable. He received harassing phone calls and scolding lectures from all sides on a fairly regular basis. Still, doing his best to salvage the situation, he worked to keep communication open among the various groups and helped create a special committee of faculty, administrators, and trustees to discuss segregation at Emory. These discussions continued throughout this tumultuous autumn.

Finally, as the spring semester opened, board chairman Henry Bowden decided it was time to act. On January 12, 1961—the day after a mob at the University of Georgia rioted outside Charlayne Hunter's dorm room when she enrolled as one of the school's first black students—Bowden appointed a committee "to study the policy of Emory University relative to the admission of negroes as students, and to recommend to the executive committee at its February 1961 meeting such changes, if any, it feels would be proper."[18] The membership of this committee resembled an Atlanta Chamber of Commerce roster, and although Bowden himself was not a member, he attended the meetings.[19]

From the beginning Bowden knew what he wanted to do and understood what the obstacles were. Like the larger Atlanta business community, he and the members of this special committee would have personally preferred to keep segregation. Their bottom-line mentality, though, as well as their privileged and insulated social position, led them to value other things more than racial separation. They would not retain traditional racial restrictions if it meant sacrificing prosperity and prestige.[20]

At their first meeting, on February 1, the committee briefly considered Emory's relationship to the Methodist Church, which was becoming more outspokenly opposed to segregation, as well as the faculty's strong support for admitting blacks.[21] The real focus of the discussion, though, was money. Bowden called attention to the Georgia legislature's grant of a tax exemption to Emory and other private schools, which applied as long as the school was maintained for whites only. Admitting blacks would potentially cost millions of dollars and end any hope of significant advancement. On the other hand, it was entirely possible that federal tax policy could soon change in ways designed to punish segregated institutions, and it was already certain that federal research grants and contracts to segregated schools were being restricted, and the president's Civil Rights Commission had recently called for a total ban on any kind of federal aid to segregated universities, a possibility that would likewise cost Emory millions of dollars and end its progress.[22]

Two days after this meeting, Walter Martin, who had met with the committee, sent a note to one of its members, Harlee Branch: "I believe, as most of you do, that desegregation is coming in all of our schools, so we might as well face it now, and in doing so settle it in our own way." This indeed was the committee's general position. Its members understood that the demise · of segregation was inevitable and they wanted to make the change at Emory with the least amount of turmoil. Early drafts of an interim report stressed continuity, citing faithfulness to the school's original and primary goal of academic excellence. This, the report suggested, would never change. The only thing that would be different was that a class of applicants that Emory had not traditionally accepted would now be eligible for admission.[23]

At issue remained whether to open admissions to the entire university or to proceed gradually, beginning with graduate divisions. Here, the committee was surprisingly willing to make the change all at once. Walter Martin strongly preferred gradual desegregation. "I am a little fearful of throwing open every school and the College to the Negro at one time. I think some of our crusaders, the NAACP, and maybe some other organizations are going to flood us with applications, and they are going to be good applications too, because the Negro high schools in Atlanta are turning out excellent products now." Bowden, and ultimately the rest of the trustees, disagreed, arguing that gradual desegregation would only drag the controversy out. It was best to get the thing finished as soon as possible.[24]

The Georgia tax exemption, though, was a sticking point. There was good reason to believe that if Emory desegregated, the state would not act to revoke that exemption. Several black colleges now admitted whites and still retained the tax status, as did the desegregated state universities. The dean of Emory's Law School, Ben Johnson, argued that any move to end Emory's exemption would have to come from the state, and he reasonably doubted that they would "invite such a crisis on their own motion." With the state universities now desegregated and Atlanta's public schools about to be, there would seem to be no point to trying to destroy Emory University. Still, Bowden and the committee members were hesitant. It was, after all, a lot to risk.[25]

In late spring 1961 the executive committee approved the special committee's final report and directed that it be presented to the full board in May. By now, both Duke and Tulane had voted to admit blacks, although neither had yet actually done so.[26] Mysteriously, however, the committee did not report to the board at this meeting, "pursuant to developments and agreements taking place immediately before the meeting on that morning." The board, though, did receive a report from the Emory Board of Visitors that called for an end to racially restricted admissions, concluding that Emory "must continue to recognize its responsibility to accept a position of leadership in resolving the problems inherited by the section of the nation in which it is located."[27] The board reserved action, noting only that segregation was now causing many "complications which can materially interfere with the ability of the University to carry out its work."[28]

Meanwhile, the campus was expecting an announcement. When they learned instead that the board had taken no action, the faculty and students reacted with dismay. Martin and Bowden received letters full of anxious disapproval. The College of Arts and Sciences Legislative Council passed a resolution deploring the board's failure, leaving Emory "in the rearguard of responsible action."[29]

To calm the situation, Walter Martin let the faculty know, through arts and sciences dean William Archie, that the board's inaction was temporary. "The Board of Trustees is not against desegregation, nor is he; that the Board of Trustees is worried about the consequences to the University, in view of the Georgia law on tax exemption, and that a declaratory judgment on the constitutionality of this law is being sought." Martin told the dean that he hoped the board would take action by November, or possibly even sooner, but he made no promises.[30]

By the time of the fall board meeting, Georgia's political atmosphere was far different than it had been a year before. The January showdown over desegregation at the University of Georgia had forced Governor Vandiver to take a stand and he judiciously chose to accept federal authority. The state university would remain open. Almost immediately, support for keeping the public schools open mushroomed and lawmakers overturned the state's massive resistance legislation in a special session. In Atlanta, after meticulous planning by the mayor and the civic elite, the public schools opened peacefully on a (barely) integrated basis.[31] Downtown, relentless boycotts and sit-ins had paralyzed business through February. White merchants, ready to negotiate, agreed to a vaguely worded statement brokered by Chamber of Commerce president Ivan Allen Jr. that committed them to desegregate their facilities at the same time as the public schools. This agreement outraged many in the student movement, but by fall the stores were desegregated and peace returned.[32]

In November, then, Emory's trustees felt that they could safely act. The special committee finally submitted its report, noting that nothing in the school's founding documents forbade the admission of blacks and that the school's admissions standards would not change. The board approved the report and announced that Emory would admit blacks to all schools at the university on the same basis as white applicants—but only "when and if it can do so without jeopardizing constitutional and statutory tax-exemption privileges essential to the maintenance of its educational program and facilities."[33]

Reaction to the announcement was largely favorable. Many faculty were relieved but cast a wary eye at the unaddressed legal issues. Trustee F. M. Bird met with the faculty on November 21 and reassured them that the board would indeed act. Martin also issued a statement promising that the board would see the matter through to its conclusion.[34] Only a handful of alumni objected, but they made up for their small numbers with their remarkable stridency. Most alumni who bothered to contact the school were pleased with the move toward desegregation.[35] The *Atlanta Constitution* praised the decision for moving Emory "a great step forward toward its ultimate position as one of the foremost seats of learning in the nation" and called on the legislature to remove the "punitive restriction" in the tax exemption.[36]

Bowden tried to interest other Georgia private colleges in joining a lawsuit to challenge the racial restriction in the tax exemption, but none would. (Rufus Harris at Mercer was more than willing, but the Mercer board would have none of it.)[37] After receiving an application to the Dental School from a qualified black student, Emory filed suit on March 21, 1962, carefully arguing that the tax exemption was valid but the racial restriction within it was not.[38] Bowden and law dean Ben Johnson argued the case, losing in the district court but prevailing at the Georgia Supreme Court.[39] The final order was entered in October 1962, and Emory admitted one black part-time graduate student, a teacher in the Decatur public schools, that fall. By spring, two black women were admitted to the graduate program in nursing. The campus received them "without any turmoil or excitement whatsoever."[40]

Although Emory's trustees made the change with relative grace and calm, there is no doubt that they would rather have kept the school white. In letter after letter Henry Bowden wrote that he would be happier if Emory could remain segregated, and that he did not want to change the custom because of "pressure from either the government or private donors who threaten to cut us off if we do not integrate." But he also implicitly admitted that this was exactly what had happened. "Whether we like it or not," he acknowledged, "the Federal Government is deeply embedded in private as well as public education. At present there is going on at Emory research involving more than $2,000,000 in Federal funds. We are of the opinion that in the not too distant future we will find Congress acting to cut off Federal funds from institutions which by charter or rules prohibit negroes from attending. If such is done and we lose this money we could continue to operate as a small ineffective college but not as a major university because our faculty will leave us if they do not have the chance to do research work." In another letter he expanded the list of outside actors who had forced the school's hand, including the foundations and the accrediting agencies. "I resent [this]," he said, "but must learn to live with it."[41] Others on the board vigorously resisted admitting what had happened. In a letter to Walter Martin written after the May board meeting, trustee Harris Purks proclaimed that in spite of his assent to desegregation, he would never support any suggestion that segregation was wrong or that Emory was giving in to outside pressure. He would never sign off on anything, he insisted, that included the following:

1. breast-beating self-righteousness,
2. unbridled implied criticism of the composite previous actions in the South with respect to race,
3. a stampede under the whip-lashing by liberals of church or press or government,
4. use of the word integration.[42]

But willing to face it or not, Emory's trustees had most certainly been forced to desegregate. Outside pressures, and internal ones too, ensured by 1961 that the school could no longer remain both a major university and segregated. The pragmatic response of the Atlanta business establishment to the state's public school crisis meant that the battle to resist changes in traditional racial relationships in Georgia, or at least in Atlanta, was already lost. There was nothing to be gained by holding out alone. Thus the board, led by Henry Bowden and dominated by members of that same Atlanta business community, did the practical thing. Emory would continue to advance, growing in size, quality, and prestige throughout the decades ahead.

One other happy consequence of the desegregation lawsuit was that it left Walter Martin free to leave Emory and return to the University System of Georgia.[43] Martin was not a man to walk away from an unfinished job and would not leave the matter of desegregation unsettled for his successor, but he began talking to friends in the Georgia system at almost the same time as the board announced its resolution on desegregation in November 1961. By Christmas, the discussions were serious. Martin announced to Emory's board his intention to accept the vice chancellorship of the University System of Georgia on April 11, 1962.[44]

Martin's ability to do the job that Emory needed done, especially the fund-raising, had been hampered from the beginning by the campus politics that surrounded his selection as president, in 1957, and that never really disappeared. The public school crisis and the tumult that accompanied it at Emory left him even weaker, exposed on all sides to sniping and outright attacks. That he accomplished anything at Emory is nearly miraculous, but he did. In his five years at Emory enrollment grew from about 3,600 to about 4,600, research grants grew from $1 million to over $3 million, and, most remarkably, despite all the controversy and bad feeling, the school's full-time faculty grew from 276 to 430. Martin had worked assiduously to improve faculty salaries and to strengthen the faculty's voice in university affairs. Perhaps his most lasting accomplishment at Emory was that he forced the trustees to face the school's most overwhelming problem—finances. By the time he left, they understood the magnitude of the fund-raising problem and accepted that the trustees must play a major role in bringing the money to campus. Almost immediately, a new development campaign became the focus of everyone's attention.[45]

With few exceptions, only after Martin's resignation did people express their appreciation of his stalwart service.[46] Those who wrote often singled out his efforts on desegregation. "I am aware of, and I thank you for, your patient, persistent efforts to move the center of sentiment among the trustees to the point where the suit was possible," wrote historian J. Harvey Young, one of the faculty's vocal proponents of desegregation. "In this touchy area, as in all others, you have won my deep appreciation—indeed, wide faculty appreciation—for your fair consideration of expressed opinion. We have known that, even when we disagreed with you or would push you harder and faster than you thought expedient, you would trust our sincerity. The genuine atmosphere of freedom of speech, with no fear of reprisal, subtle or direct, attaching to divergent views, is greatly to your credit."[47]

II

On February 19, 1960, Hollis Edens abruptly announced his resignation as Duke University's president. His announcement, unaccompanied by any convincing explanation, took the campus completely by surprise. A month later, the surprise was compounded when the Board of Trustees removed Paul Gross as vice president of the education division. Gross, a chemist who had been at Duke since 1919, had worked closely with Edens since 1949 and was heading the school's long-range planning effort when he was dismissed. Few outside the circles of the board and high administration knew what had happened.[48]

Ironically, Hollis Edens, who had so carefully tended his relationship with the Board of Trustees, fell victim to internal politics. His downfall, though, came not at the hands of the board of Duke University but rather the board of the Duke Endowment. In the early 1930s President William Preston Few's fears that the Duke Endowment might some day cut off funds to the university led him to create an institutional tie between the two boards. Three spots on the Duke University board's executive committee were filled by board members of the Duke Endowment, who were usually New Yorkers.[49] Vice President Gross had cultivated these men, who, like him, believed that Hollis Edens was not pursuing national prominence for Duke aggressively enough. For several months they had been pressuring Edens to step aside and accept a lesser role in Duke's affairs. Insulted and hurt, wanting to avoid a battle that could only divide the university, Edens resigned. While the Duke Endowment trustees on the executive committee may have been pleased, the rest of the board—seeing the door open for Gross to either become or choose the next president—was not. These other trustees, mostly North Carolinians, had had little inkling that anything was wrong. They also had no complaints about Edens, who was popular on campus and widely respected in the state.[50]

The day before the board meeting on March 23, Gross gave an interview to the *Durham Morning Herald* in which he portrayed Edens as reluctant to allow Duke to transcend its regional status and become a national university. This was simply untrue, and it deeply angered the North Carolina trustees. The meeting itself was explosive. After accepting Edens's resignation, the board asked for Gross's. Only the three Endowment trustees and two close allies opposed his removal. Before the meeting adjourned, the board also voted that minutes of every executive committee meeting be sent to every trustee.[51]

Neither the board nor Edens made any of this public. The only thing the campus knew was that Edens had resigned and that Gross, who was also popular, able, and a strong supporter of the faculty, had been dismissed from his administrative posts. Not surprisingly, havoc ensued. The faculty was angry and divided. The trustees of the Duke Endowment publicly threatened to cut off funding to the university. The campus roiled until April, when the board appointed J. Deryl Hart, chairman of surgery in Duke's Medical Center, as acting president.[52]

When Hart took office on July 1, he faced "factionalism, distrust, anxieties, a decimated top administrative staff and a resultant deterioration of morale." An established medical center administrator who was respected by all sides, Hart reached out to the faculty and staff, meeting with the various constituencies on the Duke campus. With the help of a management consulting firm he began a much-needed reorganization of the upper echelons of the administration and assembled a capable and committed staff. Taylor Cole became provost, a new title for a job that encompassed the responsibilities formerly held by the vice president of the educational division. Hart also named three vice provosts: Barnes Woodhall for the Medical Center, Frank deVyver for the other professional schools, and Marcus Hobbs for the undergraduate colleges. Although it took some time for these changes to sort themselves out, Hart and this "provost group" were working effectively by the time classes began in the fall.[53]

During the months that led up to Edens's resignation, pressure to drop segregation had continued. Duke students were pushing hard, and the sit-in movement that began just down the road in Greensboro quickly spread to Durham, where several Duke students were eager participants. The university's threat to punish students arrested in the demonstrations drew fire from all over campus.[54] In April a Student Senate referendum found 56 percent in favor of admissions based on qualifications rather than on race.[55] The Interfaith and Fellowship Committee of the University Religious Council complained to the president that they and the denominational groups were being forced to abandon activities that sometimes included black students from neighboring colleges because they could not get meals on campus "without causing embarrassment to both our guests and ourselves."[56] The Duke Bar Association submitted a resolution calling for the admission of students to the Law School without regard to race. The Divinity School reported "much greater" pressure to admit black students than in the past. Alumni continued to ask when the change was coming.[57] Black Durham minister and civil rights activist Douglas E. Moore pressed the Methodist General Conference to withhold funds from Duke, arguing that the school "receives money from the church while refusing to live up to its fundamental laws."[58]

Although the issue was understandably pushed to the back burner during the spring of 1960, by fall Hart and the provost group saw that they had an opportunity to rid the school of what was by now a real albatross. These men, all old hands at Duke, were perfectly positioned to get this done. They had close contacts among the trustees and enjoyed their respect. They could not possibly be construed as radicals or outsiders. At the same time, their commitment to national academic norms and to Duke's national reputation was a given. They could reasonably argue, too, that this troublesome problem ought to be resolved before a permanent successor to Edens was named. Once they decided to act, the change came with startling speed.

Hart and the provost group quickly developed a strategy. First, the three vice provosts prepared detailed reports on the problems caused by the restrictive admissions policy and sent them to the board. These reports intentionally ignored moral and ethical arguments. The provost group well understood that such arguments were not merely ineffective but positively damaging to their cause. Still bitterly resentful of "outside" pressure, Duke's trustees were unlikely ever to admit that segregation was wrong. The only hope of persuading the board to give up the segregated admissions policy was to overwhelm the members with evidence that it was holding Duke back, then step aside and allow them to make the decision on their own.[59]

The group moved carefully, arguing only for the desegregation of the graduate and professional schools. Taylor Cole wrote one report, which focused largely on the perceptions of external constituencies. Cole laid out the reasons why "the inability to admit the small number of duly qualified Negroes . . . has created barriers to the fullest development of Duke University and has resulted in a decline in its prestige." He presented evidence of growing difficulties in getting grants from foundations and described the negative attitudes toward Duke of accrediting organizations, professional associations, and "our own faculty and student body." Strict insistence on segregation had become "a major barrier to attaining the national and international recognition which Duke University deserves."[60]

Barnes Woodhall's report on the Medical School likewise focused on practical issues, pointing out that running a major research hospital required significant federal assistance. "As Dean of the Medical School," he wrote, "it is my opinion that continuation of the existing segregation policy of the University will seriously impair the ability of the Medical Center to further its traditional duty of 'caring for the sick' and may eventually destroy its credo of excellence."[61]

In the last report Marcus Hobbs discussed the effects of segregation on the rest of the university. Hobbs outlined the history of faculty and student support for desegregation as well as its growing intensity. Here he focused on the deepening problem of recruiting and retaining top faculty members as well as the professional difficulties that alumni of the graduate and professional schools were beginning to experience—they were hampered in the outside world by Duke's reputation as a bastion of segregation. Moving to more tangible concerns, he calculated that Duke received over $7 million in federal funds for research and training in 1960, including almost $600,000 of overhead, and then he walked through the current nondiscrimination clauses in federal contracts. Shrewdly, Hobbs did not simply conclude that segregation was too expensive to keep. Stated baldly, that argument often produced angry refusals to "sell out" the South's heritage for Yankee dollars. Instead, Hobbs linked the denial of federal funds to other problems.

> The effect of reduction of even a small fraction of the indicated revenue on the grounds of discriminatory practices could be very far reaching. The denial of a proposal by a faculty member would then be unrelated to the ability of our staff or students, or the quality of the proposed program, but would be based on a matter of policy of the University that was contrary to law and with rare exception, the strong sentiment of the faculty member. The implication of such a situation for the morale of the entire faculty and student body would be very serious indeed, even if judged in the most charitable degree. . . . Though we must be concerned with possible loss of revenue and activity because of decline of funds from this source if present admission policies are maintained, the more important effect may well be the loss of qualified staff and the general morale of the staff and students.[62]

In view of all these considerations, Hart and the provost group asked that the trustees allow the graduate and professional schools to "accept for degree programs the small number of obviously well-qualified Negro applicants," adding as a safeguard that each black applicant should be considered by an ad hoc committee of the president, provost, and dean of the school involved.[63]

The group then went out, along with Duke's vice president for public relations, Charles E. Jordan, and President Hart, to meet with small groups of trustees throughout the state, selling them on the need for change before the next meeting. In mid-January, Hart scheduled four meetings with these small groups, including one in Charlotte and one in Winston-Salem.[64] The trustees had all received copies of the reports and had the opportunity to raise any questions or objections. The administrative group managed to visit with nearly all the thirty-six board members before the March 8 board meeting.[65]

The provost group's assessment of the urgency of the matter was borne out by several events that took place while the small conferences were being held. On February 8, 1961, Dean Cushman of the Divinity School sent a petition from that faculty to Hart, who forwarded it to the board. Cushman endorsed this plea for quick desegregation, which was posed, unlike previous communications from the Divinity School, in practical rather than moral terms. Cushman too stressed the concrete consequences of failing to change in his letter to Hart. "I am frank to state that I do not believe that the Divinity School can much longer sustain, without suffering serious disabilities, the present impasse in the matter of admissions policy. Without an early alteration of this policy, the integrity of the Student Body, the Faculty, and the good reputation and national standing of the institution cannot be assured."[66]

Also in February, Dean E. R. Latty notified Hart that the Law School had received an application from a black candidate who was qualified for admission. If Duke rejected him solely because of his race, Latty warned, the Duke Law School would be censured at the next annual meeting of the Association of American Law Schools. "Such a censure," he explained, "would be a great detriment to the Duke Law School in recruiting top-caliber faculty and top-flight students and in general to our national and international prestige." Hart promised to bring the matter before the trustees and no doubt did so at the meetings.[67]

The report and the conferences had their desired effect. One of the Endowment trustees, Thomas L. Perkins, explained his thinking the week before the meeting. "It seems to me that as much as we may regret it the time has passed when we can permit our personal preferences to influence our decision in this matter. The only consideration as I see it is what is in the best interest of Duke University." Perkins accepted the arguments in the reports and, further, feared that "unless we go along gracefully with this proposal we will find that something much more unpalatable will be crammed down our throats in the near future."[68] Hart reported similar reactions from other trustees in a letter to Bunyan Womble, a strong supporter and soon to be the new chairman of the board. "In general," Hart concluded after meetings in Charlotte and Winston-Salem, "I believe they hated to see it come, they thought it inevitable, that Duke had much to lose by further delay and although it was contrary to what they had hoped would be the case they would go along with it."[69]

By the time of the board meeting on March 8, Hart had counted the votes and knew that desegregation would be approved. Because of the earlier discussions, there was not any debate. Womble, now chairman, simply asked if the trustees were ready to vote. They were. Overwhelmingly, they voted to admit qualified applicants "to the degree programs in the Graduate and Professional Schools in Duke University, effective September 1, 1961, without regard to race, creed, or national origin." A few trustees abstained, and three or four (out of the twenty-six present) voted against the change. Two of those opposed the proposal because they wanted to desegregate the entire university at once. Even those who still firmly supported segregation, though, seemed to feel no real bitterness about the decision. One opponent of the change was not at the meeting but wrote later to Womble that "I don't want you to think that I was *absolutely* opposed to what the Board did. It's only that I felt it was hurrying the situation too fast."[70]

Immediately after the board meeting, Thomas L. Perkins notified the president of the Ford Foundation, the president of the Carnegie Corporation, and the vice president of the Rockefeller Foundation. All three wrote back with approval, though with just a hint of forbearance. "I agree with you that this is a progressive move," wrote Henry Heald of the Ford Foundation, "and I am sure it will be so regarded by most of the people around the country. Of course, it would be a little better if it were not limited to the graduate and professional schools of the University, but perhaps this will come in time." Charles Cole of the Rockefeller Foundation was also understated. He understood, he said, "how hard it was to do in some respects" but allowed that "it certainly clears the air a lot and will give some other places added courage." John Gardner of the Carnegie Corporation was the most enthusiastic, commenting with an echo of Branscomb, White, and Harris that "I have always believed that the real gains on this difficult problem could be made only by the best of Southern leadership. And this certainly represents the best."[71]

Otherwise, response to the decision was overwhelmingly positive. Hart and Womble received dozens of letters from pleased alumni and only a handful from disappointed ones. Many of the angry letters came from people with no personal ties to Duke at all. Many of the happiest came from Duke alumni who were teaching at other universities and would no longer be subject to the scorn of their peers. Many Methodist ministers, as well as the director of the Methodist Board of Education, sent their congratulations. In stark contrast to the trustees, these writers saw the change as an unmitigated good. While they celebrated that the university had done what was necessary "for successful completion of the effort to move Duke past the position of being the best school in the South and into the front rank of the truly great universities of this country and the world," they also uniformly expressed delight that Duke had finally done what was morally right.[72]

The provost group's strategy of beginning with the graduate and professional schools was probably critical in getting the trustees to agree to begin desegregation at all, but once implemented it led to problems. There arose unremitting questions about which facilities were desegregated and which were not. The school's trustees and some administrators were panic stricken by the prospect of "social integration," which seemed to include anything from shared meals in dining halls to having blacks as overnight guests in the dormitories. Many Duke students were impatient with these concerns and pushed back hard, inviting blacks from North Carolina College to eat with them in the undergraduate cafeterias. Although these difficulties were not especially serious, they caused an inordinate amount of hand wringing. Otherwise, the desegregation of the graduate programs proceeded without serious incident.[73]

The Duke administrators now began talking to trustees about the next step—desegregation of the undergraduate college and all campus facilities.[74] Reporting to the board in March 1962, Taylor Cole spoke of the unhappiness on campus with the half-finished change, and in April the Undergraduate Faculty Council passed a resolution calling for an end to racial restrictions in the undergraduate schools. The University Faculty adopted this resolution on June 1.[75]

At the board meeting the next day, over a year after the decision to desegregate Duke's graduate and professional schools, the trustees considered extending the policy to the rest of the university. This may have been unplanned. Provost Cole reported on the relatively smooth course of desegregation so far and warned the board that "the question of integration at the undergraduate level receives vigorous attention at the hands of a restive faculty," but the Duke administration does not seem to have anticipated a vote that day. At the executive committee meeting the day before, Hart and the committee agreed that the university faculty's desegregation resolution would be passed on to the board "for information only." A month before, at a meeting of a trustee-faculty liaison committee, Womble and the other board members suggested that the question of undergraduate admissions would "in all probability be brought before the Trustees for discussion and decision at its November, 1962 meeting."[76] In any event, a new trustee who was attending his first meeting, Charles Rhyne, picked up on Cole's remarks and offered a motion to admit qualified applicants to the undergraduate colleges without regard to race. After ably arguing for complete desegregation on legal, moral, and practical grounds, Rhyne asked that his motion be seconded. It was, and more discussion ensued. Finally, on a secret ballot the board resolved by a large majority that "qualified applicants may be admitted to degree programs in the undergraduate colleges of Duke University without regard to race, creed, or national origin."[77]

Again, most reaction was favorable, although Hart and Womble received a few acutely angry letters. Soothing an upset alumnus, Womble downplayed the importance of the new policy.

> The new policy will, of course, be administered fairly, but on account of the very high standard of requirements for admission, I am sure very few Negroes will be admitted. In the professional and Graduate Schools, as to which the policy was changed more than a year ago, only four have been admitted for entrance this fall. Two of these are in the School of Religion. The requirements for admission to the undergraduate colleges are much more strict . . . and with the thousands of white students being turned down each year for lack of space, I shall be surprised if any Negroes applying will possess qualifications entitling them to be admitted any time soon.[78]

A. T. Spaulding, prominent black leader and executive of the black-owned North Carolina Mutual Life Insurance Company, took a more expansive, and challenging, view of what Duke had done. To Deryl Hart, Spaulding wrote:

> I sincerely believe that ten years from today every person who was instrumental in this monumental action will find more joy and satisfaction in having been a part of it than in any other one thing done by him or her during his or her connection with the University. This decision has marked a monumental milestone along the highway of Duke's history and I believe it will be looked at as a reckoning point in the years ahead, a point of reference in measuring Duke's future progress and achievement at an ever accelerating rate. For basic to all truly great achievement is freedom. Duke University has now freed

itself from an impediment which has militated against its furnishing to the South and to the Nation the great leadership of which it was otherwise capable. May she always cherish that spirit which sets men free.[79]

III

In 1960 there was a head-on collision at Vanderbilt University between the past and the future. The cautious arguments on racial change that had carried the day at Vanderbilt, rooted in the notion that white leaders must control the pace and scope of the change, came into sudden and direct conflict with the very different ideology of the student sit-in movement. In February 1960 black students from Nashville's Fisk, Tennessee A&I, and the American Baptist Theological Seminary began a series of sit-in demonstrations at downtown lunch counters. These students were in close contact with the organizers of the Greensboro, North Carolina, sit-ins, which had begun only a few days earlier. James Lawson, a black Vanderbilt divinity student and regional director of the Fellowship of Reconciliation, had devoted himself to careful preparation of the Nashville demonstrators. A serious student of Gandhian pacifism who had been sentenced to a prison term for refusing induction into the army, Lawson was eminently qualified for this role. He encouraged the protesting students and gave them a working understanding of nonviolent methods.[80]

On February 27 crowds of what Branscomb called "white rabble" attacked the sit-in demonstrators, some of whom were Vanderbilt students. Police arrested eighty-one students, and much of white Nashville became frantic, fearing that race war was about to break out.[81] On the night of February 29 nearly two hundred black ministers, including Lawson, met with Nashville Mayor Ben West. West argued that the students had the legal right to sit as long as a lunch counter was open but as soon as the owner announced that it was closed, they had to leave. Lawson, now identified publicly as a leader of the demonstrations, expressed his frustration with what he rightly saw as purposeful legal hairsplitting. He contended that this use of the law was a "gimmick" to break the movement. Nashville newspapers reported this remark, though in different versions. Lawson's advice to the students—that they continue the sit-ins—many whites now chose to interpret as intentional lawlessness, and even as contempt for law itself. Although the student demonstrators enjoyed a surprising amount of white support, many opposed them bitterly. The *Nashville Banner,* under the leadership of James Stahlman, led the charge against Lawson and the sit-ins. Stahlman was beside himself, utterly enraged, and wrote front-page editorials attacking Lawson and the demonstrators with lurid rhetoric.[82]

Branscomb was deeply worried. The possibility of mass racial violence certainly frightened him, but his main concern, as ever, was the potential for serious damage to Vanderbilt. Not the least of these dangers was that the Vanderbilt board's executive committee, spurred on by Stahlman, might do something rash. In Branscomb's eyes, far more than James Lawson was at stake. The foundation that he had so carefully laid, and upon which the institution's advancement still rested, was profoundly threatened.[83]

Branscomb's ability to convince the board to admit black students had all along depended on a firm sense of control. Branscomb's greatest fear was thus always of racial "incidents"—that is, any behavior that might draw hostile attention from either side. The near-revolt that followed the desegregation of the Law School in 1957 confirmed in his eyes that public perception that the university favored radical racial change (even if it didn't) could destroy the sense of balance and control that Branscomb needed to keep his long-term strategy of gradual desegregation on course.

The sit-ins, however, were something far worse than an "incident." The black (and some white) students who sat in at the lunch counters were far different from the naive Henry Wallace supporters of 1948, whom southern university presidents condemned for unrealistic idealism. These new students did not just disagree with acknowledged authority figures about the proper speed of racial change. Rather, with the sit-ins, they directly challenged the authority of the white establishment itself. They insisted that they, too, had a right to make decisions. To a man who worried about problems that might arise from black students playing intramural basketball with whites, this must have seemed apocalyptic.

If Lawson had been willing publicly to disavow continued leadership of these students, the episode might have ended relatively quietly. Branscomb, desperate to prevent an explosion in the Vanderbilt boardroom, wanted Lawson to repudiate the protests. Lawson was ready to give substantial ground but could not possibly end his support of the sit-ins. Several high-ranking university administrators (but not the chancellor himself, who never met Lawson during this entire episode) spent several days trying to craft some compromise statement, but time ran out.[84] A regular meeting of the board's executive committee was scheduled for March 3, 1960, Good Friday, and Branscomb raised the issue there. (Much later he admitted that this had been a mistake.) He may well have feared that the board would act unilaterally, or he may have wanted to distribute responsibility. Quite possibly, he knew that there would be no way to avoid it. Both Stahlman and Robert Sloan, a trustee whose downtown store was a particular target of demonstrators, were not likely to let Lawson's status at Vanderbilt go unremarked. Branscomb brought Robert Nelson, the dean of the Divinity School, along to the meeting, hoping, apparently, that Nelson could help persuade the trustees to delay any action until Branscomb could figure out a solution. Nelson, however, only irritated and provoked the committee with references to Christ standing before Pilate. There would be no reprieve for Lawson.[85]

Branscomb probably did not want to expel Lawson. Of all the possible moves that he could make, that was the one most likely to focus negative attention on Vanderbilt. But the arguments that he had used for years to persuade the trustees to accept gradual racial change on campus left him ill-prepared to counter their rage at Lawson and the movement in general. Since 1946 he had contended that following the judgment of educated white men was a prerequisite to peaceful, constructive race relations in the South. Now, groups of young black students openly scorned that judgment and tried to seize control of race relations from their elders, both white and black, threatening public order. Branscomb, too confident of his own ability to control events, had clearly not anticipated such a turn. When this crisis came, he found himself with his flank exposed. Nearly two decades of careful argument for controlled racial change left him with no principled basis for resisting the board's impulse to punish the "arrogant" Lawson. The executive committee gave Lawson a choice: they would allow him to withdraw from the university or face expulsion the next day. Branscomb must have desperately wanted him to withdraw and may well have been responsible for even offering the choice, but Lawson chose expulsion.[86]

By any measure, this was a bad situation. In ordinary circumstances Branscomb would have been able to temper the negative impact of the expulsion with some well-placed phone calls and letters. But these were not ordinary times. He tried to manage the story so as to minimize the damage, but his explanations seem confused. Branscomb's public justification for Lawson's expulsion was both uncharacteristically murky and singularly unconvincing. "The University's position," Branscomb repeated for months, "was not to oppose the sit-in movement, nor to discipline the individual for possible infringement of a particular law, but to state that no student could remain in good standing who in a potentially riotous situation commits himself to an organized program of deliberate violation of law."[87] This makes little sense. Other Vanderbilt students deliberately violated the law as part of an organized program and the university did not punish them. And Lawson had not, in fact, broken any laws at all—he did not participate in the sit-ins, he taught nonviolence to those who did.[88] Further, Vanderbilt itself had intentionally broken Tennessee segregation laws when it admitted Joseph Johnson to the School of Religion in 1953. Then, Branscomb argued that Vanderbilt could disobey the state statutes because they were probably unconstitutional. It is difficult to see any principled difference between that decision and Lawson's insistence that the laws requiring segregation in lunch counters did not have to be obeyed. Branscomb wrote letter after letter attempting to make his position clear but he never succeeded. This was mostly, one suspects, because he did not believe it himself and it was not the real reason for the expulsion.[89]

Far more convincing was something he said in a letter to Liston Pope of the Yale Divinity School, who was scheduled to speak at the dedication of Vanderbilt's new chapel later in March. This letter was frank and personal, written in a tone that bears no resemblance to Branscomb's stiff semi-official pronouncements.

> When we accepted Negroes without any legal requirement to do so, the protest of Vanderbilt alumni was wide spread and threatening. We succeeded in getting the Board of Trust to support the policy which had been recommended. We have, furthermore, eliminated segregation in all official university occasions and in the dining halls of the University, and in some other general respects. I had discussed with Dean Nelson moving next on the dormitory issue, if wise arrangements could be made which would start with the Divinity School students. I am frank to say that if we must support so dramatic an insistence upon civil disobedience in the face of the mayor's efforts to solve the problem by mediation and legal recourse, I have no hope of being able to hold the policy on which we are embarked.[90]

The second and far more destructive phase of this episode began when Lawson's expulsion set off a faculty rebellion. The faculty of the Divinity School followed the progress of Lawson's case with rapt concern. To them, Lawson was a man answering a high Christian call and a powerful symbol who touched deep chords of moral guilt. They were infuriated and dismayed at the shabby treatment meted out to him by Branscomb and the board. Over the next few weeks there was a tumult in and around the Divinity School. In downtown Nashville, the sit-ins continued and an atmosphere of crisis prevailed. Lawson was arrested as a co-conspirator in violating Tennessee commerce statutes and was bailed out by his former professors. Representatives from the Divinity School faculty, including Bard Thompson, James Sellers, and Lou Silberman, began a series of unsatisfactory meetings with Branscomb and Vice Chancellor Rob Roy Purdy, hoping to find some way to get Lawson reinstated. At the same time, a rift developed between Nelson and the faculty, who were unhappy with what they perceived as his weak leadership. When Liston Pope arrived to speak at the dedication of the school's new chapel, named after former dean Jack Benton, he sharply criticized Vanderbilt for expelling Lawson, reserving his only praise for the theology faculty who opposed the expulsion.[91]

Several tense and sometimes bizarre weeks of negotiations between the divinity professors and the administration followed. The faculty, at times consulting with sympathetic trustee Hugh Morgan, tried again and again to find some way to reinstate Lawson. On May 26 they tried instead to bring Lawson back for the summer session through regular admissions procedures. Branscomb was furious. Whether or not it was so intended, he took the faculty's request for Lawson's readmission by the 28th as an ultimatum and on May 30 flatly denied it. That evening eleven members of the Divinity School faculty sent their resignations to Branscomb at his home. (Dean Nelson had resigned earlier in the day.)[92]

These resignations opened a fundamental rupture between Branscomb and the board. Whatever doubts he may have harbored about Lawson's expulsion, Branscomb was more than half-convinced that he had to do it to protect Vanderbilt. This crisis, though, was another matter entirely. In the resignations that he read in his living room, he saw the death of the modern university he had dedicated his life to building. The executive committee of the Vanderbilt board, on the other hand, saw only another challenge to their personal authority. And, although there were members of the larger board with a broader view of the situation, it was largely the executive committee members—local, conservative, committed to retaining southern ways—who were responsible for dealing with the fallout of the Lawson expulsion. These men were determined above all to maintain their power, to punish anyone audacious enough to resist duly constituted authority. Some of them even received news of the resignations with something like delight, as it gave them a chance to demonstrate their resoluteness. "I am personally hopeful," wrote James Stahlman to a friend, "that the number of overdue resignations will subsequently relieve the situation on campus. You may rest assured that the Board of Trust isn't going to be pushed around by faculty, students, foundations, or what-have-you." Branscomb received similar expressions of support from quarters that must have been horribly galling. Bitter-enders, formerly his worst critics, rushed to embrace him. Sims Crownover, who had led the alumni revolt against the desegregation of Vanderbilt's Law School in 1956, sent a letter glowing with good feeling. "At that time [1956] I was concerned lest our great Southern Institution with a heritage and tradition second to none was in a process of degeneration. However, those fears have now been dissipated by the manner in which you have handled the Lawson matter. Please allow me to retract anything I may have said about you in the past and let me offer you my complete approval and cooperation. . . . I am proud of you."[93]

The losses in reputation and financing that would befall Vanderbilt because of the resignations obviously did not trouble these men. As far as they were concerned, the approval of the northern foundations was a dubious honor, many of these "highly regarded" professors were troublemakers who would not be missed, and the goodwill of alumni in Alabama and Mississippi was far more valuable than a reputation for academic excellence in the North. Trustee Robert Garner, scolding a divinity graduate student, clearly demonstrates what they perceived was at stake—the supremacy of the board's judgment and authority.

> I think it is necessary to realize that the legal existence of the University is based on the authority and responsibility of the Board of Trust. Grants and contributions, including those to the Divinity School, which over the years have made possible Vanderbilt's growth and progress have been made on the condition that they will be administered by the Chancellor under the authority of the Board. Obviously the responsibilities of the Chancellor and the Board extend to insisting that the affairs of the University be conducted in an orderly manner so that its resources can be applied to the purpose for which they were contributed. It seems to me not unreasonable to expect that those who are receiving employment and benefits out of these resources should give weight, not only to their personal sentiments and consciences, but to their responsibility and decent regard for the welfare of the University.[94]

Vance Alexander, a friend of Stahlman's, articulated a similar vision of university governance. "Personally," he wrote Stahlman, "I wouldn't care if all of [the divinity faculty] resigned. . . . I really believe that Vanderbilt would be much better off if they had no School of Religion as long as students and the faculty attempt to run the school." Alexander was not clear about who, exactly, ought to be running the school if not its faculty.[95]

Stahlman editorialized in the *Banner* that these resignations were in "the best interest of the university," but Branscomb knew better.[96] National newspapers covered the story, and outside the South the attention was entirely negative. Job offers poured in to the professors who had resigned, seminaries adopted resolutions of solidarity, and condemnations of Vanderbilt were legion. If he could not stop the departure of this faculty, Branscomb would be unable to recruit a new one of any real quality.[97]

So, on June 1 Branscomb began a new round of negotiations with the Divinity School faculty, trying to work out some compromise that would allow them to withdraw their resignations. Discussions hung up over the issue of Lawson's readmission, a bottom line requirement for the faculty. Also discouraging was Branscomb's willingness to discredit the faculty in the press, unfairly characterizing them as "unreasonable men who would not even discuss with him and Mr. Vanderbilt [their] differences."[98] Ominously, discontent began to spread to the other faculties of the university. Several professors in the Medical School and the college now also seemed likely to resign.[99]

Despite Branscomb's harsh tactics, he badly wanted to end the episode. By June 9, with the help of Dr. Charles Roos, a physics professor, Branscomb and board chairman Harold Vanderbilt worked out an agreement with the faculty members. After all the tumult, the deal was fairly simple. Lawson would receive credit for his spring semester classes by examination, and Branscomb would then recommend to the board that they grant him his degree. The divinity faculty would withdraw their resignations.[100] That afternoon Branscomb took the agreement to a meeting with the board's executive committee. In a truly reckless decision, this small group of men, unrepresentative of the larger Vanderbilt board—James Stahlman, John Sloan, Eldon Stevenson, Cecil Sims, Orrin Ingram, and William Waller—refused to accept it.[101]

When the campus found out, all bets were off. Now, large numbers of faculty outside the Divinity School became involved. On June 10, 161 professors (out of 195 contacted) signed a petition, which they distributed to the press, expressing shock at the committee's action. They urged quick resolution on the terms agreed to by Branscomb and Harold Vanderbilt. The national press returned to campus.[102]

Branscomb was left with little choice. He could do what the board members wanted and allow Vanderbilt to self-destruct. He could resign, with the same result. Or, he could make a last-ditch attempt to save the school in spite of the trustees. On June 13, over the objections of the executive committee and in the belief that the larger board would support him, Branscomb issued his own statement to the faculty.[103] He scolded the Divinity School faculty and unfairly placed the blame for the executive committee's rejection of the settlement agreement on Dean Nelson, but otherwise he recapitulated the earlier agreement in a clear and straightforward manner. He accepted Nelson's resignation, allowed the other Divinity School faculty to withdraw theirs, and provided that Lawson could receive his degree either by transfer of credits or by examination. He then pronounced the matter closed.[104]

And, surprisingly, it *was* closed, although the recriminations lasted for decades. Everyone on campus seemed to realize at the same time how close to disaster they had come.[105] The Divinity School faculty withdrew their resignations on the evening of June 15 and the Vanderbilt board acquiesced. They did not fire Branscomb, but many trustees, especially the members of the executive committee and their allies, now regarded him with fury and derision. In a cruel blow, even their own chancellor had publicly defied their authority. Vance Alexander complained angrily to Stahlman that "several Nashville students have written me that the Chancellor has gone back on the Board and has gone back on his word, and some of them are so bitter that they hope he leaves Vanderbilt. . . . He did not act in keeping with the resolutions of the Board of Trust and if he had followed the resolutions he could have gotten out of trouble and stayed out of trouble. We gave him a chance but he would not take it."[106] Two days later Alexander was still fuming. "Personally, I am afraid Branscomb is a negro sympathizer, he has shown that all along. . . . I, like you, believe that the fat is in the fire and it is going to hurt Vanderbilt much more in view of the stand taken by the Chancellor than it is going to help the school. He has made his bed, let him lie in it."[107]

Several other trustees and prominent alumni were also bitter, reaching beyond the Lawson episode to the whole array of changes that Branscomb had brought to Vanderbilt. J. P. Norfleet traced the beginning of the current woes to "one of the greatest mistakes ever made in the history of Vanderbilt University," the admission in 1953 of Reverend Joseph Johnson to the School of Religion. "I have been a great admirer of Chancellor Branscomb," Norfleet wrote to James Simpson, "but have never subscribed to his liberal views with reference to the negro problem. I think when we took the first negro into our Theological Department about 7 years ago we laid the foundation for all of the trouble we have been having."[108] Other prominent alumni, friends of the trustees, agreed. Another alumnus joined Norfleet in bemoaning the fact that blacks had ever been admitted. "The fact that they were 'theologs' did not affect the social status and that is the seat of all the trouble. Give them an inch and they will demand more. . . . That breach with Southern traditions brought no credit and plenty of grief upon the school."[109] W. F. "Babe" Murrah, a Memphis attorney and associate of both Stahlman and Vance Alexander, made it clear that he believed the root cause of the school's trouble was the changes that the chancellor had made over a period of years. These changes were the very ones that had led to steady progress in Vanderbilt's quality and reputation, but Murrah saw only "radical elements that have infiltrated the student body and faculty at Vanderbilt." His contempt for the chancellor was pretty thorough. "It takes a strong man with the right convictions at the head of an institution to keep it on the right course and combat such insidious penetration. I think Branscomb has made a miserable failure and shown inexcusable weakness in handling the situations that have arisen at Vanderbilt during the past several years, resulting in lowering the Vanderbilt standard and destroying some of its most cherished traditions."[110]

These observations contained at least some truth. Vanderbilt under Branscomb had indeed become an utterly different school than the one that these aging men had attended. Rather than lowering standards, though, Branscomb had raised them almost immeasurably. It was true that northern faculty and students now made up a large part of the campus population, and their talent and ambitions helped bring the university national prestige. The Divinity School in particular, which drew the wrath of several trustees for its betrayal of "old time" religion, was one of the most respected in the country. Branscomb's strategy of easing racial restrictions over time had made it possible for Vanderbilt to focus attention on the business of building a great university rather than on figuring out ways to fight off outsiders.

Ironically, though, these very changes had left the chancellor's *other* flank vulnerable during the Lawson episode. The new faculty members that Branscomb had aggressively recruited, whether northern or southern-born, had their eyes firmly fixed on both their own academic success and their school's national reputation. They had, by and large, bought into Branscomb's vision of Vanderbilt as an elite national research university. They would not simply sit back and watch it be destroyed in the name of an anachronistic southern tradition. However well the expulsion of Lawson may have played in Memphis or Birmingham, it was a disaster in the national academic community, calling into question Vanderbilt's commitment to fundamental principles of university governance as well as its commitment to racial justice. While the racial issues that surrounded the expulsion were inflammatory, the executive committee's total lack of regard for any faculty authority was equally important in provoking the crisis.

When all was said and done, despite the horrific national press and the deluge of horrified mail, the damage to Vanderbilt proved limited and temporary. Even during the worst days of the crisis, Branscomb kept in close contact with the people who really did have the power to hurt or help Vanderbilt—not the Alabama alumni, but the AAUP, the Rockefeller Foundation, the Carnegie Corporation, and the Ford Foundation. He kept them informed and did his best to articulate a reasoned basis for Vanderbilt's actions. He assured them that the escalating conflict did not call into question the university's commitment to a gradual program of desegregation, and that there was no chance of backtracking. This effort was effective. In September 1960, just months after the end of the crisis, the Ford Foundation announced its support of Vanderbilt with a $4 million challenge grant.[111]

The Divinity School suffered the most. In 1957, when he hired Nelson, Branscomb had confided to Duke University chaplain James Cleland that "my major contribution to education over the years is to be, I believe, the hope of bursting into full flower of the Vanderbilt Divinity School."[112] This did come to pass, but only for a brief while. Although the disgruntled faculty members returned to the Divinity School, its reputation was severely damaged. In November the American Association of Theological Schools placed the school on a year-long probation. (Although the AATS investigation was triggered by the expulsion of Lawson, its chief concern was the institutional powerlessness of the Divinity School faculty.) Gradually, its best faculty began to drift away to other schools. The search for a new dean was, not surprisingly, a difficult one. Still, the school held together and eventually recovered a good deal of strength.[113]

In spite of the fact that he shepherded Vanderbilt through to safety, Branscomb's disappointment was profound and his sense of betrayal was lifelong.[114] He was, he thought, unfairly branded as an opponent of civil rights when all along he sought only to ensure that the Vanderbilt board would not back away from the admission of blacks. He came to believe—not completely without reason—that he was the only person who cared more about the future of the university than about a personal agenda. This led him to view his opponents, especially Dean Nelson, as enemies of Vanderbilt who were intent on destroying it. At the end of that June, as the tense resolution was reached and press coverage died down, he searched for the meaning of the episode and for some kind of redemption. Attempting to salvage what remained of his long-held beliefs about racial change in the South, Branscomb indulged in uncharacteristic wishful thinking. "I believe, though it is too early to say this for sure, that we have emerged as the leader of the Southeast in this area of race relations, namely, that we are going forward with constructive steps, but do not yield to demands for radical campaigns that cannot be sanctioned or supported by institutions which are largely Southern in constituency, control, and support."[115]

After the drama of the Lawson episode, Vanderbilt's final desegregation seems an anticlimax. For roughly the next two years the university continued to admit blacks on the limited basis that Branscomb first outlined in the early 1950s but regulated the activities of the black graduate and professional students on campus with a heavy hand. Vanderbilt still did not house black students, but they were able to eat in the school's dining halls. Black student were allowed to sit with white students at sports events. When a black law student wanted to play on an intramural basketball team, though, Branscomb told his classmates that while he could play against the other graduate and professional schools, it would be best if he sat out against undergraduate teams, as there might be "episodes or controversies arising out of the heat of the battle." More than anything, Branscomb wanted to avoid "episodes." This, rather than any personal feelings of discomfort or abstract disapproval, seemed to be what drove his ad hoc regulations. Discussing the inevitable "problem of dormitories," for example, Branscomb's only concern seemed to be which students would be most likely to accept black floor mates without drawing public attention.[116]

By 1962, it had become clear that it was time to finish this off. Discussion on campus would not die, and with the growing success of the grassroots civil rights movement Vanderbilt had begun to lose the aura of being advanced on race relations that helped it in the past with grant makers. Branscomb and Harold Vanderbilt agreed that the issue must be resolved before the chancellor's retirement. In his usual thorough way Branscomb began preparing.[117]

Even in 1962, most of Vanderbilt's conservative undergraduate body opposed desegregation. The Undergraduate Senate, after acrimonious debate, narrowly defeated a resolution calling on the board to desegregate the undergraduate schools. In a February campus vote on the resolution, with about 59 percent of the student body casting ballots, it was rejected again.[118] But there was strong support for desegregation elsewhere on campus, and Branscomb marshaled it. The student newspaper, the *Hustler,* under its editor Lamar Alexander (later governor, then senator from Tennessee), urged the university to proceed without delay in removing all racial restrictions. Alexander was encouraged by Branscomb, who brought him to a board meeting to discuss probable student reaction to desegregation.[119] The Graduate Student Council also supported an open admissions policy in a March 12 vote, favoring the opening of all graduate programs, including those at the master's level, to black students. In April 1962 the faculty of the undergraduate college endorsed a resolution that recommended abolishing racial restrictions in the admissions process.[120]

Also in April, the University Senate unanimously passed a resolution recommending that admission to all schools and programs be "based solely on considerations of individual merit." This body, revived by Branscomb in 1958, consisted of the vice chancellor, the deans, and ten elected members of the faculty. Branscomb served as chairman.[121] Almost certainly, given his history of behind-the-scenes orchestration, this resolution and the report that supported it were part of the planning for the May board meeting. The Senate rehearsed precisely the same arguments that Branscomb and Harold Vanderbilt were readying for the trustees, underscoring the unanimity of opinion at the school's highest administrative levels.

Branscomb presented this Senate report to the board in closed session at its May 4 meeting.[122] Predictably, it focused on concrete problems—above all, the near certain loss of both federal and foundation funding—rather than on moral or ideological concerns. Citing the end of segregation at the South's other prominent private schools, now including Duke, Emory, and Tulane, the Senate argued that failure to finish desegregating would hobble Vanderbilt. Their conclusion was clear: "if Vanderbilt is to exert its traditional leadership it must move promptly and decisively."[123]

To make this bitter pill easier to swallow, the report stressed that in the eyes of the faculty and administration, "the merit principle is paramount to all other considerations in student admissions," and few blacks could hope to meet Vanderbilt's high standards. Vanderbilt had admitted only twenty-seven blacks since 1953 (a mere seven had graduated so far), and with proper "administrative discretion" could keep the numbers low in the future. The inevitable problems such as housing, the use of athletic facilities, and social interactions, were likewise nothing that the administration could not handle with careful planning.[124]

To buttress the report's conclusion, Branscomb brought in Vanderbilt's Director of Sponsored Research and Grants to discuss the impact of federal contracts—worth nearly $4.5 million a year at this time–on the finances of the university. Dean Wade of the Law School sent in a letter commenting on Judge J. Skelly Wright's opinion in the Tulane lawsuit, which suggested that even private institutions might be subject to the Fourteenth Amendment.[125] Finally, Harold Vanderbilt spoke. He repeated many of the Senate's arguments, provided a summary of desegregation in southern private colleges, and again pointed out the extremely low number of black students at Vanderbilt. "Vanderbilt was the first private Southern university to begin to integrate," he concluded, "but it had not since then kept pace with many other Southern universities." He was now convinced, he told his colleagues, that "complete integration of Vanderbilt can no longer be delayed if we are to preserve our status as a national institution."[126] After brief debate the board agreed. The vote, while not unanimous, did not leave any acrimony and the board was not badly split.[127]

Still, the trustees were not entirely at ease. They mandated that the chancellor use "care and discretion in implementing this policy, with the view of insuring a continuing atmosphere conducive to learning, study, and good conduct compatible with the high traditions of Vanderbilt University." They also immediately passed another resolution, introduced by James Stahlman, which required that applications from blacks, or "any other applications which might be considered questionable," be reviewed by the dean of the school, the vice chancellor of the division, and the chancellor. They were willing to admit black undergraduates but not willing to entrust their admission to the faculty.[128]

The change provoked little reaction. There are a handful of letters in the files of Branscomb and Stahlman, about evenly mixed between approval and disapproval.[129] The *Hustler,* under new editor Roy Blount, was happy.[130] The faculty of the Divinity School adopted a resolution expressing "its delight over the action" and its "profound thanks [to the Chancellor] for his leadership in the accomplishment of this epochal event." Again Branscomb turned to the major foundations, this time to report the good news.[131]

Branscomb also announced at the May 1962 board meeting that he would leave the chancellor's office on August 31 or as soon thereafter as his successor could assume his duties.[132] In a speech to the faculty, Branscomb, now a "lame duck," showed more interest in Vanderbilt's future than in its past. In a single paragraph he reviewed the accomplishments of his last sixteen years—faculty more than doubled, thirty-one new buildings, library holdings increased from 470,000 to 840,000 volumes, endowment multiplied two and one-half, a leap in the quality of teaching and research—and recounted the struggles, including that over the admission of blacks, to define the institution and its relationship to society. In the next ten pages of the speech, Branscomb talked about the university's bright prospects. The continuing support of the foundations, including another $6 million from the Ford Foundation, coupled with now substantial alumni contributions, left Vanderbilt on the verge of another leap in quality and prestige.

But Branscomb went on, almost scolding the faculty that it must remember that Vanderbilt was still in and of the South. "In the last analysis, it must be recognized that no university can be built without substantial support in its own region. You cannot build a great university out of New York or Washington. The maintenance and further development of the respect and pride of our own region is an essential for the realization of the aims and purposes of this institution. The administration and the faculty must never forget this; no institution can cut itself off from its society."[133] Such a reminder would have been utterly unnecessary when Branscomb arrived at Vanderbilt, a deeply southern institution, in 1948.

IV

At Tulane University, the search for Rufus Harris's successor began in 1959. For the first time, the Board of Administrators authorized a faculty advisory committee to assist in the task, and this committee saw desegregation as a major consideration.[134] The new president, they said, "should recognize that during his tenure of office desegregation will be one of the crucial problems facing educational institutions, private as well as public. He should be capable of furnishing leadership to the Board, the faculty, the student body, the alumni and the general public in arriving at an equitable solution of this problem which will reflect credit on both the University and the region."[135] President Harris's longtime secretary and close confidant Kathryn Davis took the bold step of writing board chairman Joseph Jones with her own thoughts on the matter. Miss Davis argued that the next head of Tulane ought to come from the ranks of Tulane's professoriate. The disadvantages of bringing someone from outside were many, "not least of which would be to find someone acceptable to not only the South but also New Orleans. Not only must he—and his wife who is a most important campus personality—be accepted here but he and she must accept us and accept segregation and drinking and Carnival (many people are against these things!) and yet go to church and know how to handle themselves with these other things."[136]

The Tulane board did not follow Miss Davis's advice, shrewd though it was. They hired instead a man who was an outsider in almost every conceivable way.[137] Herbert Longenecker was a northerner, a native of Pennsylvania. A chemist, he was educated entirely at Penn State, where he received his B.S. in 1933, his master's in 1934, and his Ph.D. in biochemistry in 1936. He went abroad as a National Research Council Fellow in the biological sciences, studying at the University of Liverpool, the University of Cologne, and Queen's University in Kingston, Canada. Longenecker taught chemistry for eight years at the University of Pittsburgh, becoming dean of research in the natural sciences in 1942. He held that position concurrently with the deanship of Pitt's Graduate School from 1946 until 1955. He came to Tulane from the University of Illinois, where he was responsible for the university's professional schools in Chicago, including a graduate college, medicine, dentistry, nursing, social work, the University of Illinois hospitals, and related research institutes.[138]

Longenecker was a generation younger than Rufus Harris and had reached professional maturity in an environment that was far different from the one that nurtured his predecessor. He had spent his entire academic career in large, northern, public institutions. His style, for both good and ill, was that of a bureaucrat. The kind of personal leadership that had always been the hallmark of small southern universities was not familiar to Longenecker. Harris's total identification with Tulane was not to be repeated, was, in fact, probably not repeatable. Harris well understood the situation Longenecker was walking into and shared his thoughts in a letter he wrote on his last day in office. "I wish," Harris told his successor, "that I could express some measure of the warm good wishes I have for you. I have every confidence in you and in your intent and ability to direct Tulane's course wisely into another generation. . . . I do know the stumbling blocks ahead, and believe me, I will be rooting for *you* and will be on *your* side, and always available to you for anything you want of me."[139]

Longenecker hit those stumbling blocks the minute he set foot on campus in April 1960.[140] With the New Orleans public schools under court order to integrate in the fall and the city's business establishment (unlike Atlanta's) unwilling to stand up to segregationists in the state government, racial tension was near a peak of hysteria.[141] As the crisis unfolded, it became a regular topic of discussion at Tulane board meetings. In May the University Senate asked the board to make a statement about the need to preserve public education in New Orleans. They refused, saying that "such a statement would be a disservice to the University and would have a detrimental result." They were more amenable to another Senate request, however, and agreed to look into the possibility of setting up a school (segregated, of course) for the children of Tulane staff, faculty, and students if the New Orleans public schools closed.[142]

Tulane administrators also spent much of May and June dancing to the tune called by the South Louisiana Citizen's Council, which had been "reliably informed" that Tulane was violating state segregation laws by allowing black employees to use "white only" drinking and toilet facilities. With offhand menace, the council's executive director, Jack Ricau, professed that he was trying to help out: "We are anxious to hear from you—to know that you will correct conditions in these matters—so that we can assuage those who have complained of the violations."[143] This letter set off a barrage of fact-finding on campus. Vice President and Comptroller Clarence Scheps had the business manager conduct a thorough census of which maids and custodians used which toilets. Scheps wound up stymied—although there seemed to be no problem with the employees, Tulane allowed black professionals to eat lunch when they attended meetings on campus, which was against the law. Despite counsel's repeated assurances that the Louisiana law was certainly unconstitutional, Scheps was troubled that he could tell the Citizen's Council only that Tulane was in compliance with the spirit of the law.[144]

Trouble came from another direction when Tulane students joined demonstrations and sit-ins organized by the Congress of Racial Equality (CORE) at New Orleans businesses. Although these sit-ins were not as successful as others around the South and soon ended, public awareness that Tulane students were involved was cause for alarm. After one of these students, Sydney Goldfinch, brought black friends to the snack bar at Tulane's University Center, the administration began to compile dossiers on the students, threatened them with the loss of their graduate school teaching positions, and generally made life difficult.[145] Tulane did not, however, expel them. The lesson of the Lawson episode at Vanderbilt had been well learned. In Longenecker's files, a copy of the *Christian Century* editorial of April 13, 1960, entitled "Vanderbilt Should Reinstate Lawson" is marked with his handwritten comment: "There is a significant lesson in the wide reaction to the hasty drastic step taken by Vanderbilt."[146] Outraged citizens, though, let Tulane know that allowing these "troublemaking students" to remain enrolled "will surely degrade your institution in the eyes of many." The South Louisiana Citizen's Council again weighed in, insinuating in an echo of the late 1940s that the students involved with CORE as well as two sympathetic Tulane professors were engaged in "subversive or Communistic activity" and that the university would do nothing about it because "Tulane is the recipient of numerous Grants from certain Foundations and therefore Tulane's hands are tied."[147]

Matters only got worse in the fall. In the face of federal court orders that required the New Orleans public schools to begin desegregating first grade, the Louisiana legislature enacted a series of laws designed to take control of the city's schools and shut them down. A restraining order from Judge J. Skelly Wright prevented this, but the state froze payroll funds meant for the city's teachers. Nonetheless, on November 4, four black children enrolled in previously white schools. White parents at these schools formed jeering, rock-throwing mobs. Mayor Morrison remained unswervingly focused on his own political future and denied any responsibility for the situation. The national press had a field day as the mobs gathered to scream and spit at children day after day.[148]

At Tulane, the faculty was unhappy. On December 14, 1960, the College of Arts and Sciences adopted a resolution that in rather intemperate terms called for an end to the street protests and for the governor and the legislature to stop fueling the discord and resolve the crisis. The next day, the graduate faculty proposed a slightly different statement, with the language toned down. This statement was signed by over three hundred Tulane faculty members and released to the press. This, together with a similar public appeal from a group of businessmen, was the first hint that anyone might possess the will to confront the crisis.[149]

As bad as all this was, however, it took money to really get the Tulane board's attention. During the fall of 1960, Longenecker and Joseph Jones had been overseeing the preparation of a proposal for a major Ford Foundation Challenge Grant. Tulane, now engaging in deep deficit spending, badly needed the money.[150] The foundation had already announced several of these very large grants, including the one to Vanderbilt, aimed at strengthening research universities. Talks with James W. Armsey, director of the Foundation's Special Program in Education, were going well and expectations were high. Armsey visited Tulane, however, at the very height of the chaos in the city's streets. He attended the board meeting on November 22, along with New Orleans Mayor DeLesseps Morrison, who apparently was there to assure Armsey that the present school crisis was temporary, that law and order would soon return, and that New Orleans was well able to solve its racial problems.[151] Armsey, though, was not assured. On December 8, at the next meeting of the board's executive committee, Joseph Jones reported that he had received a letter from the Ford Foundation "relative to Tulane's position in the matter of segregation." The following week, at a meeting of the full board, Jones explained that Armsey wanted a reply in advance of Tulane's application materials. He offered two possible statements, neither of which survives.[152]

One piece of evidence that sheds light on the board's debate about how to answer the Ford Foundation is a memorandum prepared by law committee member Marie Louise Snellings on January 24. She very quickly covered the basic legal quandary—that the original gifts to create Tulane and Newcomb (the women's college) were bound by restrictions that limited their use to the education of whites, but that Tulane later came to include the assets of the public University of Louisiana, giving the school a public aspect that would seem to require the admission of blacks. "However," she continued, "we have remained a private university, privately supported, and under the recent *Girard Case* which we followed with interest, the day is not yet here when the Supreme Court is ready to invalidate conditions such as Paul Tulane's and Mrs. Newcomb's as *contra bonos mores*. The day may come, anytime. But are we ready to seek it?"[153]

Mrs. Snellings's answer was no. While insisting that she had no personal objection to "the admission of a bona fide qualified negro applicant to Tulane University in the Graduate School," she had several reasons for declining to support such a move.

1. I fear the possible repercussions in the form of contests by the Tulane heirs and angry dissatisfaction among the alumni.
2. I do not see that we are forced to this decision at this point, and when the state of Louisiana is in a condition of upheaval and unrest in the public schools because of this question it seems an ill advised time to take such action. My loyalty to my home, my neighbors, and to the South and the burden of the problem she has had to bear compels me to say that I must vote to maintain our status quo at the present.
3. The last reason is very important to me. Any change we would make in our policy at this time would be caused, to all practical intent, by the possibility of the grant of money from the Ford Foundation. This I cannot do. Under no circumstances could I vote for a change which would appear to all the world as a sell out.

   If I had to guess, I would guess that I could vote for this change in good conscience somewhere from three to ten years hence.[154]

The letter that Jones finally sent to the Ford Foundation was exactly wrong. It was the sort of letter that might be expected from a board chairman with an inflated estimation of his own power and without any real understanding of the people, culture, and intertwined relationships of the philanthropic foundations. Jones produced an extraordinarily dense, four-page, single-spaced explanation of why Tulane would do nothing to desegregate. He leaned heavily on the language of Paul Tulane's 1882 donation, which stated that the funds were "for the promotion and encouragement of intellectual, moral, and industrial education among the white young persons in the City of New Orleans," and asserted that the administrators were bound by this language to continue barring black students. Any attempt to change this would be "improvident" because of the "dependence of the University upon the wholehearted support of the community and the very tense situation existing regionally respecting the racial question." Much of the rest of this letter is reminiscent of Hollis Edens at his windiest and touches repeatedly on the themes of the need to rely on the judgment of the board members and of Tulane's importance as a regional leader.[155]

Armsey forwarded the letter to Henry Heald, the head of the foundation, along with a very crisp summary and reaction:

> We are boxed in by legal restrictions; we cannot get out of the box except by instituting legal action; to do so now would be unwise, so we have decided officially to do nothing; we must ourselves decide our future course of action.

> In short, the legal status is segregation; the policy is to keep it that way; there is no intent to change; and there are no plans to do so.

> In this context, I don't see how we can continue to carry on discussions about a possible SPE grant to Tulane.

The following week Jones sent a supplemental statement, almost four more pages of reasons why desegregating Tulane was impossible. His patience at an end, Armsey wrote Heald what was really the bedrock statement of the situation: "Tulane *could* find ways to enroll Negroes if it really wished to. The reason it does not is not the legality of an original agreement; it is a current policy decision reached and maintained for reasons other than the founder's statement about 'white young persons.'"

Barely ten days later, Longenecker received a brief letter from Armsey declining to support Tulane's proposal.[156] Until this moment, Marie Louise Snellings had been right—the only problems caused by failing to desegregate were prospective. But by refusing to take the threats seriously, Tulane courted disaster and disaster came. And it was only that disaster, finally, that created a consensus on the board that they had to do something.

When they met on March 8, it seemed that the dithering might finally be over.[157] Longenecker had gotten a letter from Walter Martin at Emory about their desegregation, which he reported, and then he raised the matter of the Ford Foundation rejection.[158] Jones was a sudden convert, proclaiming that reconsideration of the admissions policy was now of "the utmost importance." After discussion, "it was the sense of the meeting that the Board recognize it is incumbent upon it, to the extent it legally can, to change the admissions policy, which on a controlled basis, would permit the admission of any qualified student to attend any college in the University." On April 12 the board approved the announcement of this decision. Longenecker also notified the presidents of the Ford Foundation and the Rockefeller Foundation.[159]

The dithering, though, was far from over. In spite of Joseph Jones's claim that "the action taken was bold and courageous," the statement that the administrators released was a masterpiece of equivocation. "Tulane University would admit qualified students regardless of race or color," it read, "if it were legally permissible."[160] The board maintained, however, that it was *not* legally permissible. Further, they had no plans to seek a declaratory judgment on the question. If they truly intended to desegregate the university, their failure to file such an action is difficult to understand. Although it is possible that the board feared bringing such an action because it would have to be filed in a Louisiana state court rather than in federal court, the most likely explanation of their refusal to ask for a declaratory judgment is that they were afraid of the reaction.

This concern is clear in the hiring of a public relations firm to help manage the news of their decision. In August a member of this firm accompanied Tulane's director of public relations, Horace Renegar, to New York to seek the counsel of a pioneer of American public relations, Earl Newsom. Probably not coincidentally, Newsom and his firm had deep ties to both the Ford Motor Company and the Ford Foundation.[161] Newsom, an old hand at crisis management, gave the Tulane representatives clear and cogent advice, identifying several possible strategies for dealing with "the spotlight of national attention." The first—the option he endorsed—was simply to admit qualified black students. Newsom pointed out that the administrators had acted for the past eighty years as if they were not bound by the restrictions in Paul Tulane's gift—except for the restriction against blacks. Admitting the students would "avoid a defensive posture in the face of the threatened lawsuit; it would implement the stated opinion of the Administrators on April 12; it would avoid the criticism inherent in excusing itself by legal inhibitions it had not heretofore recognized; it would align itself with the inevitable; and would take a position endorsed by a majority of the American people." A second option was to institute a suit for a declaratory judgment, which had the disadvantage of being unpredictable but was at least positive action. Finally, Newsom concluded, if the board failed to take any action on its own, they would certainly be sued and would then be left to claim that they welcomed the suit as a way to "clarify the matter." This was the worst possible choice because "it is inconsistent with the facts of University decisions over the years, and this inconsistency would immediately be exposed by thoughtful people all over the land—including editors and commentators. The Administrators would be put in the public position of recoiling timidly from prosecution of a line of action that the University has, in reality, consistently followed."[162]

The administrators, inevitably, chose the last option. One factor seemed to outweigh all others in their decision—the likelihood that most of white New Orleans, including the upper crust from which the school drew many of its students, would be angry about allowing blacks to attend Tulane. The administrators probably hoped that if they waited for someone to sue them, they would be seen by the white community as defending themselves rather than instigating more unwanted racial change in a troubled city. Rufus Harris later endorsed this explanation with his usual candor. In 1963 he wrote that Tulane had not desegregated earlier because of "a small group of illiberal members [of the board] who wanted a court decision ordering them to integrate, which they could hide behind." In 1962 an article in the student newspaper, the *Hullabaloo,* entitled "The Ford Foundation and Integration: Money Talks," stated it just as bluntly. "Sensitive as they are to public opinion in this region, [the administrators] were extremely reluctant to make any blatant shifts in admissions policy without having a fall guy on whom to pin the blame."[163]

So as applications from qualified blacks began to arrive, the Tulane board sat and waited to be sued. Too fearful to initiate legal proceedings in which they would argue for what they claimed they wanted—the right to admit any qualified student—they put themselves in the position of having to defend the exact opposite. The board minutes reveal a clear understanding that they would be sued and their carefully drafted response to black applicants seemed to beg for a lawsuit, confessing that the student would be admitted if it were legal.[164]

On September 1, 1961, Pearlie Hardin Elloie and Barbara Guillory, qualified applicants who had been rejected, filed suit in the federal district court to compel Tulane to admit them.[165] Tulane's administrators responded by vigorously trying to stop what they had announced they wanted. Not, they said, because they meant to keep blacks out—they asserted that they wanted them to come in—but because they wanted to defend the donor's wishes in an effort to find out if they were valid. Whatever it was they really thought they were doing, it did not take long before they found out they were playing with fire.[166]

On March 28, 1962, U.S. District Court Judge J. Skelly Wright, a New Orleans native and the man who had ordered the desegregation of the New Orleans public schools, granted the plaintiff's motion for summary judgment. Just as the administrators had feared throughout the late 1950s, Tulane's undeniable public aspects provided a wedge for a ruling that could strip away the school's independence. Wright declared that the racial restrictions in the original donations were unenforceable. But then he went much farther, ruling in sweeping terms that Tulane had sufficient public aspects to bring it within reach of the Fourteenth Amendment. Its refusal to admit black applicants was thus unconstitutional "state action." Wright enjoined the university to admit the plaintiffs.[167]

Tulane's trustees were horrified. They would never acquiesce in a decision that could conceivably make them subject to the whims of the Louisiana legislature. Wright's probably intentional failure to address one of the other issues—whether the heirs of Paul Tulane could now sue for the recision of his donation (or even the present value of that gift)—also caused consternation, in spite of the palpable lack of interest in such a suit on the part of the three Tulane sisters in St. Petersburg, Florida.[168]

Angered by Wright's decision and by the sarcastic language he directed at the university's board, Tulane immediately announced that it would appeal the decision. In a letter to Rice University's president, Kenneth S. Pitzer, Longenecker stressed that it was the uncertainty about Tulane's public status that prompted the appeal. "While it maybe said that Judge Wright's reference to Tulane University as a public institution is 'obiter dicta,' there is enough doubt about the meaning of his judgment to make it necessary for Tulane not to accept the decision."[169] Tulane's lawyers quickly shifted strategy when Wright was appointed to the Second Circuit Court of Appeals in Washington, DC, and was replaced on the New Orleans District bench by Frank Ellis. Rather than appeal, they filed a motion for a new trial, which Ellis granted on May 12, 1962.[170]

The board's refusal to accept Wright's decision brought varied reaction. While it certainly helped Tulane's reputation among staunch segregationists and with the Citizen's Council, it drew anger from other quarters. In correspondence with Mark Etheridge, a longtime friend and the editor of the *Louisville Courier-Journal*, Rufus Harris wrote,

> And speaking of good old Tulane, I somehow bleed for her. So much of the image of her stimulating life and action she has lost. That hurts, for it is so much easier to lose it than to form it. Better than anyone, I know her difficulty. She is in very bad trustee leadership and action. Too many new trustees came in who are too juvenile, materialistic and egotistic. They came within too short a period to be either trained or absorbed. You know so well that such training is frequently necessary if the fine university is to escape their basic ignorance and lack of sympathy or understanding of the nature of a great university and its raison d'etre. Even in the awful segregation conflagration—not to mention some other juvenile decisions—they have not permitted the University to manifest any leadership, or prepare the community for its responsible action and life in a desegregated society. Their posture of bitter enders is almost tragic.[171]

This correspondence is of particular interest because Etheridge was also a member of the board of the Ford Foundation. His reply to Harris indicates that Etheridge believed Tulane's administrators had deliberately misled the foundation about their intentions regarding desegregation (a problem that could easily have been avoided by filing a suit for a declaratory judgment):

> I share your sorrow over Tulane; in fact, I'm shocked at what seems to be the board's turnabout from what I had understood the situation to be. We on the Ford board were told that this suit was to protect the trustees, that the outcome was foregone and that the board would not vigorously appeal. That does not appear to be true. We voted Tulane $750,000, if I remember the figure correctly, in spite of the feeling of almost all the members of the board that we were not willing to vote money to private institutions which, if not legally bound by the Su-

preme Court decision, were at least morally so. I must say that in my own case had I known that Tulane was doing more than to protect itself from Paul Tulane's will, I would have voted differently.[172]

Longenecker and the board faced other complications in the spring of 1962. The local CORE chapter, reinvigorated after the 1961 Freedom Rides (in which Tulane students participated), was again organizing demonstrations and sit-ins at downtown lunch counters. Although internal problems led the now numerous Tulane student members to leave CORE in early 1962, these students were far from defeated. They responded by bringing direct action to the Tulane campus. In January and February, and again in April, they staged numerous interracial sit-ins in the cafeteria of the Tulane University Center. Longenecker and the board stepped very carefully, conscious that their litigation was pending. By and large, they simply tolerated the sit-ins, stationing security in the room but otherwise doing little. Only one student, Ed Clark, was suspended, and he was later allowed to return. Much of Tulane's faculty supported the students. The College of Arts and Sciences passed several resolutions urging that students not be suspended for the sit-ins, that the University Center be desegregated, and that black students be admitted. The board rejected these resolutions and prepared for the trial scheduled to begin that summer.[173]

The trial took place in early August, but Judge Ellis's decision was not handed down until December.[174] The months in between were difficult ones on campus. Faculty who favored desegregation suspected that the board was dragging its feet. The faculties of the College of Arts and Sciences and the School of Social Work both adopted resolutions that implicitly threatened resignations if the racial ban was not dropped soon. The College of Engineering, on the other hand, expressed its willingness to abide by whatever the board decided.[175] Students, almost equally divided on segregation, agitated on both sides. Cafeteria sit-ins began again in October, now with tempers flaring, fueled in part by the crisis over James Meredith's enrollment at the University of Mississippi. After violence nearly broke out during a cafeteria protest on October 8, the campus quieted down, but it was an anxious peace.[176]

On December 5, 1962, Judge Ellis announced his decision.[177] Tulane, he said, was a private institution that could not be compelled to admit blacks under the Fourteenth Amendment. However, following the reasoning of the United States Supreme Court in *Shelley v. Kramer,* Ellis also concluded that the racial restrictions in Tulane's founding documents were unenforceable. Whether the heirs could sue for return of the gift was uncertain, but the disinclination of Paul Tulane's relatives to do so, coupled with awareness of the federal courts' refusals to enforce any private racial restrictions, led Tulane's attorney to believe there was no danger. Two days later the board's law committee met and decided that Tulane would not appeal. On December 12 the full board endorsed this conclusion and voted to admit Barbara Guillory and Pearlie Hardin Elloie for the spring semester of 1963. Rufus Harris telegraphed his congratulations to Longenecker on December 13. Two days later, Mark Etheridge's *Louisville Courier Journal* praised Judge Ellis and the Tulane board for removing the "dead hand of the past."[178]

In the end, segregation at Tulane went out with barely a whimper. Although the university anticipated media coverage and possibly demonstrations at registration that spring, there were none. The first black student to register (out of eleven that semester), Percell Church, signed up for classes on January 24. Tulane registration officials reported, "It was an overstatement that not an eyebrow was raised. Very quiet. No one seemed to give a damn."[179]

V

At Rice, 1960 was a year of change. That January, the trustees proposed changing the school's name, replacing *institute* with the broader *university*. The new name took effect in July.[180] In August, President William Houston went on leave after suffering a heart attack. He resigned in September, when it became clear that he would not be able to resume his duties with full vigor. Provost Carey Croneis became acting president, serving while the board searched for Houston's successor.[181]

Determined to bring in a president who could lead Rice to greatness in an era of rapid change, the trustees chose Kenneth Sanborn Pitzer from the University of California at Berkeley. A native Californian, Pitzer received his B.S. in chemistry from the California Institute of Technology and his Ph.D. from Berkeley. The new president was a distinguished chemist, a member of the National Academy of Sciences, and a former chairman of the General Advisory Committee of the Atomic Energy Commission (AEC). In the late 1940s he was instrumental, as director of research for the newly established AEC, in crafting close ties between government and the universities. These ties figured large in the thinking of the Rice board, which had its sights set on greatly increasing federal research funding.[182]

The choice proved to be a wise one. Besides being a capable and well-connected administrator and politician, Pitzer, like Rice's first president

Edgar Odell Lovett, was a man of both vision and great energy. His tenure at Rice would be marked by huge gains in the quality and prestige of the school, as Pitzer dedicated himself to the expansion of the Graduate School, the strengthening of the humanities and social sciences, and above all the aggressive recruitment of talented new faculty members. He quickly put together a five-year plan that called for targeted expansion of certain departments, including a new department of space science, a substantial increase in the number of faculty, more graduate fellowships, and several new buildings. He also modernized Rice's primitive administrative structures, instituting, for example, a formal system of tenure for the first time. With his arrival came excitement and intellectual reinvigoration.[183]

Convincing Pitzer to take the job had required some concessions. Like William Houston, Pitzer was a deeply committed scholar and was determined not to take on a presidency unless he could continue his own research. George Brown and J. Newton Rayzor, the trustees who recruited him most actively, assured him that this would not be a problem. Potentially more troublesome, however, was segregation. Pitzer found the continuation of a racial bar in admissions at this time "just ridiculous" and made it clear that he would not come to Rice, indeed could not do the job that Rice wanted done, if the ban on black admissions was not removed. Surprisingly, Brown and Rayzor replied that "this was no longer a serious matter of controversy with the board." While the trustees had not actually voted on the issue, Pitzer believed that "Rayzor and Brown knew their colleagues . . . well enough" and that "there was no question in their mind, that once the legalities and . . . alumni relations, community relations, procedure, and so forth, were sorted out, that they would move."[184]

Rayzor and Brown's understanding of the need for Rice to end segregation was rooted in discussions surrounding the evolving nondiscrimination clause in federal contracts that began in the late 1950s and the effect this could have on their ambitions for a major federal research laboratory in Houston.[185] Research and instruction contracts with such a facility would provide enormous benefits to Rice in terms of money and prestige, allowing the school to use federal funds to strengthen its advanced programs in the sciences and engineering. Neither George Brown, who showed little interest in race relations at all, nor Newton Rayzor, who personally favored desegregation, would walk away from a deal that promised so much to the university in order to maintain a ban on black students.

Even before the board announced Pitzer's selection, the issue of nondiscrimination requirements came up again. In May 1961, economics professor Edgar Edwards received a grant from the Ford Foundation for a summer institute to be held on the Rice campus. The agreement required that admission be open to all qualified applicants, regardless of race. Newton Rayzor and Acting President Carey Croneis approved the contract, and two blacks attended the summer class. A likely consideration in this decision was Rice's pending application for a Ford Foundation Challenge Grant—the same grant that had been awarded to Vanderbilt in the wake of the Lawson episode and denied to Tulane just months before.[186]

At Pitzer's first board meeting as Rice's president, on September 27, 1961, his own research contract with the AEC—the one he had insisted on keeping as a condition of accepting Rice's presidency—became an issue. Newton Rayzor reported that "in view of the inclusion in the contract of a new and much more stringent non-discrimination clause," board member and Rice attorney Malcolm Lovett had reviewed the document. The board's Faculty, Student and Alumni Committee also thoroughly discussed it.[187] The majority of that committee wanted to approve the contract, but Rayzor (and certainly Brown and Pitzer) insisted that the full board face the issue. After lengthy debate, the board approved execution of the agreement.[188] The new clause, mandated by President Kennedy's Executive Order 10925 of March 1961, was much more detailed and required much more from contractors, in effect shifting the burden of compliance with federal policy onto their shoulders. It was not ambiguous. It ran to seven sections and filled a full page. The penalty for failure to comply was cancellation of the contract and loss of eligibility for future contracts.[189]

There was no mistaking the meaning of this decision. On Rayzor's motion, the trustees now directly addressed segregation at Rice:

It was also the sense of the meeting that the University's attorneys should be requested to give consideration to all restrictions contained in its charter and in the Indenture from William Marsh Rice pursuant to which the University was established, including those relating to the class or classes of persons who may be accepted as students, both undergraduate and graduate, and the charging of tuition [following the express direction of its 1891 charter, Rice imposed no tuition charges], and to advise this Board fully concerning their views and recommendations on ways and means of meeting and accommodating the operation and affairs of the University to broader policies of admission and employment more in keeping with the existing policies and requirements of other comparable institutions.[190]

Pitzer must have left this first board meeting hopeful that the problem of racial restrictions would quickly be solved. It would not, however, be quite so easy. Apart from Brown and Rayzor, two powerful voices, there was no real appetite for desegregation among the Rice trustees, no eagerness to step forward and make what they believed would be an unpopular change.

But the problem of securing badly needed money kept forcing them back to the issue. Throughout late 1961 and into 1962 the board was preoccupied with how to pay for the improvements that they had hired Ken Pitzer to oversee. In a memorandum to a board development committee, Carey Croneis (now Rice's chancellor) laid out the difficulty. To sustain any improvement, Rice would need to raise about $33 million over three years, with at least $11 million coming from foundations, including the anticipated grant from the Ford Foundation. Failure to do this, Croneis suggested, would lead to a bleak future. If the trustees decided that Rice should simply live within its current means, and with its charter restrictions against charging tuition and admitting black students, he was certain that Rice would "immediately lose all standing in the academic world. It would remain an unorthodox and altogether extraordinary anachronism in a fast-moving and constantly improving academic world. It would attract few outstanding students, hold few, if any, leading scholars, and deserve and probably receive very little additional financial support." The committee agreed to recommend to the full board that they begin a campaign to increase the endowment by $33 million by 1966.[191]

Happily, a major infusion of federal funds was now all but assured. After years of backroom politicking by George Brown and Albert Thomas—with the help of Vice President Lyndon Johnson—NASA announced on September 19, 1961 (a week before the Rice board approved Pitzer's AEC contract), that its new $60 million manned spaceflight laboratory would be built "on a thousand acres of land to be made available to the government by Rice University."[192] Well before this decision was made public, Pitzer had begun work on a comprehensive proposal for Rice to handle part of the new facility's research and instruction needs. In early August, Chancellor Croneis met twice in Washington with James Webb, NASA's administrator, and when the official site selection team visited Houston on August 24, they spent a day and a half with Rice faculty, administrators, and trustees discussing possible cooperative ventures.[193] By the end of the year Homer Newell, the director of NASA's Office of Space Sciences, had talked at length with Pitzer and Croneis about the general relationship between Rice and the Manned Space Center and had detailed negotiations with representatives of many of Rice's science and engineering departments. Although Newell made no specific promises at that time, it was clear that NASA contemplated funding a great deal of instruction and research at Rice.[194]

At the same time, the effects of the new executive order on nondiscrimination were making their way down to individual contractors. Pitzer's own 1961 research agreement with the Atomic Energy Commission was the first one that raised the issue of compliance, but it was far from the last. Throughout 1961 and 1962 Rice's lawyers and business manager struggled with the compliance forms, eager for the federal money but increasingly boxed in by the government's requirements. The national foundations also made it known to Pitzer that they had run out of patience, and that desegregation was now a prerequisite for approval of any grant proposals.[195]

At the board meeting in May 1962, eight months after the initial decision to seek legal advice on changing the charter, the close connection between the need to raise money and desegregation was apparent. "Mr. Brown opened discussion on the proposed fund drive . . . and court action to permit charging tuition, reporting on recent discussions [he] had with three of the Directors of The Ford Foundation. He stated that as a result of these discussions he was of the opinion that . . . our chances would be enhanced by dealing first with the matter of tuition and racial discrimination." Malcolm Lovett then presented a report on his firm's legal opinion regarding the proposed court action. The attorneys concluded that "the matter of a tuition charge was largely a detail of administration and not a departure from the purpose of the trust while the question of integration would be tied in more with the purpose of the trust; that if the Board is going to take this move it must go in for a specific purpose and the consent of the Trustees would be a prerequisite to such action." More than a simple board vote would be needed to make the change, although the board's approval was a first step. Rice's trustees had only deviated from charter language in the past with the express consent of the state of Texas, and they believed that such consent was necessary for this change as well.[196]

The extent to which financial consideration now set the terms of debate was evident in the discussion that followed. No one, apparently, contended that it was wrong or offensive or in violation of southern tradition to allow blacks to enroll at Rice. Instead, several trustees argued that taking steps to remove the bar on black admissions would hinder rather than help Rice's efforts to solve its financial problem. Pointing to community opposition to desegregation, they argued that "we would have a much better chance of raising funds without injecting the colored question." George Brown, however, never wavered. The issues of tuition and segregation, he answered, were secondary. The point was to bring in enough money for the school to pursue aggressively its program of expansion. Whatever it took to accomplish that was what Rice would do. And Brown, with his deep understanding of Washington, knew perfectly well that raising significant money was conditioned on changing the admissions policy.

Newton Rayzor immediately offered a motion to authorize the attorneys "to proceed forthwith to secure authority from the courts to charge tuition and admit colored people." It was seconded, but before the vote could be taken, several board members asked that before Rice acted, "an effort be made to build up sentiment in favor of these proposals." Brown was willing to go along with this but indicated that no more than another month should pass before moving forward.[197]

The board sent one of the governors, James W. Hargrove, to meet with the executive board of the Rice alumni association. At their June 5 meeting, Hargrove told the officers about the deferred motion to authorize legal action to remove the racial restrictions and the ban on tuition. After he succinctly described the financial and recruiting pressures that led the trustees to contemplate action, the group's secretary recorded that "the majority of those present felt that due to these changing times, we should set our personal feelings to one side and wholeheartedly support Rice."[198] Hargrove came back to the trustees with the impression that although some alumni would have objections, they were largely sympathetic to the moves. After yet another "full discussion," though, the board still did not vote on the original resolution authorizing legal action. This time, they decided that Malcolm Lovett needed to meet with the attorney general of Texas, who would be the defendant in any suit to change Rice's charter, to gauge *his* reaction.

While the board debated matters of timing and legal strategy, the rest of the campus remained largely in the dark. Soon after Pitzer arrived in 1961, English professor Wilfred Dowden, the chairman of Rice's chapter of the American Association of University Professors, approached him about the prospects for integration. Pitzer told Dowden that it had to happen soon and urged him to let this be known to the faculty. He also, however, suggested that the chapter not adopt a formal resolution, which he felt would be a tactical mistake.[199] In the meantime, segregation continued to hamper the recruitment of new faculty. Edgar O. Edwards, head of the Department of Economics and Business Administration, informed Pitzer of his failure to hire an established scholar for a full professorship. While the man was "greatly attracted to the opportunities which exist at Rice" and Edwards believed he had an excellent chance of bringing him on, that hope was abruptly destroyed. "When he learned that Rice was a segregated university at present," Edwards reported, "he terminated the discussion."[200]

Rice students now debated desegregation almost endlessly but seemed to have no notion that its demise on campus was near.[201] The sit-in movement captured attention at Rice as it did throughout the country. In April 1960 the *Thresher* surveyed campus opinion on the "sit downs," which had spread to Houston in March and numbered several Rice students among the participants. Every one of the nine people interviewed expressed some degree of support for the protestors, although several, including English professor Dowden, worried that race relations might be damaged by the sit-ins. In the same issue, *Thresher* staff writer Griffin Smith wrote a long piece that strongly condemned the movement on the grounds that the sit-ins violated the property rights of the store owners and suggested that only the "radical agitators of the NAACP" supported it.[202] Throughout April students wrote excited letters taking all sorts of positions, although the *Thresher* itself refused to take any editorial position at all. At the end of the month, the Rice Forum presented a panel discussion on black civil rights, bringing several Texas Southern University students and leaders of the Houston sit-ins to Rice for the event.[203]

While the local scene quickly settled down, with Houston's downtown lunch counters quietly desegregating on August 5, 1960, interest in racial issues continued to grow on campus.[204] The new staff of the *Thresher* kept the issue of desegregation alive on campus during 1961 and took an unambiguous stance against segregation. When five Rice students were arrested at a sit-in at the train station in late February, the paper praised them for their strong moral convictions. "The responsibility for the arrest of these young citizens does not lie with them. It lies with the outmoded and inhumane Southern institution of segregation. In the end, it lies with this community and all others like it which tolerate two classes of Americans."[205] In late November 1961 the Rice Student Senate passed a resolution favoring the elimination of racial restrictions in admissions and the use of Rice facilities. The Senate then sponsored a campuswide referendum on the resolution. More than 75 percent of the student body turned out for the vote, the largest total in Rice election history. The undergraduates approved the call for an end to segregation on campus by a 2 to 1 margin, the graduate students by 4 to 1, and the faculty by 8 to 1. Hopes were high that the vote would have some influence with the trustees.[206]

Alumni also pressed for change. "I realize that there are legal complications to [desegregation] because of the terms of the original endowment," wrote one alumna to Croneis in late 1961, but "surely these are not insurmountable in a time when the necessity of our witness to a belief in democracy is so important." Croneis assured the correspondent, and several others, that the matter was "receiving full consideration" from the board.[207]

In July 1962 Malcolm Lovett notified the board that attorneys in his firm were now preparing briefs on both desegregation and charging tuition and assured them that Rice would have "the full cooperation of the Attorney General."[208] Finally, on September 26 he distributed copies of the proposed resolution and the trustees voted. Unanimously, on a motion made by Newton Rayzor and seconded by Daniel Bullard, they approved a lawsuit to change Rice's charter to allow them to charge tuition and admit black students. Unanimity was achieved by having only the trustees, and not the governors, vote on the resolution. Still, apparently only one governor objected to dropping the restrictive admissions policy. At the same time, the trustees passed a resolution conveying the land for the Manned Space Center to NASA.[209]

Still, months passed and the school's attorneys did not file the petition. Pitzer grew increasingly alarmed. Sometime over the Christmas holiday in late 1962 or very early 1963 he drafted a letter to Malcolm Lovett, which he may never have sent. In it, Pitzer pleaded for action. He feared several things. First, the delay in filing the suit was holding back the desperately needed capital campaign. Pitzer worried that "enthusiasm related to Rice's part in bringing NASA to Houston and to our Semicentennial [will be] dissipated before the capital campaign can be started." What made Pitzer really uncomfortable, though, was that Rice was now alone. A joint funding proposal to a major foundation from the schools in the Council of Southern Universities had to be revised to make clear that Rice was the only one that was still segregated. Pitzer was aghast. "The longer this situation remains," he wrote, "the more Rice will be labeled as a provincial school apparently out of touch with national or even regional trends and the more trouble we will have overcoming the damage thus caused. One story in a national publication pointing out our slowness in acting to remove restrictions could do very great damage. We have been lucky so far; let us not stretch our luck further."[210]

Pitzer also feared reaction closer to home. He told Lovett that "the situation with respect to students and faculty is also becoming precarious. By the natural leakage of information . . . most of the faculty and student body are now aware of the situation and many know that the decision was really made last summer. I have been successful so far in explaining the delay on the basis of the need of legal preparation and later of the change in Attorney General. Frankly, I have no further explanation. I am seriously concerned lest the faculty and student body come to believe that this action is being intentionally delayed." In closing, Pitzer again emphasized the dire consequences of failure to act. He urged "immediate filing of our action and accompanying publication of the Board Resolution. Even a day of unnecessary delay should be avoided."[211]

Whether or not Pitzer sent this letter, the Baker and Botts attorneys began to act. On December 27, 1962, one of the partners handling the case, Dillon Anderson, wrote the new attorney general, Waggoner Carr, to inform him of the proposed suit and to seek a meeting before it was filed.[212] Finally, on February 21, 1963, Rice's attorneys filed the lawsuit. This suit, more than Emory's or Tulane's, went right to the heart of the changes in southern higher education since World War II. The outcome of Emory's action turned on an interpretation of Georgia tax law; Tulane's depended on the legal status of the university as public or private. Rice's lawsuit, though, revolved around the question of whether institutionalized racial discrimination destroyed the school's ability to advance, or even sustain itself at its current level of quality and prestige. Rice's legal team argued that the vast changes in the nation, the region, and in higher education since the time the university's charter was drafted in 1891 meant that enforcement of the restrictive clauses would undermine the broader purpose of William Marsh Rice's gift—the creation of a university of the highest order. On April 20 the Texas attorney general indicated that his office had no objection to the charter change.[213]

Reaction to the lawsuit was largely favorable. Dozens of alumni and friends of the university praised the decision. Fewer objected, although those who did were often scathing in their criticism.[214] Most alumni seemed to understand the board's reasons for the suit and to approve of them. Indeed, many correspondents expressed relief that Rice had finally taken action. "Certainly," wrote one alumnus, "a decade after the decision of the Supreme Court in the public school segregation cases is none too soon for Rice to begin considering applications from Negroes."[215]

Just as quickly, however, a misconception about the nature of the legal proceedings crept into the correspondence. Alumni, even the majority who approved of the action, understood the lawsuit to be a challenge to William Marsh Rice's will, not a petition to change the interpretation of trust language.[216] Opponents of the change made the same mistake, although more vehemently. Two enraged alumni could not wait for the postal service to convey their disapproval to the university. In a telegram, they protested: "Highly disappointed and amazed at incredible action of board seeking to destroy basic and crystal clear provisions of Rice will. Trust that court will not uphold this flagrant and arrogant violation of our benefactor's desires."[217] Pitzer, George Brown, Malcolm Lovett, and others tried repeatedly to convince opponents and supporters alike that no one was "breaking" Mr. Rice's will. In November 1963, at Rice's homecoming, Lovett gave a talk to the alumni association in which he carefully stepped through the reasoning that led to the lawsuit and the legal issues involved. These explanations, although well argued, were necessarily long and complex and were no match for the angry but simple rhetoric of the minority that wanted to stop change.[218]

Two prominent alumni were particularly determined. On September 20, John Coffee and Val Billups filed a petition in intervention, arguing that the trustees were forever bound by the literal meaning of Rice's charter, even if a literal reading destroyed the purpose of the charter. Any other interpretation, they argued through their lawyers at the Houston firm of Bracewell, Reynolds, and Patterson, would deal a fatal blow to certainty in wills and trusts. This intervention prevented the timely resolution of Rice's suit, forced a trial, and kept the university tied up in appeals for years.[219] The intervenors claimed repeatedly that they did not oppose the admission of blacks or the charging of tuition but merely cared passionately about the sanctity of testamentary documents. It is inconceivable, though, that they would not have known, if only through their lawyers, that the principle of deviation from the terms of a trust where compliance would defeat the accomplishment of its purpose was a time-tested principle of trust law.

In an astute note to Pitzer about the intervention, Carey Croneis quoted from a speech given by Robert Maynard Hutchins about twenty-five years before. "All alumni are dangerous. They see their alma mater through a rosy haze that gets thicker through the years. They do not know what the college was really like. They do not want to know what it is like now. They want to imagine that it is like what they think it was like in their time. Therefore they oppose all change. If changes are made *without* their approval, they are resentful. Since no useful change could ever be made *with* their approval, few useful changes have been made in higher education." Something like this seems to have been at the heart of Coffee and Billup's intervention in the Rice lawsuit.

Coffee revealed a good bit about his thinking in correspondence with a recent Rice graduate alumnus named James Aronson. While at Rice, Aronson had received a scholarship funded by and named after Coffee. When he heard about the intervention, he sought to return the money. In reply, Coffee asserted again that he did not object to the enrollment of blacks but claimed that the board had the authority to accomplish this without changing the charter. (Ironically, this also seems to have been Pitzer's position from the first.) The real heart of Coffee's complaint, however, was something quite different. "Investigation has shown," he told Aronson, "the Trustees decided on this course of action after repeated urging by Attorney General Kennedy, with attendant promises of huge Federal grants to our school. . . . Rice Institute as you and I know it—and it is a great school—would be no more if this happens." It is worth noting that Coffee referred to the school as "Rice Institute" rather than "Rice University," suggesting that he may have been displeased with the name change as well. That Coffee was generally unhappy with changing times is also suggested by a letter he wrote to the *Houston Press*. Coffee condemned the Rice trustees for several sins: seeking to "impose their aspirations for the growth of Rice University over the will of Wm. Marsh Rice," abandoning the undergraduate program in favor of graduate studies, wanting "instant integration," and adopting a new school song.[220]

The delay caused by the intervention created serious difficulties. Although Rice was trying to remove its racial restrictions, there was no longer any guarantee that it would succeed. By late 1963, Pitzer was desperate. That summer, the Ford Foundation told him that they would wait for the outcome of the lawsuit before deciding whether to make a grant to Rice.[221] Many other smaller complications arose. In the summer of 1963, for example, the chief of naval personnel, Vice Admiral W. R. Smedberg, let Pitzer know that he could not allow a Naval ROTC program to continue at Rice for much longer. To leave the unit in a school "where race or color would be a bar for entry to morally, mentally, and physically qualified applicants would not be within the spirit nor the intent of the [federal] equal opportunity policy."[222]

Above all, Pitzer was intensely concerned about Rice's relationship with NASA. While the university's current agreements with the Manned Spacecraft Center had been signed before new, more stringent NASA non-discrimination rules became effective, Pitzer feared that Rice would be deeply embarrassed when these agreements came up for renewal. These fears were justified. In August 1963 NASA sent him a copy of Federal Per-

sonnel Manual Letter 410–5, which prohibited federal agencies from select-
ing for training any facility that discriminated based on race. "The criterion
to be applied in each case is whether a qualified NASA employee would be
admitted to the facility without consideration of race, creed, color, or national origin." The new regulations would become effective on August 15,
1963, and included the following: "If training in process on that date is being conducted by a non-Government facility that does not qualify [under
the nondiscrimination rule] it must be terminated at the conclusion of the
current training unit." Pitzer worried that "the completion by Tulane of its
legal action with respect to racial restrictions leaves Rice exposed as the last
university of its type to complete this action. While our intentions are now
clearly on record, and this is most valuable, they alone cannot indefinitely
avoid serious detrimental effects upon the University."[223]

Also in late 1963, the Department of Health, Education, and Welfare
contacted Croneis about a faculty member's proposal for a summer language institute, calling attention to the contract's nondiscrimination clause.
In February 1964 Rice's director of placement notified Pitzer that the Internal Revenue Service refused to interview Rice students on campus. "It
was inferred from their conversation," wrote Evans, "as in the case of some
other government agencies, that they were not interviewing because of the
fact that no negroes are enrolled at Rice University."[224] Most disturbing to a
school in the midst of a new push for broad excellence, the delay left segregation as a major stumbling block in faculty recruitment. Several frustrated
department chairmen sent Pitzer copies of correspondence with heavily recruited scholars who turned down job offers over segregation.[225]

Pitzer did what he could on his own authority. At the time the board approved the petition for the charter change, Rice adopted a policy of nondiscrimination in its other relations with the black community. Pitzer outlined
this policy in a brief letter to two alumni. "In other areas, such as employment and attendance at special educational activities, lectures, etc., the University is following a non-discrimination policy. There were two Negro participants in a special summer institute for college economics teachers in
1962, and there is now one Negro employee at the professional research
level."[226]

Finally, on February 10, 1964, the case came to trial in state district court.
In one particularly revealing turn, the intervenors demanded a jury trial
and Rice's lawyers, probably fearing an appeal, agreed to it.[227] The intervenors still sought to keep the trustees bound to the four corners of the char-

ter. Rice presented overwhelming evidence that it was no longer possible for a university to be both segregated and "of the first order." The presidents of Southern Methodist University, the University of Texas, Texas Christian University, Trinity University, the University of St. Thomas, and the American Council on Education testified that segregation had been abandoned on nearly every American campus, that foundations would no longer contribute to the few segregated institutions that remained, and that federal funding for research, training, and facilities construction would also be cut off. Pitzer, George Brown, Carey Croneis, and Rice treasurer Leo Shamblin presented evidence that Rice's admissions policy, if continued, would cripple the school's ability to raise funds, keep faculty, and recruit students.[228] The jury unanimously agreed that William Marsh Rice had intended to create an outstanding university through his gift, and that maintaining segregation would make it impossible to carry out this intent. The judge, William Holland, entered judgment in favor of the university on March 9, 1964.

Although Coffee and Billups pressed appeals of the decision until 1967, this judgment allowed Rice to proceed with both desegregation and its ambitious fund-raising efforts. In his report to the board of governors in January 1965, Pitzer detailed the critical steps that had been taken. "One Negro, Mr. Raymond Johnson, with truly excellent academic qualifications, was admitted to graduate study in mathematics. . . . Also, I am signing the certification to Federal Government Agencies that we will comply with the Civil Rights Act."[229]

The fact that William Marsh Rice's will was never at issue did nothing to dissuade some angry alumni from condemning Pitzer and the board for breaking faith with a dead man. The passage of years (even decades) did not put this misperception to rest. At the end of 1966, the president of Rice's alumni association was still trying to soothe the feelings of disgruntled graduates who believed that Rice had somehow pulled a shady maneuver for its own secret purposes.[230] What these purposes might be remained somewhat vague, but more than one alumnus expressed the belief that the federal government—usually in the person of the nefarious Robert F. Kennedy—had struck a deal with the university to strip away its independence in return for cash. Although extreme, this notion reflected a more widespread distrust of the national government. This attitude baffled Pitzer, a non-southerner, who saw the federal government and its agencies as sources of sustenance rather than a threatening enemy. "I do not fully understand the attitude which seems common in this area in which people regard the Federal Government as a foreign entity rather than something which their own ancestors created and they themselves and their fellow citizens control."[231]

By 1961, the decision makers at these five universities were finally confronted with nonnegotiable demands. Whether from a foundation, the federal government, their own faculty, or all of these in combination, they received the message that there was no more room for evasion, ambiguity, or bitter-end posturing. They would either change or not. If they did, they would be rewarded. If they did not, they would be punished. Now. Not at some time in the future, after they had more time to weigh and balance, more time to consider the proper course. Now. Finally, it was the threat of immediate negative consequences that elicited a rather sudden change of heart among previously stalwart defenders of southern tradition.

Conclusion

After World War II the pace of change in the United States, and especially in the South, seemed dizzying. The region was utterly transformed in these years, becoming more urban, more industrial, and far more prosperous than ever before. Southerners, black and white, were better educated. Ties to the rest of the nation grew stronger as southerners moved North and northerners migrated to the South's cities to work for the major corporations now located there. Old economic patterns vanished and old social patterns along with them. On the region's private university campuses, a similar transformation occurred. There was a massive influx of money for research and a major expansion of graduate education. The undergraduate colleges, once all that existed of most of these schools, became less central as the institutions grew into larger, multifaceted enterprises. Faculties became less southern and more tied to their professional colleagues than their local communities. Students bodies grew more diverse and more able, challenged by standardized admissions tests and stricter entrance requirements. The campuses themselves expanded outward in every direction, sometimes growing into a tangled maze of new buildings with obscure purposes.

The presidents of these schools, because their jobs forced them to focus on the future, quickly grasped the changes in the postwar South and nation. They understood almost immediately after the war that the desegregation of their campuses was only a matter of time and that the universities could not truly excel until it came. For them, the central question was how to lead this inevitable change. Some—Harris, Branscomb, and later Deryl Hart and Ken Pitzer—led as boldly as they could. The others did their best to get by and stay out of serious trouble. There were, however, a few difficulties. The chief problem was that the university presidents did not control their universities—the trustees did. And the presidents could not make any changes, however delicate and carefully timed, without their permission. By and large, this permission was not forthcoming. To the mainly older men who served as trustees at these universities, the changes that took hold in the 1950s represented a fundamental and unwelcome upheaval. Before their eyes, their stable and secure world degenerated into something that they saw as near chaos. As the South opened up, as travel became easy and people more mobile, as a suburban middle class rose up around the cities, as blacks and whites alike owned televisions and refrigerators and graduated from high school, the relevance and the power of the local white establishment began to erode. Other influences became stronger. And the old guard could not do anything about it. They did, however, have the power to stop change on campus. No new admissions policy could be adopted without their consent. And so, frightened and angry about what they had already lost, the trustees fought with real passion to hold off any "deterioration" in the schools of their youth. Forced to swallow the camel, they strained mightily at the gnat.

The trustees uniformly claimed to endorse postwar efforts to bring these schools into the national mainstream academically, but their understanding of what that would mean was, in most cases, superficial. They were businessmen and lawyers, ministers and doctors, and they knew precious little of the intellectual life of the disciplines or of academic values. When conflict arose between the needs of academics and the values of upper-class white trustees and alumni, there was no question about which would prevail. Most of these trustees remained committed until the last possible moment to preserving the racial status quo in the South. In his memoirs, Duke chaplain Barney Jones described the problem as he saw it during Hollis Edens's tenure.

It had been my conviction for some time that, in particular, a number of clerical members of the Board were men of small stature and limited vision who were holding the University back. The generally conservative and provincial outlook of the Board was nowhere more evident than in its studied, southern-styled avoidance of the integration issue. They were determined to keep Negroes out of the University — at least as long as possible. Edens, who was conservative on the issue but able to transcend his provincialism, was determined that a wedge not be driven between himself and his Board. . . . At the same time, Edens did what he could to move the Board to take action on racial integration. He told me he would say to his Board that this was an urgent issue and that it was imperative that it be faced and resolved without delay. There would follow a prolonged silence around the table until at last the Chairman would ask, "Is there any *other* business to come before the Board?"[1]

The trustees' unwillingness to do what needed to be done only intensified as time went by. The effect of the Supreme Court's decision in *Brown v. Board of Education* was, at first, wholly destructive of hopes for peaceful desegregation of these schools. Resentment of growing outside interference, fears of the "socialist" leanings of the federal government, an unwillingness to bear even the slightest criticism from their friends and neighbors, and plain old-fashioned racism meant that a majority of trustees fiercely opposed lifting the color bar. The turmoil that followed the decision heightened all these emotions. Barney Jones captured this too. "Edens told me," he wrote, "that in his judgment had he made integration a condition of his remaining on in the presidency prior to the Supreme Court School Desegregation Decision, Duke would have integrated. But after that decision, he conceded, had he made it a condition, the board would have accepted his resignation. He reported that the mood of the Board was, 'We were about to integrate on our own, but now that the Supreme Court had ordered us to do so, be damned if we will!'"[2]

They did, though. Despite much wailing about southern tradition, when all was said and done the trustees traded southern tradition for concrete gain. The only arguments for desegregation they would listen to were those they saw as realistic or practical—that is, arguments that touched on the impact of segregation on *themselves*. Thus, moral arguments that centered on black equality in the eyes of God or democratic arguments that focused on black equality before the law fell on absolutely deaf ears. Justice, even ordinary fairness, was not a "practical" consideration. Arguments based on these notions, these men believed, were the hallmark of zealots who ignored reality. Like almost all people, though, their reality was bounded by their own vision. The fact that it was a very practical problem to a black man that he could not attend school near his family completely escaped them. Interestingly, almost no one (the only clear exceptions are Harvie Branscomb and Rufus Harris) understood that a zealous commitment to enforced racial separation was, precisely like its opposite, "a wholly doctrinaire position which ignores the facts of history and the realities of the present."[3]

It was only the imminent threat of harm to something *they* cared about that impelled the boards to accept desegregation. In and of itself, this is not unusual. It's the way people act all the time. What is remarkable, though, was that so many trustees were willing for so long to let their university be damaged rather than admit that segregation was a problem (even a practical one) or that outsiders could influence their judgment about it. A decade and a half of chronic trouble that sapped the morale of the faculty, discouraged new talent from coming to campus, made public relations a nightmare, and lowered the schools' reputations in the eyes of the nation had little effect. It took the immediate danger of drastic punishment, the prospect of decimated institutions, to make them change their admissions policies.

By 1960, though, the appallingly high cost of segregation was finally starkly clear even to the trustees. Through the relatively politically insulated mechanism of the executive order, every president since Harry Truman had strengthened the federal government's commitment to equality of opportunity. With the election of John F. Kennedy, the reach of federal nondiscrimination requirements in contracting finally extended into the admissions policies of the private southern universities. Failure to comply meant ineligibility for the federal grants and contracts that were the lifeblood of the advanced programs at these schools. In the private sector, the major philanthropies, some dedicated to southern education since before World War II, also ran out of patience. On top of that, many outsiders had somehow become insiders. Faculty members, recruited from all over the nation in the attempt to raise the quality and reputation of these schools, felt entitled to have a voice in decisions about who would study on their campuses. A new breed of university administrators also appeared on these campuses, men who were products of the complex, bureaucratic institutions of higher education that had evolved after World War II and who were above all hardheaded managers. Southern blacks themselves now insisted that their future was not a matter for the "educated white men of the South" to determine, that the time had come for the "theoretical idealism" of democracy and equal rights to be put into practice.

Where boards were led by chairmen with a broader vision of the world and a clear-eyed understanding of power politics, there was relatively gracious acquiescence. The recipe for change seemed to require both a willing president and at least one prominent board member who would exercise leadership in an effort to coax the more hidebound members of the board to act. Thus at Rice, which had seemed for years oblivious to pressure for racial change, George R. Brown firmly moved the board to initiate a lawsuit to remove the charter restriction on black enrollment. Similarly, at Emory Chairman Henry Bowden steered that board to a calm resolution. At Vanderbilt, still reeling from its open confrontation with the civil rights movement, Branscomb's final efforts at desegregating the school, aided by Harold Vanderbilt, were anticlimactic. At other schools it was not so easy. Tulane, still led by Joseph Merrick Jones, finally yielded only after it lost a major, desperately needed, foundation grant. At Duke, it took the ugly loss of Hollis Edens and a carefully plotted battle by his interim successor, Deryl Hart, to convince a majority of the trustees to do what was best for the university instead of what they personally preferred.

But the trustees, even many of those who favored making the change, denied that they had been forced to admit black students. "This action," wrote Duke trustee Bunyan Womble, "did not come as a result of any pressure or petitions but only after careful and intense consideration over the past few months." This completely ignores the fact that the careful and intense consideration was only necessary because of pressure from outside the board. Although the Emory board characterized their lawsuit as a way to battle state coercion (by removing Georgia's control over Emory's admissions policies), they too were effectively coerced into filing the suit. The major exception to all this denial was Marie Louise Snellings at Tulane, who understood clearly that a decision to desegregate in order to receive grants and federal money was a "sellout." Ironically, this honest assessment of the situation seemed to make it more difficult for Tulane to change. Backs stiffened when the pressure was perceived too clearly. It took, apparently, some measure of delusion to make the medicine go down.

The notion that these schools voluntarily desegregated is intimately tied to the concepts of control and authority that guided their actions during the decades after World War II. Even more than to segregation, the trustees of the private southern universities were committed to the belief that they had both the authority and the power to control their institutions free from any outside interference. Neither Yankees, nor "coloreds," nor the "socialistic" federal government, they believed, had the smallest right to claim any authority or to exercise any power in interference with the prerogatives of the white southern establishment. Only when authority had been openly wrested from them could racial change come.

Once it did, though, it quickly became apparent that segregation had been the last meaningful southern tradition remaining on these campuses. In the twenty years following the end of World War II, Duke, Emory, Rice, Tulane, and Vanderbilt had gradually become the same as their counterparts in other regions—better than some, worse than others, but of a piece with ambitious research universities across North America. The students had the same career goals, the faculty were trained in the same graduate programs and shared the same ethos of research and publication, the role of religion had eroded into the same oblivion as on campuses in Wisconsin or Indiana or Connecticut. Important changes in administration that had already occurred in the North, East, and West now took hold in the South. The presidents of these schools would never again be so personally rooted in the older traditions of the South or entwined so deeply with the particular culture of each campus. As the average tenure of university presidents grew shorter, they became managers rather than larger-than-life leaders with paternal commitments to their school, and the power that earlier presidents wielded was increasingly dispersed throughout a bureaucratic organization. In the clash between southern tradition and national prominence, southern tradition had been abandoned. With the demise of segregation, these elite southern universities finally joined the mainstream of American higher education. In the years to come they would compete on level ground.

Notes

INTRODUCTION

1. George B. Tindall, *The Emergence of the New South, 1913–1945* (Baton Rouge, 1967), 263–66. There are several good histories of the development of higher education in the United States, but they focus heavily on northern institutions. See, for example, Frederick Rudolph, *The American College and University: A History* (Athens, GA, 1990) and Laurence R. Veysey, *The Emergence of the American University* (Chicago, 1965). John R. Thelin's excellent *A History of American Higher Education* (Baltimore, 2004) covers southern developments much more thoroughly.

2. The development of graduate studies is discussed in Richard Storr, *The Beginnings of Graduate Education in America* (Chicago, 1953). Paul Conkin's *Gone with the Ivy: A Biography of Vanderbilt University* (Knoxville, TN, 1985) is an excellent study of Vanderbilt's evolution. John P. Dyer, *Tulane: The Biography of a University, 1834–1965* (New York, 1966) gives a good overview of the development of Tulane but lacks the interpretive vigor of Conkin's study. Similarly, Thomas H. English, *Emory University, 1915–1965: A Semicentennial History* (Atlanta, 1966) provides reliable information but little interpretation.

3. There is no comprehensive work on the impact of the cold war and McCarthyism on universities in the South. Ellen W. Schrecker touches on some southern schools, particularly Tulane, in *No Ivory Tower: McCarthyism and the Universities* (New York, 1986), 242–44. Clarence Mohr and Joseph Gordon, *Tulane: The Emergence of a Modern University, 1945–1980* (Baton Rouge, 2000), chapter 2, contains a thorough analysis of right-wing attacks on Tulane and the response of the administration. Paul Conkin, in *Gone with the Ivy*, 502–14, has a very good discussion of the problem of academic freedom in an era of political hysteria. Conkin makes clear the identification in many southern minds of "Communism" with anything they didn't like, including efforts to bring about any semblance of racial equality.

4. On the rapid transformation of the region after World War II see Numan V. Bartley, *The New South, 1945–1980* (Baton Rouge, 1995); Morton Sosna, "More Important than the Civil War? The Impact of World War II on the South," in *Perspectives on the American South: An Annual Review of Society, Politics, and Culture,* ed. James C. Cobb and Charles R. Wilson (New York, 1987), 145–61; James C. Cobb, *The Selling of the South: The Southern Crusade for Industrial Development, 1936–1980* (Baton Rouge, 1982); and Bruce J. Schulman, *From Cotton Belt to Sunbelt: Federal Policy, Economic Development, and the Transformation of the South, 1938–1990* (New York, 1991).

5. Graduate education in the South was still woefully inadequate compared to other regions. The Carnegie Foundation calculated that in 1950 in the eastern region, with a population of 44,900,000, there were 2,932 earned doctorates awarded. In the Midwest, with 40,000,000 people, there were 2,317 doctorates awarded. In the South, with a population of 31,800,000, only 317 doctorates were earned. This state of affairs provides part of the explanation for the high level of major philanthropic interest in southern higher education throughout the 1950s. See the *Annual Report of the President of Tulane University, 1950–51* (New Orleans, 1951), p. 47, and President's Report to the Board, December 11, 1951, University Archives, Special Collections, Howard-Tilton Library, Tulane University.

6. On the changes that swept through the southern universities, see Clarence Mohr, "World War II and the Transformation of Southern Higher Education," in *Remaking Dixie: The Impact of World War II on the American South,* ed. Neil R. McMillen (Jackson, MS, 1997), 33–55; Bartley, *New South,* 152–54. An excellent undergraduate honors thesis is Jeanne E. Stevens, "The Impacts of World War II on Duke University" (Duke University, 1991). On the profound transformation of Stanford University, see Rebecca S. Lowen, *Creating the Cold War University: The Transformation of Stanford* (Berkeley, CA, 1997).

7. The "outside" pressures were not always a simple product of commitment to American ideals, however. Not only were motivations complex, but the very notion that the South existed as a region apart, deviant and problematic, is a complicated one with a long history. A series of recent essays that suggests some of this intricacy is Larry J. Griffin and Don Doyle, eds., *The South as an American Problem* (Athens, GA, 1995). On the rise of new pressure on racial issues during the early part of this period see John Egerton, *Speak Now against the Day: The Generation before the Civil Rights Movement in the South* (New York, 1994), especially 409–16.

8. George W. Cable, "The Freedman's Case in Equity (1885)" and "The Silent South (1885)" in Cable, *The Negro Question,* ed. Arlin Turner (New York, 1958). On Cable see Louis D. Rubin, *George W. Cable: The Life and Times of a Southern Heretic* (New York, 1969). For discussions of Cable and the place of racial dissent in the making of southern race relations, see Paul Gaston, *The New South Creed: A Study in Southern Mythmaking* (Baton Rouge, LA, 1970), chapter 4; David Chappell, *Inside Agitators: White Southerners in the Civil Rights Movement* (Baltimore, 1994), chapter 1; and Grace Elizabeth Hale, *Making Whiteness: The Culture of Segregation in the South, 1890–1940* (New York, 1998), 44–51.

9. Cable, "The Negro Question," in *The Negro Question,* 110.

10. Gaston, *New South Creed,* 132–35, 140–50, discusses the tension in Grady's arguments between the acknowledgment of the possibility of increased black influence through merit and the stated determination to retain white dominance in any event.

11. The rise of black middle and upper classes, and the inflammatory impact of that rise on white opinion, has been well studied. The most recent work is the excellent Kevin K. Gaines, *Uplifting the Race: Black Leadership, Politics, and Culture in the Twentieth Century* (Chapel Hill, 1996), but also important are E. Franklin Frazier, *Black Bourgeoisie: Rise of a New Middle Class* (Glencoe, IL, 1957) and Willard Gatewood, *Aristocrats of Color: The Black Elite, 1880–1920* (Bloomington, IN, 1990).

12. The treatment of "exceptional" blacks as exceptions rather than as blacks was at the heart of the admissions policies of the northern elite universities at this time, where they were admitted but in tiny numbers. See Marsha Graham Synott, *The Half-Opened Door: Discrimination and Admissions at Harvard, Yale and Princeton, 1900–1970* (Westport, CT, 1979).

1. INTELLIGENT WHITE MEN OF THE SOUTH: THE LATE 1940S

1. Rufus Harris to F. C. Rand, July 3, 1946, Box V-11, James G. Stahlman Papers, Vanderbilt University Special Collections, The Jean and Alexander Heard Library, Nashville, Tennessee (cited hereinafter as VUSC). In general, the selection process that brought Branscomb to Vanderbilt was clumsily handled and reflected some long-standing divisions among the trustees. Conkin, *Gone with the Ivy,* 440–44.

2. Harvie Branscomb, *Purely Academic: An Autobiography* (Nashville, 1978), 153. The Fisk

professors wrote Branscomb asking if they would be allowed to attend these events, but they never actually attended. A similar request, also apparently exploratory, was unceremoniously rejected soon after O. C. Carmichael became chancellor. Although it was addressed to the head of the Vanderbilt Student Union, he apparently consulted the chancellor in making his reply and the correspondence is found in Carmichael's files. William A. Griffey to Byron Anglin, Nov. 4, 1937; Anglin to Griffey, Nov. 8, 1937, Box 174, RG 300, Chancellor's Office Papers, VUSC.

3. Transcript of Swint Tapes (first draft of Branscomb's memoirs), Box 20, Centennial Record Group, VUSC.

4. Transcript of Swint Tapes, Box 20, Centennial Record Group, VUSC. Birmingham College later merged with Southern University, run by the Methodists of southern Alabama, and became Birmingham-Southern.

5. Oddly enough, the first Rhodes scholarship winner from Alabama was Oliver Cromwell (O. C.) Carmichael, who preceded Branscomb at Birmingham College and again as chancellor of Vanderbilt.

6. See Wilma Dykeman and James Stokely, *Seeds of Southern Change: The Life of Will Alexander* (Chicago, 1962), chapter 5; and Egerton, *Speak Now against the Day*, 47–48.

7. Transcript of Swint Tapes, Box 20, Centennial Record Group, VUSC.

8. Branscomb, *Purely Academic*, 70–74; Lewis Howard Grimes, *A History of the Perkins School of Theology* (Dallas, 1993), 46–48.

9. Branscomb, *Purely Academic*, 101. It appears that blacks who attended chapel services were seated separately. Minutes of the Divinity Faculty, June 1, 1949, Divinity School Papers, Duke University Archives, Perkins Library, Durham, North Carolina (cited hereinafter as DUA); Conkin, *Gone with the Ivy*, 449–52.

10. This brief account is distilled from the early chapters of Conkin, *Gone with the Ivy*.

11. Branscomb, *Purely Academic*, 111–14; Conkin, *Gone with the Ivy*, 444.

12. While asserting that "we will be blind . . . if we continue to think only of Southern issues in regional terms," Branscomb contended that the university had a special contribution to make, based on southern traditions, "one which grows out of her special background and heritage." Speech to Nashville Rotary Club, October 7, 1946, Box 5, Branscomb Papers, VUSC; Clippings from *Nashville Tennessean*, November 5, 6, 1946, Box V-28, James Stahlman Papers, VUSC.

13. Branscomb, "Where Would the Money Come From," a brief paper prepared in July 1970 for the Vanderbilt Centennial History Project, Box 20, Centennial Record Group, VUSC.

14. Transcript of Swint tapes, Box 20, Centennial Record Group, VUSC.

15. Robert G. Spinney, *World War II in Nashville: The Transformation of the Homefront* (Knoxville, TN, 1998), 52–72.

16. Branscomb to James A. Simpson, September 17, 1954, Box 101, Chancellor's Office Papers, RG 300, VUSC.

17. Branscomb to Daniels, September 3, 1948, Box 101, Chancellor's Office Papers, RG 300, VUSC.

18. This understanding, naive by today's standards, was generally accepted in the 1940s and into the 1950s, remaining largely unchallenged by mainstream white historians until C. Vann Woodward, *The Strange Career of Jim Crow* (1955; reprint, New York, 1974).

19. Harvie Branscomb to Jonathan Daniels, Sept. 3, 1948, Box 101, Chancellor's Office Papers, RG 300, VUSC. Daniels was editor of the Raleigh, North Carolina, *News and Observer*. He was closely associated with the New Deal in his home state and was a close friend of Frank Porter Graham, another prominent southern liberal and president of the University of North

Carolina. See Charles W. Eagles, *Jonathan Daniels and Race Relations: The Evolution of a Southern Liberal* (Knoxville, 1982), and John Kneebone, *Southern Liberal Journalists and the Issue of Race, 1920–1944* (Chapel Hill, 1985), which discusses Daniels and four other prominent journalists. Branscomb made the same argument, stressing the presence of educated blacks in the South and the need for them to "render the largest possible service" to the region, in a statement given to a *Nashville Banner* reporter. Branscomb to Mary Jane Brooks, September 20, 1948, Box 212, Chancellor's Office Papers, RG 300, VUSC.

20. Branscomb to Donald Davidson, March 25, 1948, Box 154, Chancellor's Office Papers, RG 300, VUSC. Praising a *New York Times* article on southern racial problems, Branscomb expressed this stance succinctly. This article, he wrote, "will be a source of encouragement to those individuals who feel acutely the need for change of sentiment in certain areas but who are realistically conscious of difficulties of bringing that about, particularly in an atmosphere of criticism and fret from outside the region." Branscomb to Arthur Krock, September 13, 1948, Box 212, Chancellor's Office Papers, RG 300,VUSC.

21. "Tentative and Confidential Memorandum on the Establishment of a Graduate Center in Vanderbilt University," Harvie Branscomb, December 1949, Box 4, Branscomb Papers, VUSC.

22. Ibid.

23. Ibid.

24. Carmichael to Branscomb, January 3, 1950, Box 4, Branscomb Papers, VUSC.

25. Branscomb, *Purely Academic*, 153.

26. Branscomb, *Purely Academic*, 183.

27. Ibid.; Harvie Branscomb, "Strengthening and Enervating the Board of Trust," Box 20, Centennial Record Group, VUSC. This is an early draft of chapter 15 of Branscomb's memoir, *Purely Academic*. While the published memoir is quite similar, and makes the same general points, the draft version is often more frank.

28. Ibid.

29. Branscomb relates how he and other trustees convinced Harold Vanderbilt to join the university's board in *Purely Academic*, 185–90. The correspondence is in Box 6, Branscomb Papers, VUSC. After Vanderbilt joined the board, Branscomb carefully maintained a close relationship with him. Branscomb regularly had Vanderbilt as an overnight guest at Branscomb's Belle Meade home, talking over many contentious issues with him before he officially brought them before the trustees. Branscomb nowhere discussed explicitly Vanderbilt's role in bringing about racial change at the university, but suggestions of his critical importance abound, sometimes in the files of the other schools. For example, in gathering information for a study of desegregation in 1955, Dean James Cleland of the Duke Divinity School talked to Branscomb about how he had done it at Vanderbilt. Cleland related the conversation in a memo, stressing that Branscomb had convinced the board to move only with "the able backing of one prominent and effective Northern member of the Board." James T. Cleland to Marcus E. Hobbs, June 29, 1955, Box 5, J. T. Cleland Papers, DUA.

30. Branscomb was responding to Holley, who had sent him a copy of his new autobiography. Joseph W. Holley, *You Can't Build a Chimney from the Top* (New York, 1949). Holley was a larger than life figure, dedicated to the education of young black Georgians, who very nearly built Albany State College with his own hands. Holley's philosophy was reminiscent of Booker T. Washington's, a message of racial bootstrapping that was ultimately dependant on the willingness of whites to allow blacks to bring themselves up. This thinking found an avid supporter

in Harvie Branscomb, a white man who, apparently without any irony or ambiguity, wished southern blacks only the best in their efforts at self-improvement. On Washington see Louis Harlan, *Booker T. Washington: The Making of a Black Leader,1856–1901* (New York, 1972) and *Booker T. Washington: The Wizard of Tuskegee, 1901–1915* (New York, 1983); Gaines, *Uplifting the Race,* 62–63, 90–97.

31. Branscomb to J. W. Holly [sic], March 8, 1949, Box 212, RG 300, Chancellor's Office Papers, VUSC.

32. Branscomb to Gerald E. Wade, January 28, 1949, Box 212, RG 300, Chancellor's Office Papers, VUSC.

33. Branscomb to C. A. Craig, October 17, 1949, Box 212, RG 300, Chancellor's Office Papers, VUSC.

34. Branscomb to Dr. James Ward, November 9, 1949, Box 212, RG 300, Chancellor's Office Papers, VUSC.

35. February 1948 Report to the Board of Trust, Box 212, RG 300, Chancellor's Office Papers, VUSC. Branscomb sent a copy of this report to Goodrich White at Emory and to Rufus Harris at Tulane.

36. Ibid.

37. Ibid.

38. Robert E. Williams Jr. to Vanderbilt Chancellor's Office, May 25, 1949; Branscomb to Cecil Sims, June 15, 1949; Sims to Branscomb, June 15, 1949, Box 212, RG 300, Chancellor's Office Papers, VUSC; Branscomb, *Purely Academic,* 154. Sims's letter explaining Tennessee law is important. He cites both an unambiguous statute, Section 11395, et seq. of the Code of Tennessee, and a judicial opinion upholding that statute, *State v. Witham,* 165 S.W. 2d 378, informing Branscomb in no uncertain terms that it was against the law to enroll blacks at Vanderbilt. Branscomb and the board later chose to disregard this.

39. Goodrich White to Branscomb, May 20, 1948, Box 17, Goodrich White Papers, Emory University Archives, Special Collections, Robert Woodruff Library, Atlanta, Georgia (hereinafter EUA).

40. In two rough drafts, White reviews the then current historical literature on the era of his youth in the South and compares his own childhood experiences with the work of several historians. Box 31, White Papers, EUA.

41. Ibid.

42. For a thorough look at White's years at Emory see Sam M. Shiver and Robert F. Whitaker, "The 14th President's 15 Years," *Emory Alumnus* (April 1957), 5–23.

43. Ibid. Robert Yerkes, who designed the army's psychological tests during World War I, describes, tabulates, and interprets the results of these tests in "Psychological Examining in the United States Army," *Memoirs of the National Academy of Sciences,* vol. 15 (Washington, DC, 1921). For cogent critiques of the tests' flaws and biases see D. J. Kevles, "Testing the Army's Intelligence: Psychologists and the Military in World War I," *Journal of American History* 55 (Winter 1968): 565–81, and Stephen Jay Gould, *The Mismeasure of Man* (New York, 1981), 192–233.

44. Biographical files, EUA.

45. English, *Emory University,* 3–18. Emory College completed its move to the Atlanta campus in 1919.

46. Ibid., chapters 3 and 4.

47. Dumas Malone, "Report to the President on the Development of the Graduate School," *Bulletin of Emory University* 31 (October 1, 1945); English, *Emory University.*

48. Calvin Kytle and James Mackay, *Who Runs Georgia?* (Athens, GA, 1998); Ivan Allen Jr., *Mayor: Notes on the Sixties* (New York, 1971), 30–31. See also Floyd Hunter, *Community Power Structure: A Study of Decision Makers* (Chapel Hill, 1953).

49. See V. O. Key, *Southern Politics in State and Nation* (New York, 1949), chapter 6, and Numan V. Bartley, *From Thurmond to Wallace: Political Tendencies in Georgia, 1948–1968* (Baltimore, 1970).

50. See Key, *Southern Politics,* 117–19; and Numan Bartley, *The Creation of Modern Georgia* (Athens, GA, 1983), 161, 166, and 202–3, for how the county unit system thwarted coherent politics in the vitriolic 1946 election. Earl Black points out that Georgia was unusual within the South in the extent to which race was a campaign issue in the 1940s in *Southern Governors and Civil Rights: Racial Segregation as a Campaign Issue in the Second Reconstruction* (Cambridge, MA, 1976), 29.

51. Even in the late 1940s, the presence of a large, educated, and prosperous black community in Atlanta moderated white racism through its ability to exercise limited political power. See Jack L. Walker, "Protest and Negotiation: A Case Study in Negro Leadership in Atlanta, Georgia," *Midwest Journal of Political Science* 7 (May 1963): 99–124. In 1949, for example, black Democrats and Republicans united to form the Atlanta Negro Voters League in order to maintain what leverage the black community possessed. Clarence A. Bacote, "The Negro in Atlanta Politics," *Phylon* 16 (4th quarter, 1955): 349.

52. Ellis Arnall, a lawyer from Newnan, Georgia, the same town where Goodrich White was raised, was a progressive reformer. See generally Harold P. Henderson, *The Politics of Change in Georgia: A Political Biography of Ellis Arnall* (Athens, GA, 1991) and, for a clear exposition of the economic changes and social turmoil that helped create the political confusion of the 1940s in Georgia, Randall L. Patton, "A Southern Liberal and the Politics of Anti-Colonialism: The Governorship of Ellis Arnall," *Georgia Historical Quarterly* 74 (Winter 1990): 599–621. Arnall gives his own interpretation in *The Shore Dimly Seen* (Philadelphia, 1946).

53. *Smith v. Allwright,* 321 U.S. 649 (1944). On this case see Richard Kluger, *Simple Justice: The History of Brown v. Board of Education and Black America's Struggle for Equality* (New York, 1976), 235–37. On Georgia's 1946 and 1948 elections see Harold P. Henderson, "The 1946 Gubernatorial Election in Georgia" (M.A. thesis, Georgia Southern College, 1967), and Bartley, *Creation of Modern Georgia,* 197–207. Robert C. Mizell to John A. Griffin, February 8, 1946, Box 2, Robert C. Mizell Papers, EUA. Like White, Mizell worked vigorously to improve black higher education in Atlanta. Morris Brown College was his particular interest.

54. Goodrich White, draft of reminiscences, Box 31, White Papers, EUA.

55. On the Atlanta black elite see Hunter, *Community Power Structure,* 116–17, and August Meier and David Lewis, "History of the Negro Upper Class in Atlanta, Georgia, 1890–1958," *Journal of Negro Education* 28 (1959): 128–39. Also see Gary M. Pomerantz, *Where Peachtree Meets Sweet Auburn: The Saga of Two Families and the Making of Atlanta* (New York, 1996), for the intricacies and interactions of the black and white elites over more than a century.

56. Biographical files, Goodrich White, EUA.

57. David Andrew Harmon, *Beneath the Image of the Civil Rights Movement and Race Relations, Atlanta, Georgia, 1946–1981* (New York, 1996), 67–68; Lorraine Nelson Spritzer and Jean B. Bergmark, *Grace Towns Hamilton and the Politics of Southern Change* (Athens, 1997), 115–31. At various times during the late 1940s into the 1950s Emory tried to work out some way to help with the training of black doctors. The logistical problems were overwhelming. Discussing the problem in 1950, Dean Hugh Wood of Emory's medical school wrote to Hughes Spalding, chairman of

the Grady Memorial Authority. Wood fretted about "complications and incidents which might be embarrassing to all concerned," arguing that "such incidents, if allowed to occur, would probably hinder the goal we hope to achieve, which is better graduate and postgraduate education for the negro physician." R. Hugh Wood to Hughes Spalding, August 4, 1950, Box 5, Mizell Papers, EUA.

58. Harry Truman, "Letter of Appointment," reproduced in the commission's report, *Higher Education for American Democracy: The Report of the President's Commission on Higher Education* (Washington, DC, 1947). White gave a speech to a meeting of church-related colleges in July 1948 in which he explained the workings of the commission in great detail. He made clear that the report was no "rubber stamp," but that every section had been thoroughly debated and redrafted repeatedly both in subcommittee and by the entire commission. Goodrich White, "Speech to Meeting of Church Related Colleges," July 26, 1948, Box 25, White Papers, EUA.

59. White to George F. Zook, October 27, 1947, Box 17, White Papers, EUA.

60. Ibid.; *Higher Education for American Democracy*, 29.

61. *Higher Education for American Democracy*, 29.

62. White to George F. Zook, October 27, 1947, Box 17, White Papers, EUA.

63. White to Arthur H. Compton, December 2, 1947, Box 17, White Papers, EUA.

64. Report of the Commission Meeting, Nov. 3–4, 1947, Box 17, White Papers, EUA. This included two other southern members, F. D. Patterson, president of Tuskegee, and more surprisingly, O. C. Carmichael, former chancellor of Vanderbilt. Carmichael's refusal to dissent is explained by his new position in New York as head of the Carnegie Foundation for the Advancement of Teaching. He would go on to become president of the University of Alabama, his home state, where he would face racial difficulties that were probably unimaginable in 1947. See E. Culpepper Clark, *The Schoolhouse Door: Segregation's Last Stand at the University of Alabama* (New York, 1993), 23–25 and generally.

65. Branscomb to White, May 17, 1948, Box 17, White Papers, EUA; Harris to Snavely, April 20, 1948, Box 17, White Papers, EUA.

66. White to James A. Dombrowski, December 30, 1947; White to Joe J. Mickle, January 20, 1948, Box 17, White Papers, EUA. Dombrowski, radical in his politics, was a personal friend of several of these presidents. An affable man, he wrote frequent warm letters to them but nearly always managed at least one prod for racial change at their schools. A solid biography of Dombrowski is Frank T. Adams, *James Dombrowski: An American Heretic, 1897–1983* (Knoxville, TN, 1992). He is also a principal figure in Anthony P. Dunbar, *Against the Grain: Southern Radicals and Prophets, 1929–1959* (Charlottesville, 1981). On the Southern Conference Educational Fund, see Irwin Klibaner, *Conscience of a Troubled South: The Southern Conference Educational Fund, 1946–1966* (Brooklyn, NY, 1989).

67. White to Nace Cohen, February 4, 1948; White to DePriest, December 29, 1947, Box 17, White Papers, EUA.

68. Thomas English, *Emory University*, 212; Emory University Advisory Committee on Religious Life, Minutes, December 15, 1933, EUA Ms. Box 17. Sometime in 1936 or 1937 the Reverend Raymond Henderson of the Wheat Street Baptist Church addressed the faculty of the theology school, delivering a powerful speech entitled "A Plea for a Prophet." Henderson asked the assembled theologians to take on the task of bringing justice to black Christians in the South. They did not do so, but over time the theology school would become a persistent source of internal pressure for racial change at Emory. Raymond Henderson, "A Plea for a Prophet," undated, EUA Ms. Box 17.

69. Program, "Announcing a Series of Forums on Human Relations," Fall Quarter 1945, EUA Ms. Box 17a.

70. The existence of the admission applications by blacks was not made known at the time they were received. No explanation for the failure to consider them was offered. Dean J. Gordon Stipe of the Graduate School merely noted that "while Emory has no racial clause of any kind in its admissions regulations, it has, as a private institution, the prerogative of accepting or rejecting any application." *Emory Wheel,* October 19, 1950; *Atlanta Journal,* February 15, 1950.

71. *Emory Wheel,* February 28, 1948.

72. Memo, Boisfeuillet Jones to Goodrich White, February 21, 1948, Box 6, Mizell Papers, EUA.

73. "In re: Emory Christian Association Racial Equality Meeting set for Monday, February 23, 1948," John A. Dunaway to Goodrich White, February 20, 1948, Box 6, Mizell Papers, EUA.

74. "In re: Separation of Races," John A. Dunaway to Goodrich White, February 20, 1948, Box 3, Henry L. Bowden Papers, EUA; copy of letter, John A. Dunaway to Boisfeuillet Jones, March 19, 1948, Box 22, Rufus C. Harris Papers, Tulane University Archives, Special Collections, Howard-Tilton Library, New Orleans, Louisiana (hereinafter TUA).

75. For Wallace's political philosophy see Graham White and John Maze, *Henry A. Wallace: His Search for a New World Order* (Chapel Hill, 1995).

76. *Emory Wheel,* January 27, 1948; February 28, 1948. The "Resolution" language is found in "A Brief Documentary Account of the Integration of Emory University." This is a collection of copies of key documents in Emory's move to open admissions, gathered from many sources. Norman Smith and his colleagues in Emory's Development Office compiled it in 1966. EUA Ms. Box 10. Copy of letter from White to Robert A. Young, April 1, 1948, Box 22, Harris Papers, TUA. White sent copies of all the correspondence surrounding this incident to both Harris and Harvie Branscomb.

77. Biographical files, DUA; Robert F. Durden, "Donnybrook at Duke: The Gross-Edens Affair of 1960, Part I." *The North Carolina Historical Review* 71(July 1994), 332–34.

78. Robert F. Durden, *The Launching of Duke University, 1924–1949* (Durham, 1993), 493–97.

79. Robert Durden, *The Dukes of Durham, 1865–1929* (Durham, NC, 1975), gives a clear account of how the Duke family's fortune was built. Earl W. Porter, *Trinity and Duke, 1892–1924: Foundations of Duke University* (Durham, 1964), tells the story of Trinity's rather astonishing growth and improvement from the time it moved to Durham until it became the heart of Duke University.

80. Robert Durden explains the origins of the endowment in *Lasting Legacy to the Carolinas: The Duke Endowment, 1924–1994* (Durham, NC, 1998), 15–28, and points out its huge contribution to Duke's annual budget at page 116.

81. Durden, *The Launching of Duke University,* chapters 1 and 10.

82. Ibid., 464–67.

83. Paul Gross, "Memorandum with Reference to Conference with G. E. B. in Savannah Sunday Morning, October 16th," October 17, 1949, Box 43, A. Hollis Edens Papers, Duke University Archives, Perkins Library, Durham, North Carolina (hereinafter DUA).

84. "Information about Graduate and Professional Offerings in the South," summer 1949, compiled by Dean of the Graduate School Paul Gross, Edens Papers, Box 7, DUA. The Board of Control requested the information for Southern Regional Education. This group was formed in 1948 to increase cooperation among southern states in order to use the region's resources more efficiently. Redding S. Sugg, *The Southern Regional Education Board: Ten Years of Regional Coopera-*

tion in Higher Education (Baton Rouge, 1960). The SREB would become an annoyance to the presidents of these private universities, who grew suspicious of its motives and jealously guarded their independence.

85. Preliminary report on the financial needs of Duke University, Kersting, Brown & Co., November 21, 1947, Box 29, Flowers Papers, DUA.

86. Branscomb, *Purely Academic,* 101; Minutes of the Divinity Faculty, June 1, 1949, Divinity School Papers, DUA.

87. "Memo: Report on Racial Discrimination Policies on Campus," 1962, "D. U. Desegregation," Deryl Hart Papers, DUA.

88. Petition, May 1948, Box 21, Edens Papers, DUA.

89. Ibid. A deep-seated fear of the physical presence of blacks, especially during eating, sleeping, or washing, permeated the arguments made by the opponents of desegregation and was even common among those who tried to initiate change. See Mary Douglas's classic *Purity and Danger: An Analysis of the Concepts of Pollution and Taboo* (1966; reprint, New York, 1991). Even after these schools allowed black students to enroll, there were frequently battles about blacks living in the dorms, or using the swimming pool, or eating in the cafeteria with whites.

90. Petition, Box 21, Edens Papers, DUA.

91. Minutes of the Divinity Faculty, March 23, 1949, Divinity School Papers, DUA.

92. An account of these meetings is in the report of the committee to the Divinity School faculty, June 1, 1949, Box 21, Edens Papers, DUA.

93. Ibid. Beach recommended that the dean, Harold Bosley, bring the petition to the Board of Trustees as soon as possible.

94. Beach wrote to Benjamin Mays of Morehouse, John Satterwhite of Livingston College in North Carolina, and Neal Hughley, Beach's personal friend, of Durham's North Carolina College. All these letters and responses are in Box 21, Edens Papers, DUA.

95. J. Neal Hughley to Waldo Beach, April 23, 1949, Box 21, Edens Papers, DUA.

96. Waldo Beach to Eugene Hawk, April 12, 1949, Box 21, Edens Papers, DUA. In addition to Hawk, Dean of the Perkins School of Theology at SMU, Beach wrote Benjamin Lacy of the Union Theological Seminary in Richmond (which began admitting blacks in 1935) and Harry Richardson of Atlanta's Gammon Theological Seminary, who apparently did not reply. All of these are also in Box 21, Edens Papers, DUA.

97. Report of the Faculty Committee, Box 21, Edens Papers, DUA; Minutes of the Divinity Faculty, June 1, 1949, Divinity School Papers, DUA.

98. Minutes of the Divinity Faculty, June 1, 1949; June 2, 1949, Divinity School Papers, DUA.

99. Recommendations of the Divinity School Faculty, June 2, 1949, Box 21, Edens Papers, DUA.

100. Recommendations of the Divinity School Faculty, June 2, 1949, Box 21, Edens Papers, DUA. The "Bassett affair" has been described and analyzed from all angles. The best account of the events is in Porter, *Trinity and Duke,* 96–139. See also Durden, *Dukes of Durham,* 117–21, for the affair from the perspective of Ben Duke. William B. Hamilton, ed., *Fifty Years of the South Atlantic Quarterly* (Durham, 1952), reprints both Bassett's provocative article and the statement of the Trinity trustees in retaining him.

101. Recommendations of the Divinity School Faculty, June 2, 1949, Box 21, Edens Papers, DUA.

102. Harold A. Bosley to Edens, June 4, 1949, Box 21, Edens Papers, DUA. In his accompanying letter he stressed the "serious and thoroughly responsible discussion" that had taken

place and made clear that the faculty understood well the "magnitude of the task" they were asking the university to consider. Still, in spite of the difficult and "troublesome" nature of the problem, Bosley wrote, "we could not, in good conscience, refuse to consider the student petition, nor could we reach any more temperate position in our search for an answer." It is difficult to imagine what a more temperate position could be.

103. Edens to Bosley, June 24, 1949, Box 21, Edens Papers, DUA. Jorge Kotelanski, in his excellent senior thesis, attributes Edens's abrupt reply to Dean Bosley to the fact that there was bad blood between the two. While that is accurate, examination of Edens's entire body of correspondence reveals that the president, who wrote in a very formal style, was abrupt with nearly everyone except very close friends. Kotelanski, "Prolonged and Patient Efforts: The Desegregation of Duke University, 1948–1963" (Duke University, 1990).

104. Augustus M. Burns III and Julian M. Pleasants, *Frank Porter Graham and the 1950 Senate Race in North Carolina* (Chapel Hill, 1990); Warren Ashby, *Frank Porter Graham: A Southern Liberal* (Winston-Salem, NC, 1980), 262–68.

105. In one area the board proved to be more flexible. In 1950, the trustees allowed the Duke football team to play the University of Pittsburgh, at Durham, even though the Panthers had a black player. They received national publicity for this action, as *NBC Sports* congratulated Duke and President Edens in particular for the "democratic" decision. Jack Lightcap to Ted Mann, September 26, 1950, Box 16, Edens Papers, DUA. Lightcap wrote Mann, Duke's director of publicity, that the people at NBC in New York "felt wonderful about your stand in the matter" and enclosed a transcript of an October 3 broadcast that praised Duke heavily. Edens's explanation for this decision had less to do with democracy than with the demands of the alumni for athletic glory. In a letter to Duke Alumni Affairs Director Charles A. Dukes, Edens notes in response to an alumni complaint that "this is a matter which is beyond our control if we are to play intersectional games as so many of our alumni have urged us to do." Edens to Dukes, October 10, 1950, Box 36, Edens Papers, DUA. Once again, the issue was presented starkly. If Duke were to gain glory in the eyes of the nation, the university would have to accept the nation's standards on race. Highlighting the extent to which minor racial issues were invested with deep, and often contrary, meanings was Duke's mailbox after this game was played. Edens heard from James Dombrowski, the omnipresent director of the Southern Conference Educational Fund, who expressed his great pleasure at the game (and, as ever, nudged Edens to take more steps). Dombrowski to Edens, October 20, 1950, Box 12, Edens Papers, DUA. Trustee Chairman Willis Smith, in the midst of his intense runoff campaign against Frank Porter Graham, received a note from a supporter who also rejoiced that this game had been played. His reason, though, was that he believed Smith could use it to disprove allegations that Smith was a racist. Robert Deyton to Smith, October 2, 1950, Box 132, Willis Smith Papers, Duke University Special Collections, Perkins Library, Durham, North Carolina.

106. Biographical Files, TUA; Dyer, *Tulane,* 208–9.

107. Harris to J. W. Holley, January 15, 1948, Box 99, Herbert Longenecker Papers, TUA. Harris is answering a letter from Holley, who wrote "to congratulate you and the other southern college presidents on your protest against the plan of the President's Committee on Education [Truman's Commission on Higher Education]." Holley objected to the commission's "radical" proposals on the grounds that they were "too Utopian for the present." Holley also sought Harris's advice on his new job as head of a Georgia program to equalize black educational facilities in the state. Holley to Harris, January 6, 1948, Box 99, Longenecker Papers, TUA.

108. Governor Eugene Talmadge purged several faculty members and administrators at the

university, and then several members of the Board of Regents who objected, because he deemed them "foreigners" (that is, they had been born or educated in the North) who were "soft" on the "Negro issue." The Southern Association of Colleges and Secondary Schools withdrew accreditation. (The chairman of the investigating committee was O. C. Carmichael, then chancellor of Vanderbilt.) Talmadge argued that the issue was not about academic freedom, but rather about Negroes and liberals. Harris came in for a great deal of criticism as being himself "soft" on the Negro issue, but he held his ground. The matter became a campaign issue in the next Georgia governor's race, and Talmadge was defeated by Harris's ally and friend Ellis Arnall, who immediately began working with the Southern Association to restore the university's accreditation. Bartley, *Creation of Modern Georgia,* 193–95; Thomas G. Dyer, *The University of Georgia: A Bicentennial History, 1785–1985* (Athens, GA, 1985), 225–40; James F. Cook Jr., "Politics and Education in the Talmadge Era: The Controversy over the University System of Georgia, 1941–42" (Ph.D. dissertation, University of Georgia, 1972).

109. *New Orleans Times Picayune,* July 1, 1943.

110. Harris to J. K. Haynes, November 23, 1946, Box 33, Harris Papers, TUA.

111. In addition to his flirtation with Vanderbilt in 1946, Harris indicated interest in the Duke presidency before Edens got the job. Harris to O. C. Carmichael, March 31, 1948, Box 55, Harris Papers, TUA. Later, he even talked with Branscomb about becoming the head of Vanderbilt's Law School.

112. Dyer, *Tulane.*

113. On faculty salaries, L. J. Buchan to O. C. Carmichael, June 25, 1946, Box 27, Harris Papers, TUA.

114. Ibid. Tulane got early notice of the federal government's postwar spending plans. In 1943 Harris received a letter from a colleague who was serving as staff director for the U.S. Senate Sub-Committee on Wartime Health and Education. It said, "I might tip you off now that there is going to be a rather heavy post war building program sponsored by the federal government to head off unemployment. This is in the early stages of formulation. It may be that by getting your oar in soon, you can get a building for Tulane. . . . I know the ropes a little better now and may be able to really do something for you when the occasion arises." Randolph Feltus to Harris, August 20, 1943, Box 28, Harris Papers, TUA.

115. Harris to John R. Miles, January 13, 1949, Box 28, Harris Papers, TUA.

116. William V. Moore, "Civil Liberties in Louisiana: The Louisiana League for the Preservation of Constitutional Rights," *Louisiana History* 31 (Winter, 1990): 59–81. *Louisiana League for the Preservation of Constitutional Rights Bulletin,* November 26, 1942, Box 33, Harris Papers, TUA, gives a clear picture of the kinds of very specific civil liberties issues and incidents that concerned the league in the 1940s.

117. The brief outline of events surrounding the academic freedom disputes at Tulane that follows is based largely on the extensive account in Mohr and Gordon, *Tulane,* 78–93. On the SCHW see Thomas A. Krueger, *And Promises to Keep: The Southern Conference for Human Welfare, 1938–1948* (Nashville, 1967), and especially Numan V. Bartley, "The Southern Conference and the Shaping of Post-World War II Southern Politics," in Winfred B. Moore, Joseph F. Tripp, and Lyon G. Tyler, eds., *Developing Dixie* (New York, 1988), 179–97.

118. Harris received several letters complaining about Tulane professors teaching at SCHW institutes. He defended the loyalty of the professors as well as their rights as citizens to speak before any group that wanted to hear them. Walter M. Carter to Harris, October 3, 1947; Harris to Carter, October 8, 1947, Box 22, Harris Papers, TUA.

119. The letter is from Harris to E. Clagett Upton, printed as *Letter from Tulane*, Box 43, Harris Papers, TUA. Mohr and Gordon point out that the letter is drawn from a presentation Harris made to the Tulane board and that it was toned down, in effect made more apologetic, for public consumption. Mohr and Gordon, *Tulane*, 80–82.

120. Bartley, "The Southern Conference and Post-World War II Southern Politics," 191–93; Paul Brosman to Florence Dymond, February 19, 1948, Box 29, Harris Papers, TUA.

121. Hebert quoted in Mohr and Gordon, *Tulane*, 85–86. Ironically, the Tulane history department is now housed in Hebert Hall.

122. On Hubert Humphrey, the formation of the ADA, and the 1948 Democratic Convention fight over the civil rights plank see Robert Mann, *The Walls of Jericho: Lyndon Johnson, Hubert Humphrey, Richard Russell and the Struggle for Civil Rights* (New York, 1996), chapter 1. The ADA New Orleans chapter, headed by Tulane professor William Kolb, was singularly ineffective. Too sensitive to white fears of integration, it was never bold enough to attract any real following among either whites or blacks and folded by 1950. Adam Fairclough, *Race and Democracy: The Civil Rights Struggle in Louisiana, 1915–1972* (Athens, GA, 1995), 141.

123. Mohr and Gordon, *Tulane*, 89. The actual plank that was proposed by the ADA at the convention is as follows: "The Democratic Party commits itself to continuing its efforts to eradicate all racial, religious, and economic discrimination. We again state our belief that racial and religious minorities must have the right to live, the right to work, the right to vote, the full and equal protection of the law, on a basis of equality with all citizens as guaranteed by the Constitution. We again call upon Congress to exert its full authority to the limit of its constitutional power to assure and protect these rights." Reprinted in Mann, *Walls of Jericho*, 14.

124. Harris to F. Edward Hebert, January 11, 1949, Box 49, Harris Papers, TUA; Hebert to Harris, January 19, 1949, Box 22, Harris Papers, TUA.

125. The alumni were already nearly hysterical. They had begun to circulate a petition that called for direct supervision of all courses taught at Tulane and all literature distributed there, the monitoring of all campus organizations for subversive intent, and the immediate firing of all faculty members who expressed dissatisfaction with "the American form of government." Petition, n.d. [May, 1948], Box 29, Harris Papers, TUA.

126. Harris to Mrs. George M. Snellings, June 5, 1948, Box 29, Harris Papers, TUA. Harris asked Snellings, a lawyer and a former student of his who would serve on the Tulane board, to circulate this among Tulane alumni.

127. This letter first appears as a typed document dated February 21, 1949, Box 29, Harris Papers, TUA. It was later published as "A Letter from the President," *Letter from Tulane*, June 1949. The students who attended the interracial party were mostly members of the Young Progressives of America, the youth wing of Henry Wallace's Progressive Party. Fairclough, *Race and Democracy*, 140–41. In the aftermath of the arrests, they were all interviewed separately by their deans, who then sent detailed written reports to Harris.

128. Harris had copies of all the relevant documents from Branscomb and White in several places. All of them are gathered together in Box 42, Harris Papers, TUA, but most also appear elsewhere in his files.

129. Harris wrote White in April 1948 asking for a copy of all White's statements on race relations in higher education. This correspondence and all the copies are in Box 22, Harris Papers, TUA.

130. Harris removed language that was specific to the context of the report and added some

words of his own. Where White disagreed with the theoretical idealism of the "Commission's recommendations," Harris disagreed with the theoretical idealism of "persons who feel that democracy can be achieved by imposing laws which would level the masses."

131. Harris asked Branscomb for a copy of his statement to the Vanderbilt board. Harris to Branscomb, April 24, 1948, Box 212, Chancellor's Office Papers, RG 300, VUSC. The copy is in Box 22, Harris Papers, TUA. Here, Harris changed only two words. Where Branscomb discussed individuals leading "their race" along the slow path of improvement, Harris substituted "all Americans." Branscomb, not surprisingly, wholeheartedly endorsed this *Letter from Tulane*. Branscomb to Harris, February 5, 1948, Box 42, Harris Papers, TUA.

132. Minutes of Dean's Meeting, February 5, 1948, Box 1, Harris Papers, TUA. It appears that this meeting never took place.

133. At the time, Bunche was a senior official of the United Nations. He received the Nobel Peace Prize in 1950. See Brian Urquhardt, *Ralph Bunche: An American Life* (New York, 1993).

134. Minutes, Board of Administrators Meeting, October 18, 1949, TUA.

135. Harris to Fred Cole, October 27, 1949; Cole to Harris, October 31, 1949; George Simmons to Cole, October 30, 1949; Harris to Cole, November 1, 1949, Box 5, Harris Papers, TUA.

136. Minutes, Board of Administrators Meeting, December 13, 1949, TUA.

137. Fredericka Meiners, *A History of Rice University: The Institute Years, 1907–1963* (Houston, 1982), chapter 1, describes Rice's opening ceremonies, which were attended by many of the world's most prominent academics, an indication of Lovett's ambitions for the school. Pages 48–49 include discussion of the school's high standards.

138. Meiners, *History of Rice*, 15–16, 51.

139. For Rice during World War II see Meiners, *History of Rice*, 134–35. The chairman of Rice's Board of Trustees, J. T. Scott, gave a very upbeat assessment of Rice's financial position in the spring of 1945 in a speech to the Rice faculty, April 10, 1945, Box 36, Edgar O. Lovett Papers, Woodson Research Center, Fondren Library, Rice University, Houston, Texas (hereinafter WRC).

140. Report of the Survey Committee of the Board of Trustees, April 11, 1945, Box 36, Lovett Papers, WRC. The number of graduate students historically was quite small, never reaching one hundred in any single year.

141. "A Long Range Program for Rice Institute," July 30, 1945, Box 36, Lovett Papers, WRC.

142. H. C. Weiss, "Rice Looks Forward," address before the Association of Rice Alumni, November 9, 1945, Box 36, Lovett Papers, WRC. Weiss was a native of Beaumont, Texas, and one of the organizers of the Humble Company. He graduated from Princeton and also sat on Princeton's Board of Trustees, Biographical Files, WRC. There is no in-depth study of the important Rincon transaction, but it is discussed briefly in Meiners, *History of Rice*, 137–38, and in Kerri D. Gantz, "On the Basis of Merit Alone: Integration, Tuition, Rice University, and the Charter Change Trial, 1963–1966" (M.A. thesis, Rice University, 1991), 79–81.

143. "Charter of the William M. Rice Institute for the Advancement of Literature, Science and Art," WRC. The relevant language, found in the ninth clause of Article II, states that the trustees are "expressly forbidden ever to permit any lien, encumbrance, debt or mortgage to be placed upon any of the property, or funds, belonging now, or that may hereafter belong to the said Institute; . . . that the entire property of the Institute shall always be kept free from debt."

144. Minutes of the Rice Board of Trustees, April 23, 1941, Board of Trustees Records, WRC.

145. "A Long Range Program for Rice Institute," July 30, 1945, Box 36, Lovett Papers, WRC.

146. Two facts were critical in allowing Rice to limit its enrollment at a time when other schools were flooded with returning veterans. First and most important was its rosy financial picture. Second was the provision in Rice's charter that prevented it from charging tuition. Well funded and with no gain to be had by increasing admissions, Rice was able to keep its student body to a manageable size.

147. Weiss, "Rice Looks Forward," November 9, 1945, Box 36, Lovett Papers, WRC.

148. The search for Rice's second president had been a long one. Lovett had announced his intention to step down just before the outbreak of the Second World War, and a somewhat sporadic search had taken place during the war years, hampered by the preoccupation of the nation's scientists, from whose ranks candidates would be sought, with the war effort. At the close of the war, a more intensive search was led by a committee of three trustees. George R. Brown, Benjamin Botts Rice, and Harry Weiss sought out candidates in the traditional manner, relying on word of mouth and the recommendations of their friends and colleagues. Several leading candidates withdrew before the trustees settled on Houston, and Houston initially turned down the opportunity. A critical factor in his ultimate acceptance was the assurance that he would be able to continue his own scholarly work.

149. William V. Houston, Biographical File, WRC; Biographical Sketch, Papers of William Vermillion Houston, WRC.

150. Ibid.

151. "Charter of the William M. Rice Institute for the Advancement of Literature, Science and Art," WRC. Article II of the charter begins with a recitation of the purposes of William Marsh Rice's gift, including "the maintenance of an Institute for the Advancement of Literature, Science, Art, Philosophy and Letters," noting that these benefits are to be given "free for the white inhabitants of the City of Houston and the State of Texas." Like Rice's, Tulane's charter contained racially restrictive clauses, but those of Duke, Emory, and Vanderbilt did not. Rice was the only school in this group that could not charge tuition.

152. The controversy began in November 1948 and continued in the pages of the *Thresher* until February 1949. All the newspapers in Houston, both black and white, as well as other papers throughout the state covered the story.

153. The letter from Bill Smith, the editor of the *Daily Texan*, appeared on January 19, 1949. In it, Smith was very supportive of the Rice editor's stand on beginning racial change but also echoed, in his own way, the cautious rhetoric of Branscomb, White, and Harris. "I don't hold with the hot headed type of individual who thinks it can be done tomorrow," Smith wrote. "He's as dangerous as a KKK member, but I believe it will be the calm, plodding type of individual who will in the not too distant future show Texans what they do to themselves by their hatreds."

154. Houston to Brady Tyson, February 14, 1949, *Rice Thresher* Files, WRC. This letter was printed in the *Thresher* on February 19, 1949. The *New York Times* included a small story on this incident in its February 20, 1949, issue, noting that questions about admitting Negroes to Rice had received an "abrupt answer." The story was also given more space in the local newspapers.

155. For example, on March 2, 1949, the *Thresher* reprinted an editorial from Texas Tech in Lubbock that approved of a University of Missouri student body poll that overwhelmingly supported the admission of qualified black students.

156. *Texas Southern University Herald*, "Is it Sentiment or Law?" February-March 1949.

2. "THE SENSE OF SECURITY NO LONGER EXISTS": THE EARLY 1950S

1. See Bartley, *New South,* especially chapter 4. These changes were so noticeable that there is a large literature of contemporaneous or near-term assessment of the region's growth. See, for example, Allan P. Sindler, ed., *Change in the Contemporary South* (Durham, 1963), a collection of conference papers from a 1962 meeting at Duke on "The Impact of Political and Legal Change in the Postwar South." William H. Nicholls of the Vanderbilt Department of Economics produced several good studies of regional change during the 1950s and 1960s, including *Southern Tradition and Regional Progress* (Chapel Hill, 1960). Nicholls succinctly addressed in this work the corrosive effects of industrialization and urbanization on the southern tradition. Another interesting piece that directly addresses the impact of the changing southern economy on racial tradition is J. Milton Yinger and George E. Simpson, "Can Segregation Survive in an Industrial Society?" *Antioch Review* 28 (March, 1958), 15–24. See also James W. Silver, *Mississippi: The Closed Society* (New York, 1963).

2. Nicholas Lehmann, *The Promised Land: The Great Black Migration and How It Changed America* (New York, 1991) discusses the outpouring of blacks from the rural South to the urban North from the 1940s through the 1960s.

3. Seventy-fifth Anniversary Speech, October 21, 1950, Box 5, Branscomb Papers, VUSC.

4. Ibid.

5. See, for example, Aldon D. Morris, *The Origins of the Civil Rights Movement: Black Communities Organizing for Change* (New York, 1984). The best account of the genesis and history of the *Brown* cases is Kluger, *Simple Justice.*

6. An excellent overview of these developments is Peter Wallenstein's "Black Southerners and Non-Black Universities: Desegregating Higher Education, 1935–1967," *History of Higher Education Annual* 19 (1999): 121–48. *Sweatt v. Painter,* 210 S.W. 2d 442 (1947), 339 U.S. 629 (1950), and *McLaurin v. Oklahoma State Regents for Higher Education,* 339 U.S. 637 (1950), should have settled the issue of black admissions to most, if not all, public graduate programs but they did not. See John Hubbell, "The Desegregation of the University of Oklahoma, 1946–1950," *Journal of Negro History* 57 (October, 1972): 370–84. Some southern universities opened admissions to each graduate division or course of study only when forced to by a specific plaintiff seeking to enroll. For example, the NAACP had an early victory at the University of Maryland's Law School in the 1936 case of *Pearson v. Murray,* 169 Md. 478, 182 A. 590 (1936). But the university fought a rearguard action for over fifteen years, forcing black plaintiffs to sue for entry into each department. Most public universities accepted the inevitable, however, and a Southern Regional Council study revealed that by 1955 between 750 and 800 black students attended universities that had previously been segregated. See Guy B. Johnson, "New Ways on the Campus," *New South* 10 (February, 1955): 1–10.

7. Bartley cites an especially apt quote from a southern journalist's analysis of regional change in the early 1950s. Noting both the extent of change and the resistance to it, the writer saw "two Souths which exist side by side in each Southern state, but which are as different as Chicago and Bangkok." Bartley, *New South,* 105.

8. *Gastonia Gazette,* February 4, 1950, Box 10, Edens Papers, DUA.

9. There was no way for Edens to avoid the intrusion of race. Reminders of the growing turmoil appeared in his office on a regular basis. For example, in November 1950, the Yale University News Bureau sent him, as a courtesy, a copy of a talk given on the radio by the Dean of Yale's

Divinity School, Reverend Liston Pope. Pope, a graduate of Duke, used this address to proclaim that "a bloodless but extremely effective revolution in race relations" was "sweeping the U.S." Pope included a list of changes that contributed to this "revolution," ranging from black major league ballplayers to the role of Ralph Bunche in international affairs. Edens received this report with a wry comment: "We are always interested in what our graduates are doing." Richard C. Lee to Edens, November 16, 1950; Edens to Lee, November 18, 1950; News Release, Yale University News Bureau, October 23, 1950, Box 59, Edens Papers, DUA.

10. "Summary of Social Action Study," November 6, 1951. The students relied on official Methodist documents to bolster their argument that segregation was immoral. They quoted from *The Discipline of the Methodist Church*, 1948, section 2020: "We believe that God is Father of all peoples and races, Jesus Christ is his son, that we and all men are brothers, and that man is of infinite worth as a child of God."

11. For the desegregation of North Carolina's public universities, see Peter Wallenstein, "Higher Education and the Civil Rights Movement: Desegregating the University of North Carolina," in *Warm Ashes: Issues in Southern History at the Dawn of the Twenty-first Century*, edited by Winfred B. Moore Jr., Kyle S. Sinisi, and David H. White Jr., 280–300 (Columbia, SC, 2003).

12. Edens to Regan, November 19, 1951, Box 33, Edens Papers, DUA.

13. *Proceedings of the Annual Meeting of the Association of American Law Schools*, December 1950.

14. The amendment reads: "No school which follows a policy of excluding or segregating qualified applicants or students on the basis of race or color shall be qualified to be admitted to or to remain a member of the Association." (This was modified to include a two-year grace period.)

15. See for example, Edens to Branscomb, May 8, 1951; Branscomb to Edens, May 18, 1951, Box 7, Edens Papers, DUA.

16. The association's president, F. D. G. Ribble of the University of Virginia School of Law, appointed the committee of five. Headed by Elliot Cheatham of Columbia, this group also included representatives from Harvard, the University of Southern California, the University of Illinois, and the University of Texas. (Cheatham had taught at Emory's Law School early in his career.)

17. Edens to Dean J. A. McClain, April 17, 1951, Box 25, Edens Papers, DUA. This letter was included as part of Duke's response to an AALS questionnaire.

18. Statement by J. A. McClain Jr., December 1951, Box 25, Edens Papers, DUA. On these quotas see Synott, *The Half-Opened Door*, and David O. Levine, *The American College and the Culture of Aspiration, 1915–1940* (Ithaca, NY, 1986), 136–61. For anti-Semitism in admissions generally, see Jerome Karabel, *The Chosen: The Hidden History of Admission and Exclusion at Harvard, Yale, and Princeton* (New York, 2005).

19. Edens also made it something of a personal crusade to try to rein in the power of accrediting bodies, becoming in 1953 the chairman of the National Commission on Accrediting, a platform that he used to argue for the elimination of many accrediting bodies. While they understood and to some degree sympathized with Edens's position, Harris and Branscomb both opposed the idea of eliminating national accreditation for professional schools, fearing that it would further isolate the South and end up doing more harm than good to their schools' reputations. Box 22, Edens Papers, DUA.

20. Report of the President to the Board of Trustees, December 1951, Box 30, Edens Papers, DUA.

21. E. C. Bryson to Edens, April 20, 1951, Box 7, Edens Papers, DUA.

22. *Shelley v. Kramer,* 334 U.S. 1 (1948). On *Shelley,* see Clement Vose, *Caucasians Only: The Supreme Court, the NAACP and the Restrictive Covenant Cases* (Berkeley, 1959).

23. The Missouri case was *Weiss v. Leaon,* 359 Mo. 1054, 225 S.W. 2d 127 (1949). The Missouri Supreme Court tried to evade the clear intent of *Shelley* by ruling that while courts could not enforce racially restrictive covenants, they could award money damages where existing covenants were violated. This decision was roundly criticized in the law reviews for the transparency of its attempt to avoid the plain meaning of the Supreme Court decision. For example, see *Harvard Law Review* 63 (April, 1950), 1062–64. Similar judgments in several other states resulted in the United States Supreme Court decision in *Barrows v. Jackson,* 346 U.S. 249 (1953), which made clear that courts could not enforce restrictive covenants by any means whatsoever, including damages awards. See Vose, *Caucasians Only,* 211–46.

24. Edens to Bryson, April 21, 1950, Box 7, Edens Papers, DUA.

25. Edens to Bryson, April 24, 1950, Box 7, Edens Papers, DUA. The interns refused to simply acquiesce, but in the end Duke would not move. Bryson to Edens, April 27, 1950, Box 7, Edens Papers, DUA.

26. Anna G. Douglas to Edens, June 29, 1951; Edens to Anna Douglas, July 3, 1951, Box 12, Edens Papers, DUA.

27. Reverend W. M. Wells to Edens, February 17, 1953; Edens to Wells, February 20, 1953, Box 33, Edens Papers, DUA.

28. Virgil C. Stroud to Edens, May 26, 1950; Edens to Stroud, May 30, 1950, Box 29, Edens Papers, DUA.

29. The University Council was formed and approved by Duke's board in 1952 as part of a revision of the school's bylaws. It was the first real attempt at Duke to take faculty opinion into consideration in matters of university policy, but it remained a small (thirteen members plus the president and the vice president of the educational division) advisory group with no real teeth that never was able to truly represent the views of the rapidly growing and diverse faculty. Duke University Archives, Collection description for University Council Records.

30. Minutes of University Council of the University Faculty Meeting, December 10, 1952, Box 35, Edens Papers, DUA.

31. Minutes of University Council of University Faculty, January 21, 1953, Box 35, Edens Papers, DUA.

32. Edens to Ernest C. Colwell, June 22, 1950; Colwell to Edens, June 27, 1950, Box 10, Edens Papers, DUA.

33. Hamilton was a Mississippian, who received his doctorate from Duke in 1938 and returned to teach and edit the *South Atlantic Quarterly.* Durden, *The Launching of Duke University,* 137.

34. William B. Hamilton, "The Past and Future of the Duke University Chapter of the American Association of University Professors," a paper read to the chapter on November 21, 1952, Box 1, Edens Papers, DUA.

35. Interim Report of the President to the Board of Trustees, February 27, 1952, Box 30, Edens Papers, DUA.

36. Report of the President to the Board of Trustees, May 31, 1952, Box 30, Edens Papers, DUA.

37. Report of the President to the Board of Trustees, February 1953, Box 30, Edens Papers, DUA.

38. Mrs. Robert H. Morrison to Edens, October 8, 1953; Edens to Morrison, October 13, 1953, Box 33, Edens Papers, DUA. Morrison was not especially satisfied by Edens's reply. A year later, after the *New York Times* article on segregation, Morrison wrote him again. She respectfully held to her previous positions, arguing again that Duke should lead the South rather than wait for change to be forced on it. "If this sounds too idealistic," she observed, hinting at a role for education that Edens seemed to reject, "it is the fault of the university, for its professors of history and religion and economics have so shaped this mind." Morrison to Edens, May 4, 1954, Box 33, Edens Papers, DUA.

39. Report of the President to the Board of Trustees, February 24, 1954, Box 30, Edens Papers, DUA.

40. Report of the President to the Board of Trustees, February 24, 1954, Box 30, Edens Papers, DUA.

41. Ibid.

42. Waldo Beach to Edens, April 9, 1954, Box 33, Edens Papers, DUA. Beach also commented in this letter on Edens's rhetorical approach. "The manner in which you raise the question seems to me wise, gracious, and politic, certainly one at which no offense could be taken, even by those of the Board of Trustees who conscientiously would oppose any change of policy." The director of Duke's news bureau, Earl W. Porter, however, pointed out to Edens the problem with his rhetorical style. In response to inquiries from the education editor of the *New York Times,* Porter advised Edens to reply with a simple, direct statement of Duke's policy of excluding blacks. To make any other comment at all, he argued, could result in three things, all of them bad. Either Duke would be "linked with those who are definitely leaning toward admittance; with those who are defending staunchly the status quo—or, if we made a general statement it would have to be so vague and so general that in our attempt to avoid identification with either of the extreme views its very transparency would embarrass us." Earl W. Porter to Edens, January 21, 1954, Box 39, Edens Papers, DUA. Edens followed Porter's advice and wrote a brief, clear letter stating simply that Duke University did not admit Negro students. Porter became Edens's assistant in 1956, while also doing graduate work in history. His doctoral dissertation was published as *Trinity and Duke, 1892–1924: Foundations of Duke University* (Durham, NC, 1964).

43. Branscomb, *Purely Academic,* 154; February 1950 Report to the Board of Trust; Minutes of Board of Trust Meeting; April 1952 Report to the Board of Trust; Minutes of Board of Trust Meeting, Box 212, Chancellor's Office Papers, RG 300, VUSC.

44. The events at Sewanee in 1952 and 1953 are discussed in Donald Smith Armentrout, *The Quest for the Informed Priest: A History of the School of Theology* (Sewanee, TN, 1979), 279–309, and, in the context of the history of race relations within the Episcopal church, in chapter 2 of the excellent study by Gardiner H. Shattuck Jr., *Episcopalians and Race: Civil War to Civil Rights* (Lexington, KY, 2000).

45. Branscomb to Benton, June 11, 1952, Box 159, Chancellor's Office Papers, RG 300, VUSC.

46. Benton to Branscomb, September 24, 1952, Box 159, Chancellor's Office Papers, RG 300, VUSC. The twelve schools that responded to Benton's survey were Columbia Theological Seminary in Decatur, Georgia, The College of the Bible in Lexington, Kentucky, Louisville Presbyterian Theological Seminary, Southern Baptist Theological Seminary in Louisville, Phillips University College of the Bible in Enid, Oklahoma, Perkins School of Theology at SMU in Dallas, Southwestern Baptist Theological Seminary in Fort Worth, Brite College of the Bible in Fort Worth, Austin Presbyterian Theological Seminary in Austin, Texas, Union Theological Seminary in Richmond, the Candler School of Theology at Emory, and Duke University's Divinity School.

Vanderbilt's board was already aware that Scarritt College for Christian Workers, just across the street from Vanderbilt, had also recently begun enrolling black students.

47. Branscomb, law dean Ray Forrester, and board member and university attorney Cecil Sims decided in 1951 to "not make any formal reply or take a position" in response to the AALS actions. Branscomb to Forrester, November 20, 1951, Box 121, Chancellor's Office Papers, RG 300, VUSC. Vanderbilt's response to the offer of a conference from the AALS special committee on racial discrimination was succinct. Branscomb replied that if the committee wanted to visit the Law School, "we should be happy to extend them every courtesy and hospitality, but they cannot be of any assistance to us in working out this long-standing problem." Branscomb to F. D. G. Ribble, January 30, 1952, Box 121, Chancellor's Papers, RG 300, VUSC. Although Branscomb was taking a "wait and see" attitude toward the entire matter, he was already considering what Vanderbilt might do if the issue were forced. "If we are forced to make that choice," he wrote in a note to Forester, "I might be compelled to say that in my judgment we would lose more by bowing to an outside directive on this point and remaining in the Association than by withdrawing and endeavoring to handle the problem, which this action is attempting to force, in the ways in which I am confident we can handle it." Branscomb to Forrester, December 16, 1951, Box 121, Chancellor's Office Papers, RG 300, VUSC. Above all, Branscomb wanted to avoid an open fight, realizing that whatever the outcome Vanderbilt would be worse off. Chancellor's Statement to Closed Session Meeting of the Board of Trust, October 10, 1952, Box 212, Chancellor's Office Papers, RG 300, VUSC.

48. Branscomb to Hugh Stuntz, October 15, 1952, Box 228, Chancellor's Office Papers, RG 300, VUSC. This is Branscomb's reply to a letter from Stuntz, which must have been written in early September.

49. Excerpt from Closed Session of the Meeting of the Board of Trust, October 10, 1952, Box 212, Chancellor's Office Papers, RG 300, VUSC.

50. Branscomb, *Purely Academic*, 155; Conkin, *Gone with the Ivy*, 541–42.

51. The telegram came from a recent Vanderbilt graduate, Richard Burrows Jr., and in two lines simply objected and asked for ties with Scarritt to be broken. Branscomb, with typical zeal, responded with a two-page letter detailing the reasons for the decision. Branscomb to Burrows, February 16, 1953, Box 212, Chancellor's Papers, RG 300, VUSC.

52. Ibid.

53. Ibid.

54. On the same day that Benton sent Branscomb his report on the desegregation of southern seminaries he also sent a resolution of the faculty of the School of Religion. Unanimously adopted only the day before, with all members present and voting, this resolution simply conveyed the conviction of Vanderbilt's Religion faculty: "that if the practices of this School are to be in accord with the Christian gospel the fellowship and instruction of the School should be open to qualified students without reference to their race or color." Branscomb, *Purely Academic*, 154; Benton to Branscomb, September 24, 1952, Box 159, Chancellor's Office Papers, RG 300, VUSC. "I am transmitting this resolution to you," wrote Benton to the chancellor, "for your information and use in whatever manner seems best to you." Branscomb presented both documents to the board, urging them to take this step at the same time they decided the Scarritt issue. The trustees, though they did not act at this time, agreed that when Dean Benton had a "properly qualified negro student" the case should be presented to the board for serious consideration. Minutes of Meeting of Board of Trust, October 10, 1952, Box 212, Chancellor's Office Papers, RG 300, VUSC.

55. Chancellor's Statement to Closed Session of the Board of Trust, October 10, 1952, Box 212, Chancellor's Office Papers, VUSC. Branscomb admitted that he did not know if the reports about the foundations were true but still argued that they indicated the general direction of developments.

56. Branscomb to Rev. James Pike, March 16, 1953, RG 300, Box 212, Chancellor's Office Papers, VUSC.

57. Pike's statement was printed in the *New York Times*, February 13, 1953. He apparently learned of Vanderbilt's decision from a faculty member in the School of Religion.

58. Statement released for publication to the *Nashville Banner* on February 13, 1953, by Chancellor Harvie Branscomb, Box 159, Chancellor's Office Papers, RG 300, VUSC.

59. Stahlman to Branscomb, Box V-2, February 25, 1953, Stahlman Papers, VUSC.

60. Branscomb first noted the legal problem in his remarks to the board in October 1952. "It is my understanding from our legal counsel," he said, "that laws still stand upon the statute books of Tennessee requiring a completely dual system of education. . . . I doubt, however, that it is practical for us to avoid the problem by pleading this legal situation. The public is not likely to be convinced that what is legal in Knoxville [where the University of Tennessee had begun desegregation] is illegal in Nashville." Chancellor's Statement to Closed Session Meeting of the Board, October 10, 1952, Box 212, Chancellor's Office Papers, VUSC.

61. Branscomb to Pike, March 16, 1953, Box 212, Chancellor's Office Papers, RG 300, VUSC. Branscomb indicated that Vanderbilt's lawyer indicated his confidence that any legal challenge that might arise would result in the overturning of the Tennessee law requiring segregation in the classroom. The first time Branscomb inquired about the possibility of opening admissions to black students, five years earlier, Vanderbilt's attorney responded firmly that Tennessee law made it impossible.

62. Johnson later became a member of Vanderbilt's Board of Trustees.

63. Benton to Branscomb, April 28, 1953, Box 159, Chancellor's Office Papers, RG 300, VUSC.

64. Minutes of Meeting of Board of Trust, May 1, 1953, Box 212, Chancellor's Office Papers, RG 300, VUSC. A congratulatory letter to Branscomb from trustee John J. Tigert after the vote indicated in a very understated way the seriousness of the decision as well as the existence of division on the board on spite of the unanimous vote. "I hope the Board Meeting met your expectations," Tigert wrote. "I have never seen them so deliberate—however, it was an interesting session." Tigert went on to express his own strong approval of the admission of Johnson, telling Branscomb simply, "I am glad that Vanderbilt admitted this man." Tigert to Branscomb, May 5, 1953, Box 212, Chancellor's Office Papers, RG 300, VUSC. Tigert was the grandson of Methodist Bishop Holland McTyeire, instrumental in the founding of Vanderbilt and the school's first president. He was particularly proud of the fact that his grandfather ordained the first two black bishops of the Colored Methodist Episcopal Church, the church that Joseph Johnson served, in 1870.

65. Minutes of Meeting of Board of Trust, May 1, 1953, Box 212, Chancellor's Office Papers, RG 300, VUSC.

66. The editor of the *Vanderbilt Alumnus*, Robert McGaw, acknowledged this reasoning in a 1956 article, an attempt to explain the university's stance toward desegregation in the aftermath of heated controversy over the removal of racial bars to entry in the Law School. "The first cases, in 1952–53," he wrote, "involved religion, and therefore were easier for almost everybody to accept and even approve." Robert McGaw, "A Policy the University Can Defend: 'In the South and in the North, in the Present and in the Future,'" *Vanderbilt Alumnus* (November–December 1956).

67. Branscomb to Warren P. Norton, April 7, 1953, Box 203, Chancellor's Office Papers, RG 300, VUSC.

68. Branscomb considered Davidson a harmless irritant. "I am willing," he wrote, "to have Professor Davidson blow off within our own organization, and to say pretty much what he wants to, and pay no attention to it. If he goes outside with his criticisms and attacks that would be another matter, but thus far I know of nothing serious along this line." Branscomb to N. Baxter Jackson, September 23, 1953, Box 212, Chancellor's Office Papers, RG 300, VUSC. Davidson, in turn, did not particularly care for Branscomb. This only continued a rather long history of enmity between Vanderbilt's administration and those in the Agrarian circle. See Paul Conkin, *The Southern Agrarians* (Knoxville, TN, 1988), especially pages 144–45.

69. Davidson to Branscomb, May 3, 1953, Box 212, Chancellor's Office Papers, RG 300, VUSC. Davidson asked that his letter be read at the next board meeting but requested that Branscomb otherwise keep its contents confidential.

70. Letters of congratulations arrived from individual alumni, from the president of the Memphis Vanderbilt Club, and from the chairman of the Nashville Fellowship of Reconciliation. Objections likewise came from alumni. They are in Box 212, Chancellor's Office Papers, RG 300, VUSC.

71. Branscomb to Warren P. Norton, April 7, 1953, Box 203, Chancellor's Office Papers, RG 300, VUSC.

72. In 1951 the General Education Board gave Tulane $1,200,000, to be matched 1:1, for the improvement of its graduate programs in the social sciences. President's Report to the Board, April 10, 1951, TUA. Harvie Branscomb of Vanderbilt was a member of the GEB board and wrote Harris after the vote to offer his congratulations on the approval of the grant. "I am sure," Branscomb wrote, "that this will mean as much stimulus to your institution as a similar grant to Vanderbilt made a year ago. Of course, you are also going to have the great fun of raising that money." Branscomb to Harris, April 7, 1951, Box 28, Harris Papers, TUA. Also in 1951 Tulane received $300,000 to increase salaries for graduate teaching from the Carnegie Foundation. President's Report to the Board, April 10, 1951, TUA. Duke and Vanderbilt received identical grants.

73. President's Report to the Board, December 11, 1951, TUA.

74. Harris to William S. Howland, September 9, 1953, Box 42, Harris Papers, TUA.

75. Jones's election was announced in the *New Orleans Times-Picayune*, December 13, 1950.

76. The uncomfortable relationship between Harris and Jones is palpable in the documentary evidence. The most ordinary correspondence can be painfully formal, even strained. Minutes reveal that Harris frequently had to consult the board about things that would have been routine administrative matters at the other four schools. From time to time Harris, probably out of desperation, sent copies of articles about the proper role of governing boards to the trustees. Harris to Jones, December 30, 1952; April 9, 1954, Box 14, Harris Papers, TUA.

77. Mohr and Gordon, *Tulane*, chapter 3.

78. Minutes of the Meeting of the Full-time Faculty of the Tulane College of Law, November 20, 1950; December 8, 1950, Box 30, Harris Papers, TUA. Law professor Mitchell Franklin, a focal point for some of Harris's earlier problems with accusations of Communist influence, resolutely supported the Yale Amendment in faculty meetings. His was the only dissenting vote at this meeting.

79. Lemann to Cahn, July 10, 1951, Box 31, Harris Papers, TUA.

80. Harris's own attitude reflected, like Branscomb's, a desire to be "helpful" to the black community where he could. In 1953, for example, Harris worked with A. W. Dent, the president

of New Orleans's black college, Dillard, to place duplicate library books from Tulane in Dillard's weak collection. Dent to Harris, July 15, 1953; Garland Taylor to Harris, July 23, 1953, Box 28, Harris Papers, TUA.

81. Copy of Harris to Cheatham, May 2, 1951, in President's Report to the Board, May 8, 1951, TUA.

82. President's Report to the Board, December 9, 1953, TUA.

83. Ibid.

84. Ibid. The issue of black attendance at meetings was debated on the Tulane campus as well as in the board room. The student newspaper editorialized in favor of change, using many of the same arguments as Harris. "This problem must be met, and soon; for the university is increasingly faced with requests from New Orleans Negroes to attend public gatherings such as symphonies and lectures. If Tulane University takes the reins of leadership in this area—as it properly should—it will not advance alone. . . . We, too, can help put back the "universal" in university, and stand proud before the nation." *Tulane Hullabaloo,* December 11, 1953.

85. Minutes of Academic Dean's Council, December 4, 1952; February 5, 1953, Box 1, Harris Papers, TUA.

86. The refusal to relax this policy was made more complicated by the fact that Loyola University, immediately adjacent to the Tulane campus, voted in favor of the Yale Amendment. In fact, Loyola had already begun admitting black undergraduates and several enrolled in the fall of 1951. President's Report to the Board, December 11, 1951, TUA. "The position of the Roman Catholic Church," Harris noted, "seems to be one of non-segregation. This attitude of course makes our own more difficult."

87. Ibid.

88. President's Report to the Board, October 10, 1950, TUA.

89. President's Report to the Board, TUA.

90. Dyer to Longenecker, August 24, 1961, Tulane University Vertical Files, TUA. For a discussion of the role of the University Center see Robert G. Sherer's brief, "University College: A History of Access to Opportunity, 1942–1992," Tulane University Publications (1992). Dyer is the author of *Tulane: The Biography of a University.*

91. Dyer to Longenecker, August 24, 1961, Tulane University Archives Vertical Files, TUA.

92. Perhaps because of its location in a more complicated and cosmopolitan city, Tulane received a fairly steady flow of applications during the early 1950s from area blacks. These were all referred to Harris, who replied with a short, polite statement of Tulane's exclusionary policy. There are nearly a dozen responses to these applications collected in Box 99, Herbert Longenecker Papers, TUA.

93. Minutes, Board of Administrators, May 12, 1952, TUA. Paul Tulane specified that the gift from his estate be used for "the promotion and encouragement of intellectual, moral and industrial education among white young persons in the city of New Orleans, State of Louisiana." Tulane University Charter, reproduced in Dyer, *Tulane,* Appendix I.

94. Marie Louise Snellings, "The American Negro, Yesterday and Today," Box 99, Longenecker Papers, TUA.

95. *Emory Wheel,* January 27, 1950.

96. *Emory Wheel,* October 12, 1950.

97. Ernest Cushman Jr. to Robert C. Mizell, October 22, 1951, Box 5, Mizell Papers, EUA.

98. The records of the Law School are uncatalogued and in storage. AALS records are available but cannot be used to refer to any specific school.

99. *Emory Alumnus,* December 1957. The Candler family association with Emory began even earlier. Asa Candler's brother, Warren Akin Candler, graduated from old Emory College in 1875 and assumed its presidency in 1888. He held that post until 1898 when he was elected a bishop in the Methodist Church. English, *Emory University,* 6–7. For more detailed discussion of Emory's early days see Henry Morton Bullock, *A History of Emory University, 1836–1936* (Nashville, TN, 1936).

100. In 1947, for example, Candler donated half of the stock of the Asa G. Candler Company, essentially a real estate concern, to the university, increasing the school's endowment by about $5 million. English, *Emory University,* 76. He was also known as a "hands-on" chairman of the board. *Emory Alumnus,* December 1957.

101. Henry Bowden, "The Christian University in a Scientific Age (A Board Chairman's View)," speech given to Emory faculty group, April 5, 1959, Box 4, Bowden Papers, EUA.

102. *Emory Wheel,* February 5, 1953; November 5, 1953. The same week as the conference at Glenn Memorial was to be held, the Georgia Student Christian Conference met at Paine College, with eighteen Emory delegates present. Black and white students "roomed, ate, and square danced together without racial discrimination," said one Emory attendee. This body voted to condemn segregation as un-Christian. A few of Emory's representatives were faculty members, including Jack Boozer of the School of Theology and the university's director of religious life, Sam Laird.

103. "First Atlanta Conference on the Churches and World Order, April 6–7, 1953"; Charles Howard Candler to Goodrich White, March 26, 1953, Box 1, Robert F. Whitaker Papers, EUA.

104. White to Charles Howard Candler, March 30, 1953, Box 1, Whitaker Papers, EUA.

105. White to Charles Howard Candler, March 30, 1953, Box 1, Whitaker Papers, EUA.

106. Ibid.

107. Ibid.

108. See Meiners, *History of Rice,* 169–72.

109. Minutes of the Board of Trustees, Volume 15, February 15, 1950, Rice University.

110. On George R. Brown see Joseph A. Pratt and Christopher J. Castaneda, *Builders: Herman and George R. Brown* (College Station, TX, 1999). Chapter 8, "Building Universities," contains an extended discussion of George Brown's contributions to Rice as well as his brother Herman's role at Southwestern University in Georgetown, Texas. George Brown was one of the founders of Brown and Root, a powerful construction firm with global operations. His business holdings also included Texas Eastern, an oil and gas concern. See Christopher J. Castaneda and Joseph A. Pratt, *From Texas to the East: A Strategic History of Texas Eastern Corporation* (College Station, TX, 1993). Several biographies of Lyndon Johnson touch on his relationship with the Browns. Robert Dallek, *Lone Star Rising: Lyndon Johnson and His Times* (New York, 1991), and Robert Caro, *The Years of Lyndon Johnson: The Path to Power* (New York, 1982), both discuss Brown's financial help in Johnson's campaigns.

111. The frantic political atmosphere in Houston during the 1950s is chronicled in Don E. Carleton, *Red Scare! Right-Wing Hysteria, Fifties Fanaticism, and Their Legacy in Texas* (Austin, 1985). Carleton makes clear the link between radical anti-Communism and the commitment to segregation. For example, see his discussion of the Houston School Board's decision to investigate deputy superintendent George Ebey in 1953, pp. 201–204. William Henry Kellar, *Make Haste Slowly: Moderates, Conservatives, and School Desegregation in Houston* (College Station, TX, 1999), explores in detail the politics of the Houston School Board and the close connection between anti-Communism and resistance to desegregation.

112. The *Rice Thresher* was fascinated with these developments and in 1952 began a series of articles on UNESCO and its opposition in Houston. October 22, 1952.

113. R. A. Childers to Hollis Edens, February 19, 1952; Edens to Childers, February 21, 1952, Box 9, Edens Papers, DUA; Carleton, *Red Scare,* 142–46. Another black Atlantan, Dr. Benjamin Mays of Morehouse University, neatly summed up the connection between protesting racism and being branded a Communist: "For many decades the South has tried to make the world believe that the Southern way of life (the segregated way) was acceptable to Negroes. They trumpeted loud and long that Negroes were happy and satisfied with apartheid, Southern style, and that whenever a Southern Negro complained it was not really he who was speaking but, instead, he was being 'used' by white Yankees or by Communists." Benjamin E. Mays, *Born to Rebel: An Autobiography* (New York, 1971), 209.

114. Rice never had any denominational ties, and as a scientific and technical institute it remained largely unconcerned with the teaching of religion during these years. This is not to say that there was no religious presence on campus. Like all the other schools considered here, during the 1950s Rice had an annual Religious Emphasis Week, which brought a series of speakers from several faiths to campus for organized discussions with students. Denominational student organizations also had a significant presence. Still, the institute was hardly a haven of faith. This sometimes troubled the trustees, Newton Rayzor in particular. At a 1951 meeting of the Rice board Rayzor told his colleagues that "he had attended several open forums at Rice where such topics as 'Is There A God' and 'What Rice Institute Has Done To My Religion' were discussed, and that such meetings and discussions he had had with students revealed a definite and urgent need for a department of religion at Rice, such a department to teach the fundamentals of the three great American religions—Catholicism, Protestantism, and Judaism and to be staffed with men of equal standing with other departments at Rice; that in his opinion there was no subject deserving a more careful and detailed study than this subject." Minutes of the Board of Trustees, Volume 13, February 1, 1951, Rice University. Rayzor continued to argue for this and for the construction of a chapel on campus, but other concerns were always more pressing to the board as a whole. In 1951 Rayzor donated money for a professorship in religious thought. Minutes of the Board of Trustees, Volume 13, May 2, 1951. This position was in the Philosophy Department and was intended to be strictly nonsectarian. *Rice Thresher,* September 21, 1951. A chapel was not completed until 1958, and then it was built mainly with funds that came from Rayzor himself.

115. See for example, Kluger, *Simple Justice,* and Mark Tushnet, *The NAACP's Legal Strategy against Segregated Education, 1925–1950* (Chapel Hill, 1987).

116. At about the same time the council was formed Joseph Jones, the chairman of the Tulane board, wrote the chairmen of the Rice, Emory, Duke, and Vanderbilt boards suggesting that they too meet to discuss their common problems. His suggestion was not met with any enthusiasm.

117. Branscomb, typescript, "Some Dates," Box 20, Vanderbilt Centennial History Project, VUSC.

118. "Memorandum to the Members of the Council of Southern Universities [n.d., fall 1952], Box 10, Edens Papers, DUA. The list of attendees at this meeting includes Harvie Branscomb, William Houston, Goodrich White, and Rufus Harris. Hollis Edens could not attend but sent Duke vice president Paul Gross in his stead. Edens too would be a regular attendant in the future. Logan Wilson, a vice president at UNC who was present as a representative of that school, had spent years working with Harris, mainly as dean of Sophie Newcomb, Tulane's women's

college. Lewis Hammond from UVA and Chancellor James Hart from the University of Texas were at the meeting and were also very well known to everyone present.

119. Minutes of the Council of Southern Universities, October 24, 1952, Box 10, Edens Papers, DUA.

120. Houston to Edens, October 21, 1953, Box 10, Edens Papers, DUA; Houston to Branscomb, October 21, 1953, Box 5, Branscomb Papers, VUSC.

121. Memorandum to the Board of Governors with reference to the Council of Southern Universities, September 29, 1954, Box 2, Houston Papers, WRC. Again, Houston may have had off-the-record discussions with individual board members about the racial issues, but there is no official record. Rufus Harris, in contrast, fully informed the Tulane board of the extensive discussion of racial matters. President's Report to the Board, November 12, 1952, TUA. The council did obtain funds from the General Education Board for graduate fellowships and scholarships in the South. The grant was a substantial one, $2,500,000 over ten years, which represented the liquidation of the GEB. President's Report to the Board, December 8, 1954, TUA. Correspondence arranging this grant between Dean Rusk of the GEB, Harvie Branscomb, Goodrich White, and Logan Wilson, now president of the University of Texas, is in Chancellor's Office Papers, Box 153, GR 300, VUSC.

122. Minutes of the Board of Trustees Meeting, December 15, 1949, Board of Trustees Records, WRC.

123. *Rice Thresher,* November 7, 1952.

124. Hobby was a member of one of the most prominent and powerful families in Texas. His father, William P. Hobby Sr., had been governor of the state in the late teens and early twenties. His mother was Oveta Culp Hobby, secretary of health, education, and welfare in the Eisenhower administration. The Hobby family also owned one of Houston's major newspapers, the *Houston Post.* William Hobby Jr. would go on to become Texas's longest serving lieutenant governor.

125. *Rice Thresher,* October 27, 1950.

126. *Rice Thresher*, January 12, 19, 1951. Some black schools were invited to send unofficial delegations to the TISA meeting at Texas A&M in March 1951. ("Texas A&M hosts have solved the problems," noted the *Thresher,* "of housing and feeding accommodations for Negro delegates." March 16, 1951). There, the Texas Southern University's application for membership was unanimously accepted, "the high point of the convention" according to Rice delegate Bill Hobby. *Rice Thresher,* March 22, 1951. Rice itself hosted the TISA annual convention in 1953 and presumably made arrangements with TSU to host any black delegates that attended. A TSU student, Lloyd Riley, was elected parliamentarian that year, which, according to the *Thresher,* "serves as a symbol of recognition of ability regardless of other factors and should not be taken as a lean-over-backwards policy to the Negro race." March 27, 1953.

127. *Rice Thresher,* April 24, 1953. The poll was a very general one and included questions on religion, ethics, the balance between humanities and sciences, and the quality of Rice students as dates. There was only one question about race.

3. THE BACKLASH AGAINST BROWN: 1954

1. Harris to Arthur C. Mobley Jr., January 19, 1955, Box 39, Harris Papers, TUA.

2. *Brown v. Board of Education of Topeka, Kansas,* 345 U.S. 972 (1954).

3. Dwight D. Eisenhower, *The White House Years: Mandate for Change, 1953–1956* (New York, 1963), 234, discusses his reaction to *Brown* decisions and his attitudes toward segregation. See also Robert F. Burk, *The Eisenhower Administration and Black Civil Rights* (Knoxville, 1984), 151–73. The extent to which Eisenhower should receive credit or blame for federal policy on race after *Brown* is subject to debate. Michael S. Mayer, "With Much Deliberation and Some Speed: Eisenhower and the *Brown* Decision," *Journal of Southern History* 52 (February 1986): 75, and James C. Duram, *A Moderate among Extremists: Dwight D. Eisenhower and the School Desegregation Crisis* (Chicago, 1981), see the president as a quiet force for change. Others portray Eisenhower as dragging his feet on *Brown* in order to court the white southern vote. Jeffrey R. Young, "Eisenhower's Federal Judges and Civil Rights Policy: A Republican 'Southern Strategy' for the 1950s," *Georgia Historical Quarterly* 77 (Fall, 1994): 536–65. A recent addition to the Eisenhower literature, Geoffrey Perret, *Eisenhower* (New York, 1999), chapter 41, presents a more nuanced, but ultimately negative, portrayal of Eisenhower's actions (and lack thereof) on civil rights.

4. Fairclough, *Race and Democracy*, 165.

5. See generally Numan V. Bartley, *The Rise of Massive Resistance: Race and Politics in the South During the 1950s* (Baton Rouge, 1969).

6. Minutes of the First Meeting of the Board of Directors of the Southern Education Reporting Service (SERS), May 11, 1954, Box 222, Chancellor's Office Papers, RG 300, VUSC.

7. SERS Press Release, July 29, 1954, Box 222, Chancellor's Office Papers, RG 300, VUSC.

8. Ibid.

9. In a letter to the chairman of the SERS in 1960, Tuskegee president and SERS board member L. H. Foster laid out fundamental criticisms of *The Southern School News* standards of objectivity, starting with the refusal of the paper to include news from the black press, L. H. Foster to Frank Ahlgren, March 22, 1960, Box 222, Chancellor's Office Papers, RG 300, VUSC.

10. Kefauver acknowledged that it was theoretically possible for Congress to pass a constitutional amendment that would require segregation in the public schools, but quite reasonably he noted that northern opposition would be insurmountable. *Southern School News*, September 3, 1954.

11. A good analysis of Tennessee's complicated political climate is Dewey Grantham, "Tennessee and Twentieth-Century American Politics," in *Tennessee History: The Land, the People, and the Culture*, ed. Carroll Van West (Knoxville, TN, 1998), 343–72. On Clement, see Lee Seifert Greene, *Lead Me On: Frank Goad Clement and Tennessee Politics* (Knoxville, TN, 1982), and David Halberstam, "The End of a Populist," *Harper's* (January, 1971): 38. There are several useful studies of Kefauver, including Joseph Bruce Gorman, *Kefauver: A Political Biography* (New York, 1971); Charles L. Fontenay, *Estes Kefauver: A Biography* (Knoxville, TN, 1980); and Richard E. McFadyen, "Estes Kefauver and the Tradition of Southern Progressivism," *Tennessee Historical Quarterly* 37 (Winter 1978). Also helpful on Tennessee politics in the 1950s is Hugh Davis Graham, *Crisis in Print: Desegregation and the Press in Tennessee* (Nashville, 1967).

12. *Vanderbilt Hustler*, October 15, 1954.

13. *Vanderbilt Hustler*, October 22, 1954. The editors apparently sent copies of the editorial to Vanderbilt's trustees. One, Dan May, responded enthusiastically. "I read your editorial with much interest. . . . I happen to be a member of the Board of both Vanderbilt and Fisk and to my way of thinking your diagnosis is excellent." *Vanderbilt Hustler*, October 29, 1954.

14. *Vanderbilt Hustler*, October 29, 1954.

15. Branscomb to James A. Simpson, September 17, 1954, Box 212, Chancellor's Office Papers, RG 300, VUSC.

16. Branscomb to Charles R. Clason, July 16, 1954, Box 134, Chancellor's Office Papers, RG 300, VUSC.

17. Memorandum from John Wade to Branscomb, November 11, 1954, Box 237, Chancellor's Office Papers, RG 300, VUSC.

18. John Wade to Branscomb, November 11, 1954, Box 237, Chancellor's Office Papers, RG 300, VUSC.

19. Ibid.

20. Ibid.

21. Association of American Law Schools, Proceedings of the Annual Meeting, December 1951. The AALS proceedings are remarkable, and they include verbatim transcripts of floor debate.

22. John Wade to Branscomb, November 11, 1954, Box 237, Chancellor's Office Papers, RG 300, VUSC.

23. Privately, Wade was disappointed in these results and believed that it would be possible to change many of the "no" votes.

24. John Wade to Branscomb, November 11, 1954, Box 237, Chancellor's Office Papers, RG 300, VUSC.

25. Meeting of the Board of Trust, November 12, 1954, Box 212, Chancellor's Office Papers, RG 300, VUSC.

26. Branscomb to David Cavers, February 21, 1955, Box 237, RG 300, Chancellor's Office Papers, VUSC.

27. Dean John Benton to Rev. Joseph Johnson, April 1, 1954, Box 159, Chancellor's Office Papers, RG 300, VUSC.

28. John Benton to Dwight W. Harwell, July 28, 1954, Box 159, Chancellor's Office Papers, RG 300, VUSC.

29. *Southern School News,* September 3, 1954.

30. In this effort Talmadge either did not understand or chose to ignore the clear implications of *Sweatt v. Painter,* 339 U.S. 629 (1950), and *McLaurin v. Board of Regents,* 339 U.S. 637, both decided on June 5, 1950.

31. Bartley, *Massive Resistance,* 41–42, 54–55.

32. Mrs. Grace Wilkey Thomas, who argued that Georgia should accept the Supreme Court ruling gracefully, finished last. *New York Times,* September 9, 1954.

33. Bartley, *Massive Resistance,* 68–72. Georgia's factional politics were exceptionally complex in 1954, with three Talmadge allies as well as several anti-Talmadgites in the gubernatorial race and Talmadge himself unwilling to name his choice for the governor's seat. See Joseph L. Bernd, *Grassroots Politics in Georgia: The County Unit System and the Importance of the Individual Voting Community in Bifactional Elections, 1942–1954* (Atlanta, 1960), for a sophisticated and detailed analysis of Georgia politics in this period.

34. There was a significant black vote in the city, easily large enough to influence local politics. See Donald R. Matthews and James W. Prothro, "Negro Voter Registration in the South," in *Change in the Contemporary South,* ed. Allen P. Sindler (Durham, 1963), 119–49; and Margaret Price, *The Negro Voter in the South* (Atlanta, 1960), 1–5. This influence was largely exercised behind the scenes by leaders of the black community. See Clarence Stone, *Regime Politics: Governing Atlanta, 1946–1988* (Lawrence, KS, 1989), 46–50, 52–55. In 1953, however, Atlanta University President Rufus Clement was elected to a seat on the city's school board, carrying forty of fifty-eight precincts.

35. Bartley, *Massive Resistance*, 22–24, discusses the position of what he calls "business conservatives," urban businessmen who were the major spokesmen for the South's cities. In *Inside Agitators*, David Chappell analyzes in detail the ideology of the southern civic-commercial elite and their economic motivations for acting as peacemakers in the civil rights battles of the 1960s. For a specific and cogent discussion of the Atlanta business community and their agenda, see Harmon, *Beneath the Image of the Civil Rights Movement and Race Relations*, especially 45–82.

36. Report of the President to the Board of Trustees, October 26, 1954, EUA. This grant came with significant matching requirements, which would lead to wide-ranging difficulties in the near future.

37. Report of the Dean of the Graduate School, October, 1954, EUA.

38. Most of this interaction seems to have been in small group settings. Examples abound of Morehouse and Atlanta University professors speaking on various race-related topics at Emory. For example, Hyland Lewis, professor of sociology at Atlanta University, spoke to the Emory Sociology Club in 1950 on "The Adjustment of the American Negro to White Society." *Emory Wheel*, October 5, 1950.

39. *Journal of Public Law* (Spring 1954).

40. *Emory Wheel*, May 20, 1954.

41. Ibid.

42. Ibid. The only blacks who appear in the student papers of these universities during the 1940s and 1950s (aside from the occasional story about the retirement of an aged and beloved black custodian) are black entertainers hired to perform at fraternity functions.

43. Phi Beta Kappa Address, May 21, 1954, Box 26, White Papers, EUA.

44. Report of the President to the Board of Trustees, October 26, 1954, EUA.

45. Notes on Meeting of Committee of One Hundred at Emory University, on November 10, 1954, Box 14, Arthur J. Moore Papers, EUA. At around this same time Bishop Moore, in correspondence with Professor Claude Thompson of Emory's School of Theology, expressed his concern that responsible leaders must not outrun the people.. Thompson complained, very gently and with all due deference, that a Methodist Planning Conference that met in the fall had banned any discussion of issues likely to produce "discord," that is, segregation. Thompson, a strong proponent of black admissions to Emory and of desegregation in general, was "grieved" by the lack of leadership. "Can we not as Methodist ministers," Thompson pleaded, "give a needed leadership to our people of Georgia, occupying such a crucial position in America, a leadership declaring a clear and fearless word from the modern prophets of the Lord." Moore corrected Thompson, who had not attended the meeting, pointing out that no such censorship had taken place and that he had in fact brought Emory theology professor Leroy Loemker to the gathering specifically to address the "church's responsibility in this racial matter." He concluded with a plaintive observation: "I am seeking, with what little courage and insight I possess to give our church in Georgia progressive and wise leadership. I know that my motives are good, but I have to leave my methods to be either approved or criticized by good men like yourself." Claude Thompson to Moore, October 3, 1954; Moore to Thompson, November 4, 1954, Box 20, Arthur J. Moore Papers, EUA.

46. "The Segregation Question: Some Points of Information," *Emory Alumnus*, October 1954.

47. Ibid. The numbers cited by Fort are 49 private schools and 33 public ones. Eight were in the District of Columbia, 19 in the border states (Maryland, Oklahoma, Missouri, and West Virginia), 7 in Arkansas, 1 in Georgia, 12 in Kentucky, 6 in Louisiana, 3 in North Carolina, 1 in South Carolina, 5 in Tennessee, 14 in Texas, and 6 in Virginia. Only three southern states had no institutions that were integrated in 1954: Florida, Mississippi, and Alabama.

48. Emory's board had thirty-three members at full strength, but at the time this editorial was written there were two vacancies.

49. This was equally true of the other four schools studied here, all of which admitted students of nearly every hue as long as they were from other countries (except black Africans). These admissions were not always without problems. For example, in 1954 the Rice Mathematics Department made arrangements for a student from Lucknow, India, who was doing work toward a degree from the University of Paris, to work as a special student with one of its faculty members. While waiving his fees, the committee on graduate instruction also wanted it made clear that "every effort should be made to eliminate situations arising from his color." Minutes, Committee on Graduate Instruction, September 28, 1954, Box 1, Rice University Graduate Council Papers, WRC. Peter Wallenstein discusses these other nonwhite but not black students in "Black Southerners and Non-Black Universities: The Process of Desegregating Southern Higher Education, 1935–1965," in *Higher Education and the Civil Rights Movement: White Supremacy, Black Southerners, and College Campuses,* Peter Wallenstein, ed., *(Gainesville, FL, 2008),* 17–59.

50. *Emory Alumnus,* October 1954.

51. Minutes of the Graduate School Faculty, April 12, 1954, Box 28, Harris Papers, TUA.

52. Ibid.

53. *New Orleans Times-Picayune,* May 7, 1954; *New Orleans Item,* May 7, 1954.

54. Dean Cole gave the statement to the editors, reasoning that on a small campus it would leak out anyway. *Tulane Hullabaloo,* May 7, 1954. The statistics were taken from a *New York Times* survey of southern higher education. The editors noted that schools that had begun admitting blacks included Loyola, mere yards away from the Tulane campus. Blacks had actually been admitted to Loyola as early as 1951. See John Robert Payne, "A Jesuit Search for Social Justice: The Public Career of Louis J. Twomey, S.J., 1947–1969" (Ph.D. diss., University of Texas, 1976), for a chronicle of Loyola's struggle with racial issues during this period. Tulane's response to the changes at Loyola was strained. Elsewhere in Louisiana, the graduate schools at LSU had been ordered to desegregate in 1950 and in the summer of 1954 there were 230 blacks enrolled there. During the regular term their numbers were smaller, but still nearly 60 had been enrolled in the spring semester of 1954. *Southern School News,* September 1954.

55. *New Orleans Times-Picayune,* May 7, 1954; *New Orleans Item,* May 7, 1954.

56. Minutes of the Meeting of the Board of Administrators, May 12, 1954, TUA.

57. Dean's Council Minutes, May 20, 1954, Box 1, Harris Papers, TUA. The graduate faculty did not take Harris's advice to heart.

58. Ibid.

59. Mohr and Gordon, *Tulane,* 183–84.

60. Administrator J. Blanc Monroe prepared a memorandum that summarizes the discussion of the law committee meeting of May 13, 1954, Box 99, Longenecker Papers, TUA.

61. No copy of this statement survives, but Jones mentioned it at the next meeting of the full board. Minutes of the Meeting of the Board of Administrators, June 9, 1954, TUA.

62. Kennon, a former judge, was elected in 1952 as a major player in the anti-Long faction and an ally of Republican presidential candidate Eisenhower. Kennon was certainly a segregationist but saw no possibility of winning a war with the federal government. Black, *Southern Governors and Civil Rights,* 44; Bartley, *Massive Resistance,* 51; Fairclough, *Race and Democracy,* 170–71.

63. *Southern School News,* September, 1954.

64. Marie Louise Snellings to Harris, May 17, 1954, Snellings Correspondence File, Harris Papers, TUA.

65. President's Report to the Board, June 9, 1954, TUA.

66. Harris to Snellings, May 21, 1954, Snellings Correspondence File, Harris Papers, TUA.

67. Dean's Council Minutes, May 20, 1954, Box 1, Harris Papers, TUA. Harris repeated in November this warning to avoid "agitation" about black admissions. President's Agenda for Dean's Council Meeting, November 4, 1954, Box 1, Harris Papers, TUA.

68. See infra, pp. 11–14.

69. President's Report to the Board, October 13, 1954, TUA. Harris included in this report the correspondence between Tulane's Law School dean, Ray Forrester, and the chairman of the AALS Special Committee, Page Keeton of the University of Texas. Keeton had requested that Tulane finally provide what they had been attempting to dodge: "a forthright statement from you as to the policy that would be followed if a Negro qualified on all grounds other than color should apply for admission." Forrester still began his reply with a feint, asserting that the Law School was unaware of any application from a black student for at least the last five years. In the end, though, he gave Keeton what he wanted. "The University has had a policy since its inception of not admitting negroes. That is the present policy. As one school of the University, it is clear that we cannot follow a contrary policy." Keeton to Forrester, September 2, 1954; Forrester to Keeton, September 27, 1954. Harris considered this important enough to send a copy to Joseph Jones even before the board meeting. Harris to Jones, October 6, 1954, Box 14, Harris Papers, TUA.

70. Executive Order 10557, September 3, 1954; Herman M. Roth to Harris, December 31, 1954; Clarence Scheps to Harris, January 21, 1955, Box 99, Longenecker Papers, TUA. For an overview of Eisenhower and equal economic opportunity see Burk, *Eisenhower Administration and Black Civil Rights,* 89–108.

71. Garland F. Taylor to Harris, September 17, 1954, in President's Report to the Board, October 13, 1954, TUA. The Urban Life Research Institute was dedicated to the sociological study of southern urbanization. It sought outside funding for research on topics such as "Individual and Social Factors Affecting Political Behavior in Urban Areas" and "Personality Development of Negro Youth in the Urban South." The institute sometimes collaborated with the Dillard Sociology Department and by 1954 had hired the two black researchers. Box 6, Harris Papers, TUA, contains several grant proposals and letters about possible projects.

72. Ibid.

73. Ibid.

74. While the board was thinking the matter over, Harris told Taylor privately, the library should continue to provide services to blacks on a case-by-case basis and Taylor and his staff could be assured that, in the event of an incident, they would have the backing of the trustees. Harris Addenda, "Policy-Negroes," TUA.

75. George Norris Green, *The Establishment in Texas Politics: The Primitive Years, 1938–1957* (Westport, CT, and London, UK 1979), 121–34, discusses the politics of McCarthyism in Texas, with particular emphasis on Houston, where reactionary groups had the strongest foothold.

76. *Southern School News,* September 3, 1954; Green, *Establishment in Texas Politics,* 151–70. Yarborough was later elected to the Senate, where he was effective on several important committees. After his somewhat waffling start, he became an outspoken supporter of desegregation and was one of a handful of southern senators who supported the civil rights legislation of the 1960s. See Chandler Davidson, *Race and Class in Texas Politics* (Princeton, NJ, 1990), 29–32.

77. At Emory in particular the problem of care for Atlanta blacks was unremitting, due largely to the grossly inadequate facilities for black health care and the severe shortage of black

doctors. This issue was also intertwined with nearly endless debates about the future of Emory's health complex and its relationships with other Atlanta institutions. Various suggestions for helping to cope with the problem were offered, with little actually accomplished, throughout the 1950s.

78. Meiners, *History of Rice*, 204–205.

79. In 1955 the Rice board created the Rice Institute Research Sponsors as a formal organization for its industrial supporters. Minutes of the Meeting of the Board of Trustees, February 23, 1955; November 22, 1955, Rice University. Other schools sought and received industry support as well, but the voracious appetites of professional schools, medical schools in particular, for money meant that massive amounts of outside funding, far more than business could provide, were needed at all the other schools.

80. *Rice Thresher,* April 30, 1954.

81. *Rice Thresher,* November 5, 1954.

82. *Rice Thresher,* October 29, October 1, October 8, 1954.

83. *Raleigh News and Observer,* May 19, 1954; *Durham Herald,* May 19, 1954. These stories are identical. At least one North Carolinian sent Edens a note in response to this report. Nearly comically, he congratulated the president on his statement: "I liked the tone as well as the words. It was very typical of you." Indeed it was. George Watts Hill to Edens, May 20, 1954, Box 33, Edens Papers, DUA.

84. The profound irony of this non-confrontational stance has been pointed out by several commentators, including William Chafe, *Civilities and Civil Rights: Greensboro, North Carolina and the Black Struggle for Freedom* (New York, 1980), 3–10. A collection of essays on this topic is David S. Cecelski and Timothy B. Tyson, eds., *Democracy Betrayed: The Wilmington Race Riot of 1898 and Its Legacy* (Chapel Hill, 1998). In an afterword to this collection Chafe succinctly puts the issue: "No matter how often later generations of white politicians in North Carolina boasted of the state as a progressive example to the South . . . their rhetoric politely preserved the same social order that the white vigilantes built through the violence of 1898."

85. *Southern School News,* September 3, 1954. Luther Hodges was a businessman who had spent many years outside North Carolina. Back in his home state, he was elected lieutenant governor in an upset after running as an independent. Once in office he proved to be a stalwart of the business establishment wing of the Democratic Party, committed to economic growth and modernization. Hodges was a key player, for example, in the original development of the successful Research Triangle Park between Durham and Raleigh. Bartley, *New South,* 214; Paul Luebke, *Tar Heel Politics: Myths and Realities (Chapel Hill, 1990),* 72–73, 92–93. For a very readable account of his years as North Carolina's governor, see Hodges's memoirs, *Businessman in the Statehouse: Six Years as Governor of North Carolina* (Chapel Hill, 1962).

86. *Southern School News,* September 3, 1954.

87. *Duke Chronicle,* October 8, 1954.

88. Ibid.

89. *Duke Chronicle,* October 5, 1954. Thompson submitted a detailed report on this conference to President Edens, Vice President Paul Gross, and Sociology Chairman Howard Jensen. Thompson had planned to suggest the Durham–Chapel Hill area as the site of the next conference, after consulting with Edens, Chancellor House of UNC, and President Charles S. Johnson of Fisk, but planning centered around organization rather than future meetings, so he did not. A Report to President Hollis Edens, Vice-President Paul Gross, and Dr. Howard Jensen, October 31, 1954, Box 33, Edens Papers, DUA.

90. The *Christian Advocate,* December 15, 1954. Crum's article was the subject of a long story in the *Duke Chronicle,* December 17, 1954.

91. Report of the President to the Board of Trustees, June 5, 1954, Box 30, Edens Papers, DUA.

92. Ibid.

93. Ibid.

94. Minutes of University Council Meeting, December 15, 1954, Box 35, Edens Papers, DUA.

95. Helen Morrison to Edens, December 1, 1954, Box 33, Edens Papers, DUA.

96. Edens to Morrison, December 22, 1954, Box 33, Edens Papers, DUA.

4. UNABLE TO LEAD: THE LATE 1950S

1. Guion Griffis Johnson, "Quiet Revolution in the South," *Journal of the American Association of University Women* 52 (March, 1959): 133–36. For a conspicuous example of a school that utterly failed to integrate its black students, see Dwonna Goldstone, *Integrating the 40 Acres: The 50-Year Struggle for Racial Equality at the University of Texas* (Athens, GA, 2006).

2. Judson C. Ward Jr. to Goodrich C. White, May 4, 1959, Box 21, White Papers, EUA. Ward was part of the committee that visited Tulane to help with its 1959 self-study.

3. "The Future of Tulane University: A Proposed Blueprint," n.d., but late 1955 or early 1956, Box 24, Harris Papers, TUA.

4. Liva Baker, *The Second Battle of New Orleans: The Hundred-Year Struggle to Integrate the Schools* (New York, 1996); Edward F. Haas, *DeLesseps S. Morrison and the Image of Reform: New Orleans Politics, 1946–1961* (Baton Rouge, 1974). Pamela Tyler, in her insightful study of women in New Orleans's politics, quotes the daughter of a prominent white liberal discussing the situation after *Brown:* "At that point, you're either one of them or one of us. Especially when it turned the corner where it wasn't just 'you're a traitor to our race' but now 'you've become a Commie.'" Pamela Tyler, *Silk Stockings and Ballot Boxes: Women and Politics in New Orleans, 1920–1963* (Athens, GA, 1996), 222.

5. Marie Louise Snellings to Joseph McCloskey, January 6, 1955, Harris Papers, Addendum, "Policy—Negroes," TUA.

6. George Wilson to Joseph McCloskey, January 7, 1955, Harris Papers, Addendum, "Policy—Negroes," TUA.

7. Minutes of the Meeting of the Board of Administrators, January 12, 1955, TUA.

8. Ibid. Also under consideration that day was the law committee's report on a letter that Harris had received from the Tulane-Lyceum Association, a local cultural group that used the Tulane auditorium for concerts and lectures and proposed to accept black members. Stanley McDermott to Harris, December 1, 1954, Harris Papers, Addendum, "Policy—Negroes," TUA. The law committee reached a similar conclusion on this matter. "In permitting the use of its property by the Lyceum Association, the Board could legally either permit or refuse to permit the use of its property by non-segregated audiences of whites and negroes." In this case, though, where Tulane's de facto policy already permitted blacks to attend events in McAlister Auditorium, the board simply thanked the association for their consideration and told them that their membership decisions were of "no concern to Tulane." Ibid. Marie Louise Snellings also opposed this action in her letter to McCloskey. Allowing blacks to attend Lyceum events, she said, "would provoke comment, inquiry concerning other events, and would raise questions regarding seating, rest rooms, and the like." Snellings to McCloskey, January 6, 1955, Harris Papers, Adden-

dum, "Policy—Negroes," TUA. The board also took the rather unusual step of sending Harris a "formal, interim report" on the board's position. Even though Harris was involved in most, if not all, the deliberations on admitting black students, Jones notified him by letter that the board was "presently not prepared to alter the policy, but you are assured that this whole matter is now, and will continue to be, until it is resolved finally, the subject of most careful study." Jones to Harris, February 7, 1955, Harris Papers, Addendum, "Policy—Negroes," TUA.

9. Minutes of Meeting of Graduate Faculty, May 18, 1955, Box 28, Harris Papers, TUA.

10. Minutes of the Meeting of the Board of Administrators, February 9, 1955, Harris to A. P. Generes, March 4, 1955, Harris Papers, Addendum, "Policy—Negroes," TUA.

11. These new documents are discussed in detail in Marie Louise Snellings, Report to the Board of Administrators of the Tulane Educational Fund, July, 1955, Harris Papers, Addendum, "Policy—Negroes," TUA.

12. Marie Louise Snellings, Report to the Board of Administrators of the Tulane Educational Fund, July, 1955, Harris Papers, Addendum, "Policy—Negroes," TUA.

13. Harris to Marie Louise Snellings, September 13, 1955, Harris Papers, Addendum, "Policy—Negroes," TUA. Snellings's response to Harris's letter seems to indicate that she seriously anticipated a future policy decision to admit blacks and expressed "hope that the Board will seek to clear itself by Court action if they once make a policy decision in that direction." Marie Louise Snellings to Harris, September 26, 1955, Harris Papers, Addendum, "Policy—Negroes," TUA.

14. This point was made by the dean of the Law School, Ray Forrester, who also saw Mrs. Snellings's report. Ray Forrester to Harris, September 29, 1955, Harris Papers, Addendum, "Policy—Negroes," TUA.

15. President's Report to the Board, June 8, 1955, TUA.

16. Harris to Joseph McCloskey, November 7, 1955, Box 14, Harris Papers, TUA. McCloskey was the chairman of the educational affairs committee.

17. President's Report to the Board, November 9, 1955; Minutes of the Meeting of the Board of Administrators, November 9, 1955, TUA.

18. Agenda for Meeting of the Educational Affairs Committee, December 13, 1955, Box 14, Harris Papers, TUA. Tulane's law faculty was divided. In preparing for the annual meeting of the AALS in December 1955, where the special committee's proposal would be voted on, the faculty met to discuss Tulane's response. Professor Mitchell Franklin moved, and the motion was seconded, that Tulane should support the requirement and vote "yes" on the committee's recommendation. Other faculty, angered at the perceived meddling of the AALS, wanted to "announce at the Association meeting that it will not accept compulsion or dictation by the Association and that the imperative by the Association be disregarded." Minutes of the Meeting of the Faculty of the Tulane School of Law, December 10, 1955, Box 31, Harris Papers, TUA.

19. Elizabeth Wisner to Harris, November 4, 1955, Harris Papers, Addendum, "Policy—Negroes," TUA.

20. Health care for blacks in New Orleans was woeful. Flint-Goodridge Hospital, an adjunct of Dillard University, was the only hospital in the city that allowed black doctors in attendance and by the mid-1950s it was in desperate shape. See Tyler, *Silk Stocking and Ballot Boxes,* 213–19.

21. Harris to Robert A. Lambert, November 17, 1955, Box 63, Harris Papers, TUA. On November 7, 1955, the United States Supreme Court moved the reasoning of *Brown* beyond public schools, upholding a Fourth Circuit ruling that Baltimore could no longer segregate public recreational facilities and reversing a Fifth Circuit opinion that allowed segregated golf courses in

Atlanta. *Mayor and City Council of Baltimore City v. Dawson,* 350 U.S. 877 (1955); *Holmes v. City of Atlanta,* 350 U.S. 879 (1955). (Emory trustee Henry Bowden argued Atlanta's case for segregation at both the Fifth Circuit and the Supreme Court.) This action would have upset in particular Tulane board member Lester Lautenschlager, a former college football standout and the director of New Orleans's Recreational Department for many years. New Orleans had gone to great pains to keep black and white recreation separate and did not cease to do so even after these decisions. Fairclough, *Race and Democracy,* 152–53.

22. Harris to Lambert, November 17, 1955, Box 63, Harris Papers, TUA. Lambert was willing to wait to act to help black doctors and New Orleans's Flint–Goodrich Hospital, but he held the rather forlorn hope that "the few—very few, I'm certain—reactionaries on Tulane's Board will not delay the liberalization which you and I—along with so many others—seek to bring about. Time *is* important." Robert A. Lambert to Harris, December 1, 1955, Box 63, Harris Papers, TUA.

23. Minutes of the Meeting of the Board of Administrators, December 14, 1955, TUA.

24. Emmet Irwin to Jones, February 2, 1956, Harris Papers, Addendum, "Policy- Negroes," TUA. Irwin sent copies to prominent board members Darwin Fenner and Clifford Favrot, as well as to the Citizen's Council of New Orleans. Jones read Irwin's entire letter into the record at the next board meeting. Minutes of the Meeting of the Board of Administrators, February 8, 1956, TUA.

25. Harris drafted a brief reply for Jones's signature, but it is not clear if it was ever sent. Harris carefully thanked Irwin for his "courteous" expression of concern for Tulane but made it clear that Tulane employees did not forfeit their rights as citizens. Draft reply, February 16, 1956; Harris to Jones, February 16, 1956, Harris Papers, Addendum, "Policy—Negroes," TUA.

26. The law committee had met on March 9 and the educational affairs committee on March 14.

27. Harris's files contain Mrs. Snellings's July 1955 memo and others of varying degrees of detail from Joseph McCloskey, Ashton Phelps, Law School Dean Ray Forrester, and J. Blanc Monroe. Harris Papers, Addendum, "Policy—Negroes," TUA.

28. Minutes of the Meeting of the Board of Administrators, March 21, 1956, TUA.

29. Ibid. The educational affairs committee meeting was attended by Deans Lumiansky of the Graduate School, Wisner of the School of Social Work, Lapham of the Medical School, and Forrester of the Law School. All of them strongly supported the admission of blacks. Minutes of Meeting of Educational Affairs Committee, March 14, 1956, Box 14, Harris Papers, TUA.

30. Ibid.

31. Minutes of a Meeting of the Graduate Council, January 7, 1957, Box 28, Harris Papers, TUA.

32. *AAUP Bulletin,* June, 1957, 362–63.

33. Memo to the Members of the Graduate Faculty, December 2, 1957; Harris to Lumiansky, December 9, 1957, Box 28, Harris Papers, TUA.

34. Both Amsel and Kolb taught in Newcomb College. Dyer, *Tulane,* 330, 342.

35. Ray Forrester to Harris, January 6, 1958, Harris Papers, Addendum, "Policy – Negroes," TUA.

36. Ibid. Harris made a few editorial changes and submitted this as part of his next report to the board. President's Report to the Board, January 8, 1958, TUA.

37. Harris, of course, saw this before it was sent. Wade to Forrester, March 11, 1958; For-

rester to Wade, March 14, 1958; Forrester to Harris, March 14, 1958, Harris Papers, Addendum, "Policy—Negroes," TUA.

38. President's Report to the Board, April 9, 1958, TUA. A note in Harris's handwriting on his copy of the report indicates that the board went along with this, as long as no integrated meetings were allowed to take place on the Tulane campus. President's Report to the Board, April 9, 1958, Harris Papers, Addendum, "Policy—Negroes," TUA.

39. John H. Stibbs to Harris, March 10, 1958, Harris Papers, Addendum, "Policy—Negroes"; President's Report to the Board, March 12, 1958, TUA.

40. President's Report to the Board, March 12, 1958, TUA.

41. John Hubbard to Jack Dailey, February 24, 1958, Harris Papers, Addendum, "Policy—Negroes," TUA. President's Report to the Board, March 12, 1958, TUA.

42. Harris to Joseph Jones, January 21, 1955; Jones to Harris, February 11, 1955, Harris Papers, Addendum, "Policy—Negroes," TUA. In 1957, Colorado State abruptly pulled out of a basketball game it was to have played at Tulane, and the 1958 and 1959 games that had been scheduled with the Air Force Academy were cancelled by the academy because of Tulane's segregation policy. Annual Report of the Senate Committee on Athletics, 1958, Box 20, Harris Papers, TUA.

43. The next week's editorial, however, muddied the waters considerably. Another *Hullabaloo* editor suggested that although segregation was in fact dying, its demise should be more gradual. *Hullabaloo*, January 11, 1957; January 18, 1957. Angry responses from off campus soon arrived. R. G. Robinson to E. S. Evans, January 17, 1957; Harris to R. G. Robinson, January 23, 1957, Harris Papers, Addendum, "Policy-Negroes," TUA.

44. Russel M. Geer to Harris, March 26, 1955, Harris Papers, Addendum, "Policy—Negroes," TUA.

45. These letters, along with Tulane's letters of refusal, are scattered in several file folders in Harris Papers, Addendum, "Policy—Negroes," TUA.

46. Eugene A. Nabors to Harris, October 9, 1956, Box 31, Harris Papers, TUA.

47. The announcement of Harris's retirement from Tulane was met with skepticism from those who were familiar with the internal politics of the school. Hodding Carter, editor of the *Delta Democrat-Times* in Greenville, Mississippi, and a friend of Harris's, wrote that "I know there's more to your retirement than meets the eye. And I'm sorry this happened. You have done wonderful things for Tulane and I know the University will never forget it." Carter to Harris, May 7, 1959, Box 64, Harris Papers, TUA.

48. For an account of the desegregation of Mercer and Harris's decisive role in that episode see Will D. Campbell, *The Stem of Jesse: The Costs of Community at a 1960s Southern School* (Macon, GA, 1995).

49. At the request of its chairman, Father Theodore Hesburgh of Notre Dame, Harris began serving in 1958 on the U.S. Civil Rights Commission. Harris first made certain that Joseph Jones had no serious objections to Harris's service on the commission. Objections came from other quarters, though. Marie Louise Snellings, whose husband had refused to serve, wrote Harris about the matter. "In regard to the Civil rights Committee," she complained, "I am sorry you felt you should serve. . . . Many words, no matter how pretty, cannot alter the fundamental objective and with Tulane in its present position I regret this." Harris defended himself with a standard argument: "unless we ourselves undertake to work out some of these problems, outsiders who have no real knowledge of our situation will recklessly attempt to do so." Snellings to

Harris, February 13, 1959; Harris to Snellings, February 23, 1959; Harris to Monte Lemann and Edgar Stern, February 23, 1959, Box 59, Harris Papers, TUA.

50. "An Informal Discussion of My Personal Concepts of University Purpose, Organization, Operative Practices and Education Philosophy," December 18, 1959, Box 65, Harris Papers, TUA.

51. The New Orleans upper class was quite different from its counterparts in Atlanta or Houston. While the New Orleans elite was undeniably successful in business, the city was notable for its lack of the sort of business values that drove Atlanta and Houston. New Orleans did not seem to hunger for the acceptance of the rest of the country in quite the same way or to value money regardless of its pedigree. More tightly knit and far less open to newcomers than the elites of the more business-oriented cities, the upper class in New Orleans was, with notable exceptions, also less interested in civic improvement and reform. Although the historical corruption of Louisiana politics doubtless played a major role in this apathy, the obsession with Mardi Gras that took up so much energy, time, and money was also a factor. See Phyllis Hutton Raabe, "Status and Its Impact: New Orleans's Carnival, the Social Upper Class, and Upper Class Power" (Ph.D. diss., Pennsylvania State University, 1973); Charles Chai, "Who Rules New Orleans? A Study of Community Power Structures: Some Preliminary Findings on Social Characteristics and Attitudes of New Orleans Leaders," *Louisiana Business Survey* (October, 1971), 2–11.

52. Eugene H. Brooks, June 28, 1955, Box 7, Edens Papers, DUA.

53. The *Duke Chronicle* ran a series of articles in the fall of 1957 that examined in detail the desegregation of UNC. October 1, October 4, October 8, 1957.

54. *Charlotte Observer*, October 30, 1955. Edens received a letter urging him to do something about this situation and suggesting that the petition was the result of "a lot of Communists around Chapel Hill and Durham" who were "actively back of the NAACP" and who were probably "proselyting" [sic] the young Duke students. George F. Crook to Edens, December 12, 1955, Box 33, Edens Papers, DUA.

55. On December 13, 1955, for example, the *Chronicle* called segregation a "barbaric tradition." This editorial was the boldest condemnation of segregation published at Duke in the 1950s, arguing that the school must "rise above the provincialism of Durham" and demanding an explanation from Chairman of the Board Norman Cocke. While the *Chronicle*'s editorial stance toward segregation varied in intensity from year to year, from this point on it consistently understood segregation to be doomed.

56. Edens's efforts to help bring about a smoother transition to desegregation also extended beyond the Duke campus, with somewhat more success. For example, he helped craft a proposal for the elimination of a separate category for black colleges within the Southern Association of Colleges and Secondary Schools, which passed (without any negative votes) at the association's meeting in December 1960. Edens to Donald C. Agnew, December 12, 1956; Agnew to Edens, December 18, 1956; "Action with Regard to Colleges for Negro Youth," December 6, 1956, Box 67, Edens Papers, DUA.

57. President's Report to the Board, February 23, 1955, Box 30, Edens Papers, DUA.

58. Minutes of the Meeting of the University Council, February 16, 1955; March 17, 1955, Box 35, Edens Papers, DUA. The study of trends in desegregation was the work of a committee chaired by Dean Marcus Hobbs, which included Vice President Herbert Herring, Deans James Cleland and W. C. Davison, and Professor E. R. Latty.

59. The "Report by Committee on Trends and Experiences in Desegregation at Universi-

ties in the South" was distributed on December 14, 1955, Box 35, Edens Papers, DUA. Several of the people the committee spoke with, while stressing the relative ease of the transition, still expressed trepidation over the "delicate issue" of the swimming pool.

60. Minutes of the Meeting of the University Council, January 18, 1956, Box 35, Edens Papers, DUA. The resolution was passed by a vote of eight to four, with two abstentions.

61. Branscomb to Edens, November 11, 1955; Edens to Branscomb, November 16, 1955, Box 33, Edens Papers, DUA. The heat generated by the issue of desegregation at this time is indicated by Branscomb's bold markings on his letter to Edens: "PERSONAL AND CONFIDENTIAL."

62. Report of the President to the Board of Trustees, February 29, 1956, Box 30, Edens Papers, DUA.

63. Ibid.

64. Ibid.

65. Minutes of the Board of Trustees Meeting, February 29, 1956, DUA.

66. Waldo Beach, "Storm Warnings from the South," *Christianity and Crisis,* March 19, 1956.

67. *North Carolina Christian Advocate,* August 9, 1956.

68. George R. Wallace to Edens, August 14, 1956; Edens to George R. Wallace, August 17, 1956, Box 33, Edens Papers, DUA.

69. *Duke Chronicle,* April 27, 1956; President's Report to the Board, June 2, 1956, Box 30, Edens Papers, DUA.

70. Arthur C. Thomas to Hollis Edens, December 7, 1956; Edens to Arthur C. Thomas, December 13, 1956, Box 33, Edens Papers, DUA. The text of the petition is found in the *Duke Chronicle,* February 22, 1957.

71. Polly Price to Edens, May 8, 1956. Like nearly all incidents that involved race, this resolution was reported in the press and drew hostile reaction from the community. One correspondent admitted the women's good intentions but warned "you could not raise them [black students] to a standard of decency without to some extent being contaminated yourselves." J. R. Hester to Polly Price, May 11, 1956. As always, Edens defended the students' right to express their views to any correspondent who complained. One example is at Edens to P. J. Baugh Sr., June 30, 1956. All these documents are in Box 33, Edens Papers, DUA.

72. There are over a dozen of these letters, and a few responses, in Edens's files. For his part, the president seemed not at all alarmed by the student letters, although he warned the trustees that they were part of a campaign and suggested they not answer them. He also defended the students, noting in a letter to one trustee that "I am compelled to treat the students' attitude with respect. They are quite naïve but are sincere and by and large are not the trouble making kind." Edens to B. S. Womble, December 21, 1956. All the letters are in Box 33, Edens Papers, DUA.

73. Rodney Neal to N. E. Edgerton, n.d. but December 1956, Box 33, Edens Papers, DUA.

74. Edwin L. Jones to Anne Corpening, December 20, 1956; Corpening to Jones, December 6, 1956, Box 33, Edens Papers, DUA.

75. The notion of the university as a "family" was pervasive at all these schools. To cite just one example, a speech given to incoming freshmen at Emory in 1954 entitled "The Emory Ideal" stressed that the "Emory Family" was composed of these groups and that together they "have, since 1836, dedicated themselves to certain ideals and maintained certain principles." Box 21, Goodrich White Papers, EUA.

76. James Cannon to Edens, n.d. but about February 13, 1957, Box 33, Edens Papers, DUA.

77. Ibid.

78. Ibid.

79. Minutes of the Meeting of the Board of Trustees, February 27, 1957, DUA.

80. Sidney Alderman to Edens, March 1, 1957, Box 33, Edens Papers, DUA.

81. Edens to Sidney Alderman, March 7, 1957, Box 33, Edens Papers, DUA.

82. Barney L. Jones, "Reminiscences, 1930–1960," DUA.

83. R. Taylor Cole, *The Recollections of R. Taylor Cole: Educator, Emissary, Development Planner* (Durham, 1983), 158–59.

84. Barney L. Jones, "Reminiscences, 1930–1960," DUA.

85. Sidney Alderman to Edens, March 1, 1957; Edwin L. Jones to Edens, March 2, 1957; Edgar Nease to Edens, February 28, 1957, Box 33, Edens Papers, DUA. The supporters of desegregation clearly considered Edens an ally. Alderman, for example, wrote, "I was proud of you at the meeting of the Board on Thursday. I was proud of your courage. Your presentation of your recommendation was superb and won you the admiration of my most bitter opponents. Your recommendation was everlastingly right."

86. President's Report to the Board, February 26, 1958, Box 30, Edens Papers, DUA.

87. Reaction to the board's failure to begin desegregation was sharply divided. The immediate response from the student newspaper was something akin to contempt. *Duke Chronicle,* March 1, 1957. Some of Edens's correspondents were upset at the announcement, with one prospective divinity student even withdrawing his acceptance of admission. Richard James Wood to James Cannon, March 1, 1957; Mrs. Joseph E. Workman to Edens, March 18, 1957, Box 33, Edens Papers, DUA. Others strongly supported the board, expressing the certainty that desegregation would lead to "amalgamation" as well as the suspicion that "the present ministerial are being brainwashed," possibly by "some sinister force behind this matter other than the misguided people of this country." J. Bruce Eure to Hollis Edens, March 1, 1957. Similarly, another writer was unhappy that "some of the Doctors and Professors wearing the cloaks of Duke University have been mighty outspoken for integration and other foreign sounding doctrines." E. J. Burns to Edens, March 4, 1957, Box 33, Edens Papers, DUA.

88. These applications were simply turned away, although in one case the applicant, Lawrence Hampton, an honor student at North Carolina College, attempted to appeal the refusal to the General Conference of the Methodist Church. Boxes 49 and 33, Edens Papers, contain correspondence between Edens and Douglas Moore, a black Durham minister who was denied admission. On Moore, see also Taylor Branch, *Parting the Waters: America in the King Years, 1954–1963* (New York, 1988), 93. Other applications are found at Lorenza A. Lynch to President, Duke University, January 2, 1958; Waldo Beach to Lorenza A. Lynch, January 7, 1958, Box 48, Edens Papers, DUA; and J. E. Markee to Edens, April 24, 1959; Edens to Markee, April 29, 1959, Box 28, Edens Papers, DUA.

89. *Duke Chronicle,* April 12, 1957.

90. The newsletter of the Methodist Student Fellowship is one example. *The Crusader,* issued weekly during the late 1950s, mentioned the problem of segregation, at Duke and elsewhere, in nearly every issue. Methodist Student Center Papers, DUA. In the fall of 1957 the student body of the Divinity School began publishing *Response,* which likewise displayed a deep concern over segregation at Duke. Although staunch opposition to the racially restrictive admissions policy was widespread in the school, some division of opinion was evident, with a minority taking the position that "any fervent and vigorous criticism of present conditions would alienate our segregationist brethren." Throughout the late 1950s this issue was turned over again and again, with much agitation, in this publication. Divinity School Papers, "Publications," DUA.

91. *Duke Chronicle,* November 8, 1957; *Durham Herald,* November 10, 1957; *Raleigh News & Observer,* November 9, 1957.

92. *Durham Herald,* November 9, 13, 1957.

93. Edens to Sam B. Underwood Jr., November 15, 1957, Box 58, Edens Papers, DUA. There are about a dozen of these letters in Edens's files. Edens also sent a statement to the trustees, reminding them that they had also once been young and foolish. With few exceptions, most of them took the incident in stride. Edens, "To Members of the Board of Trustees of Duke University," November 14, 1957. Letters from individual trustees to the president are alongside this statement at Box 58, Edens Papers, DUA.

94. A Statement of Opinion, The Undersigned Members of the Episcopal Student Fellowship, Duke University, to the Board of Trustees, April, 1957; William C. Morris Jr. to Edens, April 28, 1957, Box 33, Edens Papers, DUA.

95. *Response,* December 20, 1957; December 19, 1958. Divinity School Papers, "Publications," DUA.

96. Graduate student petition, "To the Board of Trustees of Duke University," January 1959, Box 102, Edens Papers, DUA.

97. *Duke Chronicle,* February 27, 1959. There were, of course, some students who remained resolute segregationists. Often the objections they expressed in letters to the student paper to allowing blacks at Duke revolved around resentment of northerners, who allegedly "decided that the South must kneel down and obey their commands to surrender to integration." *Duke Chronicle,* November 12, 1958. Another common theme was revulsion at the prospect of miscegenation. These letters usually drew prompt and numerous rebuttals. And, as ever, letters came from off campus, protesting the student petitions and declaring "Lets keep our Methodist schools white and clean." C. W. Rothrock to Edens, January 20, 1959, Box 33, Edens Papers, DUA.

98. Edens to Edward Opton Jr., February 20, 1959; Edens to Robert Cushman, February 20, 1959, Box 33, Edens Papers, DUA.

99. Minutes of the executive committee meeting, February 24, 1959, DUA.

100. The *Duke Divinity School Bulletin* captured the mood well: "We should not be hanging our heads in sorrow, but on this matter they cannot droop much lower." May 1959.

101. *Christianity and Crisis,* April 27, 1959. *The Christian Century* condemned the Duke trustees just as explicitly, claiming that their recalcitrance on race "brings into disrepute the whole idea of what properly constitutes a university." March 25, 1959.

102. *Duke Chronicle,* April 24, 1959. The student paper published Beach's comments on the front page and the entire text of the *Christianity and Crisis* editorial on the second page.

103. Robert C. Byrd to Hollis Edens, March 28, 1959, Box 21, Edens Papers, DUA.

104. Walter W. Benjamin to Edens, March 24, 1959, Box 21, Edens Papers, DUA. Several similar letters are found in Box 21. They were answered, by and large, with Edens's usual obfuscation. Cushman, more emotional than Edens, sometimes showed irritation, especially when the criticism came from outside North Carolina. Cushman to Reverend Charles Malesky, March 28, 1959.

105. Robert Cushman to Edens, April 1, 1959, Box 21, Edens Papers, DUA.

106. In May 1959 William H. Brownlee resigned from the faculty of the Divinity School to take a position at Claremont, partly for personal advancement and partly because of "the adamant stand of the Board of Trustees . . . with regard to the maintenance of racial segregation." William H. Brownlee to Robert Cushman, May 5, 1959, Box 21, Edens Papers, DUA.

107. Latty became interim dean after the resignation of J. A. McClain Jr. in 1956.

108. Memorandum to President A. Hollis Edens and Vice President Paul M. Gross, April 14, 1958, Box 26, Edens Papers, DUA.

109. Brainerd to E. R. Latty, October 17, 1957, Box 26, Edens Papers, DUA.

110. Latty proved to be quite successful and stayed on as dean until the fall of 1966.

111. Franklin H. Cook to Hollis Edens, August 17, 1959, Box 8, Edens Papers, DUA.

112. Edens to Franklin H. Cook, September 9, 1959, Box 8, Edens Papers, DUA.

113. Report of the President to the Board of Trustees, Minutes, Board of Trustees Meeting, November 1, 1955, EUA.

114. *Emory Wheel,* December 3, 1959.

115. Randy Fort, "Cutting the Throat to Cure the Cancer," *Emory Alumnus,* April 1956.

116. Albert W. Stubbs to Randy Fort, May 8, 1956, Box 3, Henry Bowden Papers, EUA.

117. Charles Howard Candler to Albert W. Stubbs, May 11, 1956, Box 3, Henry Bowden Papers, EUA.

118. *Emory Wheel.*

119. Boone M. Bowen, *The Candler School of Theology: Sixty Years of Service* (Atlanta, 1974), 112–13.

120. Statement of the Faculty on the School of Theology and Race, n.d. but April 1957. Robert Woodruff Papers, Box 90, EUA. William Cannon became dean of the School of theology in 1953, replacing H. B. Tribble, who had been dean since 1937. Cannon had been a professor of theology at Emory for nine years. *Emory Wheel,* September 24, 1953.

121. White to Members of the Board of Trustees, n.d. but April 1957. White decided that the resolution should be sent to the board before the new president arrived in the summer. Box 90, Robert Woodruff Papers, EUA.

122. Ibid. The language of the faculty's request for a study was taken directly from the 1956 *Methodist Discipline,* paragraph 2026.

123. White to Members of the Board of Trustees, n.d. but April 1957, Box 90, Robert Woodruff Papers, EUA.

124. *Emory Alumnus,* May 1957.

125. Ibid.

126. Emory University Press Release, April 18, 1957, Box 69, Walter S. Martin Papers, Valdosta State University Archives (VSUA).

127. Minutes of the Meeting of the Board of Trustees, April 18, 1957, EUA.

128. Faculty Group to Charles Howard Candler, April 3, 1957, Box 86, Robert Woodruff Papers, EUA.

129. G. B. Connell to Martin, April 23, 1957, Box 61, Martin Papers, VSUA.

130. Martin had little success in placating his on-campus rivals for the presidency. Both Ernest Colwell, dean of the faculties and director of Emory's Graduate Institute of the Liberal Arts, and Howard Phillips, dean of the Graduate School, left Emory soon after his arrival. (Boisfeuillet Jones continued to supervise Emory's medical branch but was never close to Martin.) Martin was able to win over many on the faculty, though, and could count on the stalwart support of men like the dean of the Theology School, William Cannon, who had been Martin's student at Georgia, and his old classmate from the University of North Carolina, Judson C. Ward, whom he appointed as the new vice president and dean of faculties.

131. Martin also quickly began contacting the other southern university presidents, searching for help from those in a similar position. Understandably, he was most eager to talk to for-

mer Emory administrator Hollis Edens. Martin to Edens, May 27, 1957, June 14, 1957, November 1, 1957; Edens to Martin, June 7, 1957, September 24, 1957, Box 49, Edens Papers, DUA.

132. Dean Rusk to Martin, May 23, 1957, Box 62, Martin Papers, VSUA.

133. Report of the President to the Board of Trustees; Minutes of the Meeting of the Board of Trustees, November 14, 1957, EUA.

134. Interview with S. Walter Martin, April 28, 1999. Notes in possession of the author. In response to a student column in the *Wheel* that suggested Emory faculty members had simply given in to the administration's views on segregation, there came explicit denials from the faculty that they had been pressured to conform in any way.

135. Interview with S. Walter Martin, April 28, 1999. Notes in possession of author.

136. S. Walter Martin, "Civilization's Need: The Moral Touch," April 9, 1958, Box 68, Martin Papers, VSUA.

137. S. Walter Martin, "Washington Alumni Talk," October 7, 1959, Box 4, Martin Papers, VSUA.

138. Hartsfield was elected mayor in 1936 and, apart from a brief interruption during World War II, held that office until he was replaced by Ivan Allen Jr. in 1961. Hartsfield, dependent on black votes and the goodwill of the white business establishment, was committed to preserving a sense of racial calm and progress in Atlanta. He provided new services and facilities to black neighborhoods, hired black police officers for the first time, and generally did a masterful job of preserving segregation while allowing change to proceed steadily. Pomerantz, *Where Peachtree Meets Sweet Auburn,* 161–64, 184–88. A good biography of the colorful Hartsfield is Harold H. Martin, *William Berry Hartsfield: Mayor of Atlanta* (Athens, GA, 1978). In "The Quest for Freedom in the Post-*Brown* South: Desegregation and White Self-Interest," 70, *Chicago-Kent Law Review* 70, 2 (1994): 689–755.Davison Douglas examines a very similar dynamic in Charlotte, North Carolina.

139. Atlanta's representatives in the Georgia General Assembly had difficult lives during this period. United in their commitment to keeping the public schools open, the city's seven legislators were isolated and scorned by the rest of the General Assembly. One of these representatives was Hamilton Lokey, law partner of Emory's new chairman of the board Henry Bowden. Jeff Roche, *Restructured Resistance: The Sibley Commission and the Politics of Desegregation in Georgia* (Athens, GA, 1998), 49. This extremely useful study pulls together the strands of a very complicated political and racial situation.

140. *Vivian Calhoun, et al., v. A.C. Latimer, et al.,* 188 F.Supp. 401 (1959). In June 1959, Judge Frank A. Hooper ruled in favor of the plaintiffs and gave the Atlanta School Board until December to come up with a plan for integration.

141. Text of statement by Emory Faculty, *Atlanta Journal and Constitution,* November 30, 1958. Similar statements from the faculty of neighboring Agnes Scott College and from a group of over 400 doctors were presented in December. Emory University Archives Manuscript Box 10. Emory's graduate students also overwhelmingly favored keeping the schools open. In a May 1959 poll 94 percent disapproved of closing schools to prevent desegregation and 89 percent favored admitting blacks to Emory's graduate divisions. *Emory Wheel,* May 1, 1959.

142. In a talk at faculty orientation in the fall of 1962, history professor Harvey Young, who gathered many of the signatures, acknowledged the "thrill that came from the awareness that there was some slight hazard in the venture." Faculty orientation talk, September 25, 1962, Box 15, James Harvey Young Papers, EUA.

143. Henry Bowden, "The Christian University in a Scientific Age (A Board Chairman's View)," talk given to Emory faculty group, April 5, 1959, EUA.

144. "From 'Mr. Alumnus' to Top Trustee," *Emory Alumnus,* December 1957.

145. Bowden, "Christian University in a Scientific Age" April 5, 1959.

146. English, *Emory University,* 257. On Tuttle, see Jack Bass, *Unlikely Heroes* (Tuscaloosa, AL, 1981), especially 26–44.

147. *Emory Wheel,* February 6, 1959.

148. "Crisis in the Schools," *Emory Alumnus,* February 1959. Editors Randy Fort won the 1959 American Alumni Council award for editorial integrity and courage for this issue.

149. Arguments for keeping the public schools open and for opening admissions to Emory to blacks were by now commonplace in the *Wheel.* See, for example, November 14 and 21, December 5 and 12, 1958; January 16, 23, and 30, February 6, 1959.

150. Bowden to T. J. Wesley Jr., February 12, 1959, Box 3, Bowden Papers, EUA. Vice President and Dean of the Faculties Judson C. Ward responded in greater detail but to the same effect. Judson Ward to T. J. Wesley Jr., February 25, 1959, Box 3, Bowden Papers, EUA.

151. Walter R. Davis to Emmet B. Cartledge Jr., February 27, 1959. No written expression of Bowden's opinion survives, but correspondence from Davis and Randy Fort to him on this matter indicates that his views were largely the same as those expressed by Davis. All this correspondence, along with a few hostile letters from alumni, are in Box 4, Bowden Papers, EUA.

152. *Emory Wheel,* March 31, 1959.

153. The quote is from Branscomb's "Tentative and Confidential Memorandum on the Establishment of a Graduate Center in Vanderbilt University," December 1949, Box 4, Branscomb Papers, VUSC.

154. On the racial situation in Nashville see Don H. Doyle, *Nashville since the 1920s* (Knoxville, TN, 1985), 224–43. Cynthia G. Fleming discusses broadly the official attitudes toward public school desegregation and the various major problems that arose in "We Shall Overcome: Tennessee and the Civil Rights Movement" in *Tennessee History: The Land, the People, and the Culture,* ed. Carroll Van West (Knoxville, TN, 1998). Branscomb was a strong supporter of Governor Clement's efforts to desegregate peacefully and in a limited way the state's public schools. Frank Clement to Branscomb, January 23, 1956; Branscomb to Clement, January 26, 1956, Box 212, Chancellor's Office Papers, RG 300, VUSC. From time to time over the next several years the idea was floated, by Branscomb or others, that a group of "thoughtful" citizens ought to make some kind of "moderate, middle statement" condemning violent responses to school desegregation but urging slow, locally controlled implementation. Presciently anticipating federal intervention when local communities resisted desegregation, Branscomb proposed such a statement in 1956 about the growing trouble in Clinton but apparently never issued it. When Nashville began its own plan to desegregate the schools, Branscomb was approached by Hugh Morgan, head of the Medical School, to sponsor a similar letter, but he did not. Branscomb to Edward Lee Norton, December 17, 1956; Hugh Morgan to Branscomb, March 12, 1956; Branscomb to Hugh Morgan, March 15, 1956, Box 212, Chancellor's Office Papers, RG 300; Virginius Dabney to Branscomb, January 10, 1957, Box 154, Chancellor's Office Papers, RG 300, VUSC.

155. Earlier in 1955 Branscomb and Dean John Wade had tried, in an attempt to provide cover, to interest Duke and Tulane in some kind of joint action on desegregating their law schools, but to no avail. Branscomb to David Cavers, February 21, 1955; Branscomb to Franklin P. Gaines, July 15, 1955, Box 237, Chancellor's Office Papers, RG 300, VUSC.

156. John Wade to Branscomb, May 4, 1955, Box 237, Chancellor's Office Papers, RG 300, VUSC.

157. Branscomb to Franklin P. Gaines, July 15, 1955, Box 237, Chancellor's Office Papers, RG 300, VUSC.

158. Transcription from Minutes of Meeting of Board of Trust, May 6, 1955, Box 2510, Secretary of the University's Papers, RG 900, VUSC. Branscomb to Cavers, June 3, 1955, Box 237, Chancellor's Office Papers, RG 300, VUSC.

159. Branscomb to Franklin P. Gaines, July 15, 1955, Box 237, Chancellor's Office Papers, RG 300, VUSC. A letter from the board to the president of the alumni association, who had apparently been getting some heated responses from members, clarified this understanding: "The authorization to the Dean of the Law School in 1955 was not a modification of the 1953 resolution." W. H. Swiggart to Vernon Sharp, October 19, 1956, V-27, Stahlman Papers, VUSC.

160. Branscomb to Franklin P. Gaines, July 15, 1955; Branscomb to David Cavers, June 3, 1955; Cavers to Branscomb, June 17, 1955, Box 237, Chancellor's Office Papers, RG 300, VUSC. Branscomb told Cavers that the board wanted no publicity, that they wanted neither to "place ourselves in the position of boasting in this matter nor of inviting a great number of applications from Negroes." He also, however, assured Cavers that he was free to inform other "responsible educational officers. . . . In other words, I will have no hesitation in telling Rufus Harris or Hollis Edens what we have done . . . but I do not wish to broadcast this action." See also Oliver C. Carmichael Jr. to Branscomb, March 19, 1956; Branscomb to Carmichael, March 30, 1956, Box 212, Chancellor's Office Papers, RG 300, VUSC.

161. *Nashville Banner; Nashville Tennessean,* September 19, 1956. It is a measure of the care that Vanderbilt exercised in choosing these students that Branscomb and John Wade went to meet with Charles Johnson, president of Fisk, before they decided who should be admitted. William Waller, Memorandum of Conversation with John Wade, September 21, 1956, Box 212, Chancellor's Office Papers, RG 300, VUSC.

162. *Nashville Banner,* September 21, 1956; Sims Crownover to Alumni, Friends, and Supporters of Vanderbilt University, September 22, 1956, Box V-9, Stahlman Papers, VUSC. The Tennessee Federation for Constitutional Government was founded in the aftermath of the *Brown* decision. Its president was Vanderbilt English professor Donald Davidson. Wassell Randolph to Branscomb, April 26, 1956, Box 154, Chancellor's Office Papers, RG 300, VUSC.

163. Clyde Alley to Vernon Sharp, October 7, 1956, Box V-6, Stahlman Papers, VUSC. This organization never really caught on, despite attempts to contact and recruit all of Vanderbilt's alumni. The university denied them the alumni lists and the group faded away quickly, never having had more than about fifty members. Branscomb, *Purely Academic,* 158.

164. Branscomb and his wife were touring universities in South and East Africa for the Carnegie Corporation. "Report to the Carnegie Corporation on observations and reflections during the course of a tour of these universities in July–September 1956 by means of a Carnegie travel grant," n.d. but fall 1956, Box 134, Chancellor's Office Papers, RG 300, VUSC.

165. Branscomb to Stephen H. Stackpole, September 29, 1956, Box 136, Chancellor's Office Papers, RG 300, VUSC.

166. Branscomb to John Wade, October 12, 1956, Box 212, Chancellor's Office Papers, RG 300, VUSC.

167. Conkin, *Gone with the Ivy,* 546–47.

168. Sims Crownover to Branscomb, August 10, 1956, Box 212, Chancellor's Office Papers, RG 300, VUSC. The same letter is also in Box V-9, Stahlman Papers, VUSC.

169. D. W. Stubblefield to Branscomb, October 18, 1956, Box V-16, Stahlman Papers, VUSC.

Another alumnus expressed the same idea in 1958, responding directly to Branscomb's downplaying of the desegregation that had already taken place at Vanderbilt. "What you are trying to tell me is that just a little touch of Syphilis [sic] or just a little touch of pregnancy is not bad . . . and I don't agree—a little is all the way in these cases." Lawrence W. Long to Branscomb, January 20, 1958, Box 191, Chancellor's Office Papers, RG 300, VUSC.

170. Clyde Alley to Alumni Association, October 7, 1956, Box V-6, Stahlman Papers, VUSC.

171. One example is at Resolution, Vanderbilt Commodore Club of Hattiesburg, Mississippi, October 15, 1956, Box V-2, Stahlman Papers, VUSC.

172. *Nashville Tennessean,* October 3, 1956.

173. Minutes of Board of Directors of the West Kentucky Vanderbilt Club Meeting, October 9, 1956, Box 2510, Secretary of the University's Papers, RG 900, VUSC.

174. Dean Rusk to Branscomb, October 1, 1956. This letter is in Stahlman's files, as Branscomb surely sent him a copy to keep his courage up. Box V-15, Stahlman Papers, VUSC.

175. Branscomb's memoirs contain a brief discussion of his and Harold Vanderbilt's appearance before the upset alumni and their eventual acceptance of the board's decision. *Purely Academic,* 158–59. A more detailed explanation of the events at and surrounding this board meeting is McGaw, "A Policy the University Can Defend." The week before the board meeting the Vanderbilt Law Alumni also held a meeting and overwhelmingly defeated a resolution to censure the university for admitting the black students. Paul J. Hartman to Branscomb, October 23, 1956, Box 212, Chancellor's Office Papers, RG 300, VUSC.

176. Frank Houston to Branscomb, October 25, 1956, Box 212, Chancellor's Office Papers, RG 300, VUSC.

177. James Stahlman to E. E. Wilkinson, October 17, 1956; James Stahlman to J. C. Foshee, November 5, 1956, Box V-2, Stahlman Papers, VUSC.

178. Branscomb to J. D. Williams, March 27, 1956, Box 239, Chancellor's Office Papers, RG 300, VUSC. Branscomb wrote Williams offering to withdraw as commencement speaker on the chance that his appearance at Ole Miss might cause embarrassment to Williams on account of the race issue. Williams declined the offer.

179. Branscomb to Charles Clason, June 14, 1957, Box 134, Chancellor's Office Papers, RG 300, VUSC.

180. McGaw, "A Policy the University Can Defend." This article drew a large, appreciative response from the school's alumni. Randy Fort, editor of the *Emory Alumnus,* also wrote McGaw with high praise and requested several copies for distribution at Emory. Randolph L. Fort to Robert McGaw, January 7, 1957, Box 2510, Secretary of the University's Papers, RG 900, VUSC. At Tulane, Rufus Harris gave copies to the board members. Harris to Joseph M. Jones, January 16, 1957, Box 99, Longenecker Papers, TUA.

181. Branscomb to Lawrence A. Long, January 10, 1958, Box 212, Chancellor's Office Papers, RG 300, VUSC. Branscomb made this argument several times in the late 1950s. For example, recounting to an old friend the events surrounding the opening of the Law School, he said, "The argument made was that Vanderbilt is a private University and not amenable to the Supreme Court decision. My answer to this was that the implications of this argument were that the South would do nothing on this issue until forced to do so by the law and a policeman, and that this had never been the attitude of intelligent Southern leaders, and was not the attitude of Vanderbilt University." Branscomb to Charles Clason, June 14, 1957, Box 134, Chancellor's Office Papers, VUSC.

182. *Vanderbilt Hustler,* February 10, 1956.

183. *Vanderbilt Hustler,* September 20, 1957, October 4, 1957.

184. *Vanderbilt Hustler,* October 10, 1958.

185. This controversy was fairly long running, lasting throughout the late fall and winter of 1958–59 and picking up again the following fall. *Vanderbilt Hustler,* November 14, 1958, October 9, 1959. Similar debates, with varying degrees of acrimony, took place at Duke, Emory, Tulane, and Rice.

186. Stanton E. Smith to John Stanbaugh, May 8, 1958; Branscomb to Stanton Smith, May 26, 1958, Box 114, Chancellor's Office Papers, RG 300, VUSC.

187. Guy H. Wells to Branscomb, March 5, 1957; Branscomb to Guy H. Wells, March 14, 1957, Box 238, Chancellor's Office Papers, RG 300, VUSC.

188. Branscomb to Robert Harris, May 15, 1958, Box 175, Chancellor's Office Papers, RG 300, VUSC.

189. In a tribute to Benton soon after his death, Edwin Mims, head of Vanderbilt's excellent English Department and the author of a history of the university, praised Benton's stance on desegregation. "He was never a fanatic or extremist, never unaware of the great difficulties of this problem, but he viewed it from the standpoint of morality and religion and not of politics. He recommended the admission of qualified Negroes to the Divinity School. His example is an inspiration to those who are today trying to bring about a moderate and gradual solution of this vexing problem." A Recorded Synopsis of an Address by Dr. Edwin Mims on Dean John K. Benton before the Brotherhood Class and the Branscomb Class at West End Methodist Church, Sunday, August 26, 1956, Box 159, Chancellor's Office Papers, RG 300, VUSC.

190. *Vanderbilt Hustler,* January 11, 1957.

191. Branscomb to James Cleland, January 2, 1957; Branscomb to Jack Benton, May 17, 1956, Box 159, Chancellor's Office Papers, RG 300, VUSC.

192. Robert Nelson to Branscomb, November 25, 1957, January 20, 1958; Branscomb to Nelson, February 17, 1958, Box 202, Chancellor's Office Papers, RG 300, VUSC.

193. Branscomb to Robert Nelson, January 21, 1958, Box 202, Chancellor's Office Papers, RG 300, VUSC.

194. Ibid. Although Branscomb allowed the Divinity School to admit Miss McTyreire, she apparently never enrolled.

195. Meiners, *History of Rice,* 173–87.

196. William Houston, Memorandum on Graduate Studies at Rice, August 10, 1959, Box 2, Houston Papers, WRC. Most of the other doctorates were in chemistry, mathematics, and biology.

197. Herman M. Roth to Houston, December 31, 1954, Box 5, Houston Papers, WRC. Roth sent exactly the same letter to Rufus Harris at Tulane. Box 99, Longenecker Papers, TUA. The text of the order is at Executive Order no. 10,557 (19 *Federal Register* 5655, 3 *Code of Federal Regulations,* 1954 Supp.) The relevant part of the clause states, "In connection with the performance of work under this contract, the Seller agrees not to discriminate against any employee or applicant for employment because of race, religion, color, or national origin. The aforesaid provision shall include, but not be limited to, the following: Employment, upgrading, demotion, or transfer; recruitment or recruitment advertising; layoff or termination; rates of pay or other forms of compensation; and selection for training, including apprenticeship." This language was a significant strengthening of the previous requirements, which only included initial hiring.

198. Houston to Malcolm Lovett, May 22, 1957, Box 2, Houston Papers; Houston to George R. Brown, May 25, 1957; Houston to Lamar Fleming, May 25, 1957, Box 7, Houston Papers, WRC.

199. Baker, Botts, Andrews and Shepherd to Houston, May 29, 1957, Box 7, Houston Papers, WRC.

200. Executive Order 10,479, issued on August 13, 1953, replaced the old Committee on Government Contract Compliance with a new, more powerful Government Contract Committee. 18 *Federal Register* 5655, 3 *Code of Federal Regulations*, 1953 Supp. Throughout his presidency Eisenhower showed a marked preference for executive rather than legislative action on civil rights. Eisenhower, *The White House Years*, 234. Although there is an extensive literature on presidential policymaking, very little has been written on the use of executive orders as a policy tool. Ruth P. Morgan, *The President and Civil Rights: Policy-Making by Executive Order* (Lanham, MD, 1987), is a brief overview of the subject. The House Committee on Governmental Operations issued a report in 1957 entitled *Executive Orders and Proclamations: A Study of a Use of Presidential Powers* (Committee Print, 85th Congress, 1st Session, 1957).

201. Houston to Malcolm Lovett, May 22, 1957, Box 2, Houston Papers, WRC.

202. The first reactor proposal was submitted jointly by Rice, Texas A&M, and the University of Texas on May 19, 1956. Box 7, Albert Thomas Papers, WRC.

203. Thomas to Lewis L. Strauss, January 21, 1957; July 8, 1957, Box 7, Thomas Papers, WRC.

204. K. E. Fields to George R. Brown, August 7, 1956; Albert Thomas to William Houston, July 23, 1957; Houston to Thomas, August 16, 1953, Box 7, Thomas Papers, WRC. The proposal for the geophysics lab no doubt came from Chancellor Carey Croneis, who had headed Rice's new Geology Department. See Oral History Interview with Malcolm Lovett, conducted January 21, 1971, by Robert Merrifield, Johnson Space Center Archives, Rice University.

205. Thomas to Houston, July 23, 1957, Thomas Papers, Box 7, WRC.

206. See Pratt and Castaneda, *Builders*, especially chapters 3 and 4, and Dallek, *Lone Star Rising*, 175–76, 308–11.

207. Thomas to Lewis Strauss, July 8, 1957, September 12, 1957, Box 7, Thomas Papers, WRC.

208. Harold Vance to Albert Thomas, September 11, 1958, Box 7, Thomas Papers, WRC.

209. Thomas Keith Glennan, *The Birth of NASA: The Diary of T. Keith Glennan* (Washington, DC, 1993), p. 14; Thomas to Glennan, October 30, 1958; Glennan to Thomas, November 3, 1958, December 10, 1958, Box 7, Thomas Papers, WRC. NASA was truly a brand new entity. It was authorized in July 1958 when President Eisenhower signed the *National Aeronautics and Space Act* (Public Law 85–568, 72 *U.S. Statutes at Large*, 426) and formally established on October 1, 1958.

210. C. A. Dwyer to Girard College, July 10, 1958; Joseph P. Gaffney to C. A. Dwyer, July 14, 1958; C. A. Dwyer to Houston, July 31, 1958, Box 16, Pitzer Papers, WRC. Dwyer sent copies of his correspondence with Girard to each of Rice's trustees.

211. The Girard College case took a circuitous route through the legal system, beginning in Philadelphia's Orphan Court and ending up before the Supreme Court twice (although it was refused hearing the second time). The Pennsylvania Supreme Court upheld the Orphan Court's refusal to order admission in *Girard Will Case*, 127 A.2d 287 (1956), and the Supreme Court overturned this in *Commonwealth of Pennsylvania, et al., v. Board of Directors of City Trusts*, 353 U.S. 230 1957. The Pennsylvania Supreme Court then sustained the Orphan Court's action in appointing new trustees in *Girard College Trusteeship*, 138 A.2d 844. The United States Supreme Court refused to hear the case in June 1958, letting the change in trustees and the rejection of the applicants stand.

212. *Rice Thresher*, September 27, 1957, February 22, 1957.

213. *Rice Thresher*, February 15, 1957.

214. *Rice Thresher*, March 8, 1957.

215. *Rice Thresher,* March 22, 1957.

216. Gardner S. Bride Jr. to President of the Student Association of Rice Institute, October 31, 1959, Series I, Box 2, Rice Student Association Papers, WRC. The president of the Texas Students' Association was preparing for meeting with the board of regents that November and was looking for support for a stand in favor of complete integration.

217. Wayne Hanson to Frank Cooksey, November 9, 1959, Series I, Box 2, Rice Student Association Papers, WRC. Note that the treatment of black athletes seems to have changed significantly since the early 1950s.

218. Ibid.

5. PUSH COMES TO SHOVE: THE EARLY 1960S

1. Roche, *Restructured Resistance,* 76–80.

2. Ibid. See also Charles Boykin Pyles, "S. Ernest Vandiver and the Politics of Change," in Harold P. Henderson and Gary L. Roberts, eds. *Georgia Governors in an Age of Change: From Ellis Arnall to George Busbee* (Athens, GA, 1988), and Bartley, *Creation of Modern Georgia,* 213–17.

3. President's Report to the Board, November 1959, EUA.

4. *Emory Alumnus,* February 1960.

5. Roche, *Restructured Resistance,* 78–95. On Sibley and his relationship with Coca-Cola's Woodruff, see Frederick Allen, *Secret Formula: How Brilliant Marketing and Relentless Salesmanship Made Coca-Cola the Best-Known Product in the World* (New York, 1994), 219–22, 269, 331–33.

6. *Atlanta Constitution,* March 9, 1960; Pomerantz, *Where Peachtree Meets Sweet Auburn,* 251–258; Harvard Sitkoff, The *Struggle for Black Equality, 1954-1980 (New York, 1981),* 69–73. The *Emory Wheel* conceded, irrelevantly, that the Appeal "merits study," March 31, 1960. Other Emory students grasped the meaning of the statement rather more clearly and joined the demonstrations. *Emory Wheel,* March 31, 1960. Emory students remained divided throughout the early 1960s, with most preferring segregation or espousing an empty "moderation," but an active and vocal minority participated in demonstrations and sit-ins and condemned the student paper for spinelessness.

7. Minutes of the Faculty of the College of Arts and Sciences, March 16, 1960, Box 2, Emory University Faculty Papers, EUA.

8. Ibid.

9. S. Walter Martin, Remarks to Selected Faculty Members Concerning Race Relations at Emory, March 31, 1960, Box 86, Robert Woodruff Papers, EUA.

10. Ibid.

11. R. A. Day Jr. to Martin, April 5, 1960, Box 4, Bowden Papers, EUA.

12. Harvey Young to Martin, May 6, 1960, Box 1, Emory University Faculty Papers, EUA.

13. Copy of letter, Henry Bowden to Martin, May 12, 1960; Martin to William C. Archie, May 17, 1960, Box 1, Emory Faculty Papers, EUA.

14. Minutes of University Senate Meeting, April 6, April 27, May 25, 1960, Box 4, Emory University Senate Papers, EUA. John Buhler, dean of the School of Dentistry, wrote a furious note to Henry Bowden about this resolution, claiming it had been "railroaded" through the Senate and that the dental faculty was annoyed with arts and sciences for trying to speak for the whole university. John E. Buhler to Henry Bowden, June 11, 1960, Box 3, Bowden Papers, EUA.

15. William C. Archie to Martin, May 26, 1960, Box 3, Bowden Papers, EUA.

16. Roche, *Restructured Resistance,* 162–75.

17. On the Atlanta demonstrations see David J. Garrow, *Atlanta, Georgia, 1960–1961* (Brooklyn, NY, 1989); Walker, "Protest and Negotiation," 99–124. On Dr. King's incarceration and the national political machinations that surrounded it, see Branch, *Parting the Waters,* 351–70.

18. Bowden to Harlee Branch, January 13, 1961, Box 4, Bowden Papers, EUA. The situation at the University of Georgia was much on the trustees' minds that day. They sent a letter to that school's president, O. C. Aderhold, expressing their support and praising the "splendid manner in which you and your staff have handled the unfortunate situation on your campus." Martin to President Aderhold, January 12, 1961, Box 4, Bowden Papers, EUA. Quite prudently, Martin arranged for his daughter, who was a student at Georgia, to spend a few nights with family friends in Athens rather than stay in her room in Hunter's dorm. Martin to Birdie Bondurant, January 17, 1961, Box 4, Martin Papers, VSUA. On the desegregation of the University of Georgia, see Dyer, *University of Georgia,* 322–33, and Calvin Trillin, *An Education in Georgia: The Integration of Charlayne Hunter and Hamilton Holmes* (New York, 1964).

19. The biographical information is from questionnaires filled out by the trustees in 1959. Box 7, Bowden Papers, EUA.

20. Bowden to Tim Adams, January 24, 1961, Box 4, Bowden Papers, EUA.

21. In correspondence with the Atlanta district superintendent of the Methodist Church, Bowden was informed that the Woman's Division of Christian Service had decided against giving money to Emory's nursing school because it remained segregated. Lester Rumble to Bowden, February 7, 1961, Box 4, Bowden Papers, EUA. The Methodist Church was still not of one mind on desegregation, however, and some individual congregations expressed strong opposition to opening Emory to blacks. Martin had solicited letters from the faculty, and many responded. The special committee looked at these as well. Every such letter strongly supported desegregation, usually with powerful moral arguments as well as arguments about the university's standing in the larger academic community. Box 4, Bowden Papers, EUA.

22. Minutes of Meeting of Special Committee of the Executive Committee of the Board of Trustees of Emory University, February 1, 1961, Box 4, Bowden Papers, EUA.

23. Martin to Harlee Branch, February 3, 1961, Box 4, Bowden Papers, EUA; draft report, n.d. but February 1961, Box 4, Bowden Papers, EUA.

24. Martin to Harlee Branch, February 3, 1961; Bowden to Ernest Colwell, April 13, 1961, Box 4, Bowden Papers, EUA.

25. Ben Johnson to Henry Bowden, October 21, 1961, Box 4, Bowden Papers, EUA.

26. Bowden to Harlee Branch, April 14, 1961; Bowden to Hugh M. Dorsey, April 25, 1961; Bowden to F. M. Bird, April 25, 1961; Bowden to Randolph Thrower, May 3, 1961, Box 4, Bowden Papers, EUA. Bowden was also in close contact with Joseph Jones, chairman of the Tulane board, about their decision. Jones to Bowden, April 13, 1961; Bowden to Jones, April 14, 1961, Box 4, Bowden Papers, EUA. Walter Martin wrote friends at other private universities, asking for details of their plans for desegregation. Martin to Herbert Herring, February 23, 1961; Herring to Martin, March 16, 1961; Martin to Herring, March 20, 1961, Box 2, Herring Papers, DUA.

27. Randolph Thrower to Bowden, May 3, 1961; Report of Special Committee to Review University Policy on Admissions, May 1, 1961, Box 9, Bowden Papers, EUA.

28. Minutes of the Board of Trustees Meeting, May 4, 1961, EUA.

29. The resolution was adopted on May 9, 1961. Charles D. Hounshell to Martin, May 24, 1961, "Brief Documentary Account," Manuscript Box 10, EUA.

30. Minutes of the Faculty of the College of Arts and Sciences, May 25, 1961, Box 2, Emory Faculty Papers, EUA.

31. Roche, *Restructured Resistance*, 178–88. Robert L. Crain and Morton Inger, *School Desegregation in New Orleans: A Comparative Study of the Failure of Social Control* (Chicago, 1966), contrasts the calm desegregation in Atlanta with the chaos of New Orleans, locating the roots of the difference in the failure of the New Orleans civic establishment to take control of the issue. Goodrich White expressed a similar opinion in a letter to the president of Colgate in 1961. "The mob spirit that has manifested itself in Little Rock, New Orleans, Athens, and elsewhere can, I think, be kept under control by the kind of planning and public appeals that went on in Atlanta." White to Everett Case, November 2, 1961, Box 11, White Papers, EUA.

32. Branch, *Parting the Waters*, 395–97. Ivan Allen was elected mayor of Atlanta in November 1961, defeating segregationist Lester Maddox.

33. Report of Special Committee, adopted by the Board of Trustees, May 3, 1961, Box 9, Bowden Papers, EUA. At least one trustee, possibly more, was unhappy with this decision. United States Senator Spessard Holland of Florida objected vehemently, arguing that the line must be held or worse things would come. "The pressure groups which are insisting upon breaking down the racial barriers have made it very clear that they want to go as far as intermarriage." Spessard Holland to Martin, November 28, 1961, Box 3, Bowden Papers, EUA.

34. *Emory Wheel*, November 30, 1961. Martin's statement is in "A Brief Documentary Account," Box 10, Emory University Manuscripts, EUA.

35. Walter R. Davis Jr., Emory's alumni director, prepared a form letter defending the board's decision to disgruntled alumni. Walter R. Davis Jr. to John Doe, November 1961, Box 4, Bowden Papers, EUA.

36. Letters from faculty, staff, and alumni are in Boxes 3 and 4, Bowden Papers, EUA. *Atlanta Constitution*, November 4, 1961.

37. Minutes of the Meeting of the Board of Trust, November 2–3, 1961; Henry Bowden to Robert Woodruff, September 26, 1962, Box 88, Woodruff Papers, EUA.

38. This application and several others are in Box 4, Bowden Papers, EUA. Emory's brief and supplemental brief are in "A Brief Documentary Account," Box 10, Emory Manuscripts, EUA. The May 1962 issue of the *Emory Alumnus* contains both a reprint of the petition and an explanation of the suit by law dean Ben Johnson. Johnson stressed that "it is not necessary in this action for Emory to champion the rights of Negroes, and this action does not do so; we champion the rights of Emory, and every other private educational institution in Georgia, to choose its own admission policy in this regard."

39. *Emory University et al. v. Nash*, 218 Ga. 317 (1962). The case was decided on September 14 and DeKalb County filed an appeal on September 24, but the Georgia Supreme Court affirmed its decision on October 1. Henry Bowden immediately notified Robert Woodruff and sent him a copy of the Georgia Supreme Court's decision. He noted in his letter, "This is one of the things that the people [foundations] we talked to in New York you will recall have said Emory was behind in." Bowden to Robert Woodruff, September 26, 1962, Box 88, Woodruff Papers, EUA.

40. Judson C. Ward to Roland P. Mackay (quotation), January 18, 1963, Box 4, Bowden Papers, EUA; *Emory Wheel*, October 18, 1962. Interestingly, Emory's commencement speaker in 1962 was John A. Sibley, who spoke on "The Changing South." June 11, 1962, Box 120, John A. Sibley Papers, EUA.

41. Bowden to Spencer Walden Jr., February 27, 1961; Bowden to Hugh Comer, March 8, 1961, Box 4, Bowden Papers, EUA.

42. Harris Purks to Martin, May 9, 1961, Box 4, Bowden Papers, EUA.

43. It would be difficult to overstate Martin's relief at leaving. He seemed particularly thrilled that he wouldn't have to raise money anymore, underscoring Emory's vulnerable financial position. "This institution needs 75 million dollars over the next ten years," he wrote one friend, "and I am afraid I am not the one to deliver it." Martin to Claud B. Green, April 25, 1962, Box 65, Martin Papers, VSUA.

44. Martin to [all members of the Board of Trustees], April 11, 1962, Box 61, Martin Papers, VSUA. In 1966 Martin became president of Valdosta State, a branch of the University System, a position he held until his retirement in 1978.

45. Martin, President's Report to the Board of Trustees, November 1961, EUA; Sam A. Wilkins Jr. to Martin, March 13, 1962; Martin to Henry Bowden, March 16, 1962, Box 3, Bowden Papers, EUA.

46. One of the most prominent exceptions was William Cannon, dean of the Theology School, who always communicated that school's position on desegregation with the greatest respect and consideration for the difficult situation the administration was in. William R. Cannon to Martin, May 29, 1961, Box 4, Martin Papers, VSUA.

47. Harvey Young to Martin, April 19, 1962, Box 65, Martin Papers, VSUA.

48. This brief account follows Durden, "Donnybrook at Duke: Part I," and Durden, "Donnybrook at Duke: The Gross Edens Affair of 1960, Part II," *North Carolina Historical Review* 71 (October 1994), 451–71, which impressively recreate these events in great detail.

49. Durden, *Launching of Duke University*, 49–65. This requirement was dropped in 1968.

50. One exception was Bunyan Snipes Womble, from Winston-Salem. Edens had confided in him about the pressures from the Endowment trustees and Gross. Womble tried to help Edens steer through the trouble, an effort that was probably doomed from the start. See Durden, "Donnybrook at Duke, I."

51. Durden, "Donnybrook at Duke, II"; Minutes of the Meeting of the Board of Trust, March 23, 1960, DUA.

52. Durden, "Donnybrook at Duke, II"; Minutes of the Meeting of the Board of Trust, April 21, 1960, DUA. Hollis Edens accepted a position at the Mary Reynolds Babcock Foundation in Winston-Salem, turning down an offer from North Carolina's new governor (and later Duke president) Terry Sanford to become his assistant for special projects. Howard E. Covington Jr. and Marion A. Ellis, *Terry Sanford: Politics, Progress, and Outrageous Ambitions* (Durham, 1999), 262.

53. Deryl Hart, Presidential Report, n.d. but September 1963, Box 20, Deryl Hart Papers, DUA; Cole, *Recollections*, 155–57.

54. On the sit-ins in Durham see Branch, *Parting the Waters*, 272–76, and Jean Bradley Anderson, *Durham County: A History of Durham County, North Carolina* (Durham, 1990), 437–39. Reverend Douglas Moore was a key figure and was in close contact with James Lawson at Vanderbilt. The demonstrations and their fallout were constant topics in the *Chronicle* that spring. Support for the sit-ins came from the Divinity School student body, the Women's Student Government Association, and the Westminster Fellowship. *Duke Chronicle*, May 18, 1960. Divinity School Dean Robert Cushman sent the students' April 14 resolution, with his own support, to Edens and to the board. Robert Cushman to Edens, April 15, 1960, Box 21, Edens Papers, EUA.

55. *Duke Chronicle*, April 11, 1960.

56. Anne Thompson to Edens, November 30, 1959, Box 33, Edens Papers, EUA.

57. J. Cris Soich to the Trustees and President of Duke University, March 10, 1960, Bun-

yan Snipes Womble Papers; Memo re: Integration Situation, January 15, 1961, Box 33, Edens Papers, DUA.

58. Reverend Douglas E. Moore, Reverend W. T. Brown, Reverend O. W. Burwick to Delegates, Methodist General Conference, April 20, 1960, Box 33, Edens Papers, EUA. While the Methodists did not ignore Moore, neither did they press Duke very hard. Donald Tippett, chairman of the church's commission on ministerial education, wrote Edens to clarify the Methodist stance of nondiscrimination but went no farther. Donald Harvey Tippett to Edens, January 18, 1960; Edens to Tippett, February 2, 1960; Tippett to Edens, February 19, 1960, Box 33, Edens Papers, DUA.

59. Cole, *Recollections*, 158–59. Cole quotes from a 1972 Duke student paper about desegregation, whose author correctly observed "any effort on a moral plane would be wasted." In an interview with Duke student Jorge Kotelanski in 1990, Cole explained that although the provost group was criticized by some for avoiding moral arguments, they succeeded in their goal of getting "integration in the earliest possible time." A partial transcript of this interview and interviews with Robert Cushman, Peter Klopfer, Reverend Douglas E. Moore, and Waldo Beach are appended to Kotelanski, "Prolonged and Patient Efforts." Original tape recorded interviews are in Tape Collection, DUA.

60. Admission of Duly Qualified Negroes to the Graduate and Professional Schools of Duke University, January 1961. This report was prepared in November 1960. Minutes of the Meeting of the Administrative Committee, November 28, 1960, Box 7, Hart Papers, DUA.

61. Ibid.

62. Ibid.

63. Ibid.

64. Hart to Members of the Board of Trustees, January 17, 1961, Womble Papers, DUA.

65. A few trustees were unable to attend one of the scheduled meetings. Hart or Cole met with some individually, or at least spoke with them on the phone. Cole, *Recollections*, 159; Kotelanski, "Prolonged and Patient Efforts," Cole interview.

66. Secretary of the Divinity Faculty, to the Board of Trustees of Duke University through the President and the Vice-President in the Division of Education, January 11, 1961; Robert Cushman to Hart, February 8, 1961, Box 11, Hart Papers, DUA. It is not clear whether Hart sent this on to the trustees. His only response to Cushman was that he wanted to speak with him, and they may have decided that anything that even suggested a moral objection to segregation ought not be put in front of the board at that time. Hart to Robert Cushman, February 13, 1961, Box 11, Hart Papers, DUA. The Student Government Association of the Divinity School sent a resolution to the board on March 6, arguing that Duke should desegregate because "the love of God manifest in Jesus Christ reveals the equal importance of all men to God." Richard Weingart, To the President and Trustees of Duke University, March 6, 1961, Box 11, Hart Papers, DUA.

67. E. R. Latty to Hart, February 23, 1961; Hart to Latty, February 27, 1961, Box 11, Hart Papers, DUA.

68. Thomas L. Perkins to Don Elias, March 1, 1961, Womble Papers, DUA. Elias, a trustee from Asheville, North Carolina, wrote Perkins to tell him there would be an informal trustee meeting the evening before the board met. Perkins assumed that the purpose was to discuss the desegregation proposal and thus responded with his views.

69. Hart to Bunyan S. Womble, February 7, 1961, Womble Papers, DUA.

70. C. B. Houck to Womble (quotation), March 20, 1961; Womble to C. B. Houck, March 18,

1961, Womble Papers, DUA; Minutes of the Meeting of the Board of Trustees (quotation of resolution) March 8, 1961, DUA.

71. T. L. Perkins to Bunyan S. Womble, March 20, 1961; John W. Gardner to T. L. Perkins, March 17, 1961; Charles W. Cole to T. L. Perkins, March 15, 1961; Henry T. Heald to T. L. Perkins, March 15, 1961, Box 11, Hart Papers, DUA. At the March 8 meeting the board decided to leave all announcements of the change in the hands of the president and the chairman of the board. Dean Cushman of the Divinity School was thus censored when he wrote Charles Munson, the editor of the *Christian Advocate,* with the news. Cushman's letter to Munson was apparently too focused on the morality of the matter, and Hart had him retract it and send a more temperate statement that stressed the "removal of surviving barriers to the national standing of the University community" rather than "the soundings of the Christian conscience." Cushman was not happy. Robert E. Cushman to Charles Munson, March 16, 1961; Cushman to Hart, March 20, 1961; Cushman to Charles Munson, March 20, 1961, Box 12, Hart Papers, DUA.

72. George T. Eaton to Chairman of the Board of Trustees, April 8, 1961, Box 11, Hart Papers, DUA. Most of the letters are in Box 11, Hart Papers, and Womble Papers, DUA. Others are scattered throughout Hart's correspondence files. Hart himself wrote to one correspondent that the change "has been very favorably received on campus by both faculty and the students and a considerable number of our letters from over the country have been favorable." Hart to Norman Gamezy, March 28, 1961, Box 11, Hart Papers, DUA. Gamezy was a professor at the University of Minnesota. Faculty members also wrote from Penn State, Southern Methodist University, the University of Chicago, Florida State, and the University of Alberta.

73. R. Florence Brinkley to Hart, August 31, 1961; Hart to Brinkley, September 8, 1961, Hart Papers, Box 11, DUA; Annual Report of the Provost to the President, 1961, Box 3, Hart Papers, DUA.

74. Cole, *Recollections,* 160. Kotelanski, "Prolonged and Patient Efforts," 137.

75. Report of the Provost to the President, March 2, 1962, Box 3, Hart Papers; Minutes of the Meeting of the Executive Committee, June 1, 1962; Minutes of the Meeting of the Board, June 2, 1962, Box 3, Hart Papers, DUA.

76. Provost's Report to the President, June 2, 1962, Box 3, Hart Papers; Minutes of the Executive Committee Meeting, June 1, 1961; Report on Trustee-Faculty Liaison Committee, May 4, 1962, Womble Papers, DUA. This committee had been formed in the immediate wake of the Gross-Edens affair.

77. Charles S. Rhyne, *Working for Justice in America and Justice in the World: An Autobiography* (McLean, VA, 1995), chapter 22; Cole, *Recollections,* 160; Minutes of the Meeting of the Board of Trust, June 2, 1962, DUA.

78. B. S. Womble to Dean Boggs, June 13, 1962, Womble Papers, DUA.

79. A. T. Spaulding to Hart, June 4, 1962, Box 11, Hart Papers, DUA. On the remarkable Spaulding, see Walter B. Weare, *Black Business in the New South: A Social History of the North Carolina Mutual Life Insurance Company* (Urbana, IL, 1973), 163–66.

80. The episode at Vanderbilt that began with the expulsion of James Lawson is byzantine in its complexity and important enough to warrant book-length treatment. The best detailed chronology of the events of March through June 1960 is in Conkin, *Gone with the Ivy,* 547–74. David Halberstam, *The Children* (New York, 1998), 188–207, also deals, though less convincingly, with the university's treatment of Lawson.

81. It is only fair to point out that the sit-in movement was brand new in February and early March 1960, and no one knew what was going to happen. Frankly, expectations of massive ra-

cial discord were probably more reasonable than what did happen—the public endorsement of desegregation by Mayor West on April 20, a day after the bombing of the home of black lawyer Alexander Looby.

82. In *The Children*, Halberstam recounts the Nashville sit-ins based on interviews with participants. Branch, *Parting the Waters*, chapter 7, places the rise of the Nashville demonstrations in the larger context of the civil rights movement as a whole. Graham, *Crisis in Print*, 199–202, discusses newspaper treatments of the events.

83. Branscomb related his side of this story in a narrative entitled "The Lawson Episode—Twenty Years Later," November 15, 1980, Box 4, Branscomb Papers, VUSC. This document, while incomplete and self-serving, reveals quite clearly Branscomb's state of mind—beleaguered, angry, and very worried about the fate of Vanderbilt. His autobiography, *Purely Academic*, is so brief as to be useless on this episode. All it really shows is Branscomb's long-lived anger toward Dean Nelson of the School of Theology.

84. Robert McGaw, Vice Chancellor Rob Roy Purdy, and Dean Nelson tried to work out a statement with Lawson.

85. Arthur L. Foster's chronology of the Lawson case (hereinafter Foster Chronology), in Box 29, Centennial Record Group, RG 101,VUSC, provides a contemporaneous, day by day, sometimes hour by hour, account of the events. After a brief introduction to the sit-ins, it begins in earnest on February 25 and ends on June 27. The chronology runs 102 pages.

86. It's likely that Branscomb would have argued that Lawson should be allowed to withdraw, if only because that might not draw as much publicity. Stahlman to James Simpson, June 15, 1960, Box V-3, Stahlman Papers, VUSC.

87. Harvie Branscomb, "Is Civil Disobedience the Way?" Box 4, Branscomb Papers, VUSC. Branscomb reiterated this basic defense in dozens of letters, changing emphasis based on who he was addressing. The argument never became either clearer or more persuasive, however. Over a dozen of these long letters are in Box 186, Chancellor's Office Papers, RG 300, VUSC. He also continued *ad hominem* attacks on Lawson, Dean Nelson, and the Divinity School faculty for decades afterward, a measure of his sense of shocked betrayal at the course of events during these few months in 1960.

88. Lawson continued advising the students during this early period and began participating in the demonstrations immediately after his expulsion. He was in fact arrested on March 4 for violating state commerce laws. The charges were later dropped. Conkin, *Gone with the Ivy*, 554–55.

89. In a letter to a professor at the Yale Divinity School soon after the episode ended Branscomb asserted that objections were unfounded that the laws Lawson urged the students to violate were unconstitutional: "This puts the individual in a position of declaring what the Supreme Court will decide and acting in advance thereon." Branscomb to Reverend Roland Bainton, June 22, 1960, Box 186, Chancellor's Office Papers, RG 300, VUSC. But this is exactly what Branscomb did in 1953.

90. Branscomb to Liston Pope, March 9, 1960, Box 202, Chancellor's Office Papers, RG 300, VUSC.

91. Foster Chronology, 14–19; Branscomb wrote Pope (a Duke Divinity School graduate) the day after Lawson's expulsion to let him know what was happening. This correspondence and a copy of Pope's address are in Box 202, Chancellor's Office Papers, RG 300, VUSC.

92. Conkin, *Gone with the Ivy*, 556–60. Documentation of the readmission process and a copy of Nelson's letter of resignation are in Box 29, Centennial Record Group, RG 101, VUSC.

93. Stahlman to Whitefoord Cole, May 17, 1960, Box V-3, Stahlman Papers; Sims Crownover to Branscomb, June 2, 1960, Stahlman Papers, Box V-9, VUSC.

94. Robert L. Garner to Dallas A. Blanchard, May 2, 1960, Box 360, Chancellor's Office Papers, RG 300, VUSC.

95. V. J. Alexander to Stahlman, June 1, 1960, Box V-6, Stahlman Papers, VUSC.

96. *Nashville Banner,* May 31, 1960. The *Nashville Tennessean,* May 31, 1960, on the other hand, regretted the resignations.

97. Numerous clippings are in Box 24, Secretary of the University Papers, RG 900, and Box 78, Chancellor's Office Papers, RG 300, VUSC. The Foster Chronology also quotes from several editorials.

98. Foster Chronology, 57, Box 39, Centennial Record Group, RG 101, VUSC. Branscomb strategically leaked documents to the Nashville press and used the *Banner* in particular to wage a public relations battle with the resigning faculty.

99. A subdrama was going on in the Medical School, with four professors committed to resigning and sixty supporting the board's resolution of the Lawson case. Conkin, *Gone with the Ivy,* 564.

100. There was some difficulty about Nelson, who everyone agreed could no longer be dean. Branscomb agreed to reinstate him too on the understanding that he would again resign.

101. Foster Chronology, 61–63, 71–73.

102. Foster Chronology, 76–78; *Time,* June 13, 1960, carried the story of Lawson and the resignations.

103. Stahlman and O. H. Ingram were meeting on June 13 to plan their own strategy, which included announcing that the Lawson case was closed, accepting all proffered resignations, and authorizing the chancellor to immediately accept all resignations that would follow and to "take such other steps as appear necessary to restore tranquility and order to the campus." Copy of Memo of Meeting, June 13, 1960, Box 29, Centennial Record Group, RG 101, VUSC. Stahlman and Ingramm called Harold Vanderbilt, who was in the hospital with heart problems, to try to get him to agree to their plans. He would not.

104. Foster Chronology, 79–81; Copy of Statement to the Faculty of Vanderbilt University, June 13, 1960, Box 29, Centennial Record Group, RG 101, VUSC.

105. In a breathtaking editorial in the *Banner,* James Stahlman actually criticized Branscomb for not taking this kind of firm action sooner—in effect blaming the chancellor for not saving Stahlman from himself in a more timely manner. *Nashville Banner,* June 14, 1960. Branscomb replied privately that such action would not have worked even days before. He argued convincingly that "it was only after the faculty knew that we had made efforts to negotiate and that these had failed and the situation was in such chaos that some decision had to be made, that it was possible for this kind of statement to be effective." Branscomb to Stahlman, June 15, 1960, Box 29, Centennial Record Group, RG 101, VUSC.

106. Copy of letter to Branscomb from Divinity School Faculty, June 15, 1960, Box 29, Centennial Record Group, RG 101; V. J. Alexander to Stahlman, June 15, 1960, Box V-6, Stahlman Papers, VUSC.

107. V. J. Alexander to Stahlman, June 17, 1960, Stahlman Papers, Box V-6. VUSC.

108. J. P. Norfleet to James Stahlman, July 6, 1960; Norfleet to James Simpson, September 1, 1960, Stahlman Papers, Box V-14, VUSC.

109. Giles J. Patterson to Stahlman, July 25, 1960, Stahlman Papers, Box V-14, VUSC.

110. W. F. Murrah to Stahlman, June 30, 1960, Stahlman Papers, Box V-14, VUSC.

111. For a while in June, Branscomb was in almost daily contact with Dean Rusk, the president of the Rockefeller Foundation. Rusk's comments zeroed in on what was at stake. "I did want you to know . . . that if there was any way in which I could be helpful, I would feel a duty to make myself available. I was not thinking of the financial investment which our two Boards have made in Vanderbilt so much as the brooding and affectionate concern of my past and present colleagues that there evolve at Vanderbilt a great university. The possibility that a single incident, occurring in a period of general tension, might deeply injure decades of devoted work by those of you who had built up Vanderbilt was something on which I did not feel I could remain entirely silent." Dean Rusk to Branscomb, June 16, 1960, Box 186, Chancellor's Office Papers, RG 300, VUSC. Rusk singled out the potential "adverse effect on your ability to recruit top men for the faculty" as the most costly repercussion that might follow. Rusk to Branscomb, June 27, 1960, Box 186, Chancellor's Office Papers, RG 300, VUSC.

112. Branscomb to James Cleland, January 2, 1957, Box 159, RG 300, Chancellor's Office Papers, VUSC.

113. Branscomb, Statement to the Divinity Faculty, December 9, 1960, Box 158, Chancellor's Office Papers, RG 300, VUSC.

114. There are quite a few warm letters of support in Branscomb's files. Rufus Harris, now president of Mercer, wrote to *The Christian Century* declining to renew his subscription, arguing that the magazine had treated Branscomb unfairly. "I do not understand," wrote Harris, "how you think it proper to abuse the University for its course of action in this case in view of the firm public declaration of this particular student to persist in a violent and proclaimed course of civil disobedience and disorder. I feel this deeply despite my long sharing of what I think are your general views regarding the civil rights of, and educational opportunities for, Negro citizens."

115. Branscomb to James W. Armsey, June 20, 1960, Box 186, Chancellor's Office Papers, RG 300, VUSC. Perhaps the best epitaph for the Lawson episode was written by University Secretary Robert McGaw. "Three of us here, two on the Administration side and one on the other side and . . . nobody was closer to the center of it than any one of us, do solemnly and honestly declare that we can name NOBODY who changed sides from the beginning to the (we hope) end, over a period of 3 1/2 months. This despite the most energetic outpouring of 'facts.' It's as though a Roman Catholic and a Southern Baptist spent 3 1/2 months debating. In the matter of race . . . everybody finds the facts he wants to find, finds the meaning he wants to find, finds the villain he wants to find, finds the hero he wants to find." Robert McGaw to Lea Booth, June 21, 1960. RG 900, Secretary of the University Papers, Box 2510, VUSC.

116. Branscomb to S. Walter Martin, March 10, 1961, Box 162, RG 300, Chancellor's Office Papers, VUSC.

117. Branscomb, *Purely Academic*, 165.

118. *Vanderbilt Hustler*, February 9, 16, 1962.

119. Branscomb to Rhodes Scholarship Selection Committee, November 15, 1962, Box 119, Chancellor's Office Papers, RG 300, VUSC; Branscomb, *Purely Academic*, 165; *Vanderbilt Hustler*, April 20, 1962. Lamar Alexander went on to be elected governor (1979–87) and then senator (2002–) from Tennessee. A Republican, he also served as secretary of education in the George Bush administration (1991–93), and as the president of the University of Tennessee (1988–91).

120. *Vanderbilt Hustler*, March 16, 1962. Master's programs were not opened before because Branscomb and the board feared being "deluged with Negro students who want to go into teaching with a Master's degree." Branscomb to S. Walter Martin, March 14, 1961. RG 300, Chancellor's Office Papers, Box 162, VUSC.

121. Excerpt from Chancellor's Report to the Board of Trust of Vanderbilt University, October 24–25, 1958; Memorandum, "The University Senate," March 9, 1959, Box 217, RG 300, Chancellor's Office Papers, VUSC.

122. Digest of the Minutes, Board of Trust, Vanderbilt University, May 4–5, 1963, Box V-27, Stahlman Papers, VUSC.

123. "A communication from the University Senate to the Board of Trust adopted April 26, 1962, by unanimous vote of those members present and voting," April 26, 1962. Box 212, RG 300, Chancellor's Office Papers, VUSC.

124. Ibid.

125. Branscomb, "Present Status of this Problem," May 4, 1962, Box V-29, Stahlman Papers, VUSC. Wade discussed the Tulane case before the meeting in a letter to board chairman Harold Vanderbilt. John W. Wade to Harold Vanderbilt, April 4, 1962, Box 212, RG 300, Chancellor's Office Papers, VUSC.

126. There are several drafts of the data that Vanderbilt provided to the other trustees and a text of his long presentation to the board, which he apparently read largely verbatim, at Box 3, Harold S. Vanderbilt Papers, VUSC.

127. Branscomb to Hubert W. Morrow, May 23, 1962, Box 199, RG 300, Chancellor's Office Papers, VUSC.

128. Confidential Digest of the Minutes, Board of Trust, Vanderbilt University, May 4–5, 1962, Stahlman Papers, Box V-27, VUSC. This requirement was apparently more honored in the breach. Conkin, *Gone with the Ivy*, 577.

129. Alan W. Heldman to Branscomb, June 21, 1962; Branscomb to Alan W. Heldman, June 28, 1962, Box 176; Richard J. Burrow Jr. to Branscomb, May 23, 1962, Branscomb to Burrow, May 30, 1962, Box 135, Chancellor's Office Papers, RG 300, VUSC.

130. *Vanderbilt Hustler,* May 11, 1962. The 1963 editor, Roy Blount Jr. went on to become a well-known and prolific writer and humorist.

131. Branscomb to John W. Gardner, May 14, 1962, Box 137; William C. Finch to Branscomb, May 14, 1962, Box 158, RG 300, Chancellor's Office Papers, VUSC.

132. *Hustler,* May 11, 1962. Not surprisingly, James Stahlman knew exactly what he was looking for in a new chancellor. "I have some very definite ideas about the type of man we want," he wrote fellow trustee Devereaux Lake, "and I am determined as best I can to see that we don't get any of the left-wing boys who would like to subvert Vanderbilt, the last bastion of educational conservatism among the better institutions of higher learning." After a long search, the board settled on Alexander Heard, dean of the Graduate School at the University of North Carolina. Stahlman to Devereaux Lake, January 10, 1962, Stahlman Papers, Box V-3, VUSC. On the selection of Heard, see Conkin, *Gone with the Ivy,* 583–87. Heard, certainly no left-winger, went on to have his fair share of scrapes with Stahlman, particularly in 1967 when Stokely Carmichael spoke at a Vanderbilt forum. This incident is discussed in Conkin, *Gone with the Ivy,* 617–22, and much more circumspectly in Alexander Heard, *Speaking of the University: Two Decades at Vanderbilt* (Nashville, 1995), 92–97.

133. Harvie Branscomb, Speech to the Faculties, September 14, 1962, Box 5, Branscomb Papers, VUSC.

134. The Advisory Committee worked closely with the board in the search that resulted in the selection of Herbert Longenecker. Report of the Faculty Advisory Committee on the Selection of a President, April, 1960, Harris Papers, Box 20, TUA.

135. Advisory Committee to Joseph Jones, June 25, 1959, Harris Papers, Box 31, TUA.

136. Kathryn Davis to Joseph Jones, June 15, 1959, Harris Papers, Box 31, TUA.

137. Dr. Maxwell Lapham, dean of Tulane's Medical School since 1940, served as acting president from the time of Harris's departure in March 1960 until Longenecker assumed his duties in September.

138. Press Release, Tulane University News Bureau, December 18, 1959, Box 42, Harris Papers, TUA.

139. Harris to Longenecker, March 31, 1960, Box 42, Harris Papers, TUA.

140. Longenecker arrived on campus in the spring and attended his first board meeting on April 20, 1960. Minutes of the Meeting of the Board of Administrators, April 20, 1960, TUA.

141. On the crisis surrounding changing race relations in New Orleans, see Fairclough, *Race and Democracy,* generally, but especially chapter 9; Baker, *The Second Battle of New Orleans;* and for a blistering assessment of the behavior of the city's elite, Morton Inger, *Politics and Reality in an American City: The New Orleans School Integration Crisis in 1960* (New York, 1969). "Massive resistance" in Louisiana is analyzed in Bartley, *Rise of Massive Resistance,* chapters 10–12.

142. Minutes of the Meeting of the Board of Administrators, June 15, 1960, TUA. Plans for a Tulane elementary school are in Box 14, Longenecker Papers.

143. Jack Ricau to Tulane University Maintenance Department, April 18, 1960, Box 99, Longenecker Papers, TUA.

144. Memo, Business Manager to Clarence Scheps, April 25, 1960, Box 66, Longenecker Papers, TUA. Each black employee was assigned a specific toilet and given a drinking glass with instructions to draw water from any fountain and drink only from the glass. Clarence Scheps to Edmund McIlhenny, May 3, 1960; McIlhenny to Scheps, May 4, 1960; Scheps to McIlhenny, May 26, 1960; McIlhenny to Scheps, June 8, 1960; Scheps to Max Lapham, June 14, 1960, Box 99, TUA. Scheps advised Lapham to bring this up with the board, which he did at the June 15 meeting. They reaffirmed the policy of allowing blacks to participate in professional meetings on campus. Minutes of the Meeting of the Board of Administrators, TUA. At the same time, Citizen's Council president Joseph Viguerie objected that blacks were being allowed to take law and medical school admissions tests from the Educational Testing Service alongside whites at the Tulane testing site. Joseph E. Viguerie to M. E. Lapham, May 3, 1960; Lapham to Viguerie, May 5, 1960, Box 99, Longenecker Papers, TUA.

145. A memo entitled "Integration Problems" discusses the attempts to desegregate the snack bar at the University Center as well as the participation of Tulane students in the CORE sit-ins. October 12, 1960, Box 99, Longenecker Papers, TUA. On the formation of the New Orleans CORE chapter and the 1960 demonstrations, see Fairclough, *Race and Democracy,* 272–76.

146. Box 99, Longenecker Papers, TUA. Longenecker was also in contact with Vanderbilt administrator Rob Roy Purdy, who sent him a report of the Vanderbilt faculty, written in the wake of the Lawson episode, on proper procedures for disciplining students. R. R. Purdy to Longenecker, September 30, 1960; Longenecker to R. R. Purdy, October 4, 1960, Box 102, Longenecker Papers, TUA.

147. Copy of Confidential Police Report, Dave McGuire to Horace Renegar, October 13, 1960, Box 99, Longenecker Papers, TUA. McGuire was Mayor DeLesseps Morrison's chief administrative officer. His death in November deprived Morrison of perhaps the steadiest hand in City Hall during the worst of the school crisis. See Haas, *DeLesseps S. Morrison,* 274, and 249–82 generally on the chaos that enveloped the city in the fall and winter of 1960–61. F. C. Haley to

Longenecker, October 6, 1960 (quotation); Jack Ricau and Joseph Viguerie to Longenecker, October 25, 1960 (quotation), Box 99, Longenecker Papers, TUA.

148. Fairclough, *Race and Democracy,* chapter 9, recounts the battle between Wright and the state, as well as the battle in the streets of the city.

149. College of Arts and Sciences Resolution, December 14, 1960; Statement by Members of the Faculty of Tulane University, December 16, 1960, Box 99, Longenecker Papers, TUA. Rufus Harris, now president of Mercer, wrote to Provost Bob Lumiansky of his pleasure at the publication of the statement. He quoted a prominent New Orleanian who likewise strongly approved. "It looks like decency and dignity have a chance to come back, which already would have occurred but for the State Legislature. It would exhaust your imagination to dwell on the amassed ignorance and prejudice of our law making body. When they speak before the state and nation I have the feeling that the family half-wit has come downstairs to talk to the company." Harris to Robert Lumiansky, December 22, 1960, Box 28, Harris Papers, TUA.

150. For the Ford Foundation program, see Roger L. Geiger, *Research and Relevant Knowledge: American Research Universities since World War II* (New York, 1993), 113–15. Minutes of the Meeting of the Board of Administrators, October 12, 1960, TUA.

151. Minutes of the Meeting of the Board of Administrators, November 22, 1960, TUA. On November 14, Jones also wrote to Dean Rusk at The Rockefeller Foundation, which was considering a grant to the Medical School, asking for "sympathetic understanding" of the vise in which Tulane found itself. Joseph Jones to Dean Rusk, November 14, 1960, Box 75, Longenecker Papers, TUA. Also in November Longenecker had his first taste of the Association of American Law Schools pressure, when Dean Ray Forrester of the Law School sent him a copy of a letter from the chairman of the Committee on Racial Discrimination, who warned that "unless we indicate some steps are being taken, then those who advocate stronger measures may prevail." Ray Forrester to Longenecker, November 30, 1960; Longenecker to Forrester, December 2, 1960, Box 99, Longenecker Papers, TUA.

152. Minutes of the Meeting of the Executive Committee, December 8, 1960, Box 99, Longenecker Papers; Minutes of the Meeting of the Board of Administrators, December 14, 1960, TUA.

153. Marie Louise Snellings, To the Board of Administrators of Tulane Education Fund, January 24, 1961, Addendum, "Policy—Negroes," Harris Papers, TUA.

154. Ibid. The only other person whose opinion on this matter survives, interestingly, is Rufus Harris. He wrote to Joseph Jones, hardly his close friend, on January 30, about Tulane's dilemma with the Ford Foundation. "I deeply hope the Ford Foundation will deal generously with Tulane. I know something of your difficulty. Have you considered having Tulane publicly announce now a decision to admit qualified Negroes in September of 1962, or even in 1963, to the graduate and professional schools, the idea being that it is well to announce now such a decision, even though its consummation is set for a later date?" Harris to Jones, January 30, 1961, Box 64, Harris Papers, TUA. Jones replied only that "I would like to thank you for the thoughtful suggestion which you made in this direction." Copy of letter, Jones to Harris, February 4, 1961, Box 75, Longenecker Papers, TUA.

155. Joseph M. Jones to James W. Armsey, January 16, 1961, Grant #PA06400247, Ford Foundation Archives. The following letters of January 18, 20, and 24 are from the same source.

156. In a letter to Longenecker, Jones indicated that he had sent an answer to Armsey, and a similar letter to the Rockefeller Foundation, on February 4. Neither letter is in the files. Jones to Longenecker, February 4, 1961, Box 75, Longenecker Papers, TUA. Interestingly enough, Arm-

sey's letter, like much of this material, is only found in Rufus Harris's papers. James Armsey to Longenecker, February 15, 1961, Box 64, Harris Papers, TUA.

157. In the intervening board meeting on February 8, Longenecker raised another prospective problem, federal appropriations to segregated schools. "One of the first acts of the new housing administrator [in Washington, DC] will be an attempt to place restrictions on the new college housing loans against those institutions which have admissions policies barring Negroes. It is expected that there will be a strong effort made to attach discrimination clauses on all appropriations made by the government to institutions of higher learning." Minutes of the Board of Administrators Meeting, February 8, 1961, TUA.

158. Minutes of the Meeting of the Board of Trustees, March 8, 1961, TUA. The correspondence from Emory is S. Walter Martin to Robert Lumiansky, February 23, 1961; Longenecker to Martin, February 28, 1961; Martin to Longenecker, March 1, 1961, Box 102, Longenecker Papers, TUA. In a remarkable coincidence, the Duke Board of Trustees was meeting to decide the same question on this very same day. Duke provost Taylor Cole recounts in his memoirs that he was called out of the meeting in Durham to answer a phone call from a Tulane administrator who "wished to know what 'progress' we were making." Cole, *Recollections*, 161.

159. Minutes of the Meeting of the Board of Administrators, March 8, 1961; April 12, 1961, TUA; Longenecker to Henry Heald, October 20, 1961; Longenecker to George Harrar, October 20, 1961, Box 100, Longenecker Papers, TUA.

160. The announcement appeared in the local press the following day. *New Orleans Times-Picayune; New Orleans States-Item*, April 13, 1961. In reaction, the South Louisiana White Citizen's Council purported to be "stunned." Given the kid-glove treatment they had received from Tulane in the past, they probably were. On campus, a random sampling of student opinion found a wide range of reactions. *Tulane Hullabaloo*, April 28, 1961. An October 1962 poll revealed the same lack of consensus, with 48 percent favoring integration and 42 percent opposed. Tellingly, 90 percent of faculty members and graduate students wanted the school to desegregate. *Tulane Hullabaloo*, October 26, 1962.

161. On Newsom, see Stuart Ewen, *PR! A Social History of Spin* (New York, 1996), 352. Newsom and Co. partner W. H. Ferry advised the Ford Foundation on a wide variety of issues. Finding Aid, W. H. Ferry Papers, Public Policy Papers, Department of Rare Books and Special Collections, Princeton University Library.

162. Earl Newsom to Horace Renegar and Kenneth H. Gormin, August 29, 1961, Box 100, Longenecker Papers, TUA. Tulane officials readily acknowledged among themselves that "other than 'young white persons' have long been admitted" but took great care to keep this out of their public discourse. Horace Renegar to Joseph Jones, May 11, 1962, Box 87, Longenecker Papers, TUA.

163. Rufus Harris to Frederick Hard, March 8, 1963, Box 40, Harris Papers, TUA; *Tulane Hullabaloo*, April 13, 1962.

164. At least thirteen applications or requests for application materials were received from blacks by the middle of June. Minutes of the Meeting of the Board of Administrators, June 14, 1961, TUA. Among the first and best of these applications were those of Pearlie Hardin Elloie and Barbara Marie Guillory, both graduates of Dillard University. Dillard political science professor Paul Furey and Rosa Freeman Keller had been quietly working to prepare a legal challenge to Tulane's admissions policy and had identified these two women as potential applicants. Keller and Furey were probably unaware of the Tulane board's decision on March 8 when they

undertook this effort. Elloie's application was dated March 6, and Furey sent it to Tulane's admissions director, Cliff Wing, on March 13, after the March 8 board decision but before the April 12 announcement. Furey included both a cover letter and a brief personal note. In the note, he acknowledged that he had encouraged the application and that it was his "intention to put Tulane University squarely on the spot." In the letter, he said that he had "selected this student with the same care with which the Brooklyn Dodgers selected Jackie Robinson for big league baseball." March 13, 1961, Box 102, Longenecker Papers, TUA. On Keller's role, see Mohr and Gordon, *Tulane,* 262–65. The rejection letters are in Robert Lumiansky to Miss Barbara Marie Guillory, June 23, 1961; W. L. Kindelsperger to Pearlie Hardin Elloie, April 19, 1961, Box 100, Longenecker Papers, TUA.

165. *New Orleans Times-Picayune,* September 2, 1961; *The Tulanian,* September 1961. Mohr and Gordon, *Tulane,* 266–72, contains detailed analysis of the legal issues.

166. Despite, or perhaps because of, the clear invitation to a lawsuit, the administrators expressed frequent concern that this action not be perceived as a "friendly" suit. There is absolutely no doubt that it was not. Horace Renegar, Memorandum, March 30, 1962, Box 99, Longenecker Papers, TUA. Elloie and Guillory's attorneys crafted an argument that struck directly at Tulane's status as a private, independent university and Tulane's attorneys furiously defended that status. See Fairclough, *Race and Democracy,* 263.

167. In spite of Tulane's loud claims that Wright had "ruled" that Tulane was a public school, he did not seem to claim that Tulane was a "public university," only that it had enough public aspects to bring it under the sway of the Fourteenth Amendment. Wright found these public aspects in several areas: Tulane was originally a public university, and its name was changed by the state legislature in 1846; it retained state university property and three state government representatives as ex-officio members of its board; it operated under a special state franchise that provided a tax exemption for state property; and, most arguably, it performed a function "impressed with a public interest." *Guillory v. Administrators of Tulane University,* 203 F.Supp. 858 (March 1962). See also *New Orleans Times-Picayune,* March 29, 1962; *Tulane Hullabaloo,* April 6, 1962. On Wright, see Arthur Selwyn Miller, *A "Capacity for Outrage": The Judicial Odyssey of J. Skelly Wright* (Westport, CT, 1984).

168. Lida Tulane to Susan B. Keane, June 29, 1962; Susan Kean to Lida Tulane, July 6, 1962, Box 100, Longenecker Papers, TUA. The sisters were brought in as third party defendants in 1962.

169. Minutes of the Meeting of the Board of Administrators, April 5, 1962; Longenecker to Kenneth Pitzer, May 29, 1962, Box 102, Longenecker Papers, TUA.

170. Tulane's attorneys judged that they were better off with a new trial under a less liberal judge than in front of the activist Fifth Circuit Court of Appeals. On the Fifth Circuit, see Bass, *Unlikely Heroes.* Remarkably, just before he left New Orleans Judge Wright spoke at a large meeting sponsored by the AAUP at Tulane's University Center, discussing the Tulane case and segregation law in general. *New Orleans Times-Picayune,* April 6, 1962; *Tulane Hullabaloo,* April 13, 1962.

171. Harris to Mark Etheridge, April 11, 1962, Box 55, Harris Papers, TUA. Harris also wrote Skelly Wright, congratulating him on his appointment to the DC Circuit and on his decision in the Tulane case. "I regret to observe the assumed petulance of the Tulane Board over it," he wrote. Harris to Wright, April 6, 1962, Box 55, Harris Papers, TUA.

172. Mark Etheridge to Harris, April 16, 1962, Box 55, Harris Papers, TUA.

173. Tulane Police Report, February 7, 1962; Jesse B. Morgan to Longenecker, April 19, 1962;

Jesse B. Morgan to Clarence Scheps, January 29, 1962; Horace Renegar, Report to the Board of Trustees, May 2, 1962, Box 102, Longenecker Papers, TUA. Fairclough, *Race and Democracy,* chapter 10, is a detailed look at nonviolent direct action in Louisiana from 1960 to 1962. Mohr and Gordon, *Tulane,* 276–86, discuss Tulane students' involvement with CORE and the sit-ins at the University Center.

174. On the issues at trial, see Mohr and Gordon, *Tulane,* 286–88, and Cheryl V. Cunningham, "The Desegregation of Tulane University" (M.A. thesis, University of New Orleans, 1982), 77–91.

175. Minutes of the Faculty of the College of Arts and Sciences, Special Meeting, September 14, 1962; Minutes of the Faculty of the School of Social Work, September 28, 1962; Proposal of the Faculty of the School of Social Work, October 1, 1962, Box 87, Longenecker Papers; Statement of the Faculty of the School of Engineering, Minutes of the Meeting of the Board of Administrators, October 8, 1962, TUA. Longenecker also received a letter from a group of Newcomb faculty who deplored the university's failure to exercise responsible leadership on race relations. Cecilia Davis to Longenecker, November 5, 1962, Box 102, Longenecker Papers, TUA.

176. Tulane Police Report, October 3, October 8, 1962, Box 102, Longenecker Papers, TUA; *Tulane Hullabaloo,* October 12, 1962. On campus response to the trouble at Ole Miss, see *Tulane Hullabaloo,* October 5, October 12, November 2, 1962. More ordinary problems associated with the continuation of segregation did not dissipate either. In November, for example, Tulane turned away an NSF grant for a summer mathematics institute because it contained a nondiscrimination requirement. Edmund McIlhenny to Longenecker, November 15, 1962; Longenecker to McIlhenny, November 19, 1962, Box 99, Longenecker Papers, TUA.

177. *Guillory v. Administrators of Tulane University,* 212 F.Supp. 687 (December 1962).

178. John Pat Little to Joseph Jones, December 13, 1962, Box 100, Longenecker Papers; Minutes of the Meeting of the Board of Administrators, December 12, 1962; Harris to Kathryn Davis, December 13, 1962, Box 102, Longenecker Papers, TUA. The administrators announced the decision immediately. *New Orleans Times-Picayune,* December 13, 1962; *The Tulanian,* January 1963.

179. Horace Renegar to Longenecker, December 29, 1962, Box 100, Longenecker Papers; Interdepartmental Memo, January 25, 1963, Box 99, Longenecker Papers, TUA.

180. Meiners, *History of Rice,* 196–97; Minutes of the Meeting of the Board of Trustees, December 16, 1959, March 30, 1960, June 29, 1960, Board of Trustees Records, WRC.

181. Houston to Faculty, July 27, 1960, Box 13, Pitzer Papers, WRC; Minutes of the Meeting of the Board of Trustees, July 27, 1960, September 19, 1960, Rice University; *Rice Thresher,* September 10, 23, 1960. Houston was given the title of chancellor and appointed distinguished professor of physics. When Carey Croneis was named chancellor upon Pitzer's appointment as president, Houston's title became honorary chancellor. Minutes of the Meeting of the Board of Trustees, May 31, 1961.

182. Geiger, *Research and Relevant Knowledge,* 20.

183. Meiners, *History of Rice,* 199–200.

184. Interview with Kenneth S. Pitzer, conducted by John Boles and Louis Marchiafava, March 22, 1994, Rice History Project Oral History Series, WRC.

185. In 1959, at the suggestion of NASA director Keith Glennan, Rice was working on a proposal for a $1 million grant for materials research. This grant would carry the standard federal nondiscrimination clause.

186. Supplementary Statement Concerning the Proposed Institute Sponsored by the Department of Health, Education, and Welfare, October 16, 1963, Rice files, K-93, Baker and Botts.

This is part of a longer memo Pitzer sent to the board detailing the serious consequences that Rice was about to suffer in its relations with federal funding agencies.

187. Leo S. Shamblin, Rice's business manager, sent Malcolm Lovett a copy of the nondiscrimination clause in Pitzer's AEC contract, noting that "Dr. Pitzer is very anxious to execute this contract." L. S. Shamblin to H. Malcolm Lovett, September 21, 1961, Rice files, K-93, Baker and Botts, Houston, Texas.

188. Minutes of the Meeting of the Board of Trustees, September 27, 1961, Board of Trustees Records, WRC.

189. A copy of the clause is in L. S. Shamblin to H. Malcolm Lovett, September 21, 1961, Rice files, K-93, Baker and Botts, Houston, Texas.

190. Ibid. Several people in the room, among them Rayzor, Brown, Pitzer, and Croneis, already knew what Rice's lawyers thought. Two days before this meeting Malcolm Lovett distributed to them a 13-page legal analysis of the charter's racially restrictive admissions clause. Malcolm Lovett to George R. Brown, September 25, 1961, Box 16, Pitzer Papers, WRC. At the board's next meeting, this decision was reaffirmed when Rayzor submitted another contract for approval. This contract, also with the AEC, was for work to be done by Rice's Biology Department and "provided for additional research, an extension of the period, and certain changes in the contract language including the new non-discrimination clause." This time the board authorized Pitzer and Chancellor Croneis to execute any subsequent contracts that required compliance with the equal opportunity provisions of President Kennedy's Executive Order 10925. The trustees also restated their instructions that the school's lawyers "determine what action is necessary to enable the University to admit qualified acceptable candidates without regard to race or color." Minutes of the Meeting of the Board of Trustees, October 25, 1961, Board Of Trustees Records, WRC.

191. Carey Croneis, Memorandum, April 17, 1962; Minutes of a Meeting of Special Committee—Board of Governors, April 17, 1962, Rice files, K-93, Baker and Botts.

192. NASA Press Release, quoted in Henry C. Dethloff, *Suddenly Tomorrow Came: The History of the Johnson Space Center* (Washington, DC, 1993), 40; *Houston Chronicle*, September 19, 1961. The story covered the front pages of all of Houston's newspapers. For a detailed look at NASA's decision, see William D. Angel Jr., "The Politics of Space: NASA's Decision to Locate the Manned Space Center in Houston," *Houston Review* 6 (1984): 63–81.

193. Carey Croneis, Memorandum to Members of the Rice Board of Governors, August 31, 1961, Box 2, Houston Personal Papers, WRC; Kenneth Pitzer, Letter of Intent, Rice University and the Manned Space Flight Laboratory of the National Aeronautics and Space Administration, August 24, 1961, Apollo Series Documents, Johnson Space Center Archives, Rice University.

194. Homer E. Newell, Conference Report, December 19, 1961, Apollo Series Documents, Johnson Space Center Archives, Rice University.

195. John D. McCully Sr. to L. S. Shamblin, October 23, 1961, Rice files, K-93, Baker and Botts; Malcolm Lovett to Walter Reynolds, April 26, 1962, Box 19, Pitzer Papers, WRC; Malcolm Lovett to Leo Shamblin, October 16, 1961; Carey Croneis to Pitzer, October 18, 1961, Box 16, Pitzer Papers, WRC.

196. Memorandum, October 21, 1961, Rice files, K-93, Baker and Botts. The conclusion that charging tuition did not go to the purpose of the charter—which specified that a Rice education would be free—is an odd one.

197. Minutes of Meeting of the Board of Trustees, May 23, 1962, Rice University.

198. Association of Rice Alumni, Minutes of the Executive Board Meeting, June 5, 1962, Box 2, Chancellor's Papers, WRC. At the next meeting this minute was stricken on the grounds

that it was "an expression of opinion by the Executive Secretary and not a statement of fact." Association of Rice Alumni, Minutes of the Executive Board Meeting, September 11, 1962, Box 2, Chancellor's Papers, WRC.

199. Kenneth Pitzer, File memo, September 22, 1961, Box 19, Pitzer Papers, WRC.

200. Memorandum, Edgar O. Edwards to Kenneth S. Pitzer, January 15, 1962, Box 16, Pitzer Papers, WRC.

201. In April 1961, a rumor that Rice would soon charge tuition made the rounds on campus. It was quickly squelched by Carey Croneis, who dismissed the idea as "improbable." *Rice Thresher,* April 28, 1961.

202. *Rice Thresher,* April 9, 1960. On the sit-in movement in Houston, see Thomas R. Cole, *No Color Is My Kind: The Life of Eldrewey Stearns and the Integration of Houston* (Austin, TX, 1997), 25–57.

203. *Rice Thresher,* April 22, 29, 1960. Two of the black students who participated in the panel discussion had been appointed to the newly formed "Citizen's Relations Committee" by Houston Mayor Lewis Cutrer. On the workings of this committee, which included Rice students, see Cole, *No Color Is My Kind,* 43–46, 53.

204. On the news blackout that accompanied desegregation of the lunch counters, see Cole, *No Color Is My Kind,* 54–57. While the Houston press refused to discuss local desegregation, the national press was excoriating them for their failure to do their job. "Blackout in Houston," *Time* (September 12, 1960), p. 68; Ben H. Bagdikian, "Houston's Shackled Press," *Atlantic Monthly* (August 1966).

205. *Rice Thresher,* March 3, 1961. In September, the *Thresher* reported that one of the Rice students had been convicted on charges of unlawful assembly and that her attorney called several Rice professors, including Herbert H. Lehnert of the German Department and Louis Mackey of Philosophy, as defense witnesses. *Rice Thresher,* September 29, 1961. Another Rice student was convicted of the same offense in a separate trial. December 1, 1961.

206. *Rice Thresher,* December 1, 15, 1961; January 10, 1962. Rice Student Association president Reed Martin sent the results to Pitzer with this note: "Although this vote was termed an 'opinion poll' because it was not binding on any university policies, it was not intended to be an idle expression of opinion. It is our sincere hope that this expression of student opinion may be useful in an evaluation of this delicate and important problem." Reed Martin to Pitzer, December 21, 1961, Box 16, Pitzer Papers, WRC. The data that Martin sent to Pitzer was broken down in several ways—by residential college, by year in school, and by major. In every case but one, there was a substantial majority in favor of desegregation. Only the PE -Commerce majors—the athletes—voted against the referendum. A bare 14 percent favored it.

207. Kathleen Henderson to Carey Croneis, September 23, 1961; Croneis to Kathleen Henderson, October 2, 1961, Box 2, Houston Personal Papers, WRC.

208. Minutes of the Meeting of the Board of Trustees, June 27, July 25, 1962, Board of Trustees Records, WRC. Lovett, who had been a member of the Board of Governors, was elected a trustee at this meeting.

209. James O. Winston Jr. to George Brown, July 6, 1962, Rice files, K-93, Baker and Botts. Winston clearly understood the financial arguments in favor of the change and rejected them on moral grounds. He wrote, "It would seem appropriate that the top administration of Rice avoid in every way possible the appearance of sacrificing principle to financial expediency."

210. Draft of letter, Pitzer to Malcolm Lovett, n.d. but late 1962 to very early 1963, Box 16, Pitzer Papers, WRC.

211. Ibid.

212. Dillon Anderson to Honorable Waggoner Carr, December 27, 1962, Rice files, K-93, Baker and Botts. Anderson and Malcolm Lovett were both in close contact at this time with Joseph Merrick Jones, the chairman of the Tulane Board, about the details of Tulane's lawsuit. Joseph Jones to Dillon Anderson, December 6, 1962; Anderson to Jones, December 12, 1962; Jones to Anderson, December 13, 1962, Anderson to Jones, December 17, 1962, Rice files, K-93, Baker and Botts.

213. Petition, *William Marsh Rice University, et al., v. Waggoner Carr,* February 21, 1963, Series 1, Rice trial records, Pitzer Papers, WRC. The same day the suit was filed the student chairman of the Rice Forum Committee wrote Martin Luther King, asking him to postpone a planned visit to Rice "due to circumstances that have developed recently." Mike Jaffe to Rev. Dr. Martin Luther King Jr., February 21, 1963, Pitzer Papers, WRC.

214. Many of these letters are in Box 16, Pitzer Papers, WRC. Most of the angry letters are in the Baker and Botts files. Rice files, K-93, Baker and Botts.

215. John Urquhart to Pitzer, June 21, 1963, Box 16, Pitzer Papers, WRC.

216. W. Darwin Andrus to Pitzer, February 27, 1963, Box 16, Pitzer Papers, WRC.

217. Shirley Simons Jr. and S. A. Cochran Jr. to Board of Trustees, Rice University, February 25, 1963, Box 13, Pitzer Papers, WRC.

218. Malcolm Lovett, Speech to Rice Alumni, November 1963, Rice files, K-93, Baker and Botts. George Brown wrote the cleanest responses to the unhappy letters. In one especially concise note he defended the board's decision with reference to Rice's last charter change lawsuit: "Had we not asked the court for changes so we could buy the Rincon Oil Field, Rice University would have been a fifty million dollar loser." George R. Brown to Fred J. Stancliff, September 3, 1963, Rice files, K-93, Baker and Botts. Lovett and Brown often sent copies of Lovett's talk to the alumni to angry correspondents. This "should answer all the questions," Lovett wrote to one friend, "that you or your tormentors at the ROCC [River Oaks Country Club] may have." Lovett to J. W. Link, January 14, 1964, Rice files, K-93, Baker and Botts.

219. Petition in Intervention, June 23, 1963, Series 2, Rice trial records, Pitzer Papers, WRC. In his letter of resignation in 1968, Kenneth Pitzer singled out this intervention as one of the chief disappointments of his years at Rice. Pitzer to Malcolm Lovett, August 16, 1968, Box 8, Chancellor's Office Papers, WRC.

220. James L. Aronson to Pitzer, July 12, 1963; John B. Coffee to James L. Aronson, July 23, 1963, Box 9, Chancellor's Office Papers, WRC; *Houston Press,* March 2, 1964. Pitzer tried to use the opening provided by the conversation between Aronson and Coffee to craft a compromise that would end the intervention, but to no avail. The Hutchins quote is in Croneis to Pitzer, December 6, 1963, Box 13, Pitzer Papers, WRC.

221. Memo, Malcolm Lovett to Dillon Anderson, June 19, 1963, Rice files, K-93, Baker and Botts.

222. Pitzer to Members of the Board of Governors, October 16, 1963, Rice files, K-93, Baker and Botts; W. R. Smedberg III to Pitzer, July 8, 1963, Box 16, Pitzer Papers, WRC. Both Croneis and Pitzer replied to Smedberg, assuring him that Rice was trying to remove its racial restrictions but acknowledging that the intervention made it impossible to predict when they would actually be voided. Croneis to Smedberg, July 12, 1963; Pitzer to Smedberg, August 28, 1963, Box 16, Pitzer Papers, WRC.

223. Pitzer to Members of the Board of Governors, October 16, 1963, Rice files, K-93, Baker and Botts. Malcolm Lovett took the threat of losing the NASA relationship very seriously. "The NASA memorandum in particular raises problems that will be hard to meet," he wrote Dillon

Anderson. "The next Board meeting will be on October 30. We should endeavor to have our suggestions and plan, if any, for meeting this problem by that time." Memorandum, "To Dillon Anderson from Malcolm Lovett," October 14, 1963, Rice files, K-93, Baker and Botts.

224. Kenneth W. Mildenberger to Carey Croneis, October 4, 1963, Rice files, K-93, Baker and Botts. Rice apparently accepted the HEW restrictions on the summer program proposed by Jim Castaneda of the Spanish Department. Pitzer to Malcolm Lovett, October 10, 1963, Rice files, K-93, Baker and Botts. John B. Evans to Pitzer, February 4, 1964, Box 16, Pitzer Papers, WRC.

225. Copy of letter, Heinrich Schneider to Robert L. Kahn, October 25, 1963; Copy of letter, Francois Treve to Gerald MacLane, December 10, 1963, Box 16, Pitzer Papers, WRC.

226. Pitzer to Mr. and Mrs. L. Kent Bendall, October 28, 1963, Box 16, Pitzer Papers, WRC.

227. Trust interpretation is a matter of equity, which would normally be tried in front of a judge. This jury trial was a real oddity.

228. Memorandum, Croneis to Pitzer, January 24, 1964, Rice files, K-93, Baker and Botts. Congressman Albert Thomas helped compile nondiscrimination requirements of the major federal granting agencies. Hobart Taylor Jr. to Albert Thomas, January 21, 1964, Rice files, K-93, Baker and Botts.

229. Confidential Report of the President to the Board of Governors of Rice University, January 1965, Box 30, Pitzer Papers, WRC. Before he was admitted to the Graduate School, Raymond Johnson was employed as a research assistant in the Math Department.

230. Charles W. Hamilton to C. F. Johnson, November 21, 1966, Box 1, Chancellor's Papers, WRC. Examples abound in the files of Chancellor Croneis, Pitzer, and other Rice officials.

231. Pitzer to Samuel A. Shelburne, November 16, 1964, Box 13, Pitzer Papers, WRC.

CONCLUSION

1. Barney L. Jones, "Reminiscences, 1930–1960," DUA.

2. Ibid.

3. The language is from Goodrich White's dissent to the Truman Commission on Higher Education Report, *Higher Education for American Democracy,* 29.

Selected Bibliography

Manuscript Sources

Duke University

Duke University Archives, Perkins Library, Durham, North Carolina

> Records of the Administrative Committee
> Board of Trustees Papers
> Divinity School Papers
> A. Hollis Edens Papers
> Robert Flowers Papers
> Deryl Hart Papers
> Herbert Herring Papers
> Barney L. Jones "Reminiscences"
> Bunyan Snipes Womble Papers

Duke University Special Collections, Perkins Library, Durham, North Carolina

> Willis Smith Papers

Emory University

Special Collections, Robert W. Woodruff Library, Emory University, Atlanta, Georgia

> Records of the Board of Trustees and the Executive Committee
> Henry L. Bowden Papers
> Emory University Archives Manuscript Boxes
> Emory University Faculty Papers
> Robert Mizell Papers
> Arthur J. Moore Papers
> John A. Sibley Papers
> Judson C. Ward Papers
> Goodrich Cook White Papers
> Robert W. Woodruff Papers
> James Harvey Young Papers

Ford Foundation

Ford Foundation Archives, New York, New York

> Grant PA06400247

Rice University

Baker and Botts Historical Collection, Houston, Texas

>Rice University Files

Johnson Space Center Archives, Fondren Library, Rice University, Houston, Texas

>Apollo Series Documents

Woodson Research Center, Fondren Library, Rice University, Houston, Texas

>Board of Trustees Records
>George R. Brown Papers
>Chancellor's Office Papers
>Honorary Chancellor's Papers
>William Vermillion Houston Papers
>Edgar Odell Lovett Papers
>Kenneth Sanborn Pitzer Papers
>Rice Student Association Papers
>*Rice Thresher* Papers
>Rice University Graduate Council Papers
>Albert Thomas Papers

Tulane University

Tulane University Archives, Howard-Tilton Library, New Orleans, Louisiana

>Minutes of the Board of Administrators
>Rufus Carrollton Harris Papers
>Herbert Longenecker Papers
>President's Reports to the Board
>Vertical File

Valdosta State University

Valdosta State University Archives, Odum Library, Valdosta, Georgia

>S. Walter Martin Papers

Vanderbilt University

Special Collections, Jean and Alexander Heard Library, Vanderbilt University, Nashville, Tennessee

>B. Harvie Branscomb Papers
>Oliver C. Carmichael

Centennial History Project
Chancellor's Office Papers
Secretary of the University Papers
James G. Stahlman Papers
Harold S. Vanderbilt Papers

Newspapers and Magazines

AAUP Bulletin
Atlanta Constitution
Charlotte Observer
Christian Century
Christianity and Crisis
Duke Chronicle
Durham Herald
Emory Alumnus
Emory Wheel
Houston Chronicle
Houston Post
Houston Press
Nashville Banner
Nashville Tennessean
New Orleans Item
New Orleans Times-Picayune
New York Times
North Carolina Christian Advocate
Raleigh News and Observer
Rice Thresher
Southern School News
Tulane Hullabaloo
Vanderbilt Alumnus
Vanderbilt Hustler

Legal Cases

Barrows v. Jackson, 346 U.S. 249 (1953).
Brown v. Board of Education of Topeka, Kansas, 345 U.S. 972 (1954).
Vivian Calhoun, et. al., v. A.C. Latimer, et. al., 188 F.Supp. 401 (1959).
Commonwealth of Pennsylvania, et al., v. Board of Directors of City Trusts, 353 U.S. 230 (1957).
Emory University et al. v. Nash, 218 Ga. 317 (1962).
Girard College Trusteeship, 138 A.2d 844 (1958).
Girard Will Case, 127 A.2d 287 (1956).

Guillory v. Administrators of Tulane University, 203 F.Supp. 858 (March 1962); 212 F.Supp. 687 (December 1962).

Holmes v. City of Atlanta, 350 U.S. 879 (1955).

McLaurin v. Oklahoma State Regents for Higher Education, 339 U.S. 637 (1950).

Mayor and City Council of Baltimore City v. Dawson, 350 U.S. 877 (1955).

Pearson v. Murray, 169 Md. 478, 182 A. 590 (1936).

Shelley v. Kramer, 334 U.S. 1 (1948).

Smith v. Allwright, 321 U.S. 649 (1944).

State v. Witham, 165 S.W. 2d 378 (1942).

Sweatt v. Painter, 210 S.W. 2d 442 (1947), 339 U.S. 629 (1950).

Weiss v. Leaon, 359 Mo. 1054, 225 S.W. 2d 127 (1949).

Dissertations and Theses

Cook, James F., Jr. "Politics and Education in the Talmadge Era: The Controversy over the University System of Georgia, 1941–42." Ph.D. diss., University of Georgia, 1972.

Cunningham, Cheryl V. "The Desegregation of Tulane University." M.A. thesis, University of New Orleans, 1982.

Gantz, Kerri D. "On the Basis of Merit Alone: Integration, Tuition, Rice University, and the Charter Change Trial, 1963–1966." M.A. thesis, Rice University, 1991.

Henderson, Harold P. "The 1946 Gubernatorial Election in Georgia." M.A. thesis, Georgia Southern College, 1967.

Kotelanski, Jorge. "Prolonged and Patient Efforts: The Desegregation of Duke University, 1948–1963." Senior thesis, Duke University, 1990.

Newberry, Anthony. "Without Urgency or Ardor: The South's Middle Road Liberals and Civil Rights, 1945–1960." Ph.D. diss., Ohio University, 1982.

Payne, John Robert. "A Jesuit Search for Social Justice: The Public Career of Louis J. Twomey, S.J., 1947–1969." Ph.D. diss., University of Texas, 1976.

Raabe, Phyllis Hutton. "Status and Its Impact: New Orleans' Carnival, the Social Upper Class and Upper Class Power." Ph.D. diss., Pennsylvania State University, 1973.

Stevens, Jeanne E. "The Impacts of World War II on Duke University." Ph.D. diss., Duke University, 1991.

Books and Articles

Adams, Frank T. *James A. Dombrowski: An American Heretic, 1897–1983.* Knoxville: University of Tennessee Press, 1992.

Allen, Frederick. *Secret Formula: How Brilliant Marketing and Relentless Salesmanship Made Coca-Cola the Best-Known Product in the World.* New York: HarperCollins, 1994.

Allen, Ivan, Jr. *Mayor: Notes on the Sixties.* New York: Simon and Schuster, 1971.

Anderson, Jean Bradley. *Durham County: A History of Durham County, North Carolina.* Durham: Duke University Press, 1990.

Anderson, William. *The Wild Man from Sugar Creek: The Political Career of Eugene Talmadge.* Baton Rouge: Louisiana State University Press, 1975.

Angel, William D., Jr. "The Politics of Space: NASA's Decision to Locate the Manned Spacecraft Center in Houston." *Houston Review* 6 (1984): 63–81.

Armentrout, Donald Smith. *The Quest for the Informed Priest: A History of the School of Theology.* Sewanee, TN: School of Theology, University of the South, 1979.

Arnall, Ellis. *The Shore Dimly Seen.* Philadelphia: Lippincott, 1946.

Ashby, Warren. *Frank Porter Graham: A Southern Liberal.* Winston-Salem, NC: John F. Blair, 1980.

Ashmore, Harry. *The Negro and the Schools.* Chapel Hill: University of North Carolina Press, 1954.

Bacote, Clarence A. "The Negro in Atlanta Politics." *Phylon* 16 (4th quarter 1955): 349.

Baker, Liva. *The Second Battle of New Orleans: The Hundred-Year Struggle to Integrate the Schools.* New York: HarperCollins, 1996.

Baltzell, E. Digby. *The Protestant Establishment: Aristocracy and Caste in America.* New York: Random House, 1964.

Barkan, Elazar. *The Retreat of Scientific Racism: Changing Concepts of Race in Britain and the United States between the World Wars.* Cambridge: Cambridge University Press, 1991.

Bartley, Numan V. *The Rise of Massive Resistance: Race and Politics in the South during the 1950s.* Baton Rouge: Louisiana State University Press, 1969.

———. *From Thurmond to Wallace: Political Tendencies in Georgia, 1948–1968.* Baltimore: Johns Hopkins University Press, 1970.

———. *The Creation of Modern Georgia.* Athens: University of Georgia Press, 1983.

———. *The New South: 1945–1980.* Baton Rouge: Louisiana State University Press, 1995.

———. "The Southern Conference and the Shaping of Post-World War II Southern Politics." In *Developing Dixie,* edited by Winfred B. Moore, Joseph F. Tripp, and Lyon G. Tyler, 179–97. New York: Greenwood Press, 1988.

Bartley, Numan V., and Hugh Graham. *Southern Politics and the Second Reconstruction.* Baltimore: Johns Hopkins University Press, 1975.

Bass, Jack. *Unlikely Heroes.* New York: Simon and Schuster, 1981.

Bauman, Mark K., and Berkley Kalin. *The Quiet Voices: Southern Rabbis and Black Civil Rights, 1880s to 1990s.* Tuscaloosa: University of Alabama Press, 1997.

Bayor, Ronald H. *Race and the Shaping of Twentieth-Century Atlanta.* Chapel Hill: University of North Carolina Press, 1996.

Bernd, Joseph L. *Grassroots Politics in Georgia: The County Unit System and the Importance of the Individual Voting Community in Bifactional Elections, 1942–1954.* Atlanta: Emory University Research Committee, 1960.

Billingsley, William J. *Communists on Campus: Race, Politics, and the Public University in Sixties North Carolina.* Athens: University of Georgia Press, 1999.

Black, Earl. *Southern Governors and Civil Rights: Racial Segregation as a Campaign Issue in the Second Reconstruction.* Cambridge: Harvard University Press, 1976.

Bobo, James R. *The New Orleans Economy: Pro Bono Publico?* New Orleans: University of New Orleans Press, 1975.

Boles, John B. *University Builder: Edgar Odell Lovett and the Founding of the Rice Institute.* Baton Rouge: Louisiana State University Press, 2007.

Bolner, James, ed. *Louisiana Politics: Festival in a Labyrinth.* Baton Rouge: Louisiana State University Press, 1982.

Bowen, Boone M. *The Candler School of Theology: Sixty Years of Service.* Atlanta: Emory University Press, 1974.

Branch, Taylor. *Parting the Waters: America in the King Years, 1954–1963.* New York: Simon and Schuster, 1988.

Branscomb, Harvie. *Purely Academic: An Autobiography.* Nashville: limited edition printed by Vanderbilt University, 1978.

Bullock, Henry Morton. *A History of Emory University, 1836–1936.* Nashville: Parthenon Press, 1936.

Burk, Robert F. *The Eisenhower Administration and Black Civil Rights.* Knoxville: University of Tennessee Press, 1984.

Burns, Augustus M., III, and Julian M. Pleasants. *Frank Porter Graham and the 1950 Senate Race in North Carolina.* Chapel Hill: University of North Carolina Press, 1990.

Cable, George Washington. *The Negro Question.* Edited by Arlin Turner. New York: Doubleday, 1958.

Campbell, Will D. *The Stem of Jesse: The Costs of Community at a 1960s Southern School.* Macon, GA: Mercer University Press, 1995.

Carleton, Don E. *Red Scare! Right-Wing Hysteria, Fifties Fanaticism, and Their Legacy In Texas.* Austin: Texas Monthly Press, 1985.

Caro, Robert. *The Years of Lyndon Johnson: The Path to Power.* New York: Knopf, 1982.

Carson, Clayborne. *In Struggle: SNCC and the Black Awakening of the 1960s.* Cambridge: Harvard University Press, 1981.

Castaneda, Christopher J., and Joseph A. Pratt. *From Texas to the East: A Strategic History of Texas Eastern Corporation.* College Station: Texas A&M University Press, 1993.

Cecelski, David S., and Timothy B. Tyson, eds. *Democracy Betrayed: The Wilmington Race Riot of 1898 and Its Legacy.* Chapel Hill: University of North Carolina Press, 1998.

Cell, John T. *The Highest Stage of White Supremacy: The Origins of Segregation in South Africa and the American South.* Cambridge: Cambridge University Press, 1982.

Chafe, William H. *Civilities and Civil Rights: Greensboro, North Carolina, and the Black Struggle for Freedom.* New York: Oxford University Press, 1980.

Chaffin, Nora C. *Trinity College, 1839–1892: The Beginnings of Duke University.* Durham, NC: Duke University Press, 1950.

Chai, Charles W. "Who Rules New Orleans? A Study of Community Power Structures: Some Preliminary Findings on Social Characteristics and Attitudes of New Orleans Leaders." *Louisiana Business Survey* (October 1971): 2–11.

Chappell, David. *Inside Agitators: White Southerners in the Civil Rights Movement.* Baltimore: Johns Hopkins University Press, 1994.

Clark, E. Culpepper. *The Schoolhouse Door: Segregation's Last Stand at the University of Alabama.* New York: Oxford University Press, 1993.

Clowse, Barbara Barksdale. *Ralph McGill: A Biography.* Macon, GA: Mercer University Press, 1998.

Cobb, James C. *The Selling of the South: The Southern Crusade for Industrial Development, 1936–1980.* Baton Rouge: Louisiana State University Press, 1982.

———. *Industrialization and Southern Society, 1877–1984.* Lexington: University Press of Kentucky, 1984.

Cole, R. Taylor. *The Recollections of R. Taylor Cole: Educator, Emissary, Development Planner.* Durham, NC: Duke University Press, 1983.

Cole, Thomas R. *No Color Is My Kind: The Life of Eldrewey Stearns and the Integration of Houston.* Austin: University of Texas Press, 1997.

Commission on Higher Education. *Higher Education for American Democracy: The Report of the President's Commission on Higher Education.* Washington, DC: General Printing Office, 1947.

Conkin, Paul K. *Gone with the Ivy: A Biography of Vanderbilt University.* Knoxville: University of Tennessee Press, 1985.

———. *The Southern Agrarians.* Knoxville: University of Tennessee Press, 1988.

Covington, Howard E., Jr., and Marion A. Ellis. *Terry Sanford: Politics, Progress, and Outrageous Ambitions.* Durham, NC: Duke University Press, 1999.

Crain, Robert L., and Morton Inger. *School Desegregation in New Orleans: A Comparative Study of the Failure of Social Control.* Chicago: Aldine Publishing Company, 1966.

Crenshaw, Kimberle, et al., eds. *Critical Race Theory: The Writings that Formed the Movement.* New York: New Press, 1995.

Dalfiume, Richard M. *Desegregation of the U.S. Armed Forces: Fighting on Two Fronts, 1939–1953.* Columbia: University of Missouri Press, 1969.

Dallek, Robert. *Lone Star Rising: Lyndon Johnson and His Times.* New York: Oxford University Press, 1991.

Davidson, Chandler. *Race and Class in Texas Politics.* Princeton: Princeton University Press, 1990.

Dethloff, Henry C. *Suddenly Tomorrow Came: The History of the Johnson Space Center.* Washington, DC: General Printing Office, 1993.

Diamond, Nancy. "Catching Up: The Advance of Emory University since World War II." *History of Higher Education Annual* 19 (1999): 149–84.

Douglas, Davison M. "The Rhetoric of Moderation: Desegregating the South during the Decade after *Brown.*" *Northwestern University Law Review* 89 (1994): 92–139.

——. "The Quest for Freedom in the Post-*Brown* South: Desegregation and White Self- Interest." *Chicago-Kent Law Review* 70, no. 2 (1994): 689–755.

Douglas, Mary. *Purity and Danger: An Analysis of the Concepts of Pollution and Taboo.* New York: Routledge and Kegan Paul, 1966.

Doyle, Don H. *Nashville since the 1920s.* Knoxville: University of Tennessee Press, 1985.

Dunbar, Anthony P. *Against the Grain: Southern Radicals and Prophets, 1929–1959.* Charlottesville: University Press of Virginia, 1981.

Duram, James C. *A Moderate among Extremists: Dwight D. Eisenhower and the School Desegregation Crisis.* Chicago: Nelson-Hall, 1981.

Durden, Robert F. *The Dukes of Durham, 1865–1929.* Durham, NC: Duke University Press, 1975.

——. *The Launching of Duke University, 1924–1949.* Durham, NC: Duke University Press, 1993.

——. "Donnybrook at Duke: The Gross-Edens Affair of 1960, Part I." *North Carolina Historical Review* 71 (July 1994): 331–57.

——."Donnybrook at Duke: The Gross-Edens Affair of 1960, Part II." *North Carolina Historical Review* 71 (October 1994): 451–71.

Dyer, John P. *Tulane: The Biography of a University, 1834–1965.* New York: Harper and Row, 1966.

Dyer, Thomas G. *The University of Georgia: A Bicentennial History, 1785–1985.* Athens: University of Georgia Press, 1985.

Dykeman, Wilma, and James Stokely. *Seeds of Southern Change: The Life of Will Alexander.* Chicago: University of Chicago Press, 1962.

Eagles, Charles W. *Jonathan Daniels and Race Relations: The Evolution of a Southern Liberal.* Knoxville: University of Tennessee Press, 1982.

Egerton, John. *Speak Now against the Day: The Generation before the Civil Rights Movement in the South.* New York: Knopf, 1994.

Eisenhower, Dwight D. *The White House Years: Mandate for Change, 1953–1956.* New York: Doubleday, 1963.

English, Thomas H. *Emory University. 1915–1965: A Semicentennial History.* Atlanta: Emory University Press, 1966.

Ewen, Stuart. *PR! A Social History of Spin.* New York: Basic Books, 1996.

Fairclough, Adam. *Race and Democracy: The Civil Rights Struggle in Louisiana, 1915–1972.* Athens: University of Georgia Press, 1995.

Fleming, Cynthia G. "We Shall Overcome: Tennessee and the Civil Rights Movement." In *Tennessee History: The Land, the People, and the Culture,* edited by Carroll Van West, 436–55. Knoxville: University of Tennessee Press, 1998.

Fontenay, Charles L. *Estes Kefauver: A Biography.* Knoxville: University of Tennessee Press, 1980.

Fort, Randy. "Cutting the Throat to Cure the Cancer." *Emory Alumnus,* April 1956.

Fosdick, Raymond B. *Adventures in Giving: The Story of the General Education Board.* New York: Harper and Row, 1962.

Frazier, E. Franklin. *Black Bourgeoisie: Rise of a New Middle Class.* Glencoe, IL: Free Press, 1957.

Gaines, Kevin K. *Uplifting the Race: Black Leadership, Politics, and Culture in the Twentieth Century.* Chapel Hill: University of North Carolina Press, 1996.

Garrow, David J. *Atlanta, Georgia, 1960–1961.* Brooklyn, NY: Carlson Publishing, 1989.

Gaston, Paul. *The New South Creed: A Study in Southern Mythmaking.* Baton Rouge: Louisiana State University Press, 1970.

Gatewood, Willard. *Aristocrats of Color: The Black Elite, 1880–1920.* Bloomington: University of Indiana Press, 1990.

Geiger, Roger L. *To Advance Knowledge: The Growth of American Research Universities, 1900–1940.* New York: Oxford University Press, 1986.

———. *Research and Relevant Knowledge: American Research Universities since World War II.* New York: Oxford University Press, 1993.

Glennan, Thomas Keith. *The Birth of NASA: The Diary of T. Keith Glennan.* Washington, DC: NASA History Office, 1993.

Goldfield, David R. *Cotton Fields and Skyscrapers: Southern City and Region.* 1982. Reprint. Baltimore: Johns Hopkins University Press, 1989.

Goldstone, Dwonna. *Integrating the 40 Acres: The 50-Year Struggle for Racial Equality at the University of Texas.* Athens: University of Georgia Press, 2006.

Gorman, Joseph Bruce. *Kefauver: A Political Biography.* New York: Oxford University Press, 1971.

Gould, Steven Jay. *The Mismeasure of Man.* New York: W. W. Norton, 1981.

Graham, Hugh Davis. *Crisis in Print: Desegregation and the Press in Tennessee.* Nashville: Vanderbilt University Press, 1967.

Grantham, Dewey. "Tennessee and Twentieth-Century American Politics." In *Tennessee History: The Land, the People, and the Culture,* edited by Carroll Van West, 343–72. Knoxville: University of Tennessee Press, 1998.

Green, George Norris. *The Establishment in Texas Politics: The Primitive Years, 1938–1957.* Westport, CT, and London, UK: Greenwood Press, 1979.

Greene, Lee Seifert. *Lead Me On: Frank Goad Clement and Tennessee Politics.* Knoxville: University of Tennessee Press, 1982.

Griffin, Larry J., and Don Doyle, eds. *The South as an American Problem.* Athens, GA: University of Georgia Press, 1995.

Grimes, Lewis Howard. *A History of the Perkins School of Theology.* Dallas: Southern Methodist University Press, 1993.

Haas, Edward F. *DeLesseps S. Morrison and the Image of Reform: New Orleans Politics, 1946–1961.* Baton Rouge: Louisiana State University Press, 1974.

Halberstam, David. "The End of a Populist." *Harpers* (January 1971).

——. *The Children.* New York: Random House, 1998.

Hale, Grace Elizabeth. *Making Whiteness: The Culture of Segregation in the South, 1890–1940.* New York: Pantheon, 1998.

Hamilton, William B., ed. *Fifty Years of the South Atlantic Quarterly.* Durham, NC: Duke University Press, 1952.

Harlan, Louis. *Booker T. Washington: The Making of a Black Leader, 1856–1901.* New York: Oxford University Press, 1972.

——. *Booker T. Washington: The Wizard of Tuskegee, 1901–1915.* New York: Oxford University Press, 1983.

Harmon, David Andrew. *Beneath the Image of the Civil Rights Movement and Race Relations: Atlanta, Georgia, 1946–1981.* New York: Garland Publishing, 1996.

Harvard Law Review 63 (April 1950): 1062–64. Note.

Heard, Alexander. *Speaking of the University: Two Decades at Vanderbilt.* Nashville: Vanderbilt University Press, 1995.

Hein, Virginia H. "The Image of 'A City Too Busy to Hate': Atlanta in the 1960s." *Phylon* 33 (Fall 1972): 205–21.

Henderson, Harold P. *The Politics of Change in Georgia: A Political Biography of Ellis Arnall.* Athens: University of Georgia Press, 1991.

Henderson, Harold P., and Gary L. Roberts, eds. *Georgia Governors in an Age of Change: From Ellis Arnall to George Busbee.* Athens: University of Georgia Press, 1988.

Hine, Darlene Clark. *Black Victory: The Rise and Fall of the White Primary in Texas.* Millwood, NY: KTO Press, 1979.

Hodges, Luther. *Businessman in the Statehouse: Six Years as Governor of North Carolina.* Chapel Hill: University of North Carolina Press, 1962.

Holley, Joseph W. *You Can't Build a Chimney from the Top.* New York: William Frederick Press, 1949.

Hubbell, John. "The Desegregation of the University of Oklahoma, 1946–1950." *Journal of Negro History* 57 (October 1972): 370–84.

Hunter, Floyd. *Community Power Structure: A Study of Decision Makers.* Chapel Hill: University of North Carolina Press, 1953.

Inger, Morton. *Politics and Reality in an American City: The New Orleans School Integration Crisis in 1960.* New York: Center for Urban Education, 1969.

Inscoe, John C., ed. *Georgia in Black and White: Explorations in the Race Relations of a Southern State, 1865–1950.* Athens: University of Georgia Press, 1994.

Jacoway, Elizabeth, and David R. Colburn. *Southern Businessmen and Desegregation.* Baton Rouge: Louisiana State University Press, 1982.

Johnson, Guion Griffis. "Quiet Revolution in the South." *Journal of the American Association of University Women* 52 (March 1959): 133–36.

Johnson, Guy B. "New Ways on the Campus." *New South* 10 (February 1955): 1–10.

Karabel, Jerome. *The Chosen: The Hidden History of Admission and Exclusion at Harvard, Yale, and Princeton.* Boston and New York: Houghton Mifflin, 2005.

Kellar, William Henry. *Make Haste Slowly: Moderates, Conservatives, and School Desegregation in Houston.* College Station: Texas A&M University Press, 1999.

Kerr, Clark. *The Uses of the University.* Cambridge: Harvard University Press, 1963.

Kevles, D. J. "Testing the Army's Intelligence: Psychologists and the Military in World War I." *Journal of American History* 55 (Winter 1968): 565–81.

Key, V. O. *Southern Politics in State and Nation.* New York: Vintage Books, 1949.

Kirby, Jack Temple. *Rural Worlds Lost: The American South, 1920–1960.* Baton Rouge: Louisiana State University Press, 1987.

Klarman, Michael J. "How *Brown* Changed Race Relations: The Backlash Thesis." *Journal of American History* 81 (June 1994): 81–118.

Klibaner, Irwin. *Conscience of a Troubled South: The Southern Conference Educational Fund, 1946–1966.* Brooklyn, NY: Carlson, 1989.

Kluger, Richard. *Simple Justice: The History of Brown v. Board of Education and Black America's Struggle for Equality.* New York: Knopf, 1976.

Kneebone, John. *Southern Liberal Journalists and the Issue of Race, 1920–1944.* Chapel Hill: University of North Carolina Press, 1985.

Krueger, Thomas A. *And Promises to Keep: The Southern Conference for Human Welfare, 1938–1948.* Nashville: Vanderbilt University Press, 1967.

Kytle, Calvin, and James Mackay. *Who Runs Georgia?* Athens: University of Georgia Press, 1998.

Lehmann, Nicholas. *The Promised Land: The Great Black Migration and How It Changed America.* New York: Knopf, 1991.

——. *The Big Test: The Secret History of the American Meritocracy.* New York: Farrar, Straus and Giroux, 1999.

Levine, David O. *The American College and the Culture of Aspiration, 1915–1940.* Ithaca, NY: Cornell University Press, 1986.

Link, William A. "William Friday and the North Carolina Speaker Ban Crisis: 1963–1968." *North Carolina Historical Review* 72 (April 1995): 198–228.

Lowen, Rebecca S. *Creating the Cold War University: The Transformation of Stanford.* Berkeley: University of California Press, 1997.

Luebke, *Tar Heel Politics: Myths and Realities.* Chapel Hill: University of North Carolina Press, 1990.

McFadyen, Richard E. "Estes Kefauver and the Tradition of Southern Progressivism." *Tennessee Historical Quarterly* 37 (Winter 1978): 430–43.

McGaw, Robert. "A Policy the University Can Defend: 'In the South and in the North, in the Present and in the Future.'" *Vanderbilt Alumnus* (November–December 1956).

McMillen, Neil R. *The Citizens Council: Organized Resistance to the Second Reconstruction.* Urbana: University of Illinois Press, 1971.

——, ed. *Remaking Dixie: The Impact of World War II on the American South.* Jackson: University Press of Mississippi, 1997.

Malone, Dumas. "Report to the President on the Development of the Graduate School." *Bulletin of Emory University* 31 (October 1, 1945).

Mann, Robert. *The Walls of Jericho: Lyndon Johnson, Hubert Humphrey, Richard Russell and the Struggle for Civil Rights.* New York: Harcourt Brace, 1996.

Martin, Harold H. *William Berry Hartsfield: Mayor of Atlanta.* Athens: University of Georgia Press, 1978.

Matthews, Donald R., and James W. Prothro. "Negro Voter Registration in the South." In *Change in the Contemporary South,* edited by Allen P. Sindler, 119–49. Durham, NC: Duke University Press, 1963.

Mayer, Michael S. "With Much Deliberation and Some Speed: Eisenhower and the *Brown* Decision." *Journal of Southern History* 52 (February 1986): 43–76.

Mays, Benjamin E. *Born to Rebel: An Autobiography.* New York: Scribners, 1971.

Meier, August, and David Lewis. "History of the Negro Upper Class in Atlanta, Georgia, 1890–1958." *Journal of Negro Education* 28 (Spring 1959): 128–39.

Meiners, Fredericka. *A History of Rice University: The Institute Years, 1907–1963.* Houston: Rice University Press, 1982.

Miller, Arthur Selwyn. *A "Capacity for Outrage": The Judicial Odyssey of J. Skelly Wright.* Westport, CT: Greenwood Press, 1984.

Mims, Edwin. *History of Vanderbilt University.* Nashville: Vanderbilt University Press, 1946.

Mohr, Clarence L. "World War II and the Transformation of Southern Higher Education." In *Remaking Dixie: The Impact of World War II on the American South,* edited by Neil R. McMillen, 33–55. Jackson: University Press of Mississippi, 1997.

———. "Opportunity Squandered: Tulane University and the Issue of Racial Desegregation during the 1950s." *History of Higher Education Annual* 19 (1999): 85–120.

Mohr, Clarence L., and Joseph E. Gordon. *Tulane: The Emergence of a Modern University, 1945–1980.* Baton Rouge: Louisiana State University Press, 2000.

Moore, William V. "Civil Liberties in Louisiana: The Louisiana League for the Preservation of Constitutional Rights." *Louisiana History* 31 (Winter 1990): 59–81.

Morgan, Ruth P. *The President and Civil Rights: Policy-Making by Executive Order.* Lanham, MD: University Press of America, 1987.

Morris, Aldon D. *The Origins of the Civil Rights Movement: Black Communities Organizing for Change.* New York: Free Press, 1984.

Nicholls, William H. *Southern Tradition and Regional Progress.* Chapel Hill: University of North Carolina Press, 1960.

Patton, Randall L. "A Southern Liberal and the Politics of Anti-Colonialism: The Governorship of Ellis Arnall." *Georgia Historical Quarterly* 74 (Winter 1990): 599–621.

Perret, Geoffrey. *Eisenhower.* New York: Random House, 1999.

Pomerantz, Gary M. *Where Peachtree Meets Sweet Auburn: The Saga of Two Families and the Making of Atlanta.* New York: Scribners, 1996.

Porter, Earl W. *Trinity and Duke, 1892–1924: Foundations of Duke University.* Durham, NC: Duke University Press, 1964.

Pratt, Joseph A., and Christopher J. Castaneda. *Builders: Herman and George R. Brown.* College Station: Texas A&M University Press, 1999.

Pratt, Robert A. *We Shall Not Be Moved: The Desegregation of the University of Georgia.* Athens: University of Georgia Press, 2002.

Price, Margaret. *The Negro Voter in the South.* Atlanta: Southern Regional Council, 1960.

Reed, Linda. *Simple Decency and Common Sense: The Southern Conference Movement, 1938–1963.* Bloomington: Indiana University Press, 1991.

Rhyne, Charles S. *Working for Justice in America and Justice in the World: An Autobiography.* McLean, VA: Friends of Legal Profession Public Services, 1995.

Roche, Jeff. *Restructured Resistance: The Sibley Commission and the Politics of Desegregation in Georgia.* Athens: University of Georgia Press, 1998.

Rogoff, Leonard. "Divided Together: Jews and African Americans in Durham, North Carolina." In *The Quiet Voices: Southern Rabbis and Black Civil Rights, 1880s to 1990s,* edited by Mark K. Bauman and Berkley Kalin, 190–212. Tuscaloosa: University of Alabama Press, 1997.

Rubin, Louis D. *George W. Cable: The Life and Times of a Southern Heretic.* New York: Pegasus, 1969.

Rudolph, Frederick. *The American College and University: A History.* Athens, GA: Knopf, 1962.

Sarratt, Reed. *The Ordeal of Desegregation.* New York: Harper and Row, 1966.

Schiffrin, Andre, ed. *The Cold War and the University: Toward an Intellectual History of the Postwar Years.* New York: New Press, 1997.

Schrecker, Ellen W. *No Ivory Tower: McCarthyism and the Universities.* New York: Oxford University Press, 1986.

Schulman, Bruce J. *From Cotton Belt to Sunbelt: Federal Policy, Economic Development, and the Transformation of the South, 1938–1990.* New York: Oxford University Press, 1991.

Shattuck, Gardiner H., Jr. *Episcopalians and Race: Civil War to Civil Rights.* Lexington: University Press of Kentucky, 2000.

Sherer, Robert G. "University College: A History of Access to Opportunity, 1942–1992." Tulane University Publications, 1992.

Shiver, Sam M., and Robert F. Whitaker. "The 14th President's 15 Years," *Emory Alumnus* (April 1957), 5–23.

Silver, James W. *Mississippi: The Closed Society.* New York: Harcourt, Brace, 1963.

Sindler, Allen P., ed. *Change in the Contemporary South.* Durham, NC: Duke University Press, 1963.

Sitkoff, Harvard. *The Struggle for Black Equality, 1954–1980.* New York: Hill and Wang, 1981.

Sosna, Morton. *In Search of the Silent South: Southern Liberals and the Race Issue.* New York: Columbia University Press, 1977.

———. "More Important than the Civil War? The Impact of World War II on the South." In *Perspectives on the American South: An Annual Review of Society, Politics, and Culture,* edited by James C. Cobb and Charles R. Wilson, 145–61. New York: Gordon and Breach, 1987.

Spinney, Robert G. *World War II in Nashville: The Transformation of the Homefront.* Knoxville: University of Tennessee Press, 1998.

Spritzer, Lorraine Nelson, and Jean B. Bergmark. *Grace Towns Hamilton and the Politics of Southern Change.* Athens: University of Georgia Press, 1997.

Stone, Clarence. *Regime Politics: Governing Atlanta, 1946–1988.* Lawrence: University Press of Kansas, 1989.

Storr, Richard. *The Beginnings of Graduate Education in America.* Chicago: University of Chicago Press, 1953.

Sugg, Redding S. *The Southern Regional Education Board: Ten Years of Regional Cooperation in Higher Education.* Baton Rouge: Louisiana State University Press, 1960.

Synott, Marsha Graham. *The Half-Opened Door: Discrimination and Admissions at Harvard, Yale and Princeton, 1900–1970.* Westport, CT: Greenwood Press, 1979.

Tindall, George Brown. *The Emergence of the New South, 1913–1945.* Baton Rouge: Louisiana State University Press, 1967.

Trillin, Calvin. *An Education in Georgia: The Integration of Charlayne Hunter and Hamilton Holmes.* New York: Viking Press, 1964.

Tushnet, Mark V. *The NAACP's Legal Strategy against Segregated Education, 1925–1950.* Chapel Hill: University of North Carolina Press, 1987.

Tyler, Pamela. *Silk Stockings and Ballot Boxes: Women and Politics in New Orleans, 1920–1963.* Athens: University of Georgia Press, 1996.

Urquhardt, Brian. *Ralph Bunche: An American Life.* New York: W. W. Norton, 1993.

U.S. House of Representatives. Committee on Governmental Operations. *Executive Orders and Proclamations: A Study of a Use of Presidential Powers.* 85th Cong. 1st sess., 1957.

Van West, Carroll. *Tennessee History: The Land, the People, and the Culture.* Knoxville: University of Tennessee Press, 1998.

Veysey, Laurence R. *The Emergence of the American University.* Chicago: University of Chicago Press, 1965.

Vose, Clement. *Caucasians Only: The Supreme Court, the NAACP and the Restrictive Covenant Cases.* Berkeley: University of California Press, 1959.

Walker, Jack L. "Protest and Negotiation: A Case Study in Negro Leadership in Atlanta, Georgia." *Midwest Journal of Political Science* 7 (May 1963): 99–124.

Wallenstein, Peter. "Black Southerners and Non-Black Universities: Desegregating Higher Education, 1935–1967." *History of Higher Education Annual* 19 (1999): 121–48.

———. "Higher Education and the Civil Rights Movement: Desegregating the University of North Carolina." In *Warm Ashes: Issues in Southern History at the Dawn of the Twenty-first Century,* edited by Winfred B. Moore Jr., Kyle S. Sinisi, and David H. White Jr., 280–300. Columbia: University of South Carolina Press, 2003.

———, ed. *Higher Education and the Civil Rights Movement: White Supremacy, Black Southerners, and College Campuses.* Gainesville: University of Florida Press, 2008.

Weare, Walter B. *Black Business in the New South: A Social History of the North Carolina Mutual Life Insurance Company.* Urbana: University of Illinois Press, 1973.

White, Graham, and John Maze. *Henry A. Wallace: His Search for a New World Order.* Chapel Hill: University of North Carolina Press, 1995.

Woodward, C. Vann. *The Strange Career of Jim Crow.* New York: Oxford University Press, 1974.

Yerkes, Robert. "Psychological Examining in the United States Army," *Memoirs of the National Academy of Sciences,* vol. 15. Washington, DC: Government Printing Office, 1921.

Yinger, J. Milton, and George E. Simpson, "Can Segregation Survive in an Industrial Society?" *Antioch Review* 28 (March 1958): 15–24.

Young, Jeffrey R. "Eisenhower's Federal Judges and Civil Rights Policy: A Republican 'Southern Strategy' for the 1950s." *Georgia Historical Quarterly* 77 (Fall 1994): 536–65.

Index

African Americans/blacks, 2, 3, 10, 237; debate (among whites) concerning the place of the black elite, 5; "exceptional" blacks, 5, 6, 16, 242n12; harsh treatment of educated and middle-class blacks, 17, 243n18; health care of, 270–71n77, 132, 273n20; "militant" black students, 17–18; "new" blacks, 4; oppression of, 2; paranoid white feelings toward, 249n89

Alderman, Sidney, 278n85

Alexander, Henry, 19–20

Alexander, Lamar, 207, 295n120

Alexander, Vance, 201–2, 203, 204

Alexander, Will, 13

Allen, Ivan, Jr., 27, 184

American Association of Theological Schools (AATS), 205

American Association of University Professors (AAUP), 64, 142–43, 205; resolution of in support of desegregation, 135

American Baptist Theological Seminary, 196

American Council on Education, 232

Americans for Democratic Action (ADA), 45–46, 252n122

Amsel, Abram, 135

Anderson, Dillon, 304n212

anti-Communism, 3, 45, 57, 89, 116–17

Archie, William, 157, 178–79, 181, 184

Armsey, James A., 212–15

Arnall, Ellis, 28, 246n52, 250–51n108

Association of American Colleges, 22, 32

Association of American Law Schools (AALS), Special Committee on Racial Discrimination, 60–61, 69, 78, 79, 85, 90, 101, 160, 161, 256n16, 273n18, 298n152; move of to refuse membership to segregated universities, 131–32; sanctioning and accreditation power of over law schools, 102–3, 114, 270n69

Atlanta, 27–28, 105, 106, 246n51, 267n34, 281n139; and the "Appeal for Human Rights," 178; black elite of, 29; and public school desegregation, 151, 157, 177, 181, 281n140, 289n31; racial turmoil in, 156–57, 159–60, 177–78, 181; white elite of, 105, 268n35

Atlanta Journal and Constitution, 157

Atlanta University, 33, 49

Atomic Energy Commission (AEC), 170, 171, 172, 220, 222

Bassett, John Spencer, 40, 64

Beach, Waldo, 39–40, 67, 148, 249nn93–94, 249n96, 258n42

Benton, Jack, 68, 74, 167, 200, 259n54, 285n189

Billups, Val, 229

Bird, F. M., 185

Blount, Roy, 208

Bonner Nuclear Laboratory, 171

Borders, William Holmes, 86

Bosley, Harold, 38, 249n93, 249–50n102

Bowden, Henry, 34, 85, 108, 158, 159, 160, 182, 183, 184, 186, 237, 282n151

Branch, Harlee, 183

Branscomb, Harvie, 11, 32, 37–38, 42, 47–48, 57–58, 59, 95, 96, 98, 99, 114, 140, 237, 242n1, 244–45n30, 253n131, 259n51, 261n72, 282n155, 283n160, 283n164, 293n87, 294n98; anger of toward Dean Nelson, 293n83; attempts to solve Vanderbilt University's financial problems, 15–16; belief in change as critical to the success of the university, 15, 243n12; belief in the university's role in the "American democratic ideal," 15; belief of in white control of the desegregation process, 17–18, 244n20; and the changing legal status of